Penguin Books

THE PENGUIN BOOK OF 19TH CENTURY AUSTRALIAN LITERATURE

Michael Ackland is a senior lecturer in English at Monash University. His major teaching and research interests embrace English, North American and Australian literature. He has published widely on nineteenth-century Australian culture, and produced editions of the writings of Charles Harpur and Henry Kendall. He is currently preparing a monograph on Australian colonial verse tradition.

The Penguin Book of 19th Century Australian Literature

Edited by Michael Ackland

Penguin Books

Penguin Books Australia Ltd
487 Maroondah Highway, PO Box 257
Ringwood, Victoria 3134, Australia
Penguin Books Ltd
Harmondsworth, Middlesex, England
Viking Penguin, A Division of Penguin Books USA Inc.
375 Hudson Street, New York, New York 10014, USA
Penguin Books Canada Limited
10 Alcorn Avenue, Toronto, Ontario, Canada M4V 3B2
Penguin Books (N.Z.) Ltd
182–190 Wairau Road, Auckland 10, New Zealand

First published by Penguin Books Australia, 1993
10 9 8 7 6 5 4 3 2 1
Copyright in the Collection © Michael Ackland, 1993
For copyright of individual stories, see Acknowledgements

Typeset in 10/11¼pt Andover by Midland Typesetters, Maryborough, Victoria
Made and printed in Australia by Griffin Paperbacks, Adelaide

National Library of Australia
Cataloguing-in-Publication data:

The Penguin Book of 19th century Australian literature.

ISBN 0 14 015703 4.

1. Australian literature - 19th century. I. Ackland, Michael,
1951-   . II. Title: Book of 19th century Australian literature.

A820.8001

For Carole

ACKNOWLEDGEMENTS

For permission to reproduce material in this anthology I wish to thank the following:

Collins/Angus & Robertson Publishers and Colin Roderick for 'Conditions at Newcastle' from James Tucker's *Ralph Rashleigh*.

Mrs M Keall for entry from Louisa Clifton's *Journal 1841*;

The Trustees of the State Library of New South Wales for extracts from the Harpur manuscript collection and the staff of the Mitchell Library for their unfailing friendliness and co-operation.

Every effort has been made to contact the original source of copyright material contained in this book, although most is believed to be in the public domain. The publishers would, however, be pleased to hear from copyright holders not here acknowledged.

CONTENTS

INTRODUCTION

The quest for white dominion in Australia has been pursued from the outset in intellectual as well as material terms. While colonists and explorers were pushing out steadily from the initial beach-head at Sydney Cove, a parallel process was underway in the minds of those newly arrived, who were forearmed with eye-witness accounts of precursors like Joseph Banks and Captain James Cook, or with imaginative fantasies woven around European notions of a great unknown, southern continent. In the ensuing years, settlements would be established, barrier mountains crossed, and rich, lode-bearing veins unlocked. So, too, the initially exotic and incongruous conditions would be accepted by the Europeans, apparently insurmountable impediments to local writing overcome, and a wealth of literary resources discovered in the indigenous landscape, the convict past, and the examples of universal human nature, who were increasingly thronging city streets, or seeking to establish the basic necessities for physical survival in the outback. This collection offers an overview of some of the contributions made by writers to the conceptual shaping of white Australia, drawing both on familiar works, which most readers would recognise as part of their cultural heritage, and on less well-known compositions, made accessible by recent scholarship and innovative publishing ventures.

Part I, devoted to 'The Challenge of a New Landscape', outlines some of the intellectual imponderables confronted, consciously or unconsciously, by initial waves of educated white settlers. Physical challenges had their mental counterpart in the need to reconcile preconceptions with actualities, or as Louisa Clifton, while still on board ship, confided to her journal on 16 March 1841:

Within 4 degrees of the Australian shore we seem to feel and realise the presence of near land. What strange emotions are called up as I picture ourselves within a day or two actually surveying with our eyes instead of the imagination the scenes we have so long looked forward to as those of our future destiny, our future home and country.[1]

Most obviously, the local phenomena seen through European eyes were disconcertingly unfamiliar. These were variously labelled as curiosities, reversals or downright impossibilities and, in time, were related to received conceptions of providence and natural history, as in Barron Field's 'The Kangaroo'. Such incongruities, however, proved to be less unsettling than the dearth of objects made dear by custom and association, which threatened to rob both individual life and the arts of crucial points of orientation. An acute sense of exile, like that expressed in Field's 1822 journal entry, was an understandable reaction, whose converse appears in William Woolls's call to respond favourably to an original and unspoilt, pastoral landscape. According to Field, Australia was hardly conducive to artistic creation; whereas implicit in Woolls's emphasis on classical and biblical analogies is a suggestion that here, too, there may be subject matter comparable with that which inspired the great works of the ancients. Similar issues would also figure prominently in later, well-known pronouncements on the literary potential of *Terra Australis*, by such writers as Frederick Sinnett, Marcus Clarke and A. G. Stephens.

In terms of particular landscapes, early responses are frequently dominated by commercial motives or, as is often the case in the prose and verse of Part I, by reigning standards of the picturesque. For technically proficient artists, as well as for a trained amateur like Louisa Clifton, or for a person of broad culture such as Barron Field, the beauty of a scene depended, in large measure, on the extent to which it could be visualised as a landscape painting, of the kind popularised by the French painter Claude Lorrain. In his canvases, the eye of the beholder is typically led from an imagined vantage-point through a varied setting, enriched by patterns of light and shade, of forest and plain, by indications of settlement or cultivation, and crowned by the splendid effects of light and sky over sea or mountains. Australian nature, however, with regard to the picturesque as with so much else, did not lend itself to European expectations. Louisa Clifton recorded various attempts to sketch her immediate surroundings. But her work, as she remarks, was lacking in success and pleasure: that is, presumably her efforts did not yield the desired composite picture and its consequent enjoyment. On the other hand, she found that visits to the homes of Mr Eliot and the governor, despite their rude amenities, were rendered pleasant by engaging hospitality and resplendent vistas. Similarly, Field speaks of the colony as 'a perpetual flower-garden', and yet stresses the imagination-numbing monotony of its landscape: its trees seemed to defeat the requirements of European art, just as its native inhabitants refused to conform to treasured images of the noble savage. For although their campfires might provide pleasing, distant signs of habitation, European criteria and settler priorities soon combined to reduce the indigenous peoples to benighted and unseemly supernumeraries on the imperial stage.

Another problematic early issue concerned the desirable object of literary presentation. Was the primary role of art, in the context of colonisation, to provide information for the prospective emigrant and to mirror, as accurately as possible, the variety and nuances of natural life? Or did it have an interpretative, and more exalted, destiny? Most of the writers represented here went beyond, or used to more complex ends, the objects of simple mimetic recording. The demands of the latter are clearly conveyed in Emily Manning's 'The Weatherboard Fall'. Familiar, like her contemporaries, with the tradition of *ut pictura poesis* (that is, that poetry aspires ideally to emulate the qualities of painting, and painting to be 'a speaking picture'), her exposé of our restricted powers of representation moves easily between the two art forms, drawing consolation from the recognition that nature's uncapturable plenitude and sublimity point to an infinite, and ultimately benign creator. Charles Harpur, on the other hand, sought to free poetry in theory and practice from the demands of the particularised prospect, and to make it an instrument for broad instruction and prophetic vision. In his work, as he reminds us, rich scenic detail is there to convey universal truths, and in great art is subordinate to, or closely linked with, crucial human concerns: ideals which also informed the work of his immediate successor, Henry Kendall. In their writings, the notion of the physical creation as an objective and describable entity is replaced by concern with nature as a repository of everlasting lore, and as a participant in dramas of national consequence, such as those depicted in Harpur's 'The Creek of the Four Graves' and in Kendall's 'A Death in the Bush'.

By the second half of the century, one sign of expanding mental settlement was the increasing debate on the significance and dominant attributes of the landscape. As works by Marcus Clarke and Henry Lawson demonstrate, the process of taking imaginative possession of the country was already well advanced. In Clarke's hands, local landscape provides an immensely flexible setting, capable of accommodating diverse emotions and traditions, while his identification of indigenous scenery with 'Weird Melancholy' and dark, cognate attributes anticipates later writing such as Edward Dyson's 'The Conquering Bush'. Superficially at least, Lawson seemed determined to put an end to this process of creative encoding, as in the terse, corrective polemic entitled 'Some Popular Australian Mistakes'. But his writing is also informed by models of human action, by personal perceptions, and even by some of the traditions against which he is reacting. The opening paragraphs of 'The Drover's Wife', for example, read like a detailed rebuttal of the premises of the picturesque, while the apparently simple vignette from life in 'Rats' is carefully orchestrated to register specific values, as is revealed by its different endings. As published in *While the Billy Boils* (the 1896 version reprinted here), the swagman is an object of amusement and compassion. But with the addition of a further paragraph, as in an earlier version, the scene rebounds on the self-assured bushmen:

And late that evening a little withered old man with no corks round his hat and with a humorous twinkle instead of a wild glare in his eyes, called at a wayside shanty, had several drinks, and entertained the chaps with a yarn about the way in which he had 'had' three 'blanky fellers' for some tucker and 'half a case' by pretending to be 'barmy'.[2]

Irrespective of the ending, it is generally accepted that the story illustrates the thesis, articulated in Henry Lawson's 'The Bush Undertaker', of 'the grand Australian bush' as 'the nurse and tutor of eccentric minds, the home of the weird, and much that is different from things in other lands'[3] – a phrase heavy with the speculation of preceding generations. Early European dreaming was fast being replaced by individual interpretations of the land, which were destined to be singled out as worthy of assuming a permanent place in the national consciousness.

The role of art in moulding local perceptions is nowhere more apparent than with the convict heritage, which has gradually been made to yield up a usable past. Visualised often as an evil, founding gesture, or as a disfiguring stain on a virgin landscape, the penal system would become the object of creative transformations and revisionary myth-making which, with time, provided colonial equivalents for the dearth of those Old World fictional accessories lamented by Frederick Sinnett and others. Our selection in Part II traces this process of accretive, artistic assimilation, beginning with popular verse, which gives a human and individual voice to the otherwise yellow-clad mass of condemned felony, and underscores the sufferings caused by an, at times, brutal system. These perspectives afforded a means of sympathetically reappraising the convict past, while the strains of admonition and dissent, which emerge from such poems, distinguish successive phases. Early moralising tales, which served to 'convey useful and instructive precepts' (*Quintus Servinton*), gave way to the novelist's more complex accounts and psychological probings, and to the establishment of a distinctive, and often socially critical, fictional genre. Though a similar overview could have been based on bushranger lore, the penal system has enjoyed a dubious primacy in, and posed a far greater challenge to, the Australian imagination. It was, after all, at the basis of many local 'institutions', from law enforcement through to the idealised bushranger, whose original was the convict 'bolter' or escapee. Too central socially and historically to be ignored, convictism had to be desensitised, to be rendered nationally tolerable rather than a subject of deep shame. From the outset then, while muskets and chains set physical bounds to the convict menace, society looked to literature to wrest from dark sin matter of moral worth, and later, even after the formal cessation of transportation, letters still provided new ways of comprehending an ever-threatening past.

The major figure in this process of imaginative rehabilitation was undoubtedly Marcus Clarke, and Part II opens with an essay which exhibits his emphasis on the felon as dehumanised victim and the highly conscious reworking of factual matter, typical of later literary treatments. 'Port Arthur' is the last instalment from a series of articles published in the Melbourne *Argus* in July 1873. These recount seminal impressions from a visit to Tasmania, in 1870, that earlier had fed into his *Old Tales of a Young Country* and *His Natural Life*, both of which appeared in serialised form between 1870 and 1872. The ostensibly straightforward account of the convict hell-hole from 1873 thus arguably reflects experience gleaned on the spot, as well as its subsequent literary transformation. Is Clarke's account of the blow-hole, for example, imbued solely with impressions left by an actual visit, or is it also coloured by his famous chapter 'The Work of the Sea' in *His Natural Life*?[4] Certainly the comment that this striking phenomenon merits the treatment of a Victor Hugo had already been confirmed by his own writing, as had concluding reflections on 'the power of the press,' or literature, to resist efforts to bury an ugly past. For as novels by Leakey, Tucker and Clarke showed, here was matter worthy of sustained imaginative adaptation, and from which a wider understanding of transportation could be forged. In their works, the conventional notion of a convicted wrongdoer undergoing a justified period of correction and constraint is eclipsed by interest in how individuals respond to, or are deformed by, legally condoned procedures, better suited to generate barbaric and tyrannous abuses than productive reform. 'Port Arthur,' then, reveals more than the simple factual basis of larger fictional undertakings. The last in a series of recastings, it stands as a climactic acknowledgement of a haunting presence that 'remained–remains' for Clarke as for other Australians, and as a vivid example of that comprehensive sympathy which became a primary means of exorcising blame and opprobrium from individuals and a future nation: placing it squarely on 'a monstrous system of punishment futile for good and horribly powerful for evil'.[5]

In the wake of such creative endeavours, the convict heritage represented by the 1890s a set literary subject capable of diverse treatments, as may be seen in 'Price Warung's' 'Lieutenant Darrell's Predicament' and 'Tasma's' 'An Old-Time Episode in Tasmania'. For a writer of 'Price Warung's' democratic and socialistic predilections, the grisly extremes of transportation provided ready material with which to condemn authoritarian power structures. Other preoccupations, of course, are uppermost in 'Tasma's' writing, though in this tale, owing to penal practices, a life-transforming lesson ends uncharacteristically in the negation and reversal of love and social reintegration. Thus both stories lend weight to the revisionary readings, popularised by Clarke and others, of the system as being ultimately contrary to the dictates of the accepted moral and natural orders. Moreover, 'Warung' is not content merely to highlight such inversions through a ferocious convict saturnalia. He also arraigns the very procedures of enlightenment that spawned the modern penal regime through the figure of Lieutenant Darrell, whose genius for inventive experimentation and for improving on nature leads to greater dehumanisation. Similarly, 'Tasma's' tale affords a complementary verdict on mankind's drive for unconditional dominion, as well as a more subtle portrayal of the perilously fragile character of human motivation and Arcadian potential. By the turn of the century, the repellent nature of the immediate past had not only been rendered intellectually manageable, but it was yielding lessons for the present, together with grim insights which anticipated eerily the world of totalitarian excess projected by Franz Kafka in 'In the Penal Colony' (1919).

The period which saw the literary appropriation of convictism also witnessed increased examination of traditional gender roles, as demonstrated in Part III. Again the imaginative evolution was influenced by local sentiments, aroused initially by discussion centred on the future Australian race, and later by augmenting agitation for women's rights. Opinion on the former was divided. Many in the early days maintained that moral contamination was inevitable from a penal settlement and convict ancestry, and that an inheritance of misdemeanour and delinquency would be visited on subsequent generations. Opposed to this negative and deterministic conception was faith in the possibility of a fresh start, once freed from the burden of caste and prejudice, coupled with confidence that unspoilt nature and a beneficial climate would produce moral and racial regeneration. Overseas visitors soon remarked on a physical improvement in the founding stock, and this provided writers such as Charles Harpur with a basis for extrapolating less tangible ameliorations: 'The physical completeness of my countrymen, as a race, is undeniable, and I believe their mental and moral capacities only require adequate culture to become equally allowed and equally remarkable'.[6] Such progressivist optimism, in turn, had socio-political manifestations. Harpur, in the next breath, proposes a 'good National System of Education', and others clamoured for various freedoms, ranging from universal suffrage through to a republic. Moreover, the notion of a distinctive, native-born type generated more precise images of currency lads and lasses, of the bushman and the Australian girl. The latter, like Letty in Ada Cambridge's story 'A Sweet Day', is identified with a lack of affectation, practical aptitude, and almost masculine independence; her male counterpart, as in 'A Bush Tanquerary', with basic honesty, straightforwardness of character, and a willingness to stick by a proven mate, irrespective of the past. Women are shown to command respect and power, though not necessarily on their own terms. Even Letty's self-reliance, as manifested in her honey-making activities, is hardly a substitute for professional training or for the traditional vocation of marriage, so that her very originality, although ostensibly rewarded, in fact results in a reaffirmation of class and female stereotypes. A new race may have been in the making, but its promise was constantly endangered by convention and gender models.

As feminist advocates realised, women found themselves in a colonial society where, paradoxically, more was demanded of them at the same time as masculine values were being firmly enshrined in the national ethos. Ellen Clacy's 'Leaves from a Young Lady's Diary' conveys well the unprecedented scope for initiative available in the New World, and its limitations. The topsy-turvy conditions, induced by a largely male and fledgling settlement, leave the heroine at liberty to learn new manual skills, but ones which further ensure her domestic marketability and drudgery. Similarly, nature in the colonies seemed to sanction a putting aside of conventions. Yet the willing acquiescence of this young lady in the norms of home and motherhood underlines how real emancipation would depend, not simply on a change of setting, but on a far-reaching mental revolution, of the kind invoked by Louisa Lawson and her contemporaries.

Ensuing texts reprinted here juxtapose establishment and revisionist view-points. G. E. Evans's 'The Women of the West' exemplifies the standard rhetoric of compensation which, while seeming to give women their due in the frontier struggle, has assured their continued subjugation. Here the long catalogue of sufferings, which lacks particularised impact, weaves an elaborate myth of willing self-effacement, enacted, as the poet avows with unintentional irony, according to 'our fathers' creed'. Louisa Lawson's poem, 'Lines Written During a Night Spent in a Bush Inn', is far more successful in bringing home the grim actualities, physical and psychological, of the sacrifice demanded in the holy name of love. Similarly, Charles Harpur's 'Note to "A Wanton"' restates dominant Western attitudes, centred on identification of man with reason and woman with instinctual nature, or alternatively with essentially active and passive principles. Read alongside such pronouncements, the radical critique of accepted roles, which is one component of 'Squeaker's Mate', emerges in its full amplitude. By the 1880s the struggle for women's rights has been joined in earnest. Vigorous demands for emancipation and countering attempts at belittlement followed, with activists confronting not only sworn opponents, but also ingrained prejudice of the sort which enabled A. G. Stephens to describe literature as something 'which can be borrowed by women who never return it', or Charles Harpur to imagine himself to be a supporter of 'her rights . . . with an ultra liberality'.[7]

The realities, as experienced by women, together with a growing groundswell of revolt, conclude the section. As a prelude to them, however, 'The Rights of Woman (By a Brute)' is reprinted. This anonymous essay from Marcus Clarke's satirical journal, *Humbug*, both encapsulates the reactionary conception of the proper station and 'uses' of womankind and illustrates Louisa Lawson's contention, in 'The Strike Question', that women's issues are subjected to comic trivialisation in the press. Her essays, together with poems by Barbara Baynton and Ada Cambridge, challenge patriarchal assumptions; while 'Waif Wander's' 'The Spider and the Fly' documents a fiercely predatory world, with a subculture of codes and reactions born of subordination to male power, and to its corollaries: self-admiration and insensitive incomprehension. Masculine blindness and hubris are closely interrelated, as Louisa Lawson reminded readers of the *Bulletin* in an interview, published on 24 October 1896:

No, I don't run down men, but I run down their vanity – especially when they're talking and writing about women. A man editing a ladies' paper! or talking and writing about a woman's question in Parliament! I don't know whether to laugh or cry; they know so little about us. *We* see it. Oh, why don't the women laugh right out – not quietly to themselves; laugh all together; get up on the housetops and laugh, and startle you out of your self-satisfaction.[8]

Not surprisingly then, although Louisa's son Henry could write that 'it was in ninety-one or ninety-two, and the sex problem was booming then',[9] and himself contribute to the literary goldrush, it was women, by and large, who provided the memorable insights. Hence they are overwhelmingly represented here, pillorying double standards and a host of constraining or distorting mechanisms, as well as calling for an unfettered and morally courageous generation to stand firm against the sanctioned institutions of the past. In effect, dreams of new possibilities and of rebirth for humankind, once centred on the physical landscape, were now being displaced to the sexual compact, with a consequent opening up to the writer of new psychic and emotional prospects.

The pursuit of material well-being, epitomised by the goldrushes, saw colonial society grow in numbers and complexity, and Australian letters respond to pressures exerted by an expanded audience and by the various interest-groups, represented in Part IV. Thanks to their burgeoning population, the colonies developed into an important market for English publications, and expectations were raised among local authors of professional and economic improvements. With writing for remuneration a realistic option, the once private, creative outlets provided by correspondence and journals proved to be marketable commodities, whose inherent intimacy and immediacy of effect was put to good use by such writers as Ellen Clacy and Catherine Helen Spence. Expanded prospects for literary journalism, meanwhile, encouraged authors to try their hand in diverse mediums, and on a range of subjects. A negative aspect of this was a constant need for copy which could push the literary hack to extremes, as when James Skipp Borlase, noting the dramatic qualities of Ellen Clacy's description of nocturnal activities on the goldfields (the last paragraph of this is reprinted in our selection of *A Lady's Visit to the Gold Diggings*), coolly appropriated it to set the scene for his own tale of murder and detection in 'The Night Fossickers of Moonlight Flat'.[10] Finally, growing nationalist sentiment led to a politicising of literary vision, and to a realignment of thematic priorities. The Sydney *Bulletin* was the most influential proponent of this development, shifting emphasis away from stock themes, like the emigrant's complaint, towards the portrayal of indigenous, Australian experience, as part of its program for removing 'bias-bleared English spectacles', and for elevating heroic, rural existence over debilitating, urban culture. 'It is in the cities', A.G. Stephens asserted, 'not in the bush, that the national fibre is being in a hundred ways slackened and destroyed.'[11] An identifiable school of writing was one result. Another was eventually an undue narrowing of the spectrum of local letters, which led to neglect of many of the works reproduced in Parts IV and V.

The discovery of gold itself provided important stimulus to local writing, and sharpened dissatisfaction with the crassly acquisitive orientation of many colonists. Though the new settlements may have been lacking many of the hallowed settings of the European novel, there was now no denying their bustling, intense activity, nor their human diversity. Realism vied with romance as the dominant creative ideology, and local authors strove for parity with their English and American contemporaries. Indeed, A.G. Stephens at the turn of the century, in his Introduction to *The Bulletin Story Book*, persuasively proclaimed the thematic richness and imaginative advantages offered by the land, to those 'who will live Australia's life and utter her message'. But from among the writers who lent credibility to his boast, there sometimes emerged a less confidence-inspiring picture. Both Marcus Clarke and Henry Lawson, central figures in founding a tradition of indigenous sketches, offer a grim demystification of country and small-town existence, which contrasts starkly with the fabulous, rural projections of Stephens or 'Banjo' Paterson. Although this is often explained simply in terms of diverse, first-hand experiences, their disenchantment is also attributable to personal alienation from a society which had failed to reward its writers' efforts adequately. In 'Grumbler's Gully' Marcus Clarke speaks blunty of 'the brutal force of money . . . triumphant'. Edward Dyson's 'A Golden Shanty' shows it to be the ultimate social 'mortar', linking people irrespective of race or class, and providing a lingua franca of jurisprudence; while of the national type, as portrayed in Henry Lawson's 'Middleton's Rouseabout', it is unequivocally asserted 'Hasn't any idears'. Intellect and wealth, according to these and other male authors, seemed irremediably opposed, and in 'Men of Letters in New South Wales' Henry Kendall voices a common complaint in his depiction of genius forced to choose between dire poverty and journalistic self-abasement.

Wealth and its effects also loom large in the writing of women of the period, though their treatments reflect divergent concerns and experience. Whereas men tend to focus on distinctions between material and mental acquisition, or on clashes between hard, daily realities and idealistic visions, their female counterparts often register not only alienation from mainstream goals, but subordination within a male-dominated literary culture. In *My Brilliant Career* Miles Franklin's Sybylla depicts both the sapping narrowness of up-country life, and the peculiar difficulties encountered by a young woman trying to depart from traditional roles. The impulse to write, in particular, is perceived as pernicious day-dreaming because, as she bitterly concludes, 'I am only one of yourselves, I am only an unnecessary, little, bush commoner, I am only a – woman!'[12] Similarly, Louisa Lawson, who edited Australia's first feminist periodical, *The Dawn*, recounts what happened when a woman, against the odds, did choose to enter the foreign domain of print:

Did you ever think what it was to be a woman, and have to try to make a living by herself, with so many men's hands against her. It's all right if she puts herself under the thumb of a man – she's respectable then; but woe betide her if she strikes out for herself and tries to compete with men on what they call 'their own ground'. Who made it their own ground?[13]

Nevertheless, women did persist in putting their particular viewpoints, and in winning an international readership. For while they, too, could portray hard, grinding poverty, or the fruitless quest for wealth, they also focused tellingly on the effects of economic dependence and related sexual stereotypes. 'Waif Wander's' 'Towzer and Co.' unsparingly dissects this abject existence, idealised as 'helpless femininity'; while Ada Cambridge's poetry raises physical emotion above accepted propriety into a court of final appeal, thereby challenging established hierarchies centred on head and heart, and on woman as sanctified and well-to-do matron or poor and fallen slattern. Finally, the high cost of undervaluing sentiment or passion is traced in 'Tasma's' 'Barren Love', which also demonstrates convincingly that it is not just woman, but both sexes who are the losers, when calculation and materialism gain sway over human affairs.

Less easy to categorise, and generally less well known, has been a wide variety of writings which examine the roots of personal and social malaise, and constitute a literature of anxiety. The reasons for their relative neglect are diverse. Some were printed only in the ephemeral form of weekly or monthly journals for immediate reader consumption, and thereafter slipped into the limbo of archival holdings and special collections. There they remained largely untouched owing to a combination of factors, including limited research resources, an absence of comprehensive indexes, and a tendency to undervalue the significant contribution of literary journalism to early Australian letters. Other works fell victim to the dominant assumptions of their age, to changes of taste, or to shifting perceptions of national identity. Barbara Baynton's *Bush Studies*, for instance, was singled out by A. G. Stephens for 'uncompromising commendation' as an outstanding example of the 'first plane of realism'.[14] That is, according to the *Bulletin*'s literary editor, it described wonderfully well the immediate, visible givens, but failed to raise the particular into 'a type of its class', and ultimately into a universal statement: a verdict which demonstrates a limited understanding born of Stephens's unquestioning acceptance of those very norms which Baynton is at pains to subvert or otherwise challenge. Possibilities for incomprehension and neglect were further increased during and after the 1920s with the elevation of bush, democratic and egalitarian concerns, associated with Henry Lawson and the *Bulletin*, into hallmarks of the national literary heritage. This directed critical interest away from the achievements of an indigenous feminist tradition, and also away from works like those included in Part V, which focus on mental states and the supernatural.

Initial fictional explorations of psychological and super-rational dilemmas drew heavily on Romantic writing and its immediate literary offshoots. This is especially evident in the works of Marcus Clarke, the colonies' first major contributor to this heritage. There, familiar Romantic motifs recur, such as projections of hidden motivation or psychic impulses through the use of the double or *Doppelgänger*, the exploration of unusual states of mind, and the probing of familiar divisions between past and present, and between dream or hallucination and reality. These interests coalesce in Marcus Clarke's 'Human Repetends', where they generate open-ended speculation of a kind which sets this tale apart from most contemporary, local treatments of mystery and the supernatural. For in the colonies, as elsewhere, sensational writing was in demand, and aspiring authors wasted no time in peopling the bush with ghosts and inexplicable occurrences. Conventional motifs, such as the haunted location resulting from the murder of an innocent, proved to be easily assimilable, as did domestic versions of Gothic settings and tales of detection, like those popularised by Edgar Allan Poe's 'The Fall of the House of Usher' (1839) and 'The Murders in the Rue Morgue' (1841). Many writers, who turned to journalism for a livelihood, made at least occasional use of this matter of perennial reader interest, while some, like Mary Fortune ('Waif Wander') made it their professional staple. A prolific contributor to the

Australian Journal over many years, she was best known as a writer of detective fiction, such as 'Brockman's Folly'. Multiple viewpoints, the correlation between physical setting and mental condition, and the full range of anxiety-related motifs that were the stock-in-trade of the mystery writer, contribute to the desired atmosphere of suspense in this story. This, however, is kept within readily tolerable bounds by the rational, deductive demands of the genre. In effect, threat and the supernatural are skilfully manipulated according to a pre-established compact, as Mary Fortune displays the kinds of dreads which could be constantly and openly marketed for mass circulation, as distinct from the disquietening gender critique presented in 'The Spider and the Fly' and 'Towzer and Co.'

However much editorial perceptions of a target audience may have militated against the exploration of certain areas of malaise, they did not preclude the projection, in veiled or analogous forms, of preoccupying anxieties. Gauging the extent and repercussions of an author's involvement with his creation, however, is usually difficult. In 'Human Repetends', for instance, Marcus Clarke clearly attributed his own insights on Melbourne society to the speaker, while the latter's Old World upbringing is broadly that of his creator. But do the points of convergence end there? Clarke had private as well as literary reasons for his repeated interest in questions of fate; while the later 1881 version of the tale, reprinted here, contains an additional framing discussion of terrestrial instability and the mysterious fulfilment of destiny: issues that were gaining in personal relevance with the continuing deterioration of his affairs, as he rushed headlong towards a repetition of the paternal fate of insolvency and sudden death. Related difficulties are raised for the reader by Henry Kendall's recourse to more cosmopolitan material during a similar period of intense familial and financial pressure. In particular, his 'The Voyage of Telegonus', as it appeared initially in the *Sydney Morning Herald*, opens with contradictory signals of detachment and involvement. A detailed, explanatory note from Lemprière's *Classical Dictionary*, reproduced here as on the poem's first printing, invites the reader apparently to look for an objective reworking of received matter. But the speaker's introductory remarks link the forthcoming account with personal alienation, a challenging of ruling orthodoxies, and the presentation of the otherwise unspeakable, thereby raising the possibility that more is at stake, or being dramatised here, than Telegonus's well-documented fate:

But thou to whom these things are like to shapes
That come of darkness – thou whose life slips past

Regarding rather these with mute fast mouth –
Hear none the less how fleet Telegonus . . .

On a personal level, avowals of narrative unease, associated
with the pursuit of a difficult calling and with the utterance
of repressed dreads, seem to link the work with the often
tragic predicament of colonial writers, such as Adam Lindsay
Gordon and Marcus Clarke. This was a foreseeable destiny
which Kendall would try desperately to avoid in coming years;
while the condition of helpless estrangement from humankind
and divinity depicted here was capable of contemporary application in an age shaken by rapid change and religious doubt.

By the close of the century the sense of crisis latent in a number
of works composed around 1870 was surfacing in thoroughly
disquietening forms. The acute, existential malaise of 'The Voyage
of Telegonus', for instance, finds its discursive counterpart in
Clarke's *Civilization without Delusion* where he draws out some of
the ramifications of the widespread anguish arising from the
crumbling of faith and related certitudes. Subsequent writers, like
Barbara Baynton and Albert Dorrington, appear determined to
reveal unpalatable truths, or to jolt the uneasy dreamer into a
reflective state. Dorrington's 'Quilp' reads like a study in the roots
of social disfiguration, and testifies to a general corroding of
confidence. Here no escape seems possible, where all is willed
delusion, antagonism or misalliance. Similarly, Baynton's tales
question the possibility of a purposeful awakening from, or
transcendence of, an oppressive, nightmarish predicament. The
menacing storm conditions in 'A Dreamer' give way to a closing
tableau which encapsulates the unrelenting cycle of womanhood,
from thankless childbirth to obliterating death; while in 'The
Chosen Vessel,' the stock bush theme of threat to an isolated hut-
dweller provides the vehicle for a comprehensive and universal
critique of the forces at work against womankind, which impli-
cates not only individuals and conditioning but the institutional
pillars of society. Again, none are spared arraignment: a view
underscored in the 1917 revised version by the addition of a final
sentence: 'But the dog also was guilty.' Finally, verse by Christopher Brennan and Catherine Martin portrays the ever-
renewing human mind benumbed with disenchantment and
despair. From the city through to the sea, the once-promising
world has become a graceless place of terror and corruption,
evoking a spiritual dearth and cumulative anxiety, which
sounded the death-knell to sanguine dreams of the colonial past,
and provided a major imaginative burden for post-Federation
letters.

NOTES

1. Quoted from a typescript copy of her diary, MS 2801, National Library of Australia.
2. Henry Lawson, *Short Stories in Prose and Verse* (L. Lawson, Sydney, 1894), p. 5.
3. ibid., p. 71.
4. The original serialised version, entitled *His Natural Life,* was subsequently revised, shortened and reissued as the novel *For the Term of His Natural Life.*
5. From the conclusion of 'Port Arthur', reprinted here.
6. Note from 'The Kangaroo Hunt' reprinted in Michael Ackland (ed.), *Charles Harpur: Selected Poetry and Prose* (Penguin, Ringwood, Vic., 1986), p. 20.
7. See, respectively, 'What Is Literature?' reprinted in Leon Cantrell (ed.), *A. G. Stephens: Selected Writings* (Angus & Robertson, Sydney, 1977), p. 55, and 'Note to "A Wanton"' reprinted here.
8. 'A Poet's Mother - Louisa Lawson,' reprinted in Cantrell, op cit., p. 269-70.
9. 'The Sex Problem Again,' reprinted in Colin Roderick (ed.), *Henry Lawson: Short Stories and Sketches 1888–1922* (Angus & Robertson, Sydney, 1972), p. 306.
10. Borlase's story has recently been reissued in Stephen Knight (ed.), *Dead Witness: Best Australian Mystery Stories* (Penguin, Ringwood, Vic., 1989), pp. 17-36.
11. 'For Australians', reprinted in Cantrell, op. cit., p. 398.
12. Miles Franklin, *My Brilliant Career* (William Blackwood & Sons, London, 1901), p. 318.
13. 'A Poet's Mother - Louisa Lawson', reprinted in Cantrell, op. cit., p. 270.
14. 'One Realist and Another', reprinted in Cantrell, op. cit., p. 199.

I

THE CHALLENGE OF A NEW LANDSCAPE

LOUISA CLIFTON
from *Journal 1841*

Wednesday, 17th March 1841. *Barque Parkfield.*

Under feelings of the most intense interest and excitement I take up my pen to write the account of this day; we are laying to within sight of the Australian shores. How can I describe the emotions of this moment. My heart bounds with the deepest gratitude, and my spirits respond in feelings of delight and joy. The wind has blown very hard all day and under easy sail since at 10 we have been running at the rate of 9½ knots an hour. At noon today we were 115 miles from Cape Naturaliste and 96 from nearest land. About ½ past 5 the soul-reviving sound 'land in sight' rang from the mast-head; and then how every heart leapt for joy. I soon after went and joined all the party on deck, and there in the far horizon, in the grey colouring of coming twilight, loomed the faint outline of our adopted land. At a distance of 30 or 40 miles it rose high. The moment any eyes first rested on that 'dim discovered scene' was one the remembrance of which the longest life can never obliterate; none who have not known what it is to sigh, to long with sickening longing for land after a voyage of more than 3 months can fully understand with what ecstasy of feeling the first view and scent of land greets the weary senses. We are all in a state of excitement, softened excitement, I feel, for a review of the striking favours we have experienced as we have tracked our solitary way across these pathless oceans cannot fail to create sentiments of solemn thankfulness and joy. A native fire has been distinguished on the shore tho' we are still distant, and we are almost laying to and standing off the land till daylight dawns. The motion has been very distressful all day and I have done very little and felt wretchedly uncomfortable. Mrs. Gaudin went into hysterics on first seeing the coast; it is time she should display some feeling for she has not hitherto manifested much. I lie down to rest this night with a thankful heart and with prostrate soul. I desire to return unto thee our gracious and merciful God the sincere offering of gratitude and praise and, oh, may I never lose an abiding sense of thy loving kindness to us, thy most unworthy servants. I feel humbled before thee. Oh may I be enabled by thy holy spirit to walk henceforth as thou should guide me and offer up to thee the willing sacrifice of heart and life.

Thursday, 18th March 1841. *Parkfield.*

By 5 o'clock in the morning all the party were stirring and I got out of my berth to see the land which rose rather high (but lower than it appeared last evening) a few miles from us. Mama went up on deck about 7. I followed and all the party were soon assembled. We were just going round Cape Naturaliste, the wind blowing extremely fresh and the sea bouyant. Mr. Plowes, Bob and I attempted to take some outlines of the coast, but we passed too rapidly to succeed well. Breakfast was very acceptable at 9, for we all felt weary with our early rising. After breakfast I unpacked and repacked for a couple of hours and then I went on deck where I found Mama working hard at a bonnet she had just begun and wished to finish before arriving. We were then in sight of Leschenault and not very far off. I felt mortified at the procrastination which could put off such a tiresome occupation until so exciting and absorbing a moment as that of arriving at our distant goal. A boat was soon descried coming off from the shore, and between 2 and 3 o'clock it reached us. It proved to be Capt. Coffin, an American settler, who acts as pilot to ships coming in. The moment, I felt, was an anxious one to hear of the surveyors. Mrs. Gaudin said not a word. Papa enquired after them and heard of their safety, but that poor Mr. Gaudin was out of his mind, and had been so from first sailing. Papa immediately broke it to poor Mrs. Gaudin whose distress was of course extreme. This sad intelligence produced a general feeling of gloom and sympathy. I had always dreaded and expected it, but the shock upset me, for the more we heard of him the more affecting appears the whole case. About 6 in the evening we found ourselves in Leschenault Bay, within ½ mile of the shore, the sea perfectly smooth, the temperature more warm and balmy than can be described. We were all struck by the pretty aspect of the country at the mouth of the inlet and in parts along the shore. Masses of beautiful foliage grow down to the water's edge and in an opening of it we descried Mr. Eliot's and Mr. Stirling's little dwelling. The immediate coast rises in sandhills, but there is vegetation upon them, trees everywhere seen beyond the hills in the distance, high and reminding us forcibly of the Paris [?] hill at Sauoer [?]. The colouring as the sun began to decline became exquisitely soft and radiant, the hills robed in the brightest lakes and blues, the sky reflecting every colour in the rainbow, and yet so softly that every tint completely melted into one another. I cannot easily cease to remember the first Australian sunset, nor the feelings with which I viewed its promising coasts, and the native fires burning along the country, the smoke of which however we only saw. Papa, Bob and two of the young men went ashore and found Mr. Austen; then called upon Mr. Stirling and Mr. Eliot; heard that Australind is beautifully laid out. Everything here promises prosperity, and all excessively cut up at the change of site, which, as neither the Stirling nor the Henry have arrived, was before unknown to them. The excitement of this evening may be imagined.

*   *   *

Saturday, March 20th 1841. *Parkfield*, Port Leschenault.

A grey day; till these two days not a cloud has been seen for 6 months. An unsettled morning, tho' busy. Papa and Mr. Austen &c at business. Mr. Ommaney came and spent the morning and dined; we find him an agreeable man. His wife (a Miss Bustle) is at the Vasse. Directly after dinner Papa, Pearce, Mr. Ommaney, Mr. Austen left in the boat for Australind where they remained the night, and with a native start at daylight tomorrow on horseback for Perth. They took a blanket each and provisions for their journey which will occupy 3 days. It is an adventurous expedition. A heavy rain drove us down from the poop very early and the weather looks threatening and windy. It is lightning vividly. Gervase, Charles, Mr. Plowes remain at Australind tonight; others of the young men also remain on land. How exquisite is the being at rest. I feel intuitively in high spirits. 2 of the natives [,] dressed up for the occasion, visited the ship this morning. They were both covered, but I was more shocked than I can express at their appearance. I never witnessed so affecting a sight as this display, of the degradation of humanity. They do not look like human beings, so thin, so hideous, so filthy, oiled and painted red faces and hair, and pieces of rush passed through their hair. They danced and distressed us still more; in fact I feel distressed at the idea of living among such a people, so low, so degraded a race.

*   *   *

Thursday, 25th March 1841. *Parkfield*.

According to appointment Mr. Eliot and Mr. Stirling came off to take us on shore about ½ past 10. Nothing could induce Mama to go ashore so we three, E, M, and myself were obliged to go under Mr. Gibson's escort, for he accompanied us. We landed at Bunbury, walked to the Giants' Causeway, a basalt formation at the point over which the sea was breaking, but is not above 6 feet high so that there is nothing majestic or striking. Mr. Northey and Onslow accompanied us. We walked over the site for the town of Bunbury, a pretty situation for such a purpose. We then mounted the hills to the left of Mr. Eliot's house, and were charmed with the exquisite view of the estuary, the hills beyond, dips and dells and knolls beautifully studded with large and picturesque trees forming the nearest landscape. At length we arrived at Government House, situated on the summit of one of these high round knolls, commanding a lovely prospect, and tho' rude and rough in its construction, gave an idea of cheerfulness. A sofa, table, chairs, a small bookcase with books and writing materials in one corner, was all the furniture. A chimney-piece and fireplace for burning wood astonished us; the sides of the room whitewashed, the roof of thatch and high, the ceiling not having been built. Mr. Northey showed me his collection of dried plants, and very kindly gave me a specimen of each kind. After resting for some time we again set out. I again walked with Mr. Eliot, E with Mr. Gibson, and Mr. Stirling with M. We wandered through some sweet woods and were pleased with all we saw. We again returned to Mr. E's and had some delicious bread and butter, which I did indeed enjoy and then came off to dinner; all four gentlemen; the Capt. and his wife, Bob and his had not returned from Australind. We sat down to a dinner so scanty and so bad that we were all made really uncomfortable, and did not conceal our indignation. The gentlemen were very agreeable and did not go off till after tea; their attention and kindness to us was most gentlemanlike and considerate. I am destined to collect seeds and flowers. Mr. E gave me 62 packets of native seeds, collected by some famous botanist, a valuable present. I really enjoyed the excursion and felt quite at home with our new male friends, though I did not quite like our going alone.

Friday, 2nd April 1941. *Parkfield.*

An unsettling morning early. After finishing packing I went on to the poop and read History of Ireland. Mrs. Austen and Mrs. Gaudin came down from Australind at 3 and dined with us. Mrs. Austen returned in the evening, leaving Mrs. G. to sleep here. Mrs. A attired in the same dress as she wore at one of our soirees, and at the dejeuner, and white bonnet of flowers looked more than usually unladylike. The scenes in which she appeared in town were brought vividly before my mind. Major Irwin, Mr. Eliot and Mr. Northey dined here; the two latter were my neighbours at the dinner table and made themselves very agreeable. With the former I had a great deal of conversation. There is something about him which amuses me excessively. From laughter however we came down to gravity and almost melancholy, as we talked of England, friends, separation, colonial life &c. He expressed many feelings which reminded me much of dear Waller, and the more I see of young men, the greater similarity I find in their sentiments, on one point that of sighing for an object, ties of affection, home interests &c. His two little native boys came off in the evening; they were brought into the cuddy and tho' rather frightened at the large motley company, behaved extremely well. Guanga hung round Mr. Eliot with a sweet confiding manner and then read the English alphabet clearly and boldly. Christina sang; they looked astonished beyond measure, and listened most attentively but said little. It appeared too much for them. Dr. Carpenter in the midst of all this confusion and bustle began to write his home letters; one of which to his brother at Trinidad contained about 5 lines; he is the most heartless, conceited man I have ever met with. We had a very agreeable day. Mr. Northey accompanies Major Irwin to Perth in the *Helen*.

Although I have not been at all well, this day has been a pleasant one. We breakfasted at 8, Capt Barker with us. Papa, he, Mrs. Gaudin and some of the young men went to Australind. The day has been most lovely. I enjoyed a quiet reading in my own room for an hour or two; the more delightful in proportion to the rarity of such an employment. I then went on deck, alone [,] to try and sketch the coast, but failed. A very small party at dinner. Robert, Papa, Capt. Whiteside and Dr. Carpenter are dining at Government House. We have been sitting on deck watching the fires on shore near Shenton's store. The scene has been most beautiful, worthy and pencil of a Claude Lorraine [sic]; the moon and sky dazzlingly bright; the sea glistening and perfectly smooth; the outline of the shore dark and clear; the lurid flash and the curling grey and vermilion smoke of the fires throwing a bright redness over the scene, investing with a wildness congenial to the spot and exciting to the imagination. The *Helen* left the port this morning; the colonial schooner yesterday. Poor Mrs. Gaudin's cup of sorrow is almost overflowing. Her maid Maria turns out to be thoroughly worthless, and she is obliged to discharge her; thus depriving her of the last comfort she could look to, that of having a confidential, comfortable attendant. She left us in very low spirits.

Sunday, 4th April 1841

A day of exquisite warmth and beauty. A very small party at the reading on deck; being the last day on board, I wished to take a sketch of the coast and attempted, but had no pleasure or success in it, feeling it to be an undesirable occupation for the day. Decided not to go to Australind till Tuesday; walked the deck after tea and watched the last sunset at sea; the scene was lovely and heightened by vivid lightning. I am strangely altered when I think how seldom now I feel the thrill of enjoyment in the view of bright skies and sunny shores.

Monday, 5th April 1841.

Papa was so discomposed at our decision not to accompany him to the encampment this morning, that at the expense of a great deal of exertion we resolved to go up at 1 o'clock under the charge of Dr. Carpenter and C. Bedingfeld. A very bustling morning; just as we had completed our packing, Mr. Eliot and Mr. Stirling came on board and hearing with whom we were going, immediately offered and insisted on taking us up in their boat. Mama unhesitatingly accepted their kind escort for us, and about ½ past 1 we took leave of our kind friends the Whitesides and the barque *Parkfield*; although exulting in the joy of getting ashore, my spirits forsook me at last; the remembrance of the first time I saw the ship, with whom and with what feelings, with the train of thoughts accompanying a review of the past ran through my mind. I felt an oppression of spirit which I could not throw off, during our calm and scorching row and sail up the estuary. I made an effort to be chatty, but was silent; the last view of the *Parkfield* awakened too much thought and feeling. I here transcribe a letter I wrote to dear Waller this night.

Trent, Australind. 5th April 1841. I must attempt before I lie down for the first time in the bush, to give you some description of the picturesque romantic scenes in which we are now engaged. We have just made our beds on the ground, arranged our tent for the night, and with the moon shining brightly through the canvas over head, solemn stillness reigning around, except when broken by the merry laugh of gentlemen encamped round a log fire, the chirling [*sic*] of the grasshoppers and now and then the breaking of a wave upon the distant shore. You may fancy Mary and myself kneeling at a table we have rigged up in the centre of our abode, alternately writing and talking over this strange page in our history. Papa with a party of young men came hither this morning and left Mary and me to follow with a boat load of goods &c later in the day. Mr. Eliot and Mr. Stirling went on board the *Parkfield* just as we were going and insisted upon taking us up in their boat, a proposition we readily agreed to rather than commit ourselves to the care of Dr. Carpenter. We sailed almost all the way up this beautiful estuary, under a sky of surpassing beauty, the heat intense and scarcely a breath of wind. On arriving, we found our tent erected and 2 or 3 others scattered about, on the slope of a deep declivity a few hundred yards from the waterside, commanding a lovely view, surrounded by beautiful trees, but in a state of charming confusion, the sand, ankle deep, almost the only floor. Our kind friend Mr. E and S insisted upon getting everything to rights. We all went to work under a scorching sun to cut rushes for the carpet, turned everything out; they then spread them, arranged this table which with a nice English cover gives an air of comfort to the apartment, put up books; in fact, in the course of an hour or two we found ourselves in order. Mrs. Austen then kindly came from her settlement with a loaf of bread and cold meat, a most acceptable present after the labours of the day. An immense fire of branches was soon lighted on the level ground, a little distance below our tent, water boiled and tea made and having fortunately got up our plate chest containing knives and forks, tea cups &c, we sat down to a welcome repast, and with more comfort than we could have imagined possible. I wish you could have seen the interior of our new abode, some sitting on the ground, others on our mattresses rolled up; I making tea upon a gun case seated on a hassock in the midst. By degrees all the young men collected to this centre of comfort and sociability. I forgot to describe in due order a scene which amused us vastly. While we were engaged within, we found the Government Resident, the magistrate of the district, Mr. Eliot and Mr. Gibson, hard at work without kneading dough to make damper, in other words, unleavened bread, which has since been baked in wood ashes, and promises to do justice to the skill of the manufacturers. I cannot describe half of the amusing and curious incidents of the day nor convey to your mind an adequate idea of the picturesque appearance of a bush encampment, in such a climate and with such scenery on all sides. Papa and Mr. Plowes have a tent; Mr. Eliot and S and many others are by this time reposing on the bare ground, wrapped in blankets by the side of a large fire. We have just made our beds and are so completely tired that we are longing to lie down in them. The nights are extremely cold and we are beginning to feel very chilly, and the sand underneath strikes damp and cold. Mama, Ellen and all the party are to come up on Wednesday. I find myself involuntarily providing against the motion of the sea, altho' we have been almost entirely at rest for the last fortnight. The delight of feeling still, relieved of the burden of preparation against pitching and rolling and a thousand other charms in being on terra firma again compensates most fully for the personal exertions which will be required for some months to come; and then the indescribable blessing of not going to Port Grey. I feel a sensation of 'home' in this place; civilization is partly known. There are only 3 or 4 settlers, but there is the truest hospitality and kindness, and instead of being out of the reach of any human beings, we here at once meet with a hearty welcome and with ready assistance and co-operation. I cannot tell you how truly kind Mr. E and S have been. The former is a very agreeable gentlemanly man, and the latter is most pleasing, and tho' a colonist not less the gentleman. All is hushed and still and I must to my rest as we are to be up at 5 in the morning.

Yours, L.C.

BARRON FIELD

from *Journal of an Excursion*
across the Blue Mountains of New South Wales

Monday, 7th October, 1822

This spring month is the fittest to make this excursion in. The
winter nights are too cold, and the summer days too hot. In the
autumn the flowers are not in bloom.

The difficulties of the travel commence at Emu Ford over the
river Nepean, a branch of the Hawkesbury. Crossing this stream
is always a work of such time and trouble, and sometimes of such
difficulty and danger that the traveller should send forward his
cart or baggage-horses, to overcome it, half a day before he rides
or rows through it himself. The ferry is the property of government, who have hitherto delayed[1] either to provide a punt
themselves or to suffer the stock-holders of the colony to build
one by subscription. The consequences are frequent losses of
cattle in swimming, and injury of sheep in boating, over. Although
the river was not unusually high, we were obliged to unload our
cart before it could be drawn through the ford; and thus lost
several hours in transporting the baggage by one small boat, and
in reloading the cart.

On the banks of the Nepean, I saw almost the only deciduous
native tree in the territory, namely, the white cedar (melia
azedarach), the common bead-tree of India,[2] beautiful in itself, and
congenial to me from that singularity. All the other indigenous
trees and shrubs, that I have seen, are evergreens; the eternal
eucalyptus, with its white bark and its scanty tin-like foliage, or
the dark casuarina tall, and exocarpus funeral; all as unpic-
turesque as the shrubs and flowers are beautiful: - the various,
justly called proteaceous, banksia, and the hesperidean mimosa,[3]
the exquisite epacris, the curious grevillea, xanthorrhoea, the
sceptre of Flora, telopea the magnificent, and thysanotus the
lovely. New South Wales is a perpetual flower-garden, but there
is not a single scene in it of which a painter could make a
landscape, without greatly disguising the true character of the
trees. They have no lateral boughs, and cast no masses of shade;

but, in return, it is to this circumstance, which causes so little vegetable putrefaction, that the healthiness of the climate is mainly to be attributed. 'A part of their economy (says Mr Brown the botanist), which contributes somewhat to the peculiar character of the Australian forests, is, that the leaves both of the eucalyptus and acacia, by far the most common genera in Terra Australis, and, if taken together, and considered with respect to the mass of vegetable matter they contain (calculated from the size, as well as the number of individuals), nearly equal to all the other plants of that country, are vertical, or present their margin and not either surface towards the stem, both surfaces having consequently the same relation to lights.[4] Can this circumstance be partly the cause of their unpicturesqueness – of the monotony of their leaf? Or is it merely their evergreeness? 'In the Indies (says Linnæus) almost all the trees are evergreen, and have broad leaves; but in our cold regions, most trees cast their foliage every year, and such as do not, bear acerose, that is, narrow and acute, leaves. If they were broader, the snow which falls during the winter would collect among them, and break the branches by its weight. Their great slenderness prevents any such effect, and allows the snow to pass between them.'[5] But snow is not unknown to the eucalypti and acaciae of New Holland; and may not the verticalness of the broad leaves of some of them answer the same snow-diverting purpose as the acerose-leavedness of European evergreens? Yet the foliage of the eucalypti is always scanty; that of the acaciae acerose; and the snow of Australia is apt to melt. Be this as it may, no tree, to my taste, can be beautiful that it is not deciduous. What can a painter do with one cold olive-green? There is a dry harshness about the perennial leaf, that does not savour of humanity in my eyes. There is no flesh and blood in it: it is not of us, and is nothing to us. Dryden says of the laurel,

"From winter winds it suffers no decay;
For ever fresh and fair, and every month is May."

Now it may be the fault of the cold climate in which I was bred, but this is just what I complain of in an evergreen. 'For ever fresh,' is a contradiction in terms; what is 'for ever fair' is never fair; and without January, in my mind, there can be no May. All the dearest allegories of human life are bound up in the infant and slender green of spring, the dark redundance of summer, and the sere and yellow leaf of autumn. These are as essential to the poet as emblems, as they are to the painter as picturesque objects; and the common consent and immemorial custom of European poetry have made the change of seasons, and its effect upon vegetation, a part, as it were, of our very nature. I can therefore hold no fellowship with Australian foliage, but will cleave to the British oak through all the bareness of winter. It is a dear sight to an European to see his young compatriot trees in an Indian climate, telling of their native country by the fall of their leaf, and, in due time, becoming a spring unto themselves, although no winter has passed over them, just as their fellow countrymen keep Christmas though in the hottest weather, and, with fresh fruits about them, affect the fare and sometimes the fireside of old England. 'New Holland (says Sir James Smith) seems no very beautiful or picturesque country, such as is likely to form, or to inspire, a poet. Indeed the dregs of the community, which we have poured upon its shores, must probably subside and purge themselves, before any thing like a poet, or a disinterested lover of nature, can arise from so foul a source. There seems, however, to be no transition of seasons in the climate itself, to excite hope, or to expand the heart and fancy.[6]

NOTES

1. Since this was written, a punt has been established by government at Emu Ferry.
2. I met with this tree also in the Brazils.
3. I do not mean that the mimosa belongs to Linnæus's natural order *hesperideae*, though the eucalyptus does: my epithet is merely classical: I would say *golden*.
4. Flinders's Voyage, vol. II., p. 587.
5. Sup. to *Encyc. Brit., Art*, Botany.
6. Sup. to *Encyc. Brit., Art*, Botany.

BARRON FIELD
The Kangaroo

mixtumque genus, prolesque biformis.

    Virgil, *Aeneid*, book vi

KANGAROO, Kangaroo!
Thou Spirit of Australia,
That redeems from utter failure,
From perfect desolation,
And warrants the creation
Of this fifth part of the Earth,
Which would seem an after-birth,
Not conceiv'd in the Beginning
(For GOD bless'd His work at first,
 And saw that it was good),
But emerg'd at the first sinning,
When the ground was therefore curst; –
 And hence this barren wood!

Kangaroo, Kangaroo!
Tho' at first sight we should say,
In thy nature that there may
Contradiction be involv'd,
Yet, like discord well resolv'd,
It is quickly harmoniz'd.
Sphynx or mermaid realiz'd,
Or centaur unfabulous,
Would scarce be more prodigious,
Or Pegasus poetical,
Or hippogriff – chimeras all!
But, what Nature would compile,
Nature knows to reconcile;
And Wisdom, ever at her side,
Of all her children's justified.

She had made the squirrel fragile;
She had made the bounding hart;

But a third so strong and agile
Was beyond ev'n Nature's art;
So she join'd the former two
   In thee, Kangaroo!
To describe thee, it is hard:
Converse of the camélopard,
Which beginneth camel-wise,
But endeth of the panther size,
Thy fore half, it would appear,
Had belong'd to some 'small deer,'
Such as liveth in a tree;
By thy hinder, thou should'st be
A large animal of chace,
Bounding o'er the forest's space; –
Join'd by some divine mistake,
None but Nature's hand can make –
Nature, in her wisdom's play,
On Creation's holiday.

For howsoe'er anomalous,
Thou yet art not incongruous,
Repugnant or preposterous.
Better-proportion'd animal,
More graceful or ethereal,
Was never follow'd by the hound,
With fifty steps to thy one bound.
Thou can'st not be amended: no;
Be as thou art; thou best art so.

When sooty swans are once more rare,
And duck-moles* the Museum's care,
Be still the glory of this land,
Happiest Work of finest Hand!

---

* The *cygnus niger* of Juvenal is no *rara avis* in Australia; and time has
here given ample proof of the *ornythorinchus paradoxus*.

WILLIAM WOOLLS
The Beauties of Australia

It is a remark frequently made by persons who have immigrated to New South Wales, that this colony is not only devoid of any venerable remains of antiquity, but that it also is deficient in those interesting scenes which contribute so much to enliven and dignify the histories of other countries. To a certain extent, we ·must admit the truth of this assertion. It is true that we cannot boast of the massive structures which have been raised by the piety of our forefathers, and which are now the sacred store-houses of our predecessors, and guardians of their bones: we cannot pride ourselves upon the triumphal arch, the high-raised battlement, the moated tower, and the mouldered grandeur of days gone by; nor can we lead the traveller to the contemplation of those glorious fields on which tyranny and oppression fell beneath the sword of patriotism. We are not famous for the gigantic pyramids which were reared by kings whose names are now unknown. The lofty column and the lengthened aisle do not grace our shores. We have no plains of Marathon, no pass of Thermopylae, on which we may feel an honest pride; nor are our towns decorated with the trophies of ancient victories, and the headless busts of heroes long forgotten. But, nevertheless, Australia is not uninteresting to the lover of antiquity, for we may truly say that many of its scenes are calculated to awaken the most pleasing recollections. Can the admirer of classic lore survey the numerous flocks, which now are seen sporting over our plains, and be forgetful of those primitive ages when kings and queens tended their flocks, and valued them as their chief possessions? Can he behold the vine and the fig spreading luxuriantly over the land, and be unmindful of the beautiful passages in ancient writings which speak of them as the attendants of peace and plenty? And can he traverse the wide-spreading plain, climb the summit of the lofty range, or wander 'by gushing fount, wild wood, and shadowy dell', without calling to mind the inimitable descriptions of the ancient poets? In Australia, indeed, he may ponder with increased interest and delight on the wandering lives of the patriachs, and the sublime language of the prophets. Homer affords new beauties to him, and he appreciates many of those excellencies and eastern allusions, which are almost unintelligible in the cold and ungenial regions of the north. Nor is the Roman bard lost upon him, for the Eclogues and the Georgics, in sweet melodious numbers, instil into his breast a fondness for rural pleasures and agricultural pursuits. The man of observation, as he wends his lonely way through the woods of Australia, often recognises some object on which the poets of former days loved to dwell. Even the locust – which glorying in the scorching rays of the summer's sun – pours, far and wide, its deafening strains, reminds him of the τέττιξ, or cicada, and he recollects with satisfaction the beautiful ode of Anacreon addressed to it: –

> Μακαριζομεν σε τέττιξ,
> ὅτι δένδρεων ἐπ' ἄκρων,
> ὀλίγην δρόσον πεπωκώς,
> ϱασιλεὺς ὅπως, ἀειδεις.*

Thus it is manifest that Australia is by no means deficient in objects of interest to persons of a refined taste. She may, indeed, be poor in works of art, but she is rich in those of nature. Instead of splendid piles and victorious triumphs, she can boast of her clear Italian sky, her woolly flocks, her vine and fig; while her stupendous mountains and awful glens are far superior to all the paltry works of human skill.

---

* *We pronounce thee happy, O Cicada!*
because having sipped a little dew,
thou singest on the tops of trees, like a king.
Ode 43, 'On the Cicada'.
T. Gilpin, *The Odes of Anacreon of Teos*, London, 1806. [ed.]

'AUSTRALIE' (EMILY MANNING)
The Weatherboard Fall

A mighty crescent of grim cavern'd rock,
Red-grey, or gold-brown, with black broken rifts
Upon the bare face of the circled walls,
That bold uprise from out a sloping wealth
Of foliage rich, that in moist shadow'd depths
Revel in shelter, spread out happy leaves,
To be for ever kiss'd by dewy drops
Light-wafted from the murmuring waterfall.
   Ah, who can show the beauty of the scene?
Above, the wooded mountain summit, green,
Now gently falling into softer banks,
Emerald with fern, gleichenia, grass-tree bright,
Yet bolden'd, strengthen'd, by rough aged crags,
In bare wild outline, amber-tinged, or streak'd
With hoar grey lichen, yet oft holding too, –
Like touch of child-love in a cold stern breast, –
Cherish'd in clefts, some tender verdant nests
Of velvet moss, lone flowers, and grasses soft.
Beyond – seen 'twixt two guardian cliffs that cast
Black giant shadows on the tree-clad slopes –
An inland sea of mountains, stretching far
In undulating billows, deeply blue,
With here and there a gleaming crest of rock,
Surging in stillness, fading into space,
Seeming more liquid in the distance vague,
Transparent melting, till the last faint ridge
Blends with clear ether in the azure sky
In tender mauve unrealness; the dim line
Of mountain profile seeming but a streak
Of waving cloud on the horizon's verge.
   A few steps further – comes in fuller view
The stream that o'er the mountain summit winds,
Forcing its way with many a cascade step,
And hurrying to the rampart's brow, from which
Adown a thousand awful feet it falls,
Changing from gleaming water to white foam,

Then all dissolving into separate sprays,
Like cluster'd columns white of moving light,
Or April shower of diamond-gleaming rain,
Whereon the sun plays with his rainbow hues,
Till hid in shadow oft it disappears
Into the grateful coolness of the depths;
Resigning centred beauty for awhile,
Yet showing forth its presence by the tints
So rich enhanc'd by the bedewing love
That with soft tears refreshes budding leaves
And calls forth life.
       With artist-instinct true,
Longing to fix the beauty in his soul,
To tell to others what himself has loved,
In art to utter the impression grand,
Now Templar sits and striveth to portray
The glorious scene. Alas! No paint can match
The varying hues, no pencil may express
The foaming fall, grand amphitheatre
Of range on range in distance fairy-like,
Mark'd ever and anon by sun and shade,
And white light glint of rock bits! Down
He lays the brush in weary baffled pain,
And then essays to write. Nay, poorer yet,
The power of words to speak out Nature's soul,
Or tell her wondrous colours. E'en one rock
Has twenty divers tints for which one name
Must all suffice; no written sign can show
The glancing light of water, blend the shades
And trace the outlines fine of distant view.
  And were there power to mark the endless traits,
Still who could paint the every-varying moods?
Ere one effect is seized another comes
To transform every aspect; memory fails
To hold the past, and human cunning seems
Too slow to follow the swift-moving scenes.
Vain, vain attempt! Better in calm to watch
The 'beauty as it flies, nor bend it down'
To mock by words.
       So ceases he to strive,
But sits entranced, soul-sooth'd to harmony
With Nature's glorious work, by peaceful sounds,
Crescendo, decrescendo, of the fall
Down-pouring with a solemn sonorous bass
To rippling treble of the upland stream.

Silent, unalterable, stands the scene,
A monument of everlasting power,
By strength embuing strength, a protest grand
Against the mutability of life.
A protest? Ay, but in its *form* alone.
For changeable as man is Nature's face.
The substance, outline, firmly stand the same,
Yet seem not so; for every passing light
Varies its aspect, hides some salient points,
Or brings in prominence a new detail.
    Sometimes the bay of mountain-rippled blue
Lies clear in smiling sunshine, shadeless fair,
Till in the vault above the light clouds fly;
Then swift the pure unbroken smile is gone,
And fitting frowns pass o'er earth's countenance,
Or some great storm-cloud rises, shrouding part
Of Heaven's light, and straightway half the world
Of dreamy blue is black with angry gloom,
While some near peak glows laughing still in light.
    Yea, even bravest outlines seem to change,
As upward mounts the sun and 'lumes or shades
The various ridges, pencilling in one slope
To clear curved line, or rounding off some cliff
That hours before stood bold against the sky.
    So doth the Maker, while He sets the stamp
Of steadfast strength, yet vary all His work
With changeful joys of light and purple gloom,
Or cloud-reflected folds of soothing grey –
By vast resource of tinted picturing
And endless nature-language, e'en as much
As by His mightier powers, transcending aye
The utmost skill of art, and baffling all
The efforts vain of imitative man,
Who fain must still aspire, but – hopeless aim!
Can ne'er express in his poor human words
The glorious works of God.

CHARLES HARPUR
from *Preface* to *The Kangaroo Hunt*

Moreover, – except when a limited local reference happens to be historical to the subject, – the Poet, in picturing nature, should never pin himself to the particular, or to the locally present. The Proseman may do this at all times, and insist upon the merit of his parochial closeness; but the Poet must not: for if he do, his draft will be but a vague *account* at the best, – not a poetic picture. But he should paint her primarily through his imagination; and thus the striking features and colors of many scenes, which lie permanently gathered in his memory, becoming, with their influences, idealised in the process, will be essentially transfused upon *few*; or even upon *one* scene – one happy embodiment of her wildest freaks, or one Eden-piece embathed with a luminous atmosphere of sentiment. But never by wholesale will this transfusion be made, or indiscriminately; but in judicious keeping with the design and scope of his subject as a picture, and exactly according to its special limits and likelihoods as a landscape. And though what is thus painted may be raised in beauty or wildness above the average of any given exhibition of these qualities, it may yet, as a picture, be profoundly true to Nature, or to that flow and expression of character which such qualities best conform to, when we either locally exalt or locally concentrate her style. Thus it is truth sublimated, compressed, epitomised; – truth raised to its height, or strained away through the alembic of invention from whatever is unsightly or merely wearisome, and presented anew, though in vision, in its selectest forms and possibilities. For though, as a matter of art, it comes to *us* or is presented through the invention of the Poet, yet to *him* it came, – not literally, as in the picture before us, but in all the elements of that picture, – direct from Nature. In fine, if the Poet has been wholly true to his missionary insight in the first place, and to his re-creative instincts in the next, the license taken, and the modifications made by art, will reach only to its pictorial manner and assemblage of objects: in its spirit it will still be very Nature; while in its effect, as an aesthetic success, it will be Something yet more precious – a mind-enclosed possession, and thence a 'joy for ever'.

CHARLES HARPUR
Dawn and Sunrise in the Snowy Mountains

A few thin strips of fleecy clouds lie long
And motionless above the eastern steeps,
Like shreds of silver lace: till suddenly,
Out from the flushing centre to the ends
On either hand, their lustrous layers become
Dipt in all crimson streaked with pink and gold;
And then, at last, are edged as with a band
Of crystal fire. And now, even long before
The Sun himself is seen, off tow'rds the west
A range of mighty summits, more and more,
Blaze, each like a huge cresset, in the keen
Clear atmosphere. As if the Spirit of Light,
Advancing swiftly thence, and eastward still,
Kept kindling them in quick succession; – till
The universal company of cones
And pyramidal peaks, stand burning all
With rosy fires, like a wide ranging circ
Of God-great altars, – and even so announce
The Sun that now, with a vast flash, is seen
Pushing his rim above yon central height.

HENRY KENDALL
Bell-Birds

By channels of coolness the echoes are calling,
And down the dim gorges I hear the creek falling:
It lives in the mountain where moss and the sedges
Touch with their beauty the banks and the ledges.
Through breaks of the cedar and sycamore bowers
Struggles the light that is love to the flowers;
And, softer than slumber and sweeter than singing,
The notes of the bell-birds are running and ringing.

The silver-voiced bell-birds, the darlings of daytime!
They sing in September their songs of the May-time;
When shadows wax strong, and the thunder-bolts hurtle,
They hide with their fear in the leaves of the myrtle;
When rain and the sunbeams shine mingled together,
They start up like fairies that follow fair weather;
And straightway the hues of their feathers unfolden
Are the green and the purple, the blue and the golden.

October, the maiden of bright yellow tresses,
Loiters for love in these cool wildernesses;
Loiters, knee-deep, in the grasses, to listen,
Where dripping rocks gleam and the leafy pools glisten:
Then is the time when the water-moons splendid
Break with their gold, and are scattered or blended
Over the creeks, till the woodlands have warning
Of songs of the bell-bird and wings of the Morning.

Welcome as waters unkissed by the summers
Are the voices of bell-birds to thirsty far-comers.
When fiery December sets foot in the forest,
And the need of the wayfarer presses the sorest,
Pent in the ridges for ever and ever
The bell-birds direct him to spring and to river,
With ring and with ripple, like runnels whose torrents
Are toned by the pebbles and leaves in the currents.

Often I sit, looking back to a childhood,
Mixt with the sights and the sounds of the wildwood,
Longing for power and the sweetness to fashion,
Lyrics with beats like the heart-beats of Passion; –
Songs interwoven of lights and of laughters
Borrowed from bell-birds in far forest-rafters;
So I might keep in the city and alleys
The beauty and strength of the deep mountain valleys;
Charming to slumber the pain of my losses
With glimpses of creeks and a vision of mosses.

CHARLES HARPUR
from *The Scenic Part of Poetry*

A young critic of great promise has written: 'Who shall compute how much excellent versification has been squandered on what is called "descriptive poetry," in forgetfulness, rather than ignorance of a cardinal truth – that physical nature *beautiful* to celestial spirits, perhaps also in a modified sense of the word, to the lower brute creation in this world of ours, is *only poetical* in its immediate relation to the inner life and spirit of man'. Now this must be taken with great limitation. It would otherwise sweep away at least two-thirds of the Wordsworth, and leave us scarcely a leaf of the 'Seasons' of Thomson. But the truth is, *beautiful nature* is *poetical,* not only in its immediate, but in its whole relation to man – and further in *itself,* simply because it cannot be *unrelated* to man. As the mere richly wrought framework of his picture, (so to speak) it is *poetical* – even without the actual presence of the picture, though more so with it. It is in this region that Poetry and Painting more particularly conjoin, as Poetry and Music do in the measures and modulations of verse. What natural beauty may be in the abstract – unrelated to man – is a matter wholly foreign to the present disquisition; as it is one perhaps that is wholly without the pale of all useful enquiry. Had our young friend written – 'only poetical *in the highest sense,* & c.,' he would have been quite right. The whole canon with regard to what is poetical, includes all things that are beautiful and sublime: these, impassioned or idealised, though by contemplation only, are always and inevitably poetical, whether in immediate or remote relation to man, though the more intensely so, the nearer this relation.

CHARLES HARPUR
The Creek of the Four Graves

Part I

I verse a Settler's tale of olden times –
One told me by our sage friend, Egremont;
Who then went forth, meetly equipt, with four
Of his most trusty and adventurous men
Into the wilderness, – went forth to seek
New streams and wider pastures for his fast
Augmenting flocks and herds. On foot were all,
For horses then were beasts of too great price
To be much ventured upon mountain routes,
And over wild wolds clouded up with brush,
And cut with marshes, perilously deep.

So went they forth at dawn: and now the sun
That rose behind them as they journeyed out,
Was firing with his nether rim a range
Of unknown mountains that, like ramparts, towered
Full in their front, and his last glances fell
Into the gloomy forest's eastern glades
In golden masses, transiently, or flashed
Down on the windings of a nameless Creek,
That noiseless ran betwixt the pioneers
And those new Apennines; – ran, shaded up
With boughs of the wild willow, hanging mixed
From either bank, or duskily befringed
With upward tapering, feathery swamp-oaks –
The sylvan eyelash always of remote
Australian waters, whether gleaming still
In lake or pool, or bickering along
Between the marges of some eager stream.

Before them, thus extended, wilder grew
The scene each moment – and more beautiful!
For when the sun was all but sunk below
Those barrier mountains, – in the breeze that o'er
Their rough enormous backs deep fleeced with wood

Came whispering down, the wide upslanting sea
Of fanning leaves in the descending rays
Danced interdazzingly, as if the trees
That bore them, were all thrilling, - tingling all
Even to the roots for very happiness:
So prompted from within, so sentient, seemed
The bright quick motion - wildly beautiful.

But when the sun had wholly disappeared
Behind those mountains - O what words, what hues
Might paint the wild magnificence of view
That opened westward! Out extending, lo,
The heights rose crowding, with their summits all
Dissolving, as it seemed, and partly lost
In the exceeding radiancy aloft;
And thus transfigured, for awhile they stood
Like a great company of Archeons, crowned
With burning diadems, and tented o'er
With canopies of purple and of gold!

Here halting wearied, now the sun was set,
Our travellers kindled for their first night's camp
The brisk and crackling fire, which also looked
A wilder creature than 'twas elsewhere wont,
Because of the surrounding savageness.
And soon in cannikins the tea was made,
Fragrant and strong; long fresh-sliced rashers then
Impaled on whittled skewers, were deftly broiled
On the live embers, and when done, transferred
To quadrants from an ample damper cut,
Their only trenchers, - soon to be dispatched
With all the savoury morsels they sustained,
By the keen tooth of healthful appetite.

And as they supped, birds of new shape and plume,
And wild strange voice, nestward repairing by,
Oft took their wonder; or betwixt the gaps
In the ascending forest growths they saw
Perched on the bare abutments of the hills,
Where haply yet some lingering gleam fell through,
The wallaroo* look forth: till eastward all

----

* A kind of large Kangaroo peculiar to the higher and more difficult
  mountains.

The view had wasted into formless gloom,
Night's front; and westward, the high massing woods
Steeped in a swart but mellowed Indian hue –
A deep dusk loveliness, – lay ridged and heaped
Only the more distinctly for their shade
Against the twilight heaven – a cloudless depth
Yet luminous with sunset's fading glow;
And thus awhile, in the lit dusk, they seemed
To hang like mighty pictures of themselves
In the still chambers of some vaster world.

   The silent business of their supper done,
The Echoes of the solitary place,
Came as in sylvan wonder wide about
To hear, and imitate tentatively,
Strange voices moulding a strange speech, as then
Within the pleasant purlieus of the fire
Lifted in glee – but to be hushed erelong,
As with the night in kindred darkness came
O'er the adventurers, each and all, some sense –
Some vague-felt intimation from without,
Of danger, lurking in its forest lairs.

   But nerved by habit, and all settled soon
About the well-built fire, whose nimble tongues
Sent up continually a strenuous roar
Of fierce delight, and from their fuming pipes
Full charged and fragrant with the Indian weed,
Drawing rude comfort, – typed without, as 'twere,
By tiny clouds over their several heads
Quietly curling upward; – thus disposed
Within the pleasant firelight, grave discourse
Of their peculiar business brought to each
A steadier mood, that reached into the night.

   The simple subject to their minds at length
Fully discussed, their couches they prepared
Of rushes, and the long green tresses pulled
Down from the boughs of the wild willows near.
Then four, as pre-arranged, stretched out their limbs
Under the dark arms of the forest trees
That mixed aloft, high in the starry air,
In arcs and leafy domes whose crossing curves
And roof-like features, – blurring as they ran
Into some denser intergrowth of sprays, –

Were seen in mass traced out against the clear
Wide gaze of heaven; and trustful of the watch
Kept near them by their thoughtful Master, soon
Drowsing away, forgetful of their toil,
And of the perilous vast wilderness
That lay around them like a spectral world,
Slept, breathing deep; – whilst all things there as well
Showed slumbrous, – yea, the circling forest trees,
Their foremost boles carved from a crowded mass
Less visible, by the watchfire's bladed gleams,
As quick and spicular, from the broad red ring
Of its more constant light they ran in spurts
Far out and under the umbrageous dark;
And even the shaded and enormous mounts,
Their bluff brows glooming through the stirless air,
Looked in their quiet solemnly asleep:
Yea, thence surveyed, the Universe might have seemed
Coiled in vast rest, – only that one dim cloud,
Diffused and shapen like a spider, huge
Crept as with scrawling legs along the sky,
And that the stars, in their bright orders, still
Cluster by cluster, glowingly revealed
As this slow cloud moved on, – high over all, –
Looked wakeful – yea, looked thoughtful in their peace.

Part II

Meanwhile the cloudless eastern heaven had grown
More and more luminous – and now the Moon
Up from behind a giant hill was seen
Conglobing, till – a mighty mass – she brought
Her under border level with its cone,
As thereon it were resting: when, behold
A wonder! Instantly that cone's whole bulk
Erewhile so dark, seemed inwardly a-glow
With her instilled irradiance; while the trees
That fringed its outline, – their huge statures dwarfed
By distance into brambles, and yet all
Clearly defined against her ample orb, –
Out of its very disc appeared to swell
In shadowy relief, as they had been
All sculptured from its substance as she rose.

   Thus o'er that dark height her great orb arose,
Till her full light, in silvery sequence still
Cascading forth from ridgy slope to slope.
Like the dropt foldings of a lucent veil,
Chased mass by mass the broken darkness down
Into the dense-brushed valleys, where it crouched,
And shrank, and struggled, like a dragon doubt
Glooming some lonely spirit that doth still
Resist the Truth with obstinate shifts and shows,
Though shining out of heaven, and from defect
Winning a triumph that might else not be.

   There standing in his lone watch, Egremont
On all this solemn beauty of the world,
Looked out, yet wakeful; for sweet thoughts of home
And all the sacred charities it held,
Ingathered to his heart, as by some nice
And subtle interfusion that connects
The loved and cherished (then the most, perhaps,
When absent, or when passed, or even when *lost*)
With all serene and beautiful and bright
And lasting things of Nature. So then thought
The musing Egremont: when sudden – hark!
A bough crackt loudly in a neighboring brake,
And drew at once, as with a 'larum, all
His spirits thitherward in wild surmise.

   But summoning caution, and back stepping close
Against the shade-side of a bending gum,
With a strange horror gathering to his heart,
As if his blood were charged with insect life
And writhed along in clots, he stilled himself,
Listening long and heedfully, with head
Bent forward sideways, till his held breath grew
A pang, and his ears rung. But Silence there
Had recomposed her ruffled wings, and now
Brooded it seemed even stiller than before,
Deep nested in the darkness: so that he
Unmasking from the cold shade, grew erelong
More reassured from wishing to be so,
And to muse, Memory's suspended mood,
Though with an effort, quietly recurred.

But there again – crack upon crack! And hark!
O Heaven! have Hell's worst fiends burst howling up
Into the death-doom'd world? Or whence, if not
From diabolic rage, could surge a yell
So horrible as that which now affrights
The shuddering dark! Beings as fell are near!
Yea, Beings, in their dread inherited hate
And deadly enmity, as vengeful, come
In vengeance! For behold, from the long grass
And nearer brakes, a semi-belt of stript
And painted Savages divulge at once
Their bounding forms! – full in the flaring light
Thrown outward by the fire, that roused and lapped
The rounding darkness with its ruddy tongues
More fiercely than before, – as though even *it*
Had felt the sudden shock the air received
From those dire cries, so terrible to hear!

A moment in wild agitation seen
Thus, as they bounded up, on then they came
Closing, with weapons brandished high, and so
Rushed in upon the sleepers! three of whom
But started, and then weltered prone beneath
The first fell blow dealt down on each by three
Of the most stalwart of their pitiless foes!
But One again, and yet again, heaved up –
Up to his knees, under the crushing strokes
Of huge-clubbed nulla-nullas, till his own
Warm blood was blinding him! For he was one
Who had with Misery nearly all his days
Lived lonely, and who therefore, in his soul,
Did hunger after hope, and thirst for what
Hope still had promised him, – some taste at least
Of human good however long deferred,
And now he could not, even in dying, loose
His hold on life's poor chances of to-morrow –
Could not but so dispute the terrible fact
Of death, e'en in Death's presence! Strange it is:
Yet oft 'tis seen that Fortune's pampered child
Consents to his untimely power with less
Reluctance, less despair, than does the wretch
Who hath been ever blown about the world
The straw-like sport of Fate's most bitter blasts,
Vagrant and tieless; – ever still in him
The craving spirit thus grieves to itself:

'I never yet was happy – never yet
Tasted unmixed enjoyment, and I would
Yet pass on the bright Earth that I have loved
Some season, though most brief, of happiness;
So should I walk thenceforward to my grave,
Wherever in her green maternal breast
It might await me, more than now prepared
To house me in its gloom, – resigned at heart,
Subjected to its certainty and soothed
Even by the consciousness of having shaped
Some personal good in being; – strong myself,
And strengthening others. But to have lived long years.
Of wasted breath, because of woe and want,
And disappointed hope, – and now, at last,
To die thus desolate, is horrible!'

And feeling thus through many foregone moods
Whose lines had in the temper of his soul
All mixed, and formed *one* habit, – that poor man,
Though the black shadows of untimely death,
Inevitably, under every stroke,
But thickened more and more, – against them still
Upstruggled, nor would cease: until one last
Tremendous blow, dealt down upon his head
As if in mercy, gave him to the dust
With all his many woes and frustrate hope.

Struck through with a cold horror, Egremont,
Standing apart, – yea, standing as it were
In marble effigy, saw this, saw all!
And when outthawing from his frozen heart
His blood again rushed tingling – with a leap
Awaking from the ghastly trance which there
Had bound him, as with chill petrific bonds,
He raised from instinct more than conscious thought
His death-charged tube, and at that murderous crew
Firing! saw one fall ox-like to the earth; –
Then turned and fled. Fast fled he, but as fast
His deadly foes went thronging on his track!
Fast! for in full pursuit, behind him yelled
Wild men whose wild speech hath no word for *mercy*!
And as he fled, the forest beasts as well,
In general terror, through the brakes a-head

Crashed scattering, or with maddening speed athwart
His course came frequent. On – still on he flies –
Flies for dear life! and still behind him hears
Nearer and nearer, the so rapid dig
Of many feet, – nearer and nearer still.

Part III

So went the chase! And now what should he do?
Abruptly turning, the wild Creek lay right
Before him! But no time was there for thought:
So on he kept and from a bulging rock
That beaked the bank like a bare promontory,
Plunging right forth and shooting feet-first down,
Sunk to his middle in the flashing stream –
In which the imaged stars seemed all at once
To burst like rockets into one wild blaze
Of interwrithing light. Then wading through
The ruffled waters, forth he sprang and siezed
A snake-like root that from the opponent bank
Protruded, and round which his earnest fear
Did clench his cold hand like a clamp of steel,
A moment, – till as swiftly thence he swung
His dripping form aloft, and up the dark
O'erjutting ledge went clambering in the blind
And breathless haste of one who flies for life:
When in its face – O verily our God
Hath those in his peculiar care for whom
The daily prayers of spotless Womanhood
And helpless Infancy, are offered up! –
When in its face a cavity he felt,
The upper earth of which in one rude mass
Was held fast bound by the enwoven roots
Of two old trees, – and which, beneath the mould,
Just o'er the clammy vacancy below,
Twisted and lapped like knotted snakes, and made
A natural loft-work. Under this he crept,
Just as the dark forms of his hunters thronged
The bulging rock whence he before had plunged.

   Duskily visible, thereon a space
They paused to mark what bent his course might take
Over the farther bank, thereby intent
To hold upon the chase, which way soe'er

It might incline, more surely. But no form
Amongst the moveless fringe of fern was seen
To shoot up from its outline, - up and forth
Into the moonlight that lay bright beyond
In torn and shapeless blocks, amid the boles
And mixing shadows of the taller trees,
All standing now in the keen radiance there
So ghostly still, as in a solemn trance.
But nothing in the silent prospect stirred -
No fugitive apparition in the view
Rose, as they stared in fierce expectancy:
Wherefore they augured that their prey was yet
Somewhere between, - and the whole group with that
Plunged forward, till the fretted current boiled
Amongst their crowding trunks from bank to bank;
And searching thus the stream across, and then
Lengthwise, along the ledges, - combing down
Still, as they went, with dripping fingers, cold
And cruel as inquisitive, each clump
Of long flagged swamp-grass where it flourished high, -
The whole dark line passed slowly, man by man,
Athwart the cavity - so fearfully near,
That as they waded by the Fugitive
Felt the strong odor of their wetted skins
Pass with them, trailing as their bodies moved
Stealthily on, - coming with each, and going.

But their keen search was keen in vain. And now
Those wild men marvelled, - till, in consultation,
There grouped in dark knots standing in the stream
That glimmered past them, moaning as it went,
His vanishment, so passing strange it seemed,
They coupled with the mystery of some crude
Old fable of their race; and fear-struck all,
And silent, then withdrew. And when the sound
Of their receeding steps had from his ear
Died off, as back to the stormed Camp again
They hurried to despoil the yet warm dead,
Our Friend slid forth, and springing up the bank,
Renewed his flight, nor rested from it, till
He gained the welcoming shelter of his Home.

Return we for a moment to the scene
Of recent death. There the late flaring fire
Now smouldered, for its brands were strewn about,

And four stark corses plundered to the skin
And brutally mutilated, seemed to stare
With frozen eyeballs up into the pale
Round visage of the Moon, who, high in heaven,
With all her stars, in golden bevies, gazed
As peacefully down as on a bridal there
Of the warm Living - not, alas! on them
Who kept in ghastly silence through the night
Untimely spousals with a desert death.

  O God! and thus this lovely world hath been
Accursed for ever by the bloody deeds
Of its prime Creature - Man. Erring or wise,
Savage or civilised, still hath he made
This glorious residence, the Earth, a Hell
Of wrong and robbery and untimely death!
Some dread Intelligence opposed to Good
Did, of a surety, over all the earth
Spread out from Eden - or it were not so!
For see the bright beholding Moon, and all
The radiant Host of Heaven, evince no touch
Of sympathy with Man's wild violence; -
Only evince in their calm course, their part
In that original unity of Love,
Which, like the soul that dwelleth in a harp,
Under God's hand, in the beginning, chimed
The sabbath concord of the Universe;
And look on a gay clique of maidens, met
In village tryst, and interwhirling all
In glad Arcadian dances on the green -
Or on a hermit, in his vigils long,
Seen kneeling at the doorway of his cell -
Or on a monster battle-field where lie
In sweltering heaps, the dead and dying both,
On the cold gory ground, - as they that night
Looked in bright peace, down on the doomful Wild.

  Afterwards there, for many changeful years,
Within a glade that sloped into the bank
Of that wild mountain Creek - midway within,
In partial record of a terrible hour
Of human agony and loss extreme,
Four grassy mounds stretched lengthwise side by side,
Startled the wanderer; - four long grassy mounds
Bestrewn with leaves, and withered spraylets, stript

By the loud wintry wingéd gales that roamed
Those solitudes, from the old trees which there
Moaned the same leafy dirges that had caught
The heed of dying Ages: these were all;
And thence the place was long by travellers called
The Creek of the Four Graves. Such was the Tale
Egremont told us of the wild old times.

HENRY KENDALL
A Death in the Bush

The hut was built of bark and shrunken slabs
That wore the marks of many rains, and showed
Dry flaws, wherein had crept and nestled rot.
Moreover, round the bases of the bark
Were left the tracks of flying forest-fires,
As you may see them on the lower bole
Of every elder of the native woods.

For, ere the early settlers came and stocked
These wilds with sheep and kine, the grasses grew
So that they took the passing pilgrim in,
And whelmed him, like a running sea, from sight.

And therefore, through the fiercer summer months,
While all the swamps were rotten – while the flats
Were baked and broken; when the clayey rifts
Yawned wide half-choked with drifted herbage past,
Spontaneous flames would burst from thence, and race
Across the prairies all day long.

      At night
The winds were up, and then with fourfold speed,
A harsh gigantic growth of smoke and fire
Would roar along the bottoms, in the wake
Of fainting flocks of parrots, wallaroos,
And 'wildered wild things, scattering right and left,
For safety vague, throughout the general gloom.

Anon, the nearer hill-side growing trees
Would take the surges; thus, from bough to bough,
Was borne the flaming terror! Bole and spire,
Rank after rank, now pillared, ringed, and rolled
In blinding blaze, stood out against the dead
Down-smothered dark, for fifty leagues away.

For fifty leagues! and when the winds were strong,
For fifty more! But, in the olden time,
These fires were counted as the harbingers
Of life-essential storms; since out of smoke
And heat there came across the midnight ways
Abundant comfort, with upgathered clouds,
And runnels babbling of a plenteous fall.

So comes the Southern gale at evenfall
(The swift 'brickfielder' of the local folk)
About the streets of Sydney, when the dust
Lies burnt on glaring windows, and the men
Look forth from doors of drouth, and drink the change
With thirsty haste and that most thankful cry
Of, 'here it is – the cool, bright, blessed rain!'

The hut, I say, was built of bark and slabs,
And stood, the centre of a clearing, hemmed
By hurdle-yards, and ancients of the blacks;
These moped about their lazy fires, and sang
Wild ditties of the old days, with a sound
Of sorrow, like an everlasting wind,
Which mingled with the echoes of the noon,
And moaned amongst the noises of the night.

From thence a cattle-track, with link to link,
Ran off against the fishpools, to the gap,
Which sets you face to face with gleaming miles
Of broad Orara, winding in amongst
Black, barren ridges, where the nether spurs
Are fenced about by cotton-scrub, and grass
Blue-bitten with the salt of many droughts.

'Twas here the shepherd housed him every night,
And faced the prospect like a patient soul;
Borne up by some vague hope of better days,
And God's fine blessing in his faithful wife;
Until the humour of his malady
Took cunning changes from the good to bad,
And laid him lastly on a bed of death.

Two months thereafter, when the summer heat
Had roused the serpent from his rotten lair,
And made a noise of locusts in the boughs,
It came to this, that, as the blood-red sun

Of one fierce day of many slanted down
Obliquely past the nether jags of peaks
And gulfs of mist, the tardy night came vexed
By bolted clouds, and scuds that wheeled and whirled
To left and right about the brazen clifts
Of ridges, rigid with a leaden gloom.

Then took the cattle to the forest camps
With vacant terror, and the hustled sheep
Stood dumb against the hurdles, even like
A fallen patch of shadowed mountain snow;
And ever through the curlew's call afar
The storm grew on, while round the stinted slabs
Sharp snaps and hisses came, and went, and came,
The huddled tokens of a mighty blast
Which ran with an exceeding bitter cry
Across the tumbled fragments of the hills,
And through the sluices of the gorge and glen.

So, therefore, all about the shepherd's hut
That space was mute, save when the fastened dog,
Without a kennel, caught a passing glimpse
Of firelight moving through the lighted chinks;
For then he knew the hints of warmth within,
And stood, and set his great pathetic eyes,
In wind and wet, imploring to be loosed.

Not often now the watcher left the couch
Of him she watched; since, in his fitful sleep,
His lips would stir to wayward themes, and close
With bodeful catches. Once she moved away,
Half-deafened by terrific claps, and stooped,
And looked without; to see a pillar dim
Of gathered gusts and fiery rain.

      Anon,
The sick man woke, and, startled by the noise,
Stared round the room, with dull delirious sight,
At this wild thing and that; for, through his eyes,
The place took fearful shapes, and fever showed
Strange crosswise lights about his pillow-head.
He, catching there at some phantasmic help,
Sat upright on the bolster, with a cry
Of, 'Where is Jesus? – it is bitter cold!'
And then, because the thundercalls outside

Were mixed for him with slanders of the Past,
He called his weeping wife by name, and said,
'Come closer, darling! we shall speed away
Across the seas, and seek some mountain home,
Shut in from liars, and the wicked words
That track us day and night, and night and day.'

So waned the sad refrain. And those poor lips,
Whose latest phrases were for peace, grew mute,
And into everlasting silence passed.

As fares a swimmer who hath lost his breath
In 'wildering seas afar from any help –
Who, fronting Death, can never realise
The dreadful Presence, but is prone to clutch
At every weed upon the weltering wave;
So fared the watcher, poring o'er the last
Of him she loved, with dazed and stupid stare;
Half conscious of the sudden loss and lack
Of all that bound her life, but yet without
The power to take her mighty sorrow in.

Then came a patch or two of starry sky;
And through a reef of cloven thunder-cloud
The soft Moon looked: a patient face beyond
The fierce impatient shadows of the slopes,
And the harsh voices of the broken hills!
A patient face, and one which came and wrought
A lovely silence like a silver mist
Across the rainy relics of the storm.

For in the breaks and pauses of her light
The gale died out in gusts; yet, evermore
About the roof-tree, on the dripping eaves,
The damp wind loitered; and a fitful drift
Sloped through the silent curtains, and thwart
The dead.

        There, when the glare had dropped behind
A mighty ridge of gloom, the woman turned
And sat in darkness face to face with God,
And said – 'I know,' she said, 'that Thou art wise;
That when we build and hope, and hope and build,
And see our best things fall, it comes to pass
For evermore that we must turn to Thee!

And therefore, now, because I cannot find
The faintest token of Divinity
In this my latest sorrow, let Thy light
Inform mine eyes, so I may learn to look
On something past the sight which shuts, and blinds,
And seems to drive me wholly, Lord, from Thee.'

Now waned the moon beyond complaining depths;
And, as the dawn looked forth from showery woods
(Whereon had dropt a hint of red and gold),
There went about the crooked cavern-caves
Low flute-like echoes with a noise of wings
And waters flying down far-hidden fells.
Then might be seen the solitary owl,
Perched in the clefts; scared at the coming light,
And staring outward (like a sea-shelled thing
Chased to his cover by some bright fierce foe)
As at a monster in the middle waste.

At last the great kingfisher came and called
Across the hollows loud with early whips,
And lighted, laughing, on the shepherd's hut,
And roused the widow from a swoon like death.

This day, and after it was noised abroad,
By blacks, and straggling horsemen on the roads,
That he was dead 'who had been sick so long,'
There flocked a troop from far-surrounding runs
To see their neighbour and to bury him.
And men who had forgotten how to cry
(Rough flinty fellows of the native bush)
Now learned the bitter way, beholding there
The wasted shadow of an iron frame
Brought down so low by years of fearful pain;
And marking, too, the woman's gentle face,
And all the pathos in her moaned reply
Of 'masters we have lived in better days.'

One stooped – a stockman from the nearer hills –
To loose his wallet-strings, from whence he took
A bag of tea, and laid it on her lap;
Then, sobbing, 'God will help you, missus, yet,'
He sought his horse with most bewildered eyes,
And, spurring swiftly, galloped down the glen.

Where black Orara nightly chafes his brink,
Midway between lamenting lines of oak
And Warra's gap, the shepherd's grave was built,
And there the wild-dog pauses, in the midst
Of moonless watches: howling through the gloom
At hopeless shadows flitting to and fro,
What time the East Wind hums his darkest hymn,
And rains beat heavy on the ruined leaf.

There, while the Autumn in the cedar trees
Sat cooped about by cloudy evergreens,
The widow sojourned on the silent road,
And mutely faced the barren mound, and plucked
A straggling shrub from thence, and passed away,
Heart-broken on to Sydney; where she took
Her passage in an English vessel bound
To London, for her home of other years.

At rest! Not near, with Sorrow on his grave,
And roses quickened into beauty – wrapt
In all the pathos of perennial bloom;
But far from there, beneath the fretful clay
Of lands within the lone perpetual cry
Of hermit plovers and the night-like oaks,
All moaning for the peace which never comes.

At rest! And she who sits and waits behind
Is in the shadows; but her faith is sure,
And *one* fine promise of the coming days
Is breaking, like a blessed morning, far
On hills 'that slope through darkness up to God.'

MARCUS CLARKE
Preface to Adam Lindsay Gordon's *Sea Spray and Smoke Drift*

The poems of Gordon have an interest beyond the mere personal one which his friends attach to his name. Written, as they were, at odd times and leisure moments of a stirring and adventurous life, is not to be wondered at if they are unequal or unfinished. The astonishment of those who knew the man, and can gauge the capacity of this city to foster poetic instinct, is, that such work was ever produced here at all. Intensely nervous, and feeling much of that shame at the exercise of the higher intelligence which besets those who are known to be renowned in field sports, Gordon produced his poems shyly, scribbled them on scraps of paper, and sent them anonymously to magazines. It was not until he discovered one morning that everybody knew a couplet or two of 'How we beat the Favourite' that he consented to forego his anonymity and appear in the unsuspected character of a versemaker. The success of his republished 'collected' poems gave him courage, and the unreserved praise which greeted 'Bush Ballads' should have urged him to forget or to conquer those evil promptings which, unhappily, brought about his untimely death.

Adam Lindsay Gordon was the son of an officer in the English army, and was educated at Woolwich, in order that he might follow the profession of his family. At the time when he was a cadet there was no sign of either of the two great wars which were about to call forth the strength of English arms, and, like many other men of his day, he quitted his prospects of service and emigrated. He went to South Australia and started as a sheep farmer. His efforts were attended with failure. He lost his capital, and owning nothing but a love for horsemanship and a head full of Browning and Shelley, plunged into the varied life which gold-mining, 'overlanding', and cattle-driving affords. From this experience he emerged to light in Melbourne as the best amateur steeplechase rider in the colonies. The victory he won for Major Baker in 1868, when he rode Babbler for the Cup Steeplechase, made him popular, and the almost simultaneous publication of his last volume of poems gave him welcome entrance to the houses of all who had pretensions to literary taste. The reputation

43

of the book spread to England, and Major Whyte Melville did not disdain to place the lines of the dashing Australian author at the head of his own dashing descriptions of sporting scenery. Unhappily, the melancholy which Gordon's friends had with pain observed increased daily, and in the full flood of his success, with congratulations pouring upon him from every side, he was found dead in the heather near his home with a bullet from his own rifle in his brain.

I do not purpose to criticize the volumes which these few lines of preface introduce to the reader. The influence of Browning and of Swinburne upon the writer's taste is plain. There is plainly visible also, however, a keen sense for natural beauty and a manly admiration for healthy living. If in 'Ashtaroth' and 'Bellona' we recognize the swing of a familiar metre, in such poems as the 'Sick Stockrider' we perceive the genuine poetic instinct united to a very clear perception of the loveliness of duty and of labour.

'Twas merry in the glowing morn, among the gleaming grass,
    To wander as we've wander'd many a mile,
And blow the cool tobacco cloud, and watch the white wreaths pass,
    Sitting loosely in the saddle all the while;
'Twas merry 'mid the blackwoods when we spied the station roofs,
    To wheel the wild scrub cattle at the yard,
With a running fire of stockwhips and a fiery run of hoofs,
    Oh! the hardest day was never then too hard!

Aye! we had a glorious gallop after 'Starlight' and his gang,
    When they bolted from Sylvester's on the flat:
How the sun-dried reed-beds crackled, how the flint-strewn ranges rang
    To the strokes of 'Mountaineer' and 'Acrobat;'
Hard behind them in the timber, harder still across the heath,
    Close behind them through the tea-tree scrub we dash'd;
And the golden-tinted fern leaves, how they rustled underneath!
    And the honeysuckle osiers, how they crash'd!

This is genuine. There is no 'poetic evolution from the depths of internal consciousness' here. The writer has ridden his ride as well as written it.

The student of these unpretending volumes will be repaid for his labour. He will find in them something very like the beginnings of a national school of Australian poetry. In historic Europe, where every rood of ground is hallowed in legend and in song, the least imaginative can find food for sad and sweet reflection. When strolling at noon down an English country lane, lounging at sunset by some ruined chapel on the margin of an Irish lake, or watching the mists of morning unveil Ben Lomond, we feel all the charm which springs from association with the past. Soothed, saddened, and cheered by turns, we partake of the varied moods which belong not so much to ourselves as to the dead men who, in old days, sung, suffered, or conquered in the scenes which we survey. But this our native or adopted land has no past, no story. No poet speaks to us. Do we need a poet to interpret Nature's teachings, we must look into our own hearts, if perchance we may find a poet there.

What is the dominant note of Australian scenery? That which is the dominant note of Edgar Allan Poe's poetry – Weird Melancholy. A poem like 'L'Allegro' could never be written by an Australian. It is too airy, too sweet, too freshly happy. The Australian mountain forests are funereal, secret, stern. Their solitude is desolation. They seem to stifle, in their black gorges, a story of sullen despair. No tender sentiment is nourished in their shade. In other lands the dying year is mourned, the falling leaves drop lightly on his bier. In the Australian forests no leaves fall. The savage winds shout among the rock clefts. From the melancholy gums strips of white bark hang and rustle. The very animal life of these frowning hills is either grotesque or ghostly. Great grey kangaroos hop noiselessly over the coarse grass. Flights of white cockatoos stream out, shrieking like evil souls. The sun suddenly sinks, and the mopokes burst out into horrible peals of semi-human laughter. The natives aver that, when night comes, from out the bottomless depth of some lagoon the Bunyip rises, and, in form like monstrous sea-calf, drags his loathsome length from out the ooze. From a corner of the silent forest rises a dismal chant, and around a fire dance natives painted like skeletons. All is fear-inspiring and gloomy. No bright fancies are linked with the memories of the mountains. Hopeless explorers have named them out of their sufferings – Mount Misery, Mount Dreadful, Mount Despair. As when among sylvan scenes in places

Made green with the running of rivers,
And gracious with temperate air,

the soul is soothed and satisfied, so, placed before the frightful grandeur of these barren hills, it drinks in their sentiment of defiant ferocity, and is steeped in bitterness.

Australia has rightly been named the Land of the Dawning. Wrapped in the midst of early morning, her history looms vague and gigantic. The lonely horseman riding between the moonlight and the day sees vast shadows creeping across the shelterless and silent plains, hears strange noises in the primeval forest where flourishes a vegetation long dead in other lands, and feels, despite his fortune, that the trim utilitarian civilisation which bred him shrinks into insignificance beside the contemptuous grandeur of forest and ranges coeval with an age in which European scientists have cradled his own race.

There is a poem in every form of tree or flower, but the poetry which lives in the trees and flowers of Australia differs from those of other countries. Europe is the home of knightly song, of bright deeds and clear morning thought. Asia sinks beneath the weighty recollections of her past magnificence, as the Suttee sinks, jewel-burdened, upon the corpse of dread grandeur, destructive even in its death. America swiftly hurries on her way, rapid, glittering, insatiable even as one of her own giant waterfalls. From the jungles of Africa, and the creeper-tangle groves of the Islands of the South, arise, from the glowing hearts of a thousand flowers, heavy and intoxicating odours – the Upas-poison which dwells in barbaric sensuality. In Australia alone is to be found the Grotesque, the Weird, the strange scribblings of Nature learning how to write. Some see no beauty in our trees without shade, our flowers without perfume, our birds who cannot fly, and our beasts who have not yet learned to walk on all fours. But the dweller in the wilderness acknowledges the subtle charm of this fantastic land of monstrosities. He becomes familiar with the beauty of loneliness. Whispered to by the myriad tongues of the wilderness, he learns the language of the barren and the uncouth, and can read the hieroglyphs of haggard gum-trees, blown into odd shapes, distorted with fierce hot winds, or cramped with cold nights, when the Southern Cross freezes in a cloudless sky of icy blue. The phantasmagoria of that wild dream-land termed the Bush interprets itself, and the Poet of our desolation begins to comprehend why free Esau loved his heritage of desert sand better than all the bountiful richness of Egypt.

ADAM LINDSAY GORDON
The Sick Stockrider

Hold hard, Ned! lift me down once more, and lay me in the
    shade;
  Old man, you've had your work cut out to guide
Both horses, and to hold me in the saddle when I sway'd,
  All through the hot, slow, sleepy, silent ride;
The dawn at 'Moorabinda' was a mist rack dull and dense
  The sunrise was a sullen sluggish lamp;
I was dozing in the gateway at Arbuthnot's bound'ry fence,
  I was dreaming on the Limestone cattle camp;
We crossed the creek at Carricksford, and sharply through the
    haze,
  And suddenly the sun shot flaming forth;
To southward lay 'Katâwa' with the sandpeaks all ablaze
  And the flush'd fields of Glen Lomond lay to north –
Now westward winds the bridle path that leads to Lindisfarm,
  And yonder looms the double headed bluff;
From the far side of the first hill, when the skies are clear and
    calm,
  You can see Sylvester's woolshed fair enough.

Five miles we used to call it from our homestead to the place
  Where the big tree spans the roadway like an arch;
'Twas here we ran the dingo down that gave us such a chase
  Eight years ago – or was it nine? – last March.

'Twas merry in the glowing morn, among the gleaming grass,
  To wander as we've wander'd many a mile,
And blow the cool tobacco cloud, and watch the white wreaths
    pass,
  Sitting loosely in the saddle all the while;
'Twas merry 'mid the blackwoods when we spied the station
    roofs,
  To wheel the wild scrub cattle at the yard,
With a running fire of stockwhips and a fiery run of hoofs,
  Oh! the hardest day was never then too hard!

Ay! we had a glorious gallop after 'Starlight' and his gang,
   When they bolted from Sylvester's on the flat;
How the sun-dried reed-beds crackled, how the flint-strewn
     ranges rang
   To the strokes of 'Mountaineer' and 'Acrobat;'
Hard behind them in the timber, harder still across the heath,
   Close behind them through the tea-tree scrub we dash'd;
And the golden-tinted fern leaves, how they rustled
     underneath!
   And the honeysuckle osiers, how they crash'd!

We led the hunt throughout, Ned, on the chestnut and the
     grey,
   And the troopers were three hundred yards behind,
While we emptied our six shooters on the bushrangers at bay,
   In the creek with stunted box-tree for a blind!
There you grappled with the leader, man to man and horse to
     horse,
   And you roll'd together when the chestnut rear'd;
He blaz'd away and missed you in that shallow watercourse –
   A narrow shave – his powder singed your beard!

In these hours when life is ebbing, how those days when life
     was young
   Come back to us – how clearly I recall
Even the yarns Jack Hall invented, and the songs Jem Roper
     sung,
   And where are now Jem Roper and Jack Hall?

Ay! nearly all our comrades of the old colonial school,
   Our ancient boon companions, Ned, are gone;
Hard livers for the most part, somewhat reckless as a rule,
   It seems that you and I are left alone.

There was Hughes, who got in trouble through that business
     with the cards,
   It matters little what became of him,
But a steer ripp'd up MacPherson in the Cooraminta yards,
   And Sullivan was drown'd at Sink-or-swim,
And Mostyn – poor Frank Mostyn – died at last a fearful wreck,
   In 'the horrors' at the Upper Wandinong,
And Carisbrook the rider at the Horsefall broke his neck,
   Faith! the wonder was he saved his neck so long!

Ah! those days and nights we squandered at the Logans in the
    Glen –
  The Logans, man and wife, have long been dead,
Elsie's tallest girl seems taller than your little Elsie then,
  And Ethel is a woman grown and wed.

I've had my share of pastime, and I've done my share of toil,
  And life is short – the longest life a span –
I care not now to tarry for the corn or for the oil,
  Or for the wine that maketh glad the heart of man;
For good undone and gifts misspent and resolutions vain,
  'Tis somewhat late to trouble – This I know,
I should live the same life over, if I had to live again;
  And the chances are I go where most men go.

The deep blue skies wax dusky and the tall green trees grow
    dim,
  The sward beneath me seems to heave and fall,
And sickly, smoky shadows through the sleepy sunlight swim,
  And on the very sun's face weave their pall.
Let me slumber in the hollow where the wattle blossoms wave,
  With never stone or rail to fence my bed;
Should the sturdy station children pull the bush flowers on my
    grave,
  I may chance to hear them romping overhead.

MARCUS CLARKE
Pretty Dick

A hot day. A very hot day on the plains. A very hot day up in the ranges, too. The Australian sun had got up suddenly with a savage swoop, as though he was angry at the still coolness of early morning, and was determined to drive the cattle, who were munching complacently in the long rich grass of the swamp, back up under the hill among the thick she-oaks. It seemed to be a settled thing on the part of the sun to get up hotter and hotter every morning. He even went down at night with a red face, as much as to say, 'Take care, I shall be hotter than ever to-morrow!'

The men on the station did not get into smoking humour until he had been gone down at least an hour, and so they sat on a bench and a barrel or two outside the 'men's hut' on the hill, they looked away across the swamp to that jagged gap in the ranges where he had sunk, and seeing the red flush in the sky, nodded at one another, and said, 'We shall have a hot day to-morrow.' And they were right. For, when they had forgotten the mosquitoes, and the heat, and the many pleasant things that live in the crevices between the slabs of the hut, and gone to sleep, up he came again, hotter than ever, without the least warning, and sent them away to work again.

On this particular morning he was very hot. Even King Peter, who was slowly driving up the working bullocks from the swamp, felt his old enemy so fierce on his back, that he got up in his stirrups and cracked his whip, until the hills rang again, and Strawberry, and Punch, and Doughboy, and Damper, and all (except that cynical, wicked, Spot, who hated the world and always lived away by himself in a private clump of she-oak) straightened their tails and shook their heads, and galloped away up to the stockyard in mortal terror. The horses feel the heat, and King Peter's brother, who was looking for them on the side of the Stony Mount, had a long ride up and down all sorts of gullies before he found them out, and then they were unusually difficult to get together. The cockatoos knew it was hot, and screamed themselves away into the bush. The kangaroos, who had come down like gigantic shadows out of the still night, had all hopped away back into the scrub under the mountains, while the mist yet hung about the trees around the creek-bed. The parrots were uneasy, and the very station dogs got under the shadow-lee of the huts, in case of a hot wind coming up. As for the sheep – when Pretty Dick's father let them out in the dawn, he said to his dog, 'We shan't have much to do to-day, old woman, shall we?' At which Lassie wagged her tail and grinned, as intelligent dogs do.

But who was Pretty Dick?

Pretty Dick was the seven years' old son of Richard Fielding, the shepherd. Pretty Dick was a slender little man, with eyes like pools of still water when the sky is violet at sunset, and a skin as white as milk – that is, under his little blue and white shirt, for where the sun had touched it, it was a golden brown, and his hands were the colour of the ripe chestnuts his father used to gather in England years ago. Pretty Dick had hair like a patch of sunlight, and a laugh like rippling water. He was the merriest little fellow possible, and manly too! He understood all about milking, did Pretty Dick; and could drive up a refractory cow with anybody. He could chop wood too – that is, a little, you know, because he was not very strong, and the axe was heavy. He could ride, and a buck-jumper – that was his ambition – but he would take Molly (the wall-eyed mare) into the home station for his father's rations, and come out again quite safely.

He liked going into the station, because he saw Ah Yung, the Chinaman cook, who was kind to him, and gave him sugar. He had all the news to hear too. How another mob of travelling sheep were coming through the run; how the grey mare had slipped her foal; how the bay filly had bucked off Black Harry and hurt his wrist; how Old Tom had 'got the sack' for being impudent to the overseer, and had vowed to fire the run. Besides, there was the paper to borrow for his father, Mr. Trelawney's horses to look at, the chat with the carpenter, and perhaps a peep at the new buggy with its silver-mounted harness (worth, 'oh, thousands of pounds!' Pretty Dick thought;) perhaps, too, he might go down to the house, with its garden, and cool verandah, and bunches of grapes; might get a little cake from Mary, the cook; or even might be smiled upon by Mrs. Trelawney, the owner's young wife, who seemed to Dick to be something more than a lady – to be a sweet voice that spoke kindly to him, and made him feel as he would feel sometimes when his mother would get the Big Bible, that came all the way from England, and tell him the story about the Good Man who so loved little children.

He liked to go into the station, because everyone was so kind to him. Everyone loved Pretty Dick; even Old Tom, who had been a 'lag', and was a very wicked man, hushed the foul jest and savage oath when the curly head of Pretty Dick came within hearing; and the men always felt as if they had their Sunday clothes on in his presence. But he was not to go into the station to-day. It was not ration-day; so he sat on the step of his father's hut door, looking out through a break in the timber-belt at the white dots on the plain, that he knew to be his father's sheep.

Pretty Dick's father lived in the Log Hut, on the edge of the plains, and had five thousand sheep to look after. He was away all day. Sometimes, when the sheep would camp near home, Pretty Dick would go down with some fresh tea in a 'billy' for his father, and would have a very merry afternoon watching his father cut curious notches on his stick, and would play with Lassie, and look about for 'possums in the trees, or, with craning neck, cautiously inspect an ant-hill. And then when evening came, and Lassie had got the sheep together – quietly without any barking, you know – when father and son jogged homewards through the warm, still air, and the trampling hoofs of the sheep sent up a fragrance from the crushed herbage round the folding ground, Pretty Dick would repeat long stories that his mother had told him, about 'Valentine and Orson', and 'Beauty and the Beast', and 'Jack the Giant Killer', for Pretty Dick's mother had been maid in the rector's family in the Kentish village at home, and was a little above Pretty Dick's father, who was only a better sort of farm labourer. But they were all three very happy now in their adopted country. They were alone there, these three – Pretty Dick, and mother and father – and no other children came to divide the love that both father and mother had for Pretty Dick. So that when Pretty Dick knelt down by his little bed at night, and put his little brown hands together, and said, 'God bless my dear father and mother, and God bless me and make me a good boy,' he prayed for the whole family, you see. So they all three loved each other very much – though they were poor people – and Pretty Dick's mother often said that she would not have any harm happen to Pretty Dick for Queen Victoria's golden crown. They had called him Pretty Dick when he was yet a baby on board the *Star of Peace*, emigrant ship, and the name had remained with him ever since. His father called him Pretty Dick; and his mother called him Pretty Dick; and the people at the home station called him Pretty Dick and even the cockatoo that lived on the perch over Lassie's bark kennel, would call out 'Pretty Dick! Pretty Dick! Pretty Dick!' over and over again.

Now, on this particular morning, Pretty Dick sat gazing between the trunks of the gum trees into the blue distance. It was very hot. The blue sky was cloudless, and the sun seemed to be everywhere at once. There was a little shade, to be sure, among the gum-tree trunks, but that would soon pass, and there would be no shade anywhere. The little fenced-in water-hole in the front of the hut glittered in the sunlight like a piece of burnished metal, and the tin milk-pail that was turned topsy-turvy on the pole-paling, was quite dazzling to look at. Daisy, the cow, stood stupidly under the shade of a round, punchy little she-oak close by, and seemed too lazy even to lie down, it was so hot. Of course the blow-flies had begun, and their ceaseless buzz resounded above and around, making it seem hotter than ever, Pretty Dick thought.

How hot father must be! Pretty Dick knew those terrible plains well. He had been across them two or three times. Once in the early spring, when it was pleasant enough with a cool breeze blowing, and white clouds resting on the tops of the distant mountains, and the broad rolling levels of short, crisp, grass-land sweeping up from their feet to the horizon unceasingly. But he had been across there once in the summer, when the ground was dry and cracked, when the mountains seemed so close that he almost thought that he could touch them with his hand, when the heavens were like burning brass, and the air (crepitant with the ceaseless chirping of the grass-hopper) like the flame of a heated furnace. Pretty Dick felt quite a fresh accession of heat as he thought of it, and turned his face away to the right to cool himself by thinking of the Ranges. They were deep in the bush, past the creek that ran away the other side of the Sandy Rises; deep in the bush on the right hand, and many a weary stretch of sandy slope, and rough-grassed swamp, and solemn wood, and dismal, deserted scrub, was between him and them. He could see the lofty purple peak of Mount Clear, the highest in the range, grandly rising above the dense level tops of the gum-tree forest, and he thought how cool it must be in its mighty shadow. He had never been under the mountain. That there were some strange reaches of scrub, and sand, and dense thickets, and tumbled creeper-entwined rock in that swamp-guarded land, that lay all unseen under the shadow of the hills, he knew, for he had heard the men say so. Had he not heard how men had been lost in that awesome scrub, silent and impenetrable, which swallowed up its victims noiselessly? Had he not heard how shepherds had strayed or slept, and how at night the sheep had returned alone, and that search had been in vain, until perhaps some wandering horseman, all by chance, had lighted upon a rusty rag or two, a white skull, and perhaps a tin pannikin, with hopeless scratchings of name and date? Had he not been told fearful things about those ranges? How the bushrangers had made their lair in the Gap, and how the cave was yet visible where their leader had been shot dead by the troopers; how large sums of stolen money were buried there, hidden away behind slags and slabs of rock, flung into fathomless gullies, or crammed into fissures in the mountain side, hidden so well, that all the searching hands and prying eyes of the district had not yet discovered them? Did not Wallaby Dick tell him one night about the Murder that had been done down in the flat under the large Australian moon – when the two swagmen, after eating and drinking, had got up in the bright, still night, and beaten out the brains of the travelling hawker, who gave them hospitality, and how, the old man being found beside his rifled cart, with his gray hairs matted with blood, search was made for the Murderers, and they were taken in a tap-room in distant Hamilton-town bargaining with the landlord for the purchase of their plunder?

What stories had he not heard of wild cattle, of savage bulls, red-eyed, pawing, and unapproachable? What hideous tales of snakes, black, cold, and deadly, had not been associated in his mind with that Mountain Land? What a strange, dangerous fascinating, horrible, wonderful place that Mountain Land must be, and how much he would like to explore it! But he had been forbidden to go, and he dismissed, with a childish sigh, all idea of going.

He looked up at his clock – the sun. He was just over the top of the big gum-tree – that meant ten o'clock. How late! The morning was slipping away. He heard his mother inside singing. She was making the bread. It would be very hot in the hut when the loaf was put in the camp-oven to bake. He had nothing to do either. He would go down to the creek; it was cool there. So he went into the hut and got a big piece of sweet-cake, and put it in the pocket of his little jumper.

'Mother,' said Pretty Dick, 'I am going down to the creek.'

'Take care you don't get lost!' said she, half in jest, half in earnest.

'Lost! No fear!' said Pretty Dick.

– And when he went out, his mother began to sing again.

It was beautifully cool down by the creek. Pretty Dick knew that it would be. The creek had come a long way, and was tired, and ran very slowly between its deep banks, luscious with foliage, and rich with grass. It had a long way to go, too. Pretty Dick knew where it went. It ran right away down to the river. It ran on into the open, desolate, barren piece of ground where the road to the station crossed it, and where its bright waters were all red and discoloured with the trampling of horses and cattle. It ran by the old stockyard, and then turned away with a sudden jerk, and lost itself in the Five Mile Swamp, from whence it re-appeared again, broader and bigger, and wound along until it met the river.

But it did not run beyond the swamp now, Dick knew, because the weather had been so hot, and the creeks were all dried up for miles round – his father said – all but this one. It took its rise in the mountains, and when the rainfall was less than usual, grew thinner and thinner, until it became what it was now, a slender stream of water, trickling heavily between high banks – quite unlike the dashing, brawling, black, bubbling torrent that had rushed down the gully in flood-time.

Pretty Dick took off his little boots, and paddled about in the water, and found out all kinds of curious, gnarled roots of old trees, and funny holes under the banks. It was so cool and delicious under the stems and thick leaves of the water frondage that Pretty Dick felt quite restored again, and sang remembered scraps of his mother's songs, as he dodged round intervening trees, and slipped merrily between friendly trunks and branches. At last he came out into the open. Here his friend, the creek, divided itself into all sorts of queer shapes, and ran here, and doubled back again there, and twisted and tortured itself in an extraordinary manner, just out of pure fun and frolic.

There was a herd of cattle camped at this place, for the trees were tall, and big, and spreading. The cattle did not mind Pretty Dick at all, strange to say. Perhaps that was because he was on foot. If he had been on horseback now, you would have seen how they would have stared and wheeled about, and splashed off into the scrub. But when Pretty Dick, swinging a stick that he had cut, and singing one of his mother's songs, came by, they merely moved a little farther away, and looked at his little figure with long, sleepy eyes, slowly grinding their teeth from side to side the while. Now the way began to go up-hill, and there were big dead trees to get over, and fallen spreading branches to go round; for the men had been felling timber here, and the wasted wood lay thick upon the ground. At last Pretty Dick came to the Crossing Place. The crossing place was by the edge of the big swamp, and was a notable place for miles round. There was no need for a crossing place now though, for the limpid water was not a foot deep.

Pretty Dick had come out just on the top of a little sandy rise, and he saw the big swamp right before him speckled with feeding cattle, whose backs were just level with the tall rushes. And beyond the big swamp the ranges rose up, with the sunlight gleaming here and there upon jutting crags of granite, and with deep, cool shadows in other places, where the noble waving line of the hills sank in, and made dark recesses full of shade and coolness. The sky was bluer than ever, and the air was heavy with heat; and Pretty Dick wondered how the eagle-hawk that was poised – a floating speck above the mountain-top – could bear to swoop and swing all day long in that fierce glare.

He turned down again, and crossing the creek, plunged into the bush. There was a subtle perfume about him now; not a sweet, rich perfume like the flowers in the home station garden, but a strange intoxicating smell, evolved from the heat and the water and the many-coloured heath blossoms. The way was more difficult now, and Pretty Dick left the bank of the creek and made for the open space – sandy, and hunched with coarse clumps of grass. He went on for a long time, still upwards, and at last his little feet began to tire: and, after chasing a dragon-fly or two, and running a long way after a kangaroo rat, that started out from a patch of bloom, and ran in sharp diagonal lines away to hide itself in among the roots of a she-oak, he began to think of the piece of sweet cake in his pocket. So when, after some little time, emerging from out a dense mass of scrub, that scratched and tore at him as though it would hold him back, he found himself far up in the hills, with a great gully between him and the towering ranges, he sat down and came to the conclusion that he was hungry. But when he had eaten his sweet cake, he found that he was thirsty too, and that there was no water near him. But Pretty Dick knew there was water in the ranges; so he got up again, a little wearily, and went down the gully to look for it. But it was not so easy to find, and he wandered about for a long time, among big granite boulders, and all kinds of blind creeks, choked up with thick grass and creeping plants, and began to feel very tired indeed, and a little inclined to wish that he had not left the water-course so early. But he found it at last – a little pool, half concealed by stiff, spiky rush-grass, and lay down, and drank eagerly. How nice the first draught was! But at the second, the water felt warm, and at the third, tasted quite thick and slimy. There had been some ducks paddling about when he came up, and they flew away with a great quacking and splashing, that almost startled him. As soon as they had disappeared though, the place was quite still again, and the air grew heavier than ever. He felt quite drowsy and tired, and laid himself down on a soft patch of mossy grass, under a tree; and so, after listening a little while to the humming of the insects, and the distant crackling of mysterious branches in the forest, he put his little head on his little arm, and went fast to sleep.

How long he slept Pretty Dick did not know, but he woke up suddenly with a start, and a dim consciousness that the sun had shifted, and had been pouring its heat upon him for some time. The moment he woke he heard a great crashing and plunging, and started up just in time to see a herd of wild cattle scouring off down the side of the range. They had come up to drink while he was asleep, and his sudden waking had frightened them. How late it must be! The place seemed quite changed. There was sunlight where no sunlight had been before, and shadow where had been sunlight. Pretty Dick was quite startled at finding how late it was. He must go home, or mother would be frightened. So he began to go back again. He knew his way quite well. No fear of his losing himself. He felt a little tired though, but that would soon wear off. So he left the little pool and turned homewards. He got back again into the gully, and clambered up to the top, and went on sturdily. But the trees did not seem familiar to him, and the succession of dips in the hills seemed interminable. He would soon reach the Big Swamp again, and then he could follow up the creek. But he could not find the Swamp. He toiled along very slowly now, and at last found the open plot of ground where he had stopped in the morning. But when he looked at it a little, it was not the same plot at all, but another something like it, and the grim ranges, heavy with shadow, rose all around him.

A terrible fear came into poor little Pretty Dick's heart, and he seemed to hear his mother say, quite plainly. 'Take care you don't get lost, Pretty Dick!' Lost! But he put the feeling away bravely, and swallowed down a lump in his throat, and went on again. The cattle-track widened out, and in a little time he found himself upon a jutting peak, with the whole panorama of the Bush at his feet. A grand sight! On the right hand towered the Ranges, their roots sunk deep in scrub and dense morass, and their heads lifted into the sky, that was beginning to be streaked with purple flushes now. On the left, the bush rolled away beneath him – one level mass of tree tops, broken here and there by an open space of yellow swamp, or a thin line of darker foliage, that marked the meanderings of some dried up creek. The sun was nearly level with his face, and cast a long shadow behind him. Pretty Dick felt his heart give a great jump, and then go on beating quicker and quicker. But he would not give in. Lost! – Oh no, he should soon be home, and telling his mother all the wonders of the walk. But it *was* so late! He must make haste. What was that! – Somebody on horseback. Pretty Dick shaded his eyes with his little hand, and peered down into the valley. A man with a white puggaree on his hat, was moving along a sort of cattle-track. Joy! – It was Mr. Gaunt, the overseer. Pretty Dick cooeed. No answer. He cooeed again, – and again, but still the figure went on. Presently it emerged from the scrub, and the poor little fellow could see the rays of the setting sun gleam redly for an instant on a bright spur, like a dying spark. He gave a despairing shout. The horseman stopped, looked about him, and then glancing up at the fast clouding heavens, shook his horse's bridle, and rode off in a hand [*sic*] gallop.

Poor Pretty Dick! He knew that his cry had been un-heard – mistaken, perhaps, for the scream of a parrot, the cry of some native bear, or strange bird, but in his present strait, the departure of the presence something human, felt like a desertion. He fairly gave way, and sat down and cried. By-and-by he got up again, with quite a strange feeling of horror, and terror, and despair; he ran down the steep side of the range in the direction in which Mr. Gaunt had gone, and followed his fast fading figure, calling, and crying with choked voice. Presently he lost him altogether, and then he felt his courage utterly fail. He had no idea of where he was. He had lost all power of thought and reason, and was possessed but by one overpowering terror, and a consciousness that whatever he did, he must keep on running, and not stop a moment. But he soon could run no longer. He could only stagger along from tree to tree in the gloomy woods, and cry, 'Mother! Mother!' But there was no mother to help him. There was no human being near him, no sound but the hideous croaking of the frogs in the marshes, and the crackling of the branches under his footsteps. The sun went down suddenly behind the hills, and the air grew cool at once. Pretty Dick felt as if he had lost a friend, and his tears burst forth afresh. Utterly tired and worn out, he sat down at the foot of a tree, and sobbed with sheer fatigue. Then he got up and ran round and round, like some hunted animal, calling, 'Mother! Mother!'

But there was no reply. Nothing living was near him, saving a hideous black crow who perched himself upon the branch of a withered tree, and mocked him, seeming to the poor boy's distorted fancy to say, 'Pretty Dick! Pretty Dick! Walk! walk! walk!'

In a burst of passionate, childish despair, he flung a piece of stick at the bird, but his strength failed him, and the missile fell short. This fresh failure made him cry again, and then he got up and ran – stumbling, and falling, and crying – away from the loathsome thing. But it followed him, flapping heavily from tree to tree, and perched quite close to him at last, croaking like an Evil Presence – 'Pretty Dick! Pretty Dick! Walk! walk! walk!'

The sweet night fell, and the stars looked down into the gullies and ravines, where poor Pretty Dick, all bruised, bleeding, and despairing, was staggering from rock to rock, sick at heart, drenched with dew, hatless, shoeless, tear-stained, crying, 'Mother! mother! I am lost! I am lost! Oh, mother! mother!'

The calm, pitiless stars looked down upon him, and the broad sky spread coldly over him, and the birds flew away terrified at him; and the deadly chill of Loneliness fell upon him, and the cold, cruel, silent Night seemed to swallow him up, and hide him from human sympathy.

Poor Pretty Dick! No more mother's kisses, no more father's caresses, no more songs, no more pleasures, no more flowers, no more sunshine, no more love – nothing but grim Death, waiting remorselessly in the iron solitude of the hills. In the sad-eyed presence of the speechless stars, there, among the awful mystery and majesty of Nature, alone, a terrified little human soul, with the eternal grandeur of the forests, the mountains, and the myriad voices of the night, Pretty Dick knelt trembling down, and, lifting his little, tear-stained face to the great, grave, impassable sky, sobbed.

'Oh! take me home! Take me home! please, God, take me home!'

The night wore on – with strange sounds far away in the cruel bush, with screamings of strange birds, with gloomy noises, as of the tramplings of many cattle, with movements of leaves and snapping of branches, with unknown whirrings as of wings, with ripplings and patterings as of waterfalls, with a strange heavy pulsation in the air as though the multitudinous life of the forest was breathing around him. He was dimly conscious that at any moment some strange beast – some impossible monster, enormous and irresistible, might rise up out of the gloom of the gullies and fall upon him; – that the whole horror of the bush was about to take some tangible shape and appear silently from behind the awful rocks which shut out all safety and succour. His little soul was weighed down by the nameless terror of a solitude which was no solitude – but a silence teeming with monsters. He pictured the shapeless Bunyip lifting its shining sides heavily from the bottomless blackness of some lagoon in the shadow of the hills, and dragging all its loathsome length to where he lay. He felt suffocated; the silence that held all these indistinct noises in its bosom muffled him about like a murderous cloak; the palpable shadow of the immeasurable mountains fell upon him like a gravestone, and the gorge where he lay was like the Valley of the Shadow of Death. He screamed to break the silence, and the scream rang around him in the woods, and up above him in the mountain clefts, and beneath him in the mute mystery of the glens and swamps, – his cry seemed to be re-echoed again and again by strange voices never heard before, and repeated with indistinct mutterings and moanings in the caverns of the ranges. He dared not scream a second time lest he should wake some awful sound whose thunder should deafen him.

All this time he was staggering on, - not daring to look to right or left, or anywhere but straight on - straight on always. He fell, and tore his hands, and bruised his limbs, but the bruises did not hurt him. His little forehead was cut by a sharp stone, and his bright hair was all dusty and matted with blood. His knees shook and trembled, and his tongue clove to his mouth. He fell at every yard, and his heart seemed to beat so loud that the sound filled the air around him.

His strength was leaving him; he tottered from weakness; and at last emerging upon a little open platform of rock, white under the moon, he felt his head swim, and the black trunks, and the masses of fern-tree leaves, and the open ground, and the silent expanse of bush below him, all turned round in one crimson flash; and then the crimson grew purple-streaked, and spotted with sparks, and radiations, and bursting globes of light and colour, and then the Ranges closed in and fell upon him, and he was at once in his little bed at home - oh, so-fast-asleep!

But he woke at last, very cold and numbed, and with some feeling that he was not himself, but that he had been dreaming of a happy boy named Pretty Dick, who went away for a walk one afternoon many years ago. And then he felt for the blankets to pull them up about his shoulders, and his little fingers grasped a prickly handful of heather, and he woke with a terrible start.

Moonlight still, but a peaceful, solemn, sinking moon. She was low down in the sky, hanging, like a great yellow globe, over the swamp, that rose from far beneath him, straight up, it seemed, to a level with his face. Her clear-cut rim rested on the edge of the morass now. He could almost touch her, she looked so close to him; but he could not lift his little arm so high, and besides, he had turned everything upside down before he went to sleep, and the moon was down below him and the earth up above him! To be sure! and then he shut his eyes and went to sleep again.

By-and-by it dawned. The birds twittered, and the dew sparkled, and the mists came up and wreathed themselves all about the trees, and Pretty Dick was up in the pure cool sky, looking down upon a little figure that lay on an open space among the heather. Presently, slowly at first, and then more quickly, he found out that this little figure was himself, and that he was in pain, and then it all came back with one terrible shock, and he was Lost again.

He could bear to think of it now, though. His terrors, born of darkness, had fled with the uprising of the glorious golden sun. There was, after all, no reason to be afraid. Boys had been lost before, and found again. His father would have missed him last night, and the station would be speedily roused. Oh, he would soon be found! He got up, very painfully and stiffly, and went to look for water. No difficulty in that; and when he had drunken and washed his face and hands, he felt much better. Then he began to get hungry, and to comfort himself with the thought that he would soon be found. He could almost hear the joyful shout, and the welcome, and the questioning. How slowly the time went on! He tried to keep still in one place, for he knew now that his terror-driven feet had brought him to this pass, and that he should have kept still in the place where he saw Mr. Gaunt the night before.

At the recollection of that bitter disappointment, and the thought of how near he had been to succour, his tears began afresh. He tried hard to keep his terrors back – poor little fellow, – and thought of all kinds of things – of the stories his mother told him – of the calf-pen that father was putting up. And then he would think of the men at the station, and the remembrance of their faces cheered him; and he thought of Mrs. Trelawney, and of his mother. O – suppose he should never see his mother again! And then he cried, and slept, and woke, and forgot his fears for awhile, and would listen intently for a sound, and spring up and answer a fancied shout, and then lie in a dull, stupid despair, with burning eyes, and aching head, and a gnawing pain that he knew was Hunger. So the hot day wore out. The same heat as yesterday, the same day as yesterday, the same sights and sounds as yesterday – but oh! how different was yesterday to to-day, – and how far off yesterday seemed. No one came. The shadows shifted, and the heat burnt him up, and the shade fell on him, and the sun sank again, and the stars began to shine, – and no one came near Pretty Dick. He had almost forgotten, indeed, that there was such a boy as Pretty Dick. He seemed to have lived years in the bush alone. He did not know where he was, or who he was. It seemed quite natural to him that he should be there alone, and he had no wish to get away. He had lost all his terror of the Night. He scarcely knew it was night, and after sitting on the grass a little longer, smiling at the fantastic shadows that the moonlight threw upon the ground, he discovered that he was hungry, and must go into the hut for supper. The hut was down in the gully yonder; he could hear his mother singing; – so Pretty Dick got up, and crooning a little song went down into the Shadow.

They looked for him for five days. On the sixth, his father and another came upon something lying, half-hidden in the long grass at the bottom of a gully in the ranges. A little army of crows flew away heavily. The father sprang to earth with a white face. Pretty Dick was lying on his face, with his head on his arm.

God had taken him home.

HENRY LAWSON
Some Popular Australian Mistakes

1. An Australian mirage does not look like water; it looks too dry and dusty.

2. A plain is not necessarily a wide, open space covered with waving grass or green sward, like a prairie (the prairie isn't necessarily that way either, but that's an American mistake, not an Australian one); it is either a desert or a stretch of level country covered with wretched scrub.

3 A river is not a broad, shining stream with green banks and tall, dense eucalypti walls; it is more often a string of muddy water-holes – 'a chain of dry water-holes,' someone said.

4. There are no 'mountains' out West; only ridges on the floors of hell.

5. There are no forests; only mongrel scrubs.

6. Australian poetical writers invariably get the coastal scenery mixed up with that of 'Out Back.'

7. An Australian Western homestead is not an old-fashioned, gable-ended, brick-and-shingle building with avenues and parks; and the squatter doesn't live there either. A Western station, at best, is a collection of slab and galvanized-iron sheds and humpies, and is the hottest, driest, dustiest, and most God-forsaken hole you could think of; the manager lives there – when compelled to do so.

8. The manager is not called the 'super;' he is called the 'overseer' – which name fits him better.

9. Station-hands are not noble, romantic fellows; they are mostly crawlers to the boss – which they have to be. Shearers – the men of the West – despise station-hands.

10. Men tramping in search of a 'shed' are not called 'sundowners' or 'swaggies;' they are 'trav'lers.'

11. A swag is not generally referred to as a 'bluey' or 'Matilda' – it is *called* a 'swag'.

12. No bushman thinks of 'going on the wallaby' or 'walking Matilda', or 'padding the hoof'; he goes on the track – when forced to't.

13. You do not 'hump bluey' – you simply 'carry your swag'.

14. You do not stow grub - you 'have some tucker, mate'.

15. (Item for our Australian artists). A traveller rarely, if ever, carries a stick; it suggests a common suburban loafer, back-yards, clothes-lines, roosting fowls, watch-dogs, blind men, sewer-pipes, and goats eating turnip-parings.

16. (For Artists). No traveller out-back carries a horse-collar swag – it's too hot; and the swag is not carried by a strap passed round the chest, but round *one* shoulder. The nose (tucker) bag hangs over the other shoulder and balances the load nicely – when there's anything in the bag.

17. It's not glorious and grand and free to be on the track. Try it.

18. A shearing-shed is not what city people picture it to be – if they imagine it at all; it is perhaps the most degrading hell on the face of this earth. Ask any better-class shearer.

19. An Australian lake is not a lake; it is either a sheet of brackish water or a patch of dry sand.

20. Least said about shanties the better.

21. The poetical bushman does not exist; the majority of the men out-back now are from the cities. The real native out-back bushman is narrow-minded, densely ignorant, invulnerably thick-headed. How could he be otherwise?

22. The blackfellow is a fraud. A white man *can* learn to throw the boomerang as well as an aborigine – even better. A black-fellow is *not* to be depended on with regard to direction, distance, or weather. A blackfellow once offered to take us to better water than that at which we were camping. He said it was only half-a-mile. We rolled up our swags and followed him and his gin five miles through the scrub to a mud-hole with a dead bullock in it. Also, he said that it would rain that night; and it didn't rain there for six months. Moreover, he threw a boomerang at a rabbit and lamed one of his dogs – of which he had about 150.

23. etc. Half the bushmen are *not* called 'Bill', nor the other half 'Jim'. We knew a shearer whose name was Reginald! Jim doesn't tell pathetic yarns in bad doggerel in a shearer's hut – if he did, the men would tap their foreheads and wink.

In conclusion. We wish to Heaven that Australian writers would leave off trying to make a paradise out of the Out Back Hell; if only out of consideration for the poor, hopeless, half-starved wretches who carry swags through it and look in vain for work – and ask in vain for tucker very often. What's the good of making a heaven of a hell when by describing it as it really is, we might do some good for the lost souls there?

HENRY LAWSON
The Drover's Wife

The two-roomed house is built of round timber, slabs, and stringy bark, and floored with split slabs. A big bark kitchen standing at one end is larger than the house itself, verandah included.

Bush all round – bush with no horizon, for the country is flat. No ranges in the distance. The bush consists of stunted, rotten native apple trees. No undergrowth. Nothing to relieve the eye save the darker green of a few sheoaks which are sighing above the narrow, almost waterless creek. Nineteen miles to the nearest sign of civilization – a shanty on the main road.

The drover, an ex-squatter, is away with sheep. His wife and children are left here alone.

Four ragged, dried-up-looking children are playing about the house. Suddenly one of them yells: 'Snake! Mother, here's a snake!'

The gaunt, sun-browned bushwoman dashes from the kitchen, snatches her baby from the ground, holds it on her left hip, and reaches for a stick.

'Where is it?'

'Here! gone into the wood-heap!' yells the eldest boy – a sharp-faced, excited urchin of eleven. 'Stop there, mother! I'll have him. Stand back! I'll have the beggar!'

'Tommy, come here, or you'll be bit. Come here at once when I tell you, you little wretch!'

The youngster comes reluctantly, carrying a stick bigger than himself. Then he yells, triumphantly:

'There it goes – under the house!' and darts away with club uplifted. At the same time the big, black, yellow-eyed dog-of-all-breeds, who has shown the wildest interest in the proceedings, breaks his chain and rushes after that snake. He is a moment late, however, and his nose reaches the crack in the slabs just as the end of its tail disappears. Almost at the same moment the boy's club comes down and skins the aforesaid nose. Alligator takes small notice of this, and proceeds to undermine the building; but he is subdued after a struggle and chained up. They cannot afford to lose him.

The drover's wife makes the children stand together near the dog-house while she watches for the snake. She gets two small dishes of milk and sets them down near the wall to tempt it to come out; but an hour goes by and it does not show itself.

It is near sunset, and a thunderstorm is coming. The children must be brought inside. She will not take them into the house, for she knows the snake is there, and may at any moment come up through the cracks in the rough slab floor; so she carries several armfuls of firewood into the kitchen, and then takes the children there. The kitchen has no floor – or, rather, an earthen one – called a 'ground floor' in this part of the bush. There is a large, roughly made table in the centre of the place. She brings the children in, and makes them get on this table. They are two boys and two girls – mere babies. She gives them some supper, and then, before it gets dark, she goes into the house, and snatches up some pillows and bedclothes – expecting to see or lay her hand on the snake any minute. She makes a bed on the kitchen table for the children, and sits down beside it to watch all night.

She has an eye on the corner, and a green sapling club laid in readiness on the dresser by her side, together with her sewing basket and a copy of the *Young Ladies' Journal*. She has brought the dog into the room.

Tommy turns in, under protest, but says he'll lie awake all night and smash that blinded snake.

His mother asks him how many times she has told him not to swear.

He has his club with him under the bedclothes, and Jacky protests:

'Mummy! Tommy's skinnin' me alive wif his club. Make him take it out.'

Tommy: 'Shet up, you little — ! D'yer want to be bit with the snake?'

Jacky shuts up.

'If yer bit,' says Tommy, after a pause, 'you'll swell up, an' smell, an' turn red an' green an' blue all over till yer bust. Won't he, mother?'

'Now then, don't frighten the child. Go to sleep,' she says.

The two younger children go to sleep, and now and then Jacky complains of being 'skeezed'. More room is made for him. Presently Tommy says: 'Mother! listen to them (adjective) little 'possums. I'd like to screw their blanky necks.'

And Jacky protests drowsily:

'But they don't hurt us, the little blanks!'

Mother: 'There, I told you you'd teach Jacky to swear.' But the remark makes her smile. Jacky goes to sleep.

Presently Tommy asks:

'Mother! Do you think they'll ever extricate the (adjective) kangaroo?'

'Lord! How am I to know, child? Go to sleep.'

'Will you wake me if the snake comes out?'

'Yes. Go to sleep.'

Near midnight. The children are all asleep and she sits there still, sewing and reading by turns. From time to time she glances round the floor and wall-plate, and whenever she hears a noise she reaches for the stick. The thunderstorm comes on, and the wind, rushing through the cracks in the slab wall, threatens to blow out her candle. She places it on a sheltered part of the dresser and fixes up a newspaper to protect it. At every flash of lightning, the cracks between the slabs gleam like polished silver. The thunder rolls, and the rain comes down in torrents.

Alligator lies at full length on the floor, with his eyes turned towards the partition. She knows by this that the snake is there. There are large cracks in that wall opening under the floor of the dwelling-house.

She is not a coward, but recent events have shaken her nerves. A little son of her brother-in-law was lately bitten by a snake, and died. Besides, she has not heard from her husband for six months, and is anxious about him.

He was a drover, and started squatting here when they were married. The drought of 18— ruined him. He had to sacrifice the remnant of his flock and go droving again. He intends to move his family into the nearest town when he comes back, and, in the meantime, his brother, who keeps a shanty on the main road, comes over about once a month with provisions. The wife has still a couple of cows, one horse, and a few sheep. The brother-in-law kills one of the sheep occasionally, gives her what she needs of it, and takes the rest in return for other provisions.

She is used to being left alone. She once lived like this for eighteen months. As a girl she built the usual castles in the air; but all her girlish hopes and aspirations have long been dead. She finds all the excitement and recreation she needs in the *Young Ladies' Journal*, and, Heaven help her! takes a pleasure in the fashion-plates.

Her husband is an Australian, and so is she. He is careless, but a good enough husband. If he had the means he would take her to the city and keep her there like a princess. They are used to being apart, or at least she is. 'No use fretting,' she says. He may forget sometimes that he is married; but if he has a good cheque when he comes back he will give most of it to her. When he had money he took her to the city several times – hired a railway sleeping compartment, and put up at the best hotels. He also bought her a buggy, but they had to sacrifice that along with the rest.

The last two children were born in the bush – one while her husband was bringing a drunken doctor, by force, to attend to her. She was alone on this occasion, and very weak. She had been ill with a fever. She prayed to God to send her assistance. God sent Black Mary – the 'whitest' gin in all the land. Or, at least, God sent 'King Jimmy' first, and he sent Black Mary. He put his black face round the door-post, took in the situation at a glance, and said cheerfully: 'All right, Missis – I bring my old woman, she down alonga creek.'

One of her children died while she was here alone. She rode nineteen miles for assistance, carrying the dead child.

It must be near one or two o'clock. The fire is burning low. Alligator lies with his head resting on his paws, and watches the wall. He is not a very beautiful dog to look at, and the light shows numerous old wounds where the hair will not grow. He is afraid of nothing on the face of the earth or under it. He will tackle a bullock as readily as he will tackle a flea. He hates all other dogs – except kangaroo-dogs – and has a marked dislike to [sic] friends or relations of the family. They seldom call, however. He sometimes makes friends with strangers. He hates snakes and has killed many, but he will be bitten some day and die; most snake-dogs end that way.

Now and then the bushwoman lays down her work and watches, and listens, and thinks. She thinks of things in her own life, for there is little else to think about.

The rain will make the grass grow, and this reminds her how she fought a bush fire once while her husband was away. The grass was long, and very dry, and the fire threatened to burn her out. She put on an old pair of her husband's trousers and beat out the flames with a green bough, till great drops of sooty perspiration stood out on her forehead and ran in streaks down her blackened arms. The sight of his mother in trousers greatly amused Tommy, who worked like a little hero by her side, but the terrified baby howled lustily for his 'mummy'. The fire would have mastered her but for four excited bushmen who arrived in the nick of time. It was a mixed-up affair all round; when she went to take up the baby, he screamed and struggled convulsively, thinking it was a 'black man'; and Alligator, trusting more to the child's sense than his own instinct, charged furiously, and (being old and slightly deaf) did not in his excitement at first recognize his mistress's voice, but continued to hang on to the moleskins until choked off by Tommy with a saddle-strap. The dog's sorrow for his blunder, and his anxiety to let it be known that it was all a mistake, was as evident as his ragged tail and a twelve-inch grin could make it. It was a glorious time for the boys; a day to look back to, and talk about, and laugh over for many years.

She thinks how she fought a flood during her husband's absence. She stood for hours in the drenching downpour, and dug an overflow gutter to save the dam across the creek. But she could not save it. There are things that a bush woman cannot do. Next morning the dam was broken, and her heart was nearly broken too, for she thought how her husband would feel when he came home and saw the result of years of labour swept away. She cried then.

She also fought the *pleuro-pneumonia* – dosed and bled the few remaining cattle, and wept again when her two best cows died.

Again, she fought a mad bullock that besieged the house for a day. She made bullets and fired at him through cracks in the slabs with an old shotgun. He was dead in the morning. She skinned him and got seventeen-and-six for the hide.

She also fights the crows and eagles that have designs on her chickens. Her plan of campaign is very original. The children cry 'Crows, mother!' and she rushes out and aims a broomstick at the birds as though it were a gun, and says, 'Bung!' The crows leave in a hurry; they are cunning, but a woman's cunning is greater.

Occasionally a bushman in the horrors, or a villainous-looking sundowner, comes and nearly scares the life out of her. She generally tells the suspicious-looking stranger that her husband and two sons are at work below the dam, or over at the yard, for he always cunningly inquires for the boss.

Only last week a gallows-faced swagman – having satisfied himself that there were no men on the place – threw his swag down on the verandah, and demanded tucker. She gave him something to eat; then he expressed his intention of staying for the night. It was sundown then. She got a batten from the sofa, loosened the dog, and confronted the stranger, holding the batten in one hand and the dog's collar with the other. 'Now you go!' she said. He looked at her and at the dog, said 'All right, mum,' in a cringing tone, and left. She was a determined-looking woman, and Alligator's yellow eyes glared unpleasantly – besides, the dog's chawing-up apparatus greatly resembled that of the reptile he was named after.

She has few pleasures to think of as she sits here alone by the fire, on guard against a snake. All days are much the same to her;

but on Sunday afternoon she dresses herself, tidies the children, smartens up baby, and goes for a lonely walk along the bush-track, pushing an old perambulator in front of her. She does this every Sunday. She takes as much care to make herself and the children look smart as she would if she were going to do the block in the city. There is nothing to see, however, and not a soul to meet. You might walk for twenty miles along this track without being able to fix a point in your mind, unless you are a bushman. This is because of the everlasting, maddening sameness of the stunted trees – that monotony which makes a man long to break away and travel as far as trains can go, and sail as far as ships can sail – and further.

But this bushwoman is used to the loneliness of it. As a girl-wife she hated it, but now she would feel strange away from it.

She is glad when her husband returns, but she does not gush or make a fuss about it. She gets him something good to eat, and tidies up the children.

She seems contented with her lot. She loves her children, but has no time to show it. She seems harsh to them. Her surroundings are not favourable to the development of the 'womanly' or sentimental side of nature.

It must be near morning now; but the clock is in the dwelling-house. Her candle is nearly done; she forgot that she was out of candles. Some more wood must be got to keep the fire up, and so she shuts the dog inside and hurries round to the wood-heap. The rain has cleared off. She seizes a stick, pulls it out, and – crash! the whole pile collapses.

Yesterday she bargained with a stray blackfellow to bring her some wood, and while he was at work she went in search of a missing cow. She was absent an hour or so, and the native black made good use of his time. On her return she was so astonished to see a good heap of wood by the chimney, that she gave him an extra fig of tobacco, and praised him for not being lazy. He thanked her, and left with head erect and chest well out. He was the last of his tribe and a King; but he had built that wood-heap hollow.

She is hurt now, and tears spring to her eyes as she sits down again by the table. She takes up a handkerchief to wipe the tears away, but pokes her eyes with her bare fingers instead. The handkerchief is full of holes, and she finds that she has put her thumb through one, and her forefinger through another.

This makes her laugh, to the surprise of the dog. She has a keen, very keen, sense of the ridiculous; and some time or other she will amuse bushmen with the story.

She has been amused before like that. One day she sat down 'to have a good cry,' as she said – and the old cat rubbed against her dress and 'cried too.' Then she had to laugh.

It must be near daylight. The room is very close and hot because of the fire. Alligator still watches the wall from time to time. Suddenly he becomes greatly interested; he draws himself a few inches nearer the partition, and a thrill runs through his body. The hair on the back of his neck begins to bristle, and the battle-light is in his yellow eyes. She knows what this means, and lays her hand on the stick. The lower end of one of the partition slabs has a large crack on both sides. An evil pair of small, bright, bead-like eyes glisten at one of these holes. The snake – a black one – comes slowly out, about a foot, and moves its head up and down. The dog lies still, and the woman sits as one fascinated. The snake comes out a foot further. She lifts her stick, and the reptile, as though suddenly aware of danger, sticks his head in through the crack on the other side of the slab, and hurries to get his tail round after him. Alligator springs, and his jaws come together with a snap. He misses, for his nose is large and the snake's body down in the angle formed by the slabs and the floor. He snaps again as the tail comes round. He has the snake now, and tugs it out eighteen inches. Thud, thud comes the woman's club on the ground. Alligator pulls again. Thud, thud Alligator gives another pull and he has the snake out – a black brute, five feet long. The head rises to dart about, but the dog has the enemy close to the neck. He is a big, heavy dog, but quick as a terrier. He shakes the snake as though he felt the original curse in common with mankind. The eldest boy wakes up, seizes his stick, and tries to get out of bed, but his mother forces him back with a grip of iron. Thud, thud – the snake's back is broken in several places. Thud, thud – its head is crushed and Alligator's nose skinned again.

She lifts the mangled reptile on the point of her stick, carries it to the fire, and throws it in; then piles on the wood, and watches the snake burn. The boy and dog watch, too. She lays her hand on the dog's head, and all the fierce, angry light dies out of his yellow eyes. The younger children are quieted, and presently go to sleep. The dirty-legged boy stands for a moment in his shirt, watching the fire. Presently he looks up at her, sees the tears in her eyes, and, throwing his arms round her neck, exclaims:

'Mother, I won't never go drovin'; blast me if I do!'

And she hugs him to her worn-out breast and kisses him; and they sit thus together while the sickly daylight breaks over the bush.

EDWARD DYSON
The Conquering Bush

Ned 'picked up' his wife in Sydney. He had come down for a spell in town, and to relieve himself of the distress of riches – to melt the cheque accumulated slowly in toil and loneliness on a big station in the North. He was a stockrider, a slow, still man naturally, but easily moved by drink. When he first reached town he seemed to have with him some of the atmosphere of silence and desolation that surrounded him during the long months back there on the run. Ned was about thirty-four, and looked forty. He was tall and raw-boned, and that air of settled melancholy, which is the certain result of a solitary bush life, suggested some romantic sorrow to Mrs. Black's sentimental daughter.

Darton, taught wisdom by experience, had on this occasion taken lodgings in a suburban private house. Mrs. Black's home was very small, but her daughter was her only child, and they found room for a 'gentleman boarder'.

Janet Black was a pleasant-faced, happy-hearted girl of twenty. She liked the new boarder from the start, she acknowledged to herself afterwards, but when by some fortunate chance he happened to be on hand to drag a half-blind and half-witted old woman from beneath the very hoofs of a runaway horse, some-what at the risk of his own neck, she was enraptured, and in the enthusiasm of the moment she kissed the hand of the abashed hero, and left a tear glittering on the hard brown knuckles.

This was a week after Ned Darton's arrival in Sydney.

Ned went straight to his room and sat perfectly still, and with even more than his usual gravity watched the tear fade away from the back of his hand. Either Janet's little demonstration of artless feeling had awakened suggestions of some glorious possibility in Ned's heart, or he desired to exercise economy for a change; he suddenly became very judicious in the selection of his drinks, and only took enough whisky to dispel his native moodiness and taciturnity and make him rather a pleasant acquisition to Mrs. Black's limited family circle.

When Ned Darton returned to his pastoral duties in the murmuring wilds, he took Janet Black with him as his wife. That was their honeymoon.

Darton did not pause to consider the possible results of the

71

change he was introducing into the life of his bride – few men would. Janet was vivacious, and her heart yearned towards humanity. She was bright, cheerful, and impressionable. The bush is sad, heavy, despairing; delightful for a month, perhaps, but terrible for a year.

As she travelled towards her new home the young wife was effervescent with joy, aglow with health, childishly jubilant over numberless plans and projects; she returned to Sydney before the expiration of a year, a stranger to her mother in appearance and in spirit. She seemed taller now, her cheeks were thin, and her face had a new expression. She brought with her some of the brooding desolation of the bush – even in the turmoil of the city she seemed lost in the immensity of the wilderness. She answered her mother's every question without a smile. She had nothing to complain of: Ned was a very good husband and very kind. She found the bush lonesome at first, but soon got used to it, and she didn't mind now. She was quite sure she was used to it, and she never objected to returning.

A baby was born, and Mrs. Darton went back with her husband to their hut by the creek on the great run, to the companionship of bears, birds, 'possums, kangaroos, and the eternal trees. She hugged her baby to her breast, and rejoiced that her little mite would give her something more to do and something to think of that would keep the awful ring of the myriad locusts out of her ears.

Man and wife settled down to their choking existence again as before, without comment. Ned was used to the bush – he had lived in it all his life – and though its influence was powerful upon him he knew it not. He was necessarily away from home a good deal, and when at home he was not companionable, in the sense that city dwellers know. Two bushmen will sit together by the fire for hours, smoking and mute, enjoying each other's society; 'in mute discourse' two bushmen will ride for twenty miles through the most desolate or the most fruitful region. People who have lived in crowds want talk, laughter, and song. Ned loved his wife, but he neither talked, laughed, nor sang.

Summer came. The babe at Mrs. Darton's breast looked out on the world of trees with wide, unblinking, solemn eyes, and never smiled.

'Ned,' said Jane, one bright, moonlight night, 'do you know that 'possum in the big blue gum is crazy? She has two joeys, and she has gone mad.'

Janet spent a lot of her time sitting in the shade of the hut on a candle-box, gazing into her baby's large, still eyes, listening to the noises of the bush, and the babe too seemed to listen, and the mother fancied that their senses blended, and they both would some day hear something awful above the crooning of the insects and the chattering of the parrots. Sometimes she would start out of these humours with a shriek, feeling that the relentless trees which had been bending over and pressing down so long were crushing her at last beneath their weight.

Presently she became satisfied that the laughing jackasses were mad. She had long suspected it. Why else should they flock together in the dim evening and fill the bush with their crazy laughter? Why else should they sit so grave and still at other times, thinking and grieving?

Yes, she was soon quite convinced that the animals and birds, even the insects that surrounded her, were mad, hopelessly mad, all of them. The country was now burnt brown, and the hills ached in the great heat, and the ghostly mirage floated in the hollows. In the day-time the birds and beasts merely chummered and muttered querulously from the deepest shades, but in the dusk of evening they raved and shrieked, and filled the ominous bush with mad laughter and fantastic wailings.

It was at this time that Darton became impressed by the peculiar manner of his wife, and a great awe stole over him as he watched her gazing into her baby's eyes with that strange look of frightened conjecture. He suddenly became very communicative; he talked a lot, and laughed, and strove to be merry, with an indefinable chill at his heart. He failed to interest his wife; she was absorbed in a terrible thought. The bush was peopled with mad things – the wide wilderness of trees, and the dull, dead grass, and the cowering hills instilled into every living thing that came under the influence of their ineffable gloom a madness of melancholy. The bears were mad, the 'possums, the shrieking cockatoos, the dull grey laughing jackasses with their devilish cackling, and the ugly yellow-throated lizards that panted at her from the rocks – all were mad. How, then, could her babe hope to escape the influence of the mighty bush and the great white plains beyond, with their heavy atmosphere of despair pressing down upon his defenceless head? Would he not presently escape from her arms, and turn and hiss at her from the grass like a vicious snake; or climb the trees, and, like a bear, cling in day-long torpor from a limb; or, worst of all, join the grey birds on the big dead gum, and mock at her sorrow with empty, joyless laughter?

These were the fears that oppressed Janet as she watched her sad, silent baby at her breast. They grew upon her and strengthened day by day, and one afternoon they became an agonizing conviction. She had been alone with the dumb child for two days, and she sat beside the hut door and watched the evening shadows thicken, with a shadow in her eyes that was more terrible than blackest night, and when a solitary mopoke began calling from the Bald Hill, and the jackasses set up a weird chorus of laughter, she rose, and clasping her baby tighter to her breast, and leaning over it to shield it from the surrounding evils, she hurried towards the creek.

Janet was not in the hut when Ned returned home half an hour later. Attracted by the howling of his dog, he hastened to the waterhole under the great rock, and there in the shallow water he found the bodies of his wife and child and the dull grey birds were laughing insanely overhead.

HENRY LAWSON
Rats

'Why, there's two of them, and they're having a fight! Come on.'

It seemed a strange place for a fight – that hot, lonely, cotton-bush plain. And yet not more than half-a-mile ahead there were apparently two men struggling together on the track.

The three travellers postponed their smoke-ho! and hurried on. They were shearers – a little man and a big man, known respectively as 'Sunlight' and 'Macquarie', and a tall, thin, young jackeroo whom they called 'Milky'.

'I wonder where the other man sprang from? I didn't see him before,' said Sunlight.

'He muster bin layin' down in the bushes,' said Macquarie. 'They're goin' at it proper, too. Come on! Hurry up and see the fun!'

They hurried on.

'It's a funny-lookin' feller, the other feller,' panted Milky. 'He don't seem to have no head. Look! he's down – they're both down!! They must ha' clinched on the ground. No! they're up an' at it again ... Why, good Lord! I think the other's a woman!'

'My oath! so it is!' yelled Sunlight. 'Look! the brute's got her down again! He's kickin' her! Come on, chaps; come on, or he'll do for her!'

They dropped swags, water-bags and all, and raced forward; but presently Sunlight, who had the best eyes, slackened his pace and dropped behind. His mates glanced back at his face, saw a peculiar expression there, looked ahead again, and then dropped into a walk.

They reached the scene of the trouble, and there stood a little withered old man by the track, with his arms folded close up under his chin; he was dressed mostly in calico patches; and half-a-dozen corks, suspended on bits of string from the brim of his hat, dangled before his bleared optics to scare away the flies. He was scowling malignantly at a stout, dumpy swag which lay in the middle of the track.

'Well, old Rats, what's the trouble,' asked Sunlight.

'Oh, nothing, nothing,' answered the old man, without looking round. 'I fell out with my swag, that's all. He knocked me down, but I've settled him.'

'But look here,' said Sunlight, winking at his mates, 'we saw you jump on him when he was down. That ain't fair, you know.'

'But you didn't see it all,' cried Rats, getting excited. 'He hit *me* down first! And, look here, I'll fight him again for nothing, and you can see fair play.'

They talked awhile; then Sunlight proposed to second the swag, while his mates supported the old man, and after some persuasion, Milky agreed, for the sake of the lark, to act as time-keeper and referee.

Rats entered into the spirit of the thing; he stripped to the waist, and while he was getting ready the travellers pretended to bet on the result.

Macquarie took his place behind the old man, and Sunlight up-ended the swag. Rats shaped and danced round; then he rushed, feinted, ducked, retreated, darted in once more, and suddenly went down like a shot on the broad of his back. No actor could have done it better; he went down from that imaginary blow as if a cannon-ball had struck him in the forehead.

Milky called time, and the old man came up, looking shaky. However, he got in a tremendous blow which knocked the swag into the bushes.

Several rounds following with varying success.

The men pretended to get more and more excited, and betted freely; and Rats did his best. At last they got tired of the fun, Sunlight let the swag lie after Milky called time, and the jackeroo awarded the fight to Rats. They pretended to hand over the stakes, and then went back for their swags, while the old man put on his shirt.

Then he calmed down, carried his swag to the side of the track, sat down on it and talked rationally about bush matters for awhile; but presently he grew silent and began to feel his muscles and smile idiotically.

'Can you len' us a bit o'meat?' said he suddenly.

They spared him half-a-pound; but he said he didn't want it all, and cut off about an ounce, which he laid on the end of his swag. Then he took the lid off his billy and produced a fishing-line. He baited the hook, threw the line across the track, and waited for a bite. Soon he got deeply interested in the line, jerked it once or twice, and drew it in rapidly. The bait had been rubbed off in the grass. The old man regarded the hook disgustedly.

'Look at that!' he cried. 'I had him, only I was in such a hurry. I should ha' played him a little more.'

Next time he was more careful, he drew the line in warily, grabbed an imaginary fish and laid it down on the grass. Sunlight and Co. were greatly interested by this time.

'Wot yer think o' that?' asked Rats. 'It weighs thirty pound if it weighs an ounce! Wot per think o' that for a cod? The hook's half-way down his blessed gullet?'

He caught several cod and a bream while they were there, and invited them to camp and have tea with him. But they wished to reach a certain shed next day, so – after the ancient had borrowed about a pound of meat for bait – they went on, and left him fishing contentedly.

But first Sunlight went down into his pocket and came up with half-a-crown, which he gave to the old man, along with some tucker. 'You'd best push on to the water before dark, old chap,' he said, kindly.

When they turned their heads again, Rats was still fishing: but when they looked back for the last time before entering the timber, he was having another row with his swag; and Sunlight reckoned that the trouble arose out of some lies which the swag had been telling about the bigger fish it caught.

II

THE BURDEN OF THE PAST

MARCUS CLARKE
Port Arthur

The asylum was chiefly remarkable for the number of old men which it contained. Port Arthur, in the year in which we visited it, was a hospital for cripples, and decrepit, blear-eyed convicts basked in the sunshine of the yard, or warmed their maimed limbs at the fire in the keeping-room, with a senile complacency that was almost as affecting as is the helplessness of an infant.

Having passed Smith O'Brien's cottage – pointed out to us with a reverence which spoke much for the gentle breeding of that rash but patriotic Irishman – we were conducted into the asylum. Visitors to Bedlam will remember Cibber's statues, 'Melancholy and Madness.' The living statues whom we saw were mere reproductions of the hideous stone. Some leant listlessly against the walls, some raved locked in cells. In ordinary lunatic asylums one sees in one's melancholy progress a variety of character – the mad folks sing, laugh, relate anecdotes, imagine themselves to be endowed with good fortune, or to possess claims to reverence. Here were no such pleasurable emotions. The criminal lunatics were of but two dispositions – they cowered and crawled like whipped fox-hounds to the feet of their keepers, or they raged, howling blasphemous and hideous imprecations upon their gaolers. I was eager to see my poacher of 13 years. The warder drew aside a peep-hole in the barred door, and I saw a grizzled, gaunt, and half-naked old man coiled in a corner. The peculiar wild-beast smell which belongs to some forms of furious madness exhaled from the cell. The gibbering animal within turned, and his malignant eyes met mine. 'Take care,' said the gaoler; 'he has a habit of sticking his finger through the peep-hole to try and poke someone's eye out!' I drew back, and a nail-bitten hairy finger, like the toe of an ape, was thrust with rapid and simian neatness through the aperture. 'That is how he amuses himself,' said the good warder, forcing-to the iron slote; 'he'd best be dead, I'm thinking.'

From the asylum we visited the quarters of the stipendiaries, saw the neat theatre erected for the edification of those gentle-men, and examined the books in the library. 'I will take you round by the church and the chaplain's house,' said Mr. Dale, 'and it

will be then time for you to return to Government-cottage.' We
saw the church, a handsome building, built in 1836, and heard
the legend of the stolen money which was supposed to have been
built into the wall of it. 'A curious place!' cried Cool, when we
reached our cottage. 'Very curious. ("Have a touch of this rum,
Mr. Dale".) Pray how many prisoners have you here now?' 'Mrs.
Glamorgan,' says Dale, 'oblige me with a pen. By the way, there
are goats in the garden, Mrs. Glamorgan; you know the commandant's objection to goats. Here is the list, sir, as forwarded
to Hobart Town by the schooner. Gentlemen, my compliments.'
And with a bow (and a touch of rum) he departed.

The list was as follows:—

Convicts	301
Do., invalids	13
Do., insane	8
	322
Paupers not under sentence	166
Lunatics do.	86
	252
26th Jan., 1870.	574

How shorn of its glories was Babylon! How ill had the world
wagged with it since the days of the settlement of Port Phillip
in 1835, when the prison owned 911 men and 270 boys, their
labour for the year being valued at £16,000! As we slept beneath
the hospitable roof of Government-cottage, we, travellers from
despised Port Phillip, were cognisant that over the doorway of
our shelter was even then written the melancholy 'Ichabod. Thy
glory hath departed.'

Next morning came the whale-boat to take us to Dead Man's
Island, and we embarked under the noses of a guard. Cockney
travellers, anxious to find foreign similes for their local conven-
iences, have long persisted in calling gondolas the hackney cabs
of Venice. Following the same humour, I may say that the whale-
boats are the omnibuses of Port Arthur. Six convicts of good
character represent the horses, while a free coxswain, having
loaded revolver in his belt and carbine ready to his hand, sits in
the stern sheets and represents the mild cad who is so careful
of his sixpences from the Marble Arch to Bayswater.

Dead Man's Isle, or *L'Isle des Morts*, as the maps term it, is a
foolish little sand island hummocked with graves. There many
scoundrels mingle their dust with that of more fortunate men.

May (the murderer of the Italian image boy) is rotting there; so also is Robert Young, 51st Regiment, accidentally drowned; so also are three seamen of the schooner 'Echo', together with many of the 21st, 51st and 63rd Regiments. I trampled over the graves in full humour to be orthodox, and to look with abhorrence upon the clay that suffered in life beneath a yellow jacket, but decided upon the exercise of Christian charity when I found myself gazing with virtuous indignation at the headstone of one, the wife of Private Gibbons, 21st Regiment, and who (poor woman) died virtuously in childbed.

From the Island of the Dead our whaleboat took us to Long Bay, and landed us there at the wooden pier. In the 'good times' before mentioned, the isthmus between Long Bay and Norfolk Bay was bridged by the railroad of clever Captain Booth, and travellers like ourselves were dragged in waggons by harnessed murderers or burglars. In the decadence of convict discipline, however, this gratification was denied us, and we walked over sandy-soil and through prickly scrub, while a taciturn convict of unprepossessing appearance drove a cart containing our baggage. In this happy manner we reached the corresponding pier at Norfolk Bay, where, tossing in the chill waves, lay another whaleboat with another convict crew and other armed coxswain. So embarking – not without a touch of the inevitable rum – we passed Woody Island, and made for the famed Eaglehawk Neck.

Eaglehawk Neck is a strip of sand some 500 yards across. On the western side of this isthmus lies Eaglehawk Bay, opening out into Port Bunche, and guarded by the signal station of Woody Island and the peninsula of One-tree Point; on the eastern side the Southern Ocean breaks unchecked upon the rocky point of Cape Surville, rages in white wrath upon the long length of Descent Beach, or burrows in treacherous silence beneath the honeycomb rocks that guard the southern horn of Pirate's Bay. Across the isthmus is built a plank-road, in the midst of which is a guard-house. Sentinels patrol night and day, while the eye of the new comer is startled by the sight of dogs set out upon stages extending far into the shallows on either side. To reach the further shore the escaping convict must – like the adventurous Cash and his companions – dare the sharks and swim the rapids of Pirate's Bay, but to land upon the barren sand of Forrestier's Peninsula, blocked by another isthmus, which leads to civilization and recapture.

Our boat, beached upon the further shore, was met by the sergeant in charge, who received us with military honours, turned out the guard in respect to Cool's forage cap, and conducted us to his house. In old days a commissioned officer, with a subaltern's guard (and a rationed shark as legends go), looked after this important spot, and the line of neat white huts upon the sand testified to the presence of troops. At the time of our visit, Hezekias Macklewain was judged sufficient protection. To describe Sergeant Macklewain is not my intention. Suffice it to say that he was an 'old soldier', and that he fulfilled the promise of hospitality, artfulness, and discipline, which those two words imply. It is my fortune to have many friends who hold the Queen's commission, and Macklewain seemed to have relatives in every regiment in the service. 'The Fighting Onety-oneth? Me cousin Tim was colour-sergeant at Badajos!' 'Did ye say the Princess's Plungers? Me brother was batman to the ould divil of a colonel, and me wife's father knew your uncle well. Och – '

'Have a touch of rum,' says Cool. 'What's the motto of the Tearing Tenty-tenth – *Risky, frisky, whiskey*, eh?'

'By the wooden man, sir, but Sally's great uncle, Corney O'Keefe, was – – – '

'Oh, have a touch of rum,' cries Hacker.

'And so you're a grandson of General Barry, are ye? Roaring Harry Barry, of Barry Oge – him they called Barry Lyndon. Och – '

'Have another touch of rum,' said Cool.

I trust that I shall not be misunderstood when I say that we spent a merry night – within the limits of becoming mirth, of course. We related anecdotes of moving accident, we told campstories – of a Shandean order, not unfrequently; we sang military songs, and that jolly sergeant and his wife danced a reel, or I am much mistaken, to the music of Cool's melodious whistle. Then, having been all bedded down, in the sergeant's best bedroom you may be sure, with all the good-wife's blankets heaped above us, we slept the sleep of the just, lulled by the music of the murmuring waves, as they ran in upon the ocean beach.

At daylight the sergeant aroused us. 'To the Blow-hole!' The Blow-hole is a curious freak of nature. At the southern horn of Pirate's Bay the sea has bored an enormous cavern, and having – in remote ages – forced its way upwards through the roof of this tunnel, there now remains an arch of rock, called by the first discoverers of it 'Tasman's Arch'. To this spot, by a rough track, did our jovial sergeant lead us. We advanced through the scrub, and saw suddenly open at our feet an immense chasm, at the bottom of which the sea was lazily lapping. Beyond this chasm the scrub continued apparently unbroken, but upon skirting the enormous hole we felt the salt-breeze lick our faces, and a few steps further placed us at the brink of the cliff. The morning was an exquisitely calm and bright one, and the tide was low. We looked down through a funnel nearly 200 ft. deep, and saw at the bottom but wet and weed-girt rocks. Our sergeant informed us that in times of violent storm the water, driven in with the full violence of the wave which breaks upon the cliff, is spouted up through the funnel into air! I was long inclined to doubt this statement, until I found it confirmed by Dr. Ross, who records that, visiting the place on a comparatively calm day, he saw, 'between me and the light, little sparkles of spray rising up several feet into the air;' and, after stating that the impression of terror produced upon his mind by the 'awful depths of the "boilers of Buchan" ' was many degrees inferior to that induced by the Blow-hole, he says that 'the spectator could observe, at a depth of 150 ft. or 200 ft., the waters rolling in by a subterraneous channel, and *dashing the spray in his face.'* The aspect of this spot during a gale must be as marvellous as that of the Douvres. The Blow-hole, in fact, repeats at the antipodes the marvels of the Channel Islands, for, descending by a narrow pathway to the foot of the precipice, we found ourselves on a ledge of rock which at high-water is covered by furious surf, and the huge cavern, intersected and bored into by several smaller ones, bore an aspect sufficiently romantic to have warranted its selection as the scene of a drama of the sea scarcely less wonderful than that one played at the order of Victor Hugo by Gilliatt and the *pieuvre* on the Man-rock of Guernsey.

Cool and I bathed in a pool of water some 10 ft. wide, and heaven knows how deep, left by the retired sea at the base of the cliff. The sides of this natural bath were covered with sea-weeds, and its depths were inhabited by a variety of oceanic life, which the clearness of water allowed to be distinctly seen. It was as though we had plunged into an acquarium. Refreshed by our bath, and a walk over the beach to the guard-house, we break-fasted heartily, and took leave of our hospitable entertainers to embark in the ready whale-boat which was to convey us back to civilisation. The boat voyage was not remarkable for aught save weariness. The wind had freshened, and for some hours we laboured against the tide, beguiling the time with anecdote and story. The coxswain related to us the history of Cash and Cavenagh, told of the exploits of the "Jaguar", the acuteness of Mr. John Evenden, chief constable, and the unfortunate death of one 'Hangman Thompson', who, being recognized at the diggings by some of his old prison mates, was dragged to pieces with bullocks. At these tales we laughed and shuddered by turns, but no expression of merriment or of disgust moved our stolid crew. They did not seem to listen, or, listening, did not appear to heed. We free men talked in the presence of these prisoners as if they had been dogs. 'You bathe in sight of your slaves,' said someone to the Empress Theodora. 'Well, they are but slaves,' was the reply. When we landed at Ralph's Bay, waiting for our cart to jog towards Kangaroo Point, I said to Cool, busy in distributing tobacco to the boat's crew, 'What do you think of it?' Cool looked at the prisoners, at the sea, at the sky, and at Hacker. 'I respect the power of the press,' said he; 'have a touch of rum.' 'See,' said I, reversing the flask, 'it is empty!' 'Ay, only the smell of it left, your honour!' said a prisoner, breaking silence for the first time.

This exclamation of our prisoner's, rude but true, is, in fact, an admirable summing up of the convict system. When safely seated after supper in the comfortable coffee-room of the Ark, we began to compare ideas and impressions of our recent experiences, the remark of the convict oarsman recurred to me again and again. The frightful blunder had become a thing of the past, the victims of it were dead or insane. Everybody admitted that 'mistakes had been made in the old times,' and begged that the loathly corpse of this dead wickedness called Transportation might be comfortably buried away and ignored of men and journalists. But 'the smell of it' remained – remains. Cripples, self-maimed, lest worse might have befallen them, walk the streets of Hobart Town. In out-of-the-way corners, in shepherds' huts or roadside taverns, one meets 'old hands' who relate terrible and true histories. In the folio reports of the House of Commons can be read statements which make one turn sick with disgust, and flush hot with indignation. Officialdom, with its crew of parasites and lickspittles, may try to palliate the enormities committed in the years gone by; may revile, with such powers of abuse as are given to it the writers who record the facts which it blushes for; but the sad grim truth remains. For half a century the law allowed the vagabonds and criminals of England to be subjected to a lingering torment, to a hideous debasement, to a monstrous system of punishment futile for good and horribly powerful for evil; and it is with feelings of the most profound delight that we record the abolition of the last memorial of an error fraught with so much misery.

ANONYMOUS
The Female Transport

Come all young girls, both far and near, and listen unto me,
While unto you I do unfold what proved my destiny,
My mother died when I was young, it caused me to deplore,
And I did get my way too soon upon my native shore.

Sarah Collins is my name, most dreadful is my fate,
My father reared me tenderly, the truth I do relate,
Till enticed by bad company along with many more,
It led to my discovery upon my native shore.

My trial it approached fast, before the judge I stood,
And when the judge's sentence passed it fairly chilled my
      blood,
Crying, 'You must be transported for fourteen years or more,
And go from hence across the seas unto Van Diemen's shore.'

It hurt my heart when on a coach I my native town passed by;
To see so many I did know, it made me heave a sigh;
Then to a ship was sent with speed along with many more,
Whose aching hearts did grieve to go unto Van Diemen's shore.

The sea was rough, ran mountains high, with us poor girls
      'twas hard,
No one but God to us came nigh, no one did us regard.
At length, alas! we reached the land, it grieved us ten times
      more,
That wretched place Van Diemen's Land, far from our native
      shore.

They chained us two by two, and whipped and lashed along,
They cut off our provisions if we did the least thing wrong;
They march us in the burning sun until our feet are sore,
So hard's our lot now we are got to Van Diemen's shore.

We labour hard from morn to night until our bones do ache,
Then every one they must obey, their mouldy beds must make;
We often wish when we lay down we ne'er may rise no more
To meet our savage Governor upon Van Diemen's shore.

Every night when I lay down I wet my straw with tears.
While wind upon that horrid shore did whistle in our ears,
Those dreadful beasts upon that land around our cots do roar,
Most dismal is our doom upon Van Diemen's shore.

Come all young men and maidens, do bad company forsake,
If tongue can tell our overthrow it will make your heart to ache;
Young girls I pray be ruled by me, your wicked ways give o'er,
For fear like us you spend your days upon Van Diemen's shore.

'FRANK THE POET'
(FRANCIS MACNAMARA)
A Convict's Lament on the Death of Captain Logan

I am a native of Erin's island
    But banished now from my native shore;
They tore me from my aged parents,
    And from the maiden I adore.
In transient storms as I set sailing,
    Like mariner bold my course did steer;
Sydney Harbour was my destination –
    That cursed place at length drew near.

I then joined banquet in congratulation
    On my safe arrival from the briny sea;
But, Alas, Alas! I was mistaken –
    Twelve years transportation to Moreton Bay!
Early one morning, as I carelessly wandered,
    By the Brisbane waters I chanced to stray;
I heard a prisoner sadly bewailing,
    Whilst on the sunny river-banks he lay.

He said: 'I've been a prisoner at Port Macquarie,
    At Norfolk Island and Emu Plains;
At Castle Hill and cursed Toongabbee –
    At all those places I've worked in chains:
But of all the places of condemnation,
    In each penal station of New South Wales,
To Moreton Bay I found no equal,
    For excessive tyranny each day prevails.

Early in the morning when day is dawning,
    To trace from heaven the morning dew,
Up we are started at a moment's warning,
    Our daily labour to renew.
Our overseers and superintendents –
    These tyrants' orders we must obey,
Or else at the triangles our flesh is mangled –
    Such are our wages at Moreton Bay!

For three long years I've been beastly treated;
   Heavy irons each day I wore;
My back from flogging has been lacerated,
   And oftimes painted with crimson gore.
Like the Egyptians and ancient Hebrews,
   We were oppressed under Logan's yoke,
Till kind Providence came to our assistance,
   And gave this tyrant his mortal stroke.

Yes, he was hurried from that place of bondage,
   Where he thought he would gain renown;
But a native black, who lay in ambush,
   Gave this monster his fatal wound.
My fellow-prisoners, be exhilarated –
   That all such monsters such a death may find:
For it's when from bondage we are extricated,
   Our former sufferings will fade from mind.'

HENRY SAVERY
from *Preface* to *Quintus Servinton*

It was not wholly a desire of fame, nor the hope of profit, nor, he trusts, an over-weening vanity, that led the author to 'o'erstep the modesty of nature,' and venture to compose a book; but it was the idea that he might convey useful and instructive precepts under their most attractive guise – the force of example. Let him not be understood, however, as wishing to convey that he feels indifferent upon the point, either of honor or of a fair remuneration for his time; for, were he regardless of the first, he might be enticed into a careless laxity, quite irreconcilable with prudence on the part of one, who treads so dangerous and uncertain a path as that of Literature, when intended for the amusement of others; and so far as the second is concerned, there are few, similarly circumstanced to the Author – whose chief dependence is the allegiance due to his King and Country, who can afford to consider it altogether immaterial, whether they devote many long and wearisome hours to an employment, 'free, gratis, and all for nothing,' or, whether they reap some advantage from their labours. Perhaps, therefore, each of the inducements has had some weight in the production of Quintus Servinton.

*   *   *

Still, is he not dismayed; because, strip him even of all other laurels, he defies the hand that may be lifted against the moral tendency of his tale; and he has not now to learn the great influence this ever has, in creating favor with the British Public. Had time and occasion served, perhaps he could have made the work more perfect in its form, its style, and language; yet, the correctness of its details could not have been improved. Such as it is, therefore, he entrusts it with some degree of confidence, to the countenance and support of the English Nation.

Van Diemen's Land, 1830

MARY THERESA VIDAL
The Convict Laundress

It was a bright, clear day – how bright, how blue, and how clear, none but those who have been out of the British isles can understand. It was Christmas day; but instead of frost and snow, and cold, and leafless trees, and blazing fires, there was intense heat, and the trees looked, as they always do in Australia, a dingy blueish tint, but still full of leaf and blossom: and here and there, where marks of cultivation peeped through the interminable forest or bush, there were strips of the brightest green maize, refreshing indeed to the eye, and contrasting pleasantly with the brown grass, and the tall white trunks of the gums. The house, or rather weather-boarded cottage, was four or five miles from the settlement, where there was a wooden church. Thither the family had repaired on this morning. There was but one service, for the clergyman proceeded to another congregation, eight miles beyond. There had been beef and plum pudding for dinner, the government men, or convicts, partaking in the Christmas fare; and there were thoughts of those far away, and many a lingering regret for the old associations of the season. Yet as the evening breeze sprung up, and stirred the gums and acacias, and breathing through the cottage refreshingly cool, the spirits of all rose, and with one accord they went out into the forest at the back of the house. The merry voices were echoed round and round, and I could see the farm-servants and working men as they strolled under the trees. Every one being out, I went to the back, to see that all was safe. There was a large waste piece of ground with the men's huts, the stables and barn, and nearer the house stood the kitchens and store. Two or three dogs lay about, the poultry were busy picking up their food, and a pet cockatoo came jumping up to my side, begging for a bone in its peculiarly unharmonious voice. As I stood, feeling rather lonely, I heard a dull, melancholy noise; it came from the kitchen. I thought every one had been out: I listened again. Yes, it was from the kitchen, and it was certainly some one in grief: heavy sobs and a low moaning formed a strange contrast to the distant sounds of mirth and merriment!

On approaching the kitchen I found one of the servants, a convict, leaning on the table – a solitary, heart-broken creature! Hour after hour, day after day, did that woman work, and often till late at night, and never was there more faithful or more devoted service than hers. Was there a trouble, or an ailment, or an extra job, it was, 'Go to Grace Allen.' Did the children want a string, or a stick, or a cake, or a kind word – Grace was there. Early and late she was at her washing-tub, or bestowing dainty care on all the old clothes that came from England, because she said she knew 'the Missis set more value on them than on any thing new.' There was the poultry which throve doubly after they were given into her charge. Early in the morning, with light and gentle step, did she stand with a cup of coffee, made with the utmost care, because she knew 'the Missis was used to it at home.' Late at night she was there to see if all was right; and after an absence from home, Grace was sure to be the first to spy the horses, and to fly to the slip-rail with 'You're kindly welcome back, your reverence; you're kindly welcome home, ma'am, and the children are well, the jewels!'

Slight of figure and of graceful form was Grace, and there was every mark to show how pretty she once had been. There was a refined and graceful turn in every feature and limb; but she was no longer young, her hair was growing grey, her eyes were hollow, and her cheeks sunken; and now, as she raised her pale face on hearing steps, what a withered, crushed expression was there! She had been glad to let them all go out, and leave her to weep alone. Nor was it only the thoughts of her kindred, her children, her old home, which oppressed her heart; Grace was under a deadly bondage, worse than that of being a convict; there was sin as well as sorrow, and the bright blossoms of her love, her faithful clinging heart, were weighed down, crushed, soiled!

From time to time I heard all her history, and for three years tried to save her, but in vain. The following sketch will not, I think, be without interest to others; and it is a pleasure, mingled as it is with deep pain, to recall her words and vivid descriptions, though they must lose their freshness from inability to give them in her own Irish phraseology: and while I do not hide her faults, I cannot help lingering awhile on that devoted, unselfish love which battled to the last with her infirmities, which survived the wreck of her happiness, and was permitted to comfort and interest those to whom she was assigned in that far-off land, Australia.

[Here follows an account of Grace's marriage, and of her turning away from true divinity to 'household gods', first her husband

and then her son, whom she loses in successive tragedies. Stunned and grief-stricken, she finds relief, not in 'God and resignation', but 'a cordial'. – ed.]

And this was the first coil of the rope which afterwards so tightly bound Grace.

Days passed in alternate agony and stupefaction; and then one morning, when she was all alone, and Patty was gone back to her own home, Grace determined to go to Belfast herself, for she craved for further tidings, and she wished to get everything that belonged to her son. She was glad. Patty was away – she wished to go secretly, why she did not know, but she made up a small bundle of linen, locked up the cottage, hanging the key in a particular spot over the door; and, looking on all sides to see if any one were in sight, she set forth for her long journey. Weak and worn as she was, excitement kept her up. She staid at night at a small pot-house on the road, and by the afternoon of the second day she reached Belfast.

When she was fairly in the streets, a stranger not knowing where to go, faint and tired, her heart failed her, and she wished she had never come. She stopped to look about her, and seeing a woman standing outside a small shop-door, she asked her what was the name of the street, and then where Messrs. Panton and Co. lived. The woman said, 'Oh! a great way off,' and proceeded to describe the way; but poor Grace felt she could not take many steps more. 'Could you tell me of a decent and quiet lodging to be had any where near?' said she. The woman said there were several; she herself had a tidy little bed which she often let, and charged low for it: she was a widow, she added, and glad to do anything to turn a penny, for she had four small children to maintain.

Grace sighed. 'You're tired: come, step in, and take a cup of tea; sure you've come a long way seemingly.' Grace followed, and agreed to take the small room which was to let, while her business kept her in Belfast.

Mrs. Cady was active and civil, and very talkative. She told Grace that she sold cotton and lace, and tapes, and pins, and such like things; and sometimes she got a little washing, but it was hard work to make both ends meet, and she had found it a world of trouble, whatever others did. Grace's miserable looks struck Mrs. Cady, and when she heard she could not sleep, she advised her to take the least 'drop of whiskey' just as she stepped into bed: she had found from experience how good it was for sorrow.

Grace did not refuse, and she too found that it 'drove off the pain and brought sleep.'

Mrs. Cady's girl shewed Grace the next day to Messrs. Panton and Co., where she heard many particulars about her son. As she said, they were very kind, and gave her all that was due to him and his clothes, and spoke very handsomely of the lad.

How her fingers trembled and her heart beat as she folded and unfolded the shirts, the waist-coats and neck-cloths; but very few new things were added to this old stock. 'No,' as she said afterwards with glistening eyes but quivering lips, 'he was saving money for his mother; he never thought of himself; it was for me, – for me!'

Could her brother or any of her old friends have seen Grace at this time, they would scarcely have recognized her to be the same person. All her activity, her spirit was gone. She sat staring vacantly out of window, or moved about the room in feverish restlessness: her person was uncared for and neglected, she did not mend her clothes, she sat in dirt rather than sweep a room or dust a table.

Mere animal energy, even long practised habits, will fail us under a stunning blow. The most buoyant spirit will sink at last, and woe to us, if, like poor Grace, we have no other support at hand. The tempter, it is said, lurks in glittering scenes, in prosperity, in wealth, in fulfilled happiness. He also hovers over the dim room of agony. He has his weights with which he seeks to crush the bleeding heart.

Mrs. Cady persuaded Grace to remain on where she was for a while: she coaxed and flattered her, and tried to tempt her to eat and to drink; her cordials and her drops were often offered and accepted to still the beating and aching of the heart. She was not pressed to pay for her lodging, but by degrees she was persuaded into investing a small sum in the shop, and at last to take a passive share in the concern. Mrs. Cady was sharp and talkative; Grace doubted her, as she afterwards said, yet she was glad to be led. She shrank from returning home, or from any exertion, and she looked for the evening, the unlocking the corner cupboard, the long-necked bottle, and the dead, heavy sleep which followed, as she had once looked for an approving smile from her husband.

One morning, heart-sick, miserable, feverish and heavy-eyed, Grace stood at the door leaning over that part of it which was shut. Many persons passed; – carriages and beggars, nurses and children, and men going to their work. Shrill cries, laughter, buzzing and rattling, all mingled in confusion, and she looked out on the bright sunshine, and thought of her forsaken home – the little garden. No one had sought her, no one cared a pin for her, she thought. Did they think she had drowned herself in the river!

what, if she were to return and find the cottage occupied? The thought roused her. 'I wouldn't like to give it up to ruin – but I hav'n't the strength; if I had, I could pay the bit of rent by washing, and I'd like to die in the old place!' And she shuddered as she thought of a last illness and Mrs. Cady's sharp face over her pillow. She remembered one night feeling a hand under her head, and seeing in the dim light Mrs. Cady's confused face; from that hour Grace placed her money elsewhere. 'She has been kind to me to be sure, but I can pay her now: I've a great mind to go, but I am weak!' and she looked down at her worn shoes. For the first time she felt ashamed at her untidy state. 'Oh! ma'am,' she said in after years, 'it was fate, I was doomed for destruction. Just as I was thinking this way, Mrs. Cady called out from in the back room: "Mrs. Allen, here's some cheap, illegant shoes, jist your very pattern, a rare bargain." I went in and fitted them on, and paid the money, just half-price. I felt glad, for I thought, "now I can walk home when I like." Not three hours afterwards in came some constables. Mrs. Cady and I were seized for buying stolen goods; we were put into jail.'

Mrs. Cady was known as a very doubtful character, which told against Grace. Grace was tried and found guilty. It was clear and just, as she said, she knew she could'nt deny it: she heard her sentence, seven years' transportation, with scarcely a sigh, and with no effort to save herself. She did not write to her friends; she scorned the notion of being the one to bring disgrace to the M'Leans. 'Her daughters,' she said, 'should never know what their mother was, till the broad ocean rolled betwixt them.'

Grace was sent from Belfast to Dublin; and while waiting for the ship, she gained the good will of the matron of the jail. While she was out of the reach of temptation her old habits of industry and her obliging temper showed itself. She made herself useful in the jail and on board the ship: in the latter she was appointed nurse to the sick, and she often showed a Bible, given by the surgeon, with her name written in it; a testimonial of which she was very proud.

From the ship in Sydney harbour she was sent to the female convict barracks at Paramatta, where she says it made her heart sick to hear the horrible language; – old abandoned sinners and quite young girls crowded together. Grace loathed the place, resolved to try and get assigned out, and there to work and to toil, and try to resist temptation, – any thing to be free from such a place. She begged the matron to try and get her a place.

Accordingly, one day the matron called her from the work-room, and told her she had received an application for a laundress in a clergyman's family; she was desired to recommend one, and had chosen her. Grace was thankful at the prospect.

The next day a man came with a cart, received Grace's small bundle, while she herself, in her convict's dress, seated on the straw, soon left the barracks at Paramatta for a new, strange scene.

The roads were edged with wattles in full bloom, their golden blossoms shedding fragrance around. The country was flat and monotonous; the sun hot and burning. The man, - he had been a convict himself, - joked her on her dress, and being sent out at the Queen's expense; and bade her hold up her head, for that 'Government folks were not so bad.' But Grace said her heart sank within her, so forcibly did her shame and situation press upon her. They suddenly stopped at the bottom of a lane, and then the horse slowly mounted the hill, and children's voices rang out clear from the bank, - and as one, a fair-haired boy, reminding her at once of her own child, sprang out to take the whip and reins, she sobbed outright.

The bright stars cast a clear light over the farm that night, and all was still, save the buzzing of insects, and the croaking of frogs. Grace sat up on her little bed, and looked at the rough wooden planks which formed the walls of her room, at her marked dress. She was once more among respectable people she thought, but she was a convict! Rough were the accommodations of the place, but Grace's spirit revived as the morning breeze rose; she resolved to show that she could work. She went to collect sticks from the wood-heap, as her fellow-servant told her she must light a fire, and prepare for a 'heavy wash.' While so doing, the lady of the house came out and spoke to her; Grace never lifted her eyes from the ground as she answered the questions; the thin, blue lips quivered, the hand was often drawn hastily over the downcast eyes. 'I never forget I'm a convict, ma'am,' she often said.

Grace lived long with that family, to whom she attached herself with that deep devotion which formed so strong a feature in her character; she followed them in their wanderings, was hard-working, and faithful, and gentle, and skilful in sickness and in hours of pain. It was hoped that she would end her days with them, either in that country, or 'at home.' But old recollections came thronging back. Sorrow and bereavement will be received, - it rests with us *how*. If we shut the door for a time, there will be a moment in which they find too sure entrance; we may stifle, stun, and poison them, - they do not die. They came back to Grace, and there were times when the old remedy could be procured. Then followed weeks of remorse - bitter remorse; sorrowful reproaches from her friends; taunts and sneers from those who were inclined to envy the favour shown her by her employers. Grace's bodily strength began to fail, yet she would never give up; she said working was the only way to keep down her sorrows, and work she did for every one. Then came a change from the secluded bush to the suburbs of a town, and it was no longer possible to guard her, as had been done. There were dreadful pangs as she again saw the sea, and its crested waves. She sat like one broken-hearted, gazing at it, or, flinging her arms wildly, saying her son was there, and she must go to him. None but the boy whom she idolised had power to move her; nothing but spirits or opium, which she found means to procure and hide, ever gave her sleep. A veil must be drawn over this latter part of her history.

It would be too painful to write or to read of the struggles and agony which ended in loss of reason – Grace died in a lunatic asylum! She was truly a prey to strong passionate affections, and keen sensibilities, which were unsanctified. She had turned from God to worship idols, and when they were crushed, the pain was lulled by stupifying and intoxicating draughts. May her end be a warning to any of my readers who is tempted 'to drown sorrow,' – often God's last and best gift!

FREDERICK SINNETT
from *The Fiction Fields of Australia*

Man can no more do without works of fiction than he can do
without clothing, and, indeed, not so well; for, where climate is
propitious, and manners simple, people often manage to loiter
down the road of life without any of the 'lendings' that Lear cast
away from him; yet, nevertheless, with nothing between the blue
heaven and their polished skins, they will gather in a circle round
some dusky orator or vocalist, as his imagination bodies forth the
forms of things unknown, to the entertainment and elevation of
his hearers. To amend our first proposition, then, works of fiction
being more necessary, and universally disseminated, than clothing, they still resemble clothing in this, that they take different
shapes and fashions in different ages. In the days of Chaucer –

'First warbler, whose sweet breath
   Preluded those melodious bursts that fill
The spacious times of great Elizabeth
   With sounds that echo still – '

didactic and descriptive poetry was almost the only recognized
vehicle of fiction. Then came the bursts that Chaucer preluded;
and in Shakespeare's days the dramatic form prevailed over all
others. For some time afterwards every kind of feeling and
thought found its expression in miscellaneous verse; and (though
he was, of course, not the first novelist) Fielding, probably, set
the fashion of that literary garment of the imagination, which has
since been almost exclusively worn – the novel.

In the shape of novels, then, civilized man, at the present day,
receives the greater part of the fictitious clothing necessary to
cover the nakedness of his mind; and our present inquiry is to
the feasibility of obtaining the material for this sort of manufacture
from Australian soil. We are not, of course, questioning the
practicability of writing novels in Australia. Thackeray might
have begun *The Newcomes* in Kensington, and finished the book
in Melbourne, as well as on the Continent. Our inquiry is into
the feasibility of writing Australian novels; or, to use other words,
into the suitability of Australian life and scenery for the novel

writer's purpose; and, secondly, into the right manner of their treatment.

*   *   *

In the first place, then, it is alleged against Australia that it is a new country, and, as Pitt said, when charged with juvenility, 'this is an accusation which I can neither palliate nor deny'. Unless we go into the Aboriginal market for 'associations', there is not a single local one, of a century old, to be obtained in Australia; and, setting apart Mr. Fawkner's pre-Adamite recollections of Colonel Collins, there is not an association in Victoria mellowed by so much as a poor score of years. It must be granted, then, that we are quite debarred from all the interest to be extracted from any kind of archaeological accessories. No storied windows, richly dight, cast a dim, religious light over any Australian premises. There are no ruins for that rare old plant, the ivy green, to creep over and make his dainty meal of. No Australian author can hope to extricate his hero or heroine, however pressing the emergency may be, by means of a spring panel and a subterranean passage, or such like relics of feudal barons, and refuges of modern novelists, and the offspring of their imagination. There may be plenty of dilapidated buildings, but not one, the dilapidation of which is sufficiently venerable by age, to tempt the wandering footsteps of the most arrant parvenu of a ghost that ever walked by night. It must be admitted that Mrs Radcliffe's genius would be quite thrown away here; and we must reconcile ourselves to the conviction that the foundations of a second *Castle of Otranto* can hardly be laid in Australia during our time . . .

[But this, according to Sinnett, need not be an insuperable handicap, as the great themes, 'feelings and passions', which are the staple of novelists, exist here, together with the advantages of 'fresh scenery, fresh costumes, and fresh machinery' – ed.]

We explain the absence of any really first-class Australian novels simply by a reference to the mathematical doctrine of probabilities. It is only once in many years that there steps forth from among the many millions of the British people a novelist able to break up new ground, and describe phases and conditions of life undescribed before. The great mass of those that load the circulating library shelves

'Remodel models rather than the life.'

They only sing the same old song over again, 'with variations'. Like most painters, they fancy that they are imitating nature when they are only imitating pictures of nature previously painted. Just as hack orators can only quote from quotations, so hack novelists can only deal with such scenes and characters as have been put on the stage before. Give them a set of circumstances, for the mode of handling which, for novelistic purposes, they have no precedent, and they know not what to make of it. Show them an actual living man, some type of whom is not to be found in already existing novels, and they can make no use of the material at all. They pass him as they pass thousands of good human materials every day without recognizing their worth. When the real genius has once laid hold of the new material, however, and shown them how to mould him to the purposes of art, they can 'remodel the model' *ad infinitum*, so much easier is it to steal out of books than to accept the gifts of nature.

Well, then, we argue, if only now and then out of the population of all England there arises a novelist capable of breaking up fresh ground, it is not to be wondered at that no such man has yet risen here. Geniuses are like tortoiseshell tom-cats – not impossible, only rare. Every ten years one is born unto Great Britain, but probably none exists in Australia, and a reason precisely analagous to this makes it improbable that we have at present among us any one capable of doing justice to Australian materials of fiction. There are not cats enough in Australia to entitle us to a tortoiseshell tom yet, according to the doctrine of averages.

We have to confess that we labour under the same disadvantages as afflict the hacks and copyists, and we cannot, therefore, point out how the great untouched Australian quarry is to be rightly worked. Only as we roam about the motley streets, or ride through the silent bush, we have just sense enough to feel that, when the capable eye comes to look upon them, all these rude amorphous materials may be arranged in form of the highest and most artistic beauty. The recorders are tuneless only because there is no one who knows how to play upon them; in the right hands they will 'discourse most eloquent music'.

'OLINÉ KEESE'
(CAROLINE LEAKEY)
from *The Broad Arrow*
Prelude to assignment on shore

Bridget clung to her uncle's arm as they passed through rows of prisoners, who were variously employed in working, reading, and learning, it being their school-hour. Each file arose and curtsied as the party passed.

Ever and anon Miss Perkins issued orders to some unfortunate.

'Mary Gull, tie your cap. What, Mary Pike, yours off! The next offence you'll go down stairs.' Mary understood the allusion, and hastily put on her cap.

'Sarah Gubb, you are talking there. Jane Dawson, where's your curtsey? Why don't you rise, Ellen Bracket? Muggins, I shall complain of you.'

'Would you like to walk through the cells, sir?'

They went below. In one cell was a captive, kicking and stamping violently. Miss Perkins thought fit to soothe her by rapping at the door.

'You don't think that's the way to get out, do you, Stooks?'

''Twas you got me in, you *did*, you beast?'

'If I wasn't very indulgent, Stooks, I should get you double for that,' said the maternal Perkins.

'Is the devil indulgent, I should like to know, you old cant?' cried Stooks.

With a deprecating smile at Bridget, Miss Perkins stopped at Number 10, whence issued an imploring voice –

'Do beg for me; I'm quite subdued, indeed I am, Miss Love. Oh! it's Miss Perkins. I beg pardon, ma'am, I thought 'twas Miss Love,' the prisoner was heard to sigh.

Passing on, they came to stalls where different trades – cobblery, bonnet-making, etc. – were being carried on.

'Do let us go, uncle; it is so dreadful to have these poor creatures made a show of,' whispered Bridget.

'They are accustomed to it,' answered Miss Perkins to the second clause of Bridget's speech.

'As the eels are, eh, Miss Perkins?' asked Mr. Evelyn.

'Oh, they keep each other in countenance. We look at them as a lot, not as individuals.'

Here her eyes fell on Martha Grylls, who was waiting, bundle in hand, at the grating.

'Follow us, and don't be talking there, Grylls. I don't wish to lose sight of you.'

'Come along, my woman,' said Mr. Evelyn kindly.

'*No*; walk before us, if you please, Grylls. I don't wish to lose sight of you, I repeat.'

Martha obeyed without a word.

All the women tried to give her a nod on the sly; and many anxious eyes followed the party as the grated door closed, and an audible sigh was simultaneously heaved by those whom it imprisoned. Each prisoner envied Martha, and wished it had been her lot to fall to so sweet a looking lady as that bright-eyed girl who smiled on her in passing.

What lay beyond those gates not one could tell. They were as the gates of death – all doubt and mystery beyond. None ever returned to tell of the untried world to which they led.

Strange and vague are the mental picturings the prisoned female forms of the land of her exile, which she knows lies little further than a stone's throw from her. Some think, on leaving the 'Anson,' they are to be turned adrift to all the horrors of an unexplored region; others that they will be driven to market for sale. The cunning and malicious amongst them delight in filling the minds of their less gifted associates with the most terrible apprehensions of the barbarities awaiting them on their departure from their probation. It is with a thrill of cruel suspense that such prisoners first plant their foot on Tasmanian ground.

In this respect the male convicts do not suffer so acutely. Their doubts, hopes, and fears are answered, realised, or crushed almost immediately on arriving at the colony. Their probationary course does not add suspense to sorrow. At once formed into gangs, they learn the worst, and are sent to labour in the roads, or work on public buildings. The torture of suspense is not added to it.

Miss Perkins accompanied Mr. Evelyn and his niece to the deck, where she mysteriously beckoned Bridget aside –

'I hope you do not mean to employ Grylls about children.'

She gave a significant wink. 'Of course, though, you don't. You guess why? It is not usual to tell the crime; but really I think it my duty to break rule to you. Do you understand me?'

Bridget looked a negative.

Martha had drawn near enough to hear Miss Perkins's friendly caution. Casting a glance of unutterable contempt on little

Perkins, she stepped to Miss D'Urban, and herself solved the significant wink.

'Miss Perkins wishes you to know that I am sent out for murder. She would suggest the impropriety of making me a nurse.'

Bridget turned very pale, and cast an imploring look on the little officer, who, boiling over with injured prerogative, was on the point of reprimanding Martha's audacity, when Mr. Evelyn called them to be quick – the boat was waiting.

'Good morning, Miss Perky. We are much favoured by your civilities.'

The officer was hurt at the inharmonious name bestowed upon her, and vented her spite by exclaiming, as Martha was on the first step of the companion:

'I hope you'll behave better *now*, Grylls, or you'll soon learn the difference between factory and here.'

Martha turned abruptly on her. A second more, and she had been on her way back to the cells, instead of on the road to Hobarton. The crimson cheek, flashing eye, and quivering lip, a second more had met their chastisement; but Bridget's beseeching gesture once more prevailed. Quietly turning from her persecutor, Martha descended the ladder.

'Good morning, Miss Perky,' waved Mr. Evelyn abstractedly, as though his voice mechanically embodied his opinion in a *name* expressive of the little upstart, pecking at him from the deck.

'That horrid woman!' cried Bridget.

A quick nod and frown from Mr. Evelyn stopped what further she would have said.

A slight smile overspread the prisoner's face; but it soon faded into a look of anxious sadness. It mattered not to her whether the coast was beautiful or barren; whether the landscape was rendered vital by the upward wreathing of the blue smoke from pleasant homesteads; or whether its desolate grandeur was made more dreary by the long blank masonry of penal life.

She started as from a dream when the boat jerked against the jetty. A ghastly pallor struck her every feature as she stept ashore. For an instant she covered her face; then, gradually withdrawing her hands, the Maida Gwynnham of olden days discovered herself in the unabated dignity of that uprearing head, and in the strength of purpose out-shining from the purple depths of those undimmed eyes.

A strength of purpose that even now was to be tried; and if the trial, surprising an unguarded post, be victorious for a season, who shall exult?

She was prepared to confront the hardships of convict existence. She was prepared for taunts, for jibes, for suspicions, for
enemies, and felt that she could face them; but she was not
prepared to meet any of these as they were now about to assail
her.

JAMES TUCKER
from *Ralph Rashleigh*
Conditions at Newcastle

They were duly marched on board and were stripped quite naked before they were permitted to descend into the hold, that appeared to have been prepared for their reception, a rough floor having been laid over the shingle ballast. As fast as each man got below he was secured by his fetters to a chain, which in its turn was strongly fastened to the planking beneath, so that it was absolutely impossible for him to walk, even if the height of their place of confinement had permitted such a motion. But this was by no means the case, as, from Rashleigh's description of it, the distance from the floor to the upper deck could not have been more than three and a half feet at the furthest, and the vessel being very small, the number of men referred to were actually squeezed in so tight that it was perfectly impossible for them to lie in any other position than upon their sides, while from their close proximity one to the other, they quickly began to perspire so profusely that reeks of vapour almost as dense as smoke could be perceived rolling up the hatchway, the closing of which, if it were but for half an hour, must have resulted in inevitable suffocation to the whole herd of hapless wretches.

Ralph had read a great deal respecting the horrors of the slave trade, but never until now had he any faint conception of the shocking reality; and the only thing from which he could draw consolation was that as they had got but about a hundred miles in all to sail, the voyage and consequent suffering would be but of brief duration.

In a short time the vessel unmoored and the wind being fair, soon cleared the harbour and got out to sea, where a fresh gale appeared to be blowing; for the *Alligator* pitched heavily and shipped many billows, which, of course, making their way through the open hatchway into the hold, were at first hailed with delight by the parched sufferers below, whose feverish bodies were cooled by this immersion in the briny fluid. But in a little while the water increased in their prison to such an extent that they were obliged to adopt very painful positions in order to keep their heads above it. For several hours did this continue, until the captain was obliged by a shift of wind to put into a haven under his lee called Broken Bay; and then the unhappy convicts thought themselves fortunate in having the water pumped off, leaving them the wet floor to repose upon.

In brief, their voyage lasted forty-eight hours, during which period they were parched with thirst, very few being so fortunate as to obtain a single drink of water. Half a rotten and mouldy biscuit to each man formed their sole sustenance; and to crown all, they were cramped into a noxious hole, rather than hold, where the mephitic vapour arising from the breath of 130 men was increased by ordure, urine and excrement of every kind, among which the sufferers lay perforce.

This scene of complicated horrors, the intensity of which was in no whit lessened by the ruthless character of the inmates of this floating hell, was at length brought to a close by their arrival at Newcastle, where they shortly afterwards landed, naked as they were, upon the beach, and were compelled to perform sundry very necessary ablutions before their clothing was returned to them.

Here they remained until they were inspected by the military commandant, a personage of stern and uncompromising severity, the absolute rigour of whose sway well merited the appellation bestowed upon him of 'King of the Coal River.' Immediately on the close of this muster they were told off to various scenes of labour; and it fell to the lot of Rashleigh, with seventeen others, to be drafted for employment in the *old* coal mine, so called to distinguish it from another shaft, which had been recently commenced.

At the mouth of this work they were received by an overseer, the natural fierceness of whose grim physiognomy was not lessened by a plentiful griming of coal dust. He quickly called his clerk 'to take the likenesses' of those whose ill fortune had newly subjected them to his oppression. The clerk, a miserable, half-starved, downcast-looking, ragged being, soon performed his avocation with fear and trembling at the oft-repeated rude threats of his stern superior, and the men were lowered consecutively into the darksome orifice that appeared to gape for them.

On their arrival at the bottom of the chasm, a scene that had at least novelty to recommend it to our adventurer met his wondering gaze. Seven low passages appeared, that opened into the space around the termination of the shaft. They were dimly illuminated by small lamps; but at the farther extremity of each avenue there was a perfect coruscation of blazing lights, in front of which various groups of men were plying different branches of their thrift in toilsome haste, their extra diligence being apparently occasioned by the presence of the superior who had received the new-comers, a specimen of whose brutality they had an early opportunity of witnessing; for no sooner had he landed from the *skep* (bucket) in which he descended than his vigilant eye rested on one of the waggons that a party of prisoners had dragged along one of the passages. This not being filled to his liking, he, without any ceremony, but with many distasteful terms of abuse and energetic oaths, began to lay about him with a stout cudgel he carried, and dispensed his forcible favours so heartily that in a few seconds not one of the luckless gang belonging to the waggon in question was standing erect. After having thus knocked them all down, he began next to beat them until they arose again, and fairly cudgelled them off out of sight with the waggon.

On his return after this *agreeable* exercise, rather out of breath, he turned his attention to the new-comers, and dividing them into parties of six, he gave each subdivision charge of a waggon; and these led the way through one of the long galleries, followed by the waggons, until they all arrived at the end, which was an open area of considerable extent, where two or three large fires of coal were burning, by whose light, aided by that of their lamps; the miners were delving out masses of coal, at an immense heap of which he finally paused, directing a man who appeared to be overseer of this part of the work, to 'take the new chums in charge, and set them on'. This was quickly done. They were told to fill their waggons with coal, to draw them back to the opening, and there to upset the contents as the man at the shaft should direct them.

They continued to do this, stimulated by the blows and threats of their harsh taskmaster, until night, when each received a small portion of boiled grains of maize and much less rotten salt beef, which, with water, formed their whole food. The wretched miners soon after lay down in any part of the works they thought fit, bedding being here totally unknown except to the deputy overseers, and clothing of any kind whatever unworn by the workmen. In fact, the extreme heat of this subterranean place of abode, arising from want of air, and enhanced by the numerous fires maintained, would have rendered the lightest apparel an encumbrance. As for beds or blankets, there were various heaps of sand, which, being loose, were soft enough; and on these such of the convicts as were curious about lying *luxuriously* used to repose themselves.

The luckless wretches condemned to this kind of labour only left the mine once a week, on Saturday afternoons, when they were all drawn up and compelled to wash themselves and their clothing in the salt water; and after the latter articles were dry, all were marched to the convict barracks, where they abode until daylight on Monday morning, at which period they resumed their labour.

The first Saturday afternoon of our adventurer's sojourn at this miserable spot, as they were all bathing together in the sea, he noticed that not one of those who had been there longer than himself was without certain highly significant marks upon the back or breech, most frequently, indeed, on both, that told of the recent and severe application of the *cat*. A man to whom he remarked that 'punishment was plentiful enough here apparently', replied with a grin, 'Aye. There's plenty of *that*, anyway; and so you will say soon, for to-morrow is *pay* day.'

Ralph did not choose to ask any further questions, and they were soon after, to the number of five hundred, shut up in a spacious room of the prisoners' barracks, where they were left to pass the night on the floor as they thought fit.

Just at dawn the next day, *being Sunday*, they were aroused by the hoarse voice of a convict barrack officer, who turned them out into the yard of that edifice, where they were all drawn up around some implements, which the increasing light soon showed Rashleigh were triangles for securing men about to be flogged. Beside these implements was placed a table, at which sat apparently a clerk; and four scourgers stood beside the triangles, having their instruments of torture laid in fell array upon a long bench near them.

Our exile had scarcely completed his survey of all these dread preparations when the clash of arms and the roll of a drum announced the approach of the haughty potentate who was to set all this machinery of suffering in motion. An opening was quickly made in the ranks of assembled convicts, and the 'Captain' marched in, attended by the sergeant's guard of soldiers, who fell into a double rank behind him as he took his seat at the table.

'Dash my old rags,' said a fellow standing near Rashleigh, upon observing that the commandant was dressed in his suit of full regimental uniform. 'Look out, my lads! The *cove* has got on his fighting jacket. It's a-going to be a regular field day!' And full many a wretch who knew the signification and truth of this prediction writhed his back in anticipation of the warm infliction so many of them were doomed to taste ere long.

The clerk now opened his book. The overseer of the coal mines was first called on. He made his appearance, and a loutish reverence, to the awful authority, who ordered him sternly to begin his punishment list.

'Charles Chattey' stood foremost on his black beadroll, and when his name was shouted by the stentorian lungs of one of the scourgers, a little duck-legged Londoner stood forth.

'What's he been doing?' enquired the 'Captain'.

'Neglected his work, Your Honour,' was the brief reply.

'One hundred lashes,' was the equally prompt sentence. And the luckless wight was stripped and tied up in a twinkling at one of the triangles.

Three others were *tried* in as many minutes and took their places at the remaining sets.

The drummer, having received the signal, began to tap his drum in a slow and deliberate manner, marking time for the lashes, as they were inflicted by the willing and brawny arms of the flagellators, who were selected for this office from among the most muscular prisoners that would accept such a hideous berth, which, as before remarked, entailed upon them ever after the execrations of their fellow-convicts. And even while they held it, in this place, they were looked upon with distrust by their superiors, a constable always standing behind the back of the operating scourger with a stout stick, with which he scrupled not to strike the striker when his blows did not fall heavily enough upon the back of the culprit who was undergoing punishment.

MARCUS CLARKE
from *For the Term of His Natural Life*
The fate of the escapees

Two more days pass, and the three, eyeing each other suspiciously, resume their march. The third day – the sixteenth of their awful journey – such portions of the carcase as they have with them prove unfit to eat. They look into each other's famine-sharpened faces, and wonder 'who next?'

'We must all die together,' said Sanders quickly, 'before anything else must happen.'

Vetch marks the terror concealed in the words, and when the dreaded giant is out of earshot, says, 'For God's sake, let's go on alone, Alick. You see what sort of a cove that Gabbett is – he'd kill his father before he'd fast one day.'

They made for the bush, but the giant turned and strode towards them. Vetch skipped nimbly on one side, but Gabbett struck the Moocher on the forehead with the axe. 'Help! Jem, help!' cried the victim, cut, but not fatally, and in the strength of his desperation tore the axe from the monster who bore it, and flung it to Vetch. 'Keep it, Jemmy,' he cried, 'let's have no more murder done!'

They fare again through the horrible bush until nightfall, when Vetch, in a strange voice, called the giant to him.

'He must die.'

'Either you or he,' laughs Gabbett. 'Give me the axe.'

'No, no,' said the Crow, his thin, malignant face distorted by a horrible resolution. 'I'll keep the axe. Stand back! You shall hold him, and I'll do the job.'

Sanders, seeing them approach, knew his end was come, and submitted, crying, 'Give me half an hour to pray for myself.' They consent, and the bewildered wretch knelt down and folded his hands like a child. His big, stupid face worked with emotion. His great cracked lips moved in desperate agony. He wagged his head from side to side, in pitiful confusion of his brutalized senses. 'I can't think o' the words, Jem!'

'Pah,' snarled the cripple, swinging the axe, 'we can't starve here all night.'

Four days had passed, and the two survivors of this awful journey sat watching each other. The gaunt giant, his eyes gleaming with hate and hunger, sat sentinel over the dwarf. The dwarf, chuckling at his superior sagacity, clutched the fatal axe. For two days they had not spoken to each other. For two days each had promised himself that on the next his companion must *sleep* – and die. Vetch comprehended the devilish scheme of the monster who had entrapped five of his fellow-beings to aid him by their deaths to his own safety, and held aloof. Gabbett watched to snatch the weapon from his companion, and make the odds even for once and for ever. In the day-time they travelled on, seeking each a pretext to creep behind the other. In the night-time when they feigned slumber, each stealthily raising a head caught the wakeful glance of his companion. Vetch felt his strength deserting him, and his brain overpowered by fatigue. Surely the giant, muttering, gesticulating, and slavering at the mouth, was on the road to madness. Would the monster find opportunity to rush at him, and, braving the blood-stained axe, kill him by main force? or would he sleep, and be himself a victim? Unhappy Vetch! It is the terrible privilege of insanity to be sleepless.

On the fifth day, Vetch, creeping behind a tree, takes off his belt, and makes a noose. He will hang himself. He gets one end of the belt over a bough, and then his cowardice bids him pause. Gabbett approaches: he tries to evade him, and steal away into the bush. In vain. The insatiable giant, ravenous with famine, and sustained by madness, is not to be shaken off. Vetch tries to run, but his legs bend under him. The axe that has tried to drink so much blood feels heavy as lead. He will fling it away. No – he dares not. Night falls again. He must rest, or go mad. His limbs are powerless. His eyelids are glued together. He sleeps as he stands. This horrible thing must be a dream. He is at Port Arthur, or will wake on his pallet in the penny lodging-house he slept at when a boy. Is that the Deputy come to wake him to the torment of living? It is not time – surely not time yet. He sleeps – and the giant, grinning with ferocious joy, approaches on clumsy tiptoe and seizes the coveted axe.

On the north-east of Van Diemen's Land is a place called St. Helen's Point, and a certain skipper, being in want of fresh water landing there with a boat's crew, found on the banks of the creek a gaunt and blood-stained man, clad in tattered yellow, who carried on his back an axe and a bundle. When the sailors came within sight of him, he made signs to them to approach, and opening his bundle with much ceremony offered them some of its contents. Filled with horror at what the maniac displayed, they seized and bound him. At Hobart Town he was recognized as the only survivor of the nine desperadoes who had escaped from Colonel Arthur's 'Natural Penitentiary.'

A. G. STEPHENS
from *Marcus Clarke's Minor Writings*

When Clarke was at his best he had a peg to hang his thoughts on. Some of his presentations of old Australian stories are wonderfully well done. He has taken a dull record and sown it with flashes of wit and phrase, as Dumas sowed the work of his collaborators, till the whole page shines and glitters. And he brings usually a shrewd, critical head to aid his commentary.

One inclines to believe, then, that much of the force of *His Natural Life* must have lain *perdu* in the records on which Clarke based his story. But Clarke had a fine faculty of dramatic insight and dramatic expression. Given the ore he could refine it; given the situation, the scene, the men, he could bring all the contours and contrasts into prominence. His style is an admirable journalist's style, but not always good from the point of literature. It is full of light, but lacks colour and harmony. The clean, staccato sentences grow monotonous; they want a varied rhythm and sweep. In *His Natural Life*, Clarke has often tried to get these things, and often succeeded. His brain was highly receptive and impressible, and seems to have largely reflected the motion and hue of the medium in which it had just previously been merged. Some passages of Clarke seem modelled on Balzac; some on Hugo; some on Disraeli, Thackeray, and Dickens. He took his literary property where he found it; and his contemporaries called him a not too scrupulous borrower. Perhaps he followed the Thackerayan model more closely than any other, since in mental vision he was nearly kin with Thackeray. But he lacked Thackeray's breadth and depth. It is sufficient that he is himself, and that the book which concentrates himself can never in Australia be forgotten.

'PRICE WARUNG'
(WILLIAM ASTLEY)
Lieutenant Darrell's Predicament

Lieutenant Darrell, of the —rd Regiment, second officer of the detachment stationed at the Hell's Gates of Macquarie Harbour, V.D.L., was in a predicament, in which the element of strangeness, while considerable, was much less than that of mortal danger.

Lieutenant Darrell was the victim of reversed conditions. In place of commanding a prisoners' guard, he and his guard were in charge of a score of prisoners. That was the singular thing in this situation.

And the prisoners who had so defied the King's Majesty and all the proprieties as to suppress the liberties of Lieutenant Darrell, instead of ordering themselves humbly towards the officer (as the Catechism urged them), and obeying him with abject slavishness (as the Regulations commanded them), had just placed him in such a position that his life was literally depending upon his own toss-up of a coin. That was the dangerous element in the case.

He stands now in the centre of the rough, large dormitory, with forty fierce, unpitying eyes fixed upon him. He is stripped to the waist – a good specimen of the well-fed English middle-class boy of nineteen or twenty; and he evidently has the courage of his years and race. He balances a guinea on his thumb-nail preparatory to flipping it into the air with all its heavy burden of destiny on its glittering surface, and, save that his face is a trifle paler than usual, not a symptom of fear is discernible about him. He would rather that the wretches who are environing him with their bodily loathsomeness and the putrescence of their tainted spirits, should definitely fix his doom themselves. He had said as much to them, and that was his solitary attempt at influencing them as they played their murderous game. They had rejected his suggestion. They wished, by a refinement of cruelty, to constitute the young officer the arbiter of his own fate, and their leader had told him so. And the blanching of his cheek had followed upon the convict's retort. A natural and not unmanly question, surely, for what man is there who would not sooner receive his doom from the hands of another, than choose it himself after ten minutes of the dreadful suspense that 'fluctuates 'twixt blind hope and blind despair'?

A circle of steel points – bayonet tips! – is pressing upon Darrell as he stands there. The stocks of the muskets are held by convicts' hands, and so close are the weapons held to his naked body, that the action of his arm in tossing the coin, causing as it does a momentary protrusion of his back, drives his flesh on one of the points.

The coin ascends – shimmers a golden ring for a moment on the sight – and falls duly to the earthen floor.

The parti-coloured figures – some grey, some brown, some yellow and black – stoop over it, and there is a cry of 'Heads! He goes by the left door!'

The encircling bayonets are withdrawn a few inches to let the officer face to the left. The chief of the felon-gang picks up the guinea, and tenders it to the Lieutenant. The plucky boy takes it, and flings it into the other's face with a taunt.

'Here, keep it,' he sneered. 'You'll be the sooner dead because of it. It's an even chance that any one of you would murder another for a single shilling. It's therefore twenty-one chances to one that you'll be killed now you've got a guinea.'

Then he strode down to the door behind which his fate was lurking for him. At the sixth or seventh step he paused, and, wincing as his sudden stoppage brought him on to the bayonet again, cast another gibe at the convict: 'That's the first guinea, I'll swear, you ever had in your possession that you didn't steal!'

Laughing, he resumed his walk. At the door he found – but, perhaps, we ought to have begun at the beginning.

A convict who had escaped from the settlement at Sarah Island in company with seven others, returned *alone*, five weeks later. He had, he reported, lost his companions ten days after the escape, and had sustained life in the interval on wild berries, fish caught in the streams, and the pith of the grass-tree. His plump appearance gave the lie to his story, and a certain slavering of the mouth left those familiar with the annals of Hell's Gates (which, though few, were already full of indescribable ghastlinesses) no doubt whatever as to the means by which he had succeeded in maintaining his physical vigour. He was accordingly given his choice as to whether he would be hanged there and then as an absconder, or be first flogged 'for absenting himself from work', and then be sent to Hobart Town to be tried (and hanged) for the murder of his fellow-escapees. Naturally, the wretch preferred the latter course. Death was equally certain in either case, but the Hobart Town trip offered the supreme enjoyment of a change of scene and a glass of hot spirit the night before execution. Grog was scarce at the Harbour, and the luxuries permissible to the Condemned on the night previous to, and the morning of, their 'working-off' were neither so various nor so excellent in quality as in the Capital. For which most cogent of reasons the ex-escapee chose the present scourging and the future hanging instead of an immediate execution. While there was life there was always the chance of 'baccy and grog.

Now, while he was waiting for the departure of the *Cyprus*, the Government vessel, which was to take him and some six or seven other candidates for Brother Dougherty's (the Hobart Town hangman) tender ministrations, from the Settlement, this man learnt, in the genial gossip of the condemned cell, that a particular species of pine-timber was in request from the Capital, and that the Commandant was at a loss to obtain a sufficient supply. It occurred to his lively intellect to make a bargain with that august personage.

'Give me, yer honour, a gill o' rum an' a fig o' 'baccy ev'ry day till I'm scragged, an' I'll put yer on to as fine a block o' pine as yer ever seed!' And as the fellow described the locality with an exact circumstantiality, the Commandant, Captain Bankes, conditionally assented to the proposal. The departure of the *Cyprus* was delayed for a fortnight pending the dispatch and return, of course under guard, of the finder of the new pine-patch. And, his statement being verified, it is pleasing to relate that for the brief remainder of his life he revelled in grog and 'the weed'.

It was the Commandant's resolve to utilize the undoubtedly important discovery that had led to Lieutenant Darrell's predicament.

The pine forest was situated in the delta formed by the junction of the Franklin and the Gordon, some twenty-five miles distant from the debouchment of the latter splendid river into Macquarie Harbour. Of an area and a density to occupy at least twenty convicts for a twelve-month, the timber was too far away from the main settlement for the workers and their guards to traverse the distance daily, and hence it became necessary to erect barracks on the spot. This had been done, and the rude structure – a prisoners' dormitory and meal room, 40 ft by 20 ft, a guard-room of half the dimensions for the soldiers, and two small rooms for the officer in charge – had been tenanted by Lieutenant Darrell and his *entourage* some weeks before the day of the revolt.

Darrell was of metal from which the die of nobler circumstances would have struck out a good man and a chivalrous officer. The system, however, put him into its dehumanizing press – the System at this time was more military than civil – and moulded the golden ore of his youth into a shape that retained only one feature worthy of admiration – an absolute fearlessness. Demons, if we may believe the legends, share that quality with men, and Darrell, who had the stuff of a hero in him, simply became a devil.

He could not understand what fear meant. Neither could he understand what significance there was in the word humanity. All qualities included in the latter term, justice, generosity, pity, were to this lad meaningless abstractions.

At an age when most other boys of his class were at school, he was placed in a position of unchecked control over the most degraded of mankind. His whim was the destiny of scores of human beings. In a caprice and without reason, he could, if he so chose, send men to the triangles and the gallows, and, unless the sparse records of the epoch lie, like one of Parson Ford's pet convict-converts, he made the choice on at least one occasion. In other words, a folio in a Sarah Island Register records, tersely, that convict Such-an-one was hanged 'By Order of Lieutenant Darrell'. Nothing more. No statement of offence, no note of any inquiry. Why should there be? It was only one ruffian the less on the roll of Macquarie Harbour, and about thirty pounds per annum saved to the Colonial Treasury. If the System seemed at times wasteful of human life, the wastefulness was only apparent. Underneath there was a solid economy. For every man hanged saved the System so much money.

Darrell, boy as he was, had, prior to his receiving command of the logging party, achieved reputation both among the Authorities and the prisoners as a brilliant administrator. He gave his days to formal duty, and – meritorious young man! – his nights to qualifying himself for higher positions in the hierarchy of the System. Like the John Price of a later period, he formed intimacies with the convicts in order to ascertain their modes of thought, their secret practices, and their mysterious modes of communication. And, as though the soil of the System, imbued as it was with the sweat of pain and blood drawn by lash and bayonet, could not blossom into a sufficiently luxuriant brutality to please him, he studied to invent new punishments and to adopt old ones to present exigencies.

He took an unused 'cat' and experimented with it till he had arranged a new cracker to each tail to his satisfaction. He had plaited into the strands of whip-cord a length of *copper-wire*.

He made another alteration. He added a tenth tail. But he found that the additional lash subtracted from the value of the instrument of chastisement. It clung to the other tails so as to produce no more than six or seven welts, as against nine caused by the old-style whip. 'Ah!' he said, 'King Billy knew what he was about when he kept to the nine. You can't use more with benefit!' And forthwith he abandoned the altered scourge for the old pattern.

He read somewhere an account of the way the *forçats* of France were locked up at night, and with the eagerness of youth over a new game, was all anxiety to introduce the method into Van Diemen's Land.

'Fancy!' he exclaimed to Captain Bankes, 'I'll knock all their rioting and devil's business on the head!'

The plan which was to attain that highly desirable result was to run two iron bars the full length of each dormitory, and at a height from the floor of six inches. As the prisoners lay on the ground in a double row, heads against either wall, their feet would be chain-locked to the bars.

'They'd never sleep,' rejoined Bankes. 'And what if a man were taken ill?'

'Oh, prisoners sleep anyhow and anywhere, and nine-tenths of the illness is only shamming Abraham to avoid work.'

This was reasoning which quite commended itself to Captain Bankes's judgement, and he reported favourably upon the scheme. Colonel Sorell, however, squelched it. His Honour couldn't see his way to the expense, much to Darrell's regret.

Then again, Lieutenant Darrell was the originator of the marooning system.

Within musket shot of Sarah Island were three islets. The largest was the burial-place of the convict dead, and was known as Halliday's Island, after the first prisoner who was buried there. The next in size was noted on the charts as Settlement Isle. Here were interred the remains of the 'Free' dead – the officers and soldiers who died while on duty at the Harbour. This separation, by the way, of the 'Bond' and the 'Free' after death was one of the few merciful acts of which the System was every guilty. It left the prisoner in the kindly embrace of the Great Emancipator undisturbed by companionship with the dust of his oppressors. The third islet, a rock so small that the waves frequently swept its surface, was known as the Pilot or Grummet Rock. 'Here,' writes an historian, with a truthfulness in detail that a mere tale-monger cannot rival, 'cells were excavated for the reception of such incorrigibles as were unsubdued by the Bastille of the Harbour. Conveyed in a boat to within a few yards of the rock, the doomed man had to wade through the surf with his provisions, to clamber up into one of those comfortless recesses, and was left for days and weeks to add his yell to the seabird's scream and the dreary moan of the Western wind.' Lieutenant Darrell was the inventor of this ingenious method of subjugating the unsubduable. And, not to rob him of a single leaf of his laurels, we may as well say that his plan went a step further than that described by the historian above. He provided for the chaining down of any peculiarly untractable spirit to the exposed rock.

There were other excellencies of the System which owe their creation to the Lieutenant's fertile ingenuity, but it is needless to recount them here. We have said enough to show that the juvenile officer was a *connoisseur* of what Lord Stanley termed the 'reformatory agencies'. The lad made but one mistake. Most geniuses are born too early; Darrell committed the blunder of being born too late. The System did its best to utilize his peculiar gifts, but he was comparatively wasted in an enlightened age. He would have graced the agonies of Count Ugolino with a fresh torture, have proved an invaluable auxiliary to Torquemada, and as a deputy to my Lords of the Star Chamber he would have relieved their policy from the stigma of monotonous blood-thirstiness which attached to it, for he would have suggested so many pretty refinements. Altogether, a very promising youth, Lieutenant Darrell.

Most officers would have kicked against the fiat that sent them for three months at a time to the depths of the forest with no other company than a score of desperate malefactors and a handful of illiterate soldiers. Not so Darrell. He revelled in the prospect of carrying out certain experiments on the temper of his gang, and particularly anticipated, with positive enjoyment, the employment of a novel style of gag, the introduction of which into the routine of Sarah Island Captain Bankes had prohibited.

'I'll leave you a free hand with your own men, Darrell,' had said the Commandant in issuing final instructions for the trip up the Gordon, 'because there is no knowing what may happen. But take my advice – don't use that new spring gag of yours. They'll murder you if you do! The thing is too painful altogether.'

'Not they, sir,' had replied Darrell, 'they only murder men who're afraid of them. But I promise you I'll only use the gag once, just to see how it works.'

He kept his word: he applied the newly-designed instrument but once. Which, however, by a very annoying distastefulness on the part of the prisoners to its operation, proved once too often. The way of the inventor is often hard.

The gang, linked to a long chain, were engaged in rafting some newly-felled timber one Saturday afternoon, when a storm of almost cyclonic violence burst upon them. A sleety rain, then hail, then a mad, whirling wind that snapped off the giant pines sixty or seventy feet from the ground and thirty or forty from their crests. The rain and hail cut the prisoners' faces and hands like knives, and the falling timber, though it was borne as easily on the breath of the gale as thistledown on a summer breeze, came crashing round them in an affrighting fashion, and, naturally enough, the men impulsively moved to shelter as speedily as the chain to which they were ironed would allow. Had they waited a moment longer, Darrell, who, with the guard, was likewise exposed to the fury of the storm, would have ordered the prisoners into safety, but for the men to seek cover without instructions – why, 'twas rank mutiny! He ground his teeth as he saw the workers leave the logs.

'To the cliff, men,' he called to the soldiers. 'And protect your locks.' The guard placed their muskets under their tunics and rushed across the narrow clearing which separated the fringe of forest from an overhanging cliff by the river-bank, beneath whose walls were already grouped the convicts. Darrell followed them. When under the shelter of the granite mass he commanded the guard to examine their priming.

'Right, No. 1?' 'Yes, sir.' And so on, down the short line.

He was facing the privates, and standing between them and the prisoners as he asked them if the weapons were fireable. On being answered, he turned on his heel, and ordered the huddled 'Gov'ment men' to resume work.

The storm was at its height. Against the snow-topped Frenchman's Gap to the northward, lightning was darting in terrific dashes as though titanic warriors were hacking at the monolith with gleaming swords. Thunder rolled magnificently through the ranges, but its receding reverberations were unheard amid the roar of the wind and of the foaming current which, the one above the other below, swept down the gorge of the Gordon. And though by the clock, nightfall was still some hours ahead, the low-hung clouds soon filled the clearing with an unearthly shadow. The convicts clanked their fetters in the tremors of their superstitious horror as they peered at the elemental war from their entrenchment in the cavelike recess, and it is doubtful whether they heard the Lieutenant's order, though he stood but fifteen paces distant.

He repeated it, and in the same breath ordered the guard to the 'Present'.

The muskets, better than the words, carried significance to the brutish minds. Several of the felons, more cowardly than the rest, flung themselves to the earth. The others, amazed, stood as motionless as the tightened chain would let them.

'Do you hear, prisoners?' said Darrell, and to make quite sure that they *did* hear, he stepped forward a couple of paces: 'Go back to the logs!'

'In this rain, sir?' asked, with marked civility, one Robins. Robins, a man originally of good station, was a wiry, grey-headed, lithe figure, aged forty-four years. Landed at Sydney seventeen years before with a 'life'-sentence, he had been dispatched in 1823 to Macquarie Harbour, to serve as many years as Nature and the System would permit him of the *seventy-five* which colonial sentences had piled upon his original penalty. In short, he was a monster. Nevertheless, a very civil monster at times. His mates on the gang-chain shrank from him to the utmost limit of their iron tether when he spoke to anyone with an oily politeness. For Dick Robins was then in his most devilish mood.

'In this rain, sir?' was what he asked – with the especial grace of tone which had won for him the title of 'Dancing-school Dick'.

'In this rain!' repeated Lieutenant Darrell, ironically.

'I'll see you d—d first!' was Mr. Robins' rejoinder. And he folded his arms to wait for what would come next.

Darrell calmly put his hand into the pocket of his jacket and brought out his new gag. The idea of it was not altogether original, perhaps, for something like it had been used for rebellious servants by the great Richelieu, but still, Darrell's invention had 'points' of its own. It was, for one thing, cheaply made. Two pieces of hoop-iron were curved into a pear-like protuberance. Into the ends, riveted so as to form a hollow stair, was doubled a length of flexible steel. This latter bit of metal, pushed into the 'swell' of the pear, would fly open, act as a spring, and distend the bars of iron.

Robins had never seen the sweet thing before, and looked at it curiously.

'What did you say?' enquired Darrell.

Robins opened his mouth to reply, and, in a second, the boy officer had flung himself upon the convict, and the gag was between the convict's jaw. A pressure of the Lieutenant's thumb and a clicking sound were evidence that the pretty invention had acted perfectly. A weak humanitarian might have said too perfectly, for the sudden distension of the gag ripped open the cheeks, and Robins's mouth was widened a quarter of an inch on either side.

You could always depend upon an official of the System for improving upon Nature. Nature connected men's vertebrae and endowed men with perfect windpipes. The System was never so pleased as when it was breaking the former, except when the rope severed the latter. Nature gave men whole skins. The System was partial to the investigation of the problem – How many men could survive after the cuticle of their backs was stripped off? And, in the matter of men's mouths, Nature seldom errs on the side of smallness. The System, however, was not satisfied. It had, by Lieutenant Darrell's agency, undertaken to enlarge men's natural mouths.

Robins clapped his hand to his bleeding jaws. A curious sound came through his fingers – an idiot-like gurgle. Darrell laughed, quite pleased.

'You'll go to work now, Robins, my man, and you won't leave it without orders again, will you? Now – march!'

From Robins's right arm was dangling a manacle. He wore it always, for he, alone of all the gang, was locked to the wall of the dormitory during the night. Perhaps there were two pounds' weight in these irons, not reckoning the ball.

Robins, at Darrell's last words, moved as though to obey. And then – exerting all the immense strength stored in his muscles by the arduous gang-labour, he slashed the dangling manacles into his tyrant's face, and, repeating the blow, brought him stunned and bleeding to the ground. The military guard of six men had still their muskets at the level, and each one of the six pulled his trigger. One only of the weapons went off, and that fruitlessly: the others snapped harmlessly, the moisture of the atmosphere having penetrated to the pans. The soldiers had not time to replace the priming before the chain with its human and metallic links had encircled them in a deathly embrace. The military, unfortified by the example or voice of their officer, were powerless before that charge of fiends, through whose veins were now coursing the long damned-up floods of revenge and hate, of lust for blood and the ferocity of despair. In the next few moments the felons had balanced their account with the System for years of punishment. As has happened at so many periods and in so many climes, it was poor Tommy Atkins who bore the brunt of his superiors' wickedness and folly.

The grave of five out of the six men may be still seen on Settlement Island. The sixth man lingered for a few weeks – long enough for him to be rescued, to be sent to Hobart Town, and to tell the story to drunken old Sorell, who stood by his bedside in the General Hospital. He was buried in Davey Street cemetery.

Their first frenzy expended, the gang proceeded to estimate their position. The whole affair had consumed no more than three or four minutes, but in that time their world had been turned topsy-turvy. Before the gagging they had, one and all, though ironed and sunk into the depths of physical wretchedness and moral shame, been still free of the gallows. Now, the rope was virtually round all their necks. On the other hand, they had been the sport of a tyrant, and victims pushed before the Juggernaut car of the System. Now, at least, they were free!

Their first care was to free Robins from the gag. With great difficulty, and with something of tenderness of touch, one of their number withdrew the gory metal from the jagged mouth. Their next impulse was to free themselves from the chain. With stoic fortitude Robins bade them draw up to line, and then led them till they formed a circle round the body of young Darrell, who had not yet returned to full consciousness.

Robins motioned to the man on the last couple. 'Search him,' he said, with painful utterance, 'for the key. I don't – want to touch – him – yet. If – I – get my hands on him – I'll kill him – and I don't want to – yet.'

The recipient of the order obeyed. He dragged his length of chain to the centre of the circle, and, kneeling down, fumbled in the pockets of the prostrate officer till he found his bunch of keys. His action partially awoke Darrell to himself.

'What are you up to?' he mumbled dazedly.

'Lug 'im in the jaw!' shouted a convict.

The words suggested an idea to Robins.

'The gag – where is it?' he cried. And, one who had held it mechanically since it had been taken from Robins's mouth, held it up.

Robins took it, and examined it carefully. But he was unacquainted with the trick of readjusting the steel spring, and, throwing it to the prisoner kneeling by Darrell, told him to 'put it in just as it was'.

Darrell, barely apprehending their object, and not yet understanding what had happened to the guard, tried to struggle to his feet, and called on the soldiers. He was forced back, other convicts went to the first man's assistance, and – Lieutenant Darrell was gagged with his own invention. If it did not act quite as effectively in his case as in Robins's (it did not tear open the corners of *his* mouth) we must concede a little to the convicts' unfamiliarity with the ingenious thing. They had not, as Darrell had, the advantage of preliminary experimentalizing.

All this time, the storm had been raging, and the prisoners had scarcely had their individual chains unlocked from the common cable, before a sudden change in the wind brought its force round the angle of the cliff and thrust leaves and branches and sleet into their shelter.

'We'll have to make for the huts,' said one, and the rest assented. They were loth to tempt the storm, but the rock protected them no longer, and besides they had no wish to remain in company with the lifeless forms now that night was drooping over the ghastly place.

'What'll we do with th' off'ser?' queried another. To which silly inquiry there could be, of course, but one reply. As if they were going to encumber themselves with the boy! But Robins suggested they should make him safe. So they dragged the wreck of a big tree behind the rock, and with some of their own chains bound him thereto. Twenty full-grown men placing bonds on a boy for their personal protection was a spectacle for laughter, surely; but the felon wretches realized in their animal instincts that they were binding more than Darrell. They were putting the gyves on Law and Authority.

And so they left Lieutenant Darrell to the mercy of the elements all that awful Saturday night. Gagged and bound, faint from the loss of blood which had issued from an opening Robins's manacles had made in his scalp, sick and food-craving, drenched from the ice-cold rain, and in momentary danger from hurtling timber, he yet lived through it. At a place and in a day when endurance under bodily torture was not heroic, because it was manifested by criminals or their keepers, Darrell's survival was not phenomenal. In any other place and time, he would have been apostrophized in odes, and eloquence would have lamented its inability to do him justice.

On Sunday morning Robins, the one man who had kept sober during the orgy which had marked the late hours of the furious night, strolled from the huts to the place where Darrell had been left. The air was as pure and the sunshine as bright as ever visited that sombre region, for the malarial vapours that customarily filled the gloomy aisles of the forest had vanished before the storm; and, what with the brightness of the day and the sense of freedom, Mr. Robins was in gay spirits. It was sufficient for him to know that in the store behind him there was grog enough and food enough to last a month, that the force which could alone recapture him and his associates was twenty-odd miles away, and that a few hundred yards in front of him lay, bound and fettered, an enemy with whose sufferings he proposed to entertain himself. It would, under the circumstances, have been surprising if he had refrained from waking the primeval echoes by whistle and song.

Darrell welcomed him with a grunt which might have been an oath. Wet, shivering with cold and feverish weakness, and cramped by the weight of irons, the lad had will enough to gibe and taunt the convict. Robins listened with an amiable smile to the grunting.

'That's right, Mr. Darrell, fire away. I don't objec' if it does you good.' And then he asked him, with solicitude in his voice, 'What would his Honour like for breakfast? There was some prime bacon at the store – would a rasher satisfy his Honour, and would he have cocoa or coffee? A tot of brandy first, or after? And would his Honour shave at once, or wait till he had breakfasted?'

The officer's ankles and hands were tied, and the convict loosened the knottings of the former so that Darrell could shuffle along. Then he hauled the officer to his feet, and suggested they should start for the huts. To leave no room for contradiction on the point, Robins, picking up one of the muskets with a fixed bayonet, quietly prodded his late Commandant!

'I'm always grateful, Lieutenant,' the convict said pleasantly. 'Always! You've done that aforetime to me to help me over a rough place when I've had a log on my shoulder, and though you ain't got a log to carry, you're in *rather* a tight place, and so I'll just give you a lift – so!' And Mr Darrell's progress was again gently facilitated by the bayonet-tip.

To describe the indignities these enfranchized wretches heaped on the young officer would be impossible. And yet this much has to be said about them. Indescribable as many are, nameless as most shall be, Robins took care that in the gang's treatment of Darrell they did no more than parody the System.

They did not give Darrell a hot breakfast. They mixed him some cold flour and water, and, removing the gag from his swollen lips, forced the nauseous stuff down his throat with a leaden spoon. The System used to feed 'em on that flour and water.

They prepared some grog; stirred it right under his nose; put the pannikin to his very lips – and then dashed its contents in his face. Which was a favourite amusement of Lieutenant Darrell himself.

They lathered his face with a shameful concoction – and scraped it off with hoop-iron, to which clung also some flakes of skin and tufts of whisker. Captain Bankes's exclusive joke, this. Nearly every commanding officer has his own patent method for deriving pleasure from convicts' contortions.

They trussed him, like a fowl. Next to the seduction of soldiers' wives, and the execution without trial of convicts, few things used to confer a greater degree of happiness on Colonel Foveaux (sometime Lieutenant Governor of Norfolk Island and afterwards Administrator of New South Wales) than to truss prisoners.

They held a Prayer Book before him. The System issued to Superintendents and Commandants a 'Form of Prayer' *bound up* with the Regulations, and prescribed the reading of the *whole*

contents of the book every Sunday. Darrell refused to open his
lips. The gang cancelled his objections with the prick of the
bayonet. He had mumbled half a page when Robins bade him
stop. Then that eminently ingenious rogue found for him 'The
order for the Burial of the Dead', and made him read it through.

'There,' cried the blasphemous wretch as Darrell finished, 'not
many men can say they've read their own burial service. But you
have, my boy! Ain't you proud, sonny?'

Before he began the reading they had flogged him. Each man had
taken the cat – Darrell's own copper-wired cat – and had given
him one blow. 'Don't hit hard, lads,' begged Robins, 'leave some
life in him – for the afternoon.' (For a man with festering lips,
Robins did an astounding amount of talking that day!) And the
convicts obeyed, and did no more than raise puffy stripes on the
flesh – where the System would have put gashes.

After the reading, they flung a rope over a branch of a tree.
However, they didn't quite hang him. It isn't the first sudden haul
up to the beam that breaks the neck or chokes the wind-pipe – it's
the after suspension. And a bucketful of water brought Lieutenant
Darrell back to his senses. Here, again, there was another
departure from the System. The System would never have
brought the bucket into requisition.

Towards four o'clock, the men desired to bring the matter to a
climax. They wished to be done with Darrell, once and for all, and
to get to the grog again. And so they permitted him to rest while
they discussed the matter of his death. For, of course, the moment
they reversed the conditions, both he and they knew he would
have to die.

In that ribald conclave, some were for shooting him, others for
hanging him outright, others for repeating the grim Sydney
episode of '15 when certain convicts hunted out an ants' nest,
and pegged a gang-overseer on it to be eaten alive. But Captain
Robins had his plan.

'Look here, lads, Darrell, you know, can't find his way anywhere
unless he's guided. Put him a hundred yards from the Settlement,
and he'll lose himself!' This was quite true – Darrell, abnormally
intelligent in most things, was absolutely deficient in the sense
of locality.

'Well, what then?' suspiciously asked one of the gang. 'You ain't
a-goin' to be fool enough to let 'im loose?'

'Why, that 'ud be the best fun – take him ten miles up the
stream and turn him loose. Why, he'd starve, and he'd have no
mates to keep him alive!'

That last ghastly shot told on two of his hearers. Like the discoverer of the pine-patch, they had mysteriously sustained life in the forest wilderness.

Robins went on: –

'But we'll give him his choice how he'll die – whether he'll be turned out to starve, or whether he'll take his death standing. Now, my idea's this: – This dormitory has two doors – one at the east and the other at the west end. Outside of one end two of us take up our stations with axes, and if he comes out of that door, we just *let him have it*. If he comes out of the other door he has to go into the forest. He can't cross the junction without our seeing him, and even if he could he'd never find his way to the Harbour. So he's bound to starve. Only *we* don't starve him in that case. *We* give him his freedom. And supposing he goes out of the other door, and the axes *do* tumble on him – well, that'll be a voluntary act, too, won't it? *We* don't compel him to go out of that door. And none of the chaps inside know which door the lads with the axes go to, d'ye see?'

At first there was demurring to their leader's plan, but the more it was discussed the more its devilish ingenuity grew upon the gang. Finally, it was approved, the objection of those who would have preferred to behold Darrell's dying agonies being demolished by the consideration that the suspense would add new tortures to his sufferings.

They cut his bonds and brought him from the soldiers' hut into the dormitory. Robins explained the position. 'We have placed the men,' explained that distinguished villain, 'but no one inside knows which door they are behind. They make their own choice outside. You've to make yours inside!'

Robins was leaning against the north wall of the dormitory as he spoke. Darrell was facing him.

'You won't give me any inkling which door these men are at?'

'I couldn't if I would. And I wouldn't if I could,' answered Robins.

Darrell looked round. The eager eyes, gluttonous of his pain, glared at him. But in no glance was there any index to point to the door of freedom. He smiled disdainfully, and then took a few steps towards the right-hand, the eastern door. Half-way, however, he paused, wavered, and went as near to the other door.

As they saw his dreadful vacillation, and that great beads of sweat were dewing his forehead, although the contemptuous smile was still retained – by how strenuous an effort. God knows! – on his lips, they exulted, and thanked Robins for his happy idea!

Up and down went the boy, trying to peer through the cracks of the logs, leaning his ear against the end walls as though he would learn their station from the sentinels' breathing; up and down; up and down, not counting his paces, but every step being unerringly checked off in his brain; up and down, till the gang grew impatient, taunted him, prodded him.

Then Robins threw him one of his own guineas. 'Toss up for the door,' sneered the felon.

Darrell caught the coin eagerly. At least, it would save him the pain of decision!

'Heads, the left, the west door,' shouted Robins, 'tails, the east door.'

And the coin was spun as we have told. And Darrell went to the left door, and opened it –.

'TASMA' (JESSIE COUVREUR)
An Old-Time Episode in Tasmania

The gig was waiting upon the narrow gravel drive in front of the fuchsia-wreathed porch of Cowa Cottage. Perched upon the seat, holding the whip in two small, plump, ungloved hands, sat Trucaninny, Mr Paton's youngest daughter, whose straw-coloured, sun-steeped hair, and clear, sky-reflecting eyes, seemed to protest against the name of a black gin that some 'clay-brained cleric' had bestowed upon her irresponsible little person at the baptismal font some eight or nine years ago. The scene of this outrage was Old St David's Cathedral, Hobart, – or, as it was then called, Hobart *Town*, – chief city of the Arcadian island of Tasmania; and just at this moment, eight o'clock on a November morning, the said cathedral tower, round and ungainly, coated with a surface of dingy white plaster, reflected back the purest, brightest light in the world. From Trucaninny's perch – she had taken the driver's seat – she could see, not only the cathedral, but a considerable portion of the town, which took the form of a capital S as it followed the windings of the coast. Beyond the wharves, against which a few whalers and fishing-boats were lying idle, the middle distance was represented by the broad waters of the Derwent, radiantly blue, and glittering with silver sparkles; while the far-off background showed a long stretch of yellow sand, and the hazy, undulating outline of low-lying purple hills. Behind her the aspect was different. Tiers of hills rose one above the other in grand confusion, until they culminated in the towering height of Mount Wellington, keeping guard in majestic silence over the lonely little city that encircled its base. This portion of the view, however, was hidden from Trucaninny's gaze by the weatherboard cottage in front of which the gig was standing, – though I doubt whether in any case she would have turned her head to look at it; the faculty of enjoying a beautiful landscape being an acquisition of later years than she had attained since the perpetration of the afore-mentioned outrage of her christening. Conversely, as Herbert Spencer says, the young man who was holding the horse's head until such time as the owner of the gig should emerge from the fuchsia-wreathed porch, fastened his eyes upon the beautiful scene before him with more than an artist's appreciation in their gaze. He was dressed in the rough clothes of a working gardener, and so much of his head as could be seen beneath the old felt wide-awake that covered it, bore ominous evidence of having been recently shaved. I use the word ominous advisedly, for a shaven head in connection with a working suit had nothing priestly in its suggestion, and could bear, indeed, only one interpretation in the wicked old times in Tasmania. The young man keeping watch over the gig had clearly come into that fair scene for his country's good; and the explanation of the absence of a prison suit was doubtless due to the fact he was out on a ticket-of-leave. What the landscape had to say to him under these circumstances was not precisely clear. Perhaps all his soul was going out towards the white-sailed wool-ship tacking down the Bay on the first stage of a journey of most uncertain length; or possibly the wondrous beauty of the scene, contrasted with the unspeakable horror of the one he had left, brought the vague impression that it was merely some exquisite vision. That a place so appalling as his old prison should exist in the heart of all this peace and loveliness, seemed too strange an anomaly. Either that was a nightmare and this was real, or this was a fantastic dream and that was the revolting truth; but then which was which, and how had he, Richard Cole, late No. 213, come to be mixed up with either?

As though to give a practical answer to his melancholy question, the sharp tingle of a whip's lash made itself felt at this instant across his cheek. In aiming the cumbersome driving-whip at the persistent flies exploring the mare's back, Trucaninny had brought it down in a direction she had not intended it to take. For a moment she stood aghast. Richard's face was white with passion. He turned fiercely round; his flaming eyes seemed literally to send out sparks of anger. 'Oh, please, I didn't mean it,' cried the child penitently. 'I wanted to hit the flies. I did indeed. I hope I didn't hurt you?'

The *amende honorable* brought about an immediate reaction. The change in the young man's face was wonderful to behold. As he smiled back full reassurance at the offender, it might be seen that his eyes could express the extremes of contrary feeling at the very shortest notice. For all answer, he raised his old felt wide-awake in a half-mocking though entirely courtly fashion, like some nineteenth century Don César de Bazan, and made a graceful bow.

'Are *you* talking to the man, Truca?' cried a querulous voice at this moment from the porch, with a stress on the you that made the little girl lower her head, shame-faced. 'What do you mean by disobeying orders, miss?'

The lady who swept out upon the verandah at the close of this tirade was in entire accord with her voice. 'British matron' would have been the complete description of Miss Paton, if fate had not willed that she should be only a British spinster. The inflexibility that comes of finality of opinion regarding what is proper and what is the reverse, - a rule of conduct that is of universal application for the true British matron, - expressed itself in every line of her face and in every fold of her gown. That she was relentlessly respectable and unyielding might be read at the first glance; that she had been handsome, in the same hard way, a great many years before Truca was maltreated at the baptismal font, might also have been guessed at from present indications. But that she should be the 'own sister' of the good-looking, military-moustached, debonair man (I use the word debonair here in the French sense) who now followed her out of the porch, was less easy to divine. The character of the features as well as of the expression spoke of two widely differing temperaments. Indeed, save for a curious dent between the eyebrows, and a something in the nostrils that seemed to say he was not to be trifled with, Mr. Paton might have sat for the portrait of one of those jolly good fellows who reiterate so tunefully that they 'won't go home till morning,' and who are as good as their word afterwards.

Yet 'jolly good fellow' as he showed himself in card-rooms and among so-called boon companions, he could reveal himself in a very different light to the convicts who fell under his rule. Forming part of a system for the crushing down of the unhappy prisoners, in accordance with the principle of 'Woe be to him through whom the offence cometh,' he could return with a light heart to his breakfast or his dinner, after seeing some score of his fellow-men abjectly writhing under the lash, or pinioned in a ghastly row upon the hideous gallows. 'Use,' says Shakespeare, 'can almost change the stamp of Nature.' In Mr. Paton's case it had warped as well as changed it. Like the people who live in the atmosphere of Courts, and come to regard all outsiders as another and inferior race, he had come to look upon humanity as divisible into two classes – namely, those who were convicts, and those who were not. For the latter, he had still some ready drops of the milk of human kindness at his disposal. For the former, he had no more feeling than we have for snakes or sharks, as the typical and popular embodiments of evil.

Miss Paton had speedily adopted her brother's views in this respect. Summoned from England to keep house for him at the death of Trucaninny's mother, she showed an aptitude for introducing prison discipline into her domestic rule. From constant association with the severe *régime* that she was accustomed to see exercised upon the convicts, she had ended by regarding disobedience to orders, whether in children or in servants, as the unpardonable sin. One of her laws, as of the Medes and Persians, was that the young people in the Paton household should never exchange a word with the convict servants in their father's employ. It was hard to observe the letter of the law in the case of the indoor servants, above all for Truca, who was by nature a garrulous little girl. Being a truthful little girl as well, she was often obliged to confess to having had a talk with the latest importation from the gaol, – an avowal which signified, as she well knew, the immediate forfeiture of all her week's pocket-money.

On the present occasion her apologies to the gardener were the latest infringement of the rule. She looked timidly towards her aunt as the latter advanced austerely in the direction of the gig, but, to her relief, Miss Paton hardly seemed to notice her.

'I suppose you will bring the creature back with you, Wilfrid?' she said, half-questioningly, half-authoritatively, as her brother mounted into the gig and took the reins from Truca's chubby hands. 'Last time we had a drunkard *and* a thief. The time before, a thief, and – and a – really I don't know which was worse. It is frightful to be reduced to such a choice of evils, but I would almost suggest your looking among the – you know – the – *in-fan-ti-cide* cases this time.'

She mouthed the word in separate syllables at her brother, fearful of pronouncing it openly before Truca and the convict gardener.

Mr. Paton nodded. It was not the first time he had been sent upon the delicate mission of choosing a maid for his sister from the female prison, politely called the Factory, at the foot of Mount Wellington. For some reason it would be difficult to explain, his selections were generally rather more successful than hers. Besides which, it was a satisfaction to have some one upon whom to throw the responsibility of the inevitable catastrophe that terminated the career of every successive ticket-of-leave in turn.

The morning, as we have seen, was beautiful. The gig bowled smoothly over the macadamized length of Macquarie Street. Truca was allowed to drive; and so deftly did her little fingers guide the mare that her father lighted his cigar, and allowed himself to ruminate upon a thousand things that it would have been better perhaps to leave alone. In certain moods he was apt to deplore the fate that had landed – or stranded – him in this God-forsaken corner of the world. Talk of prisoners, indeed! What was he himself but a prisoner, since the day when he had madly passed sentence of transportation on himself and his family, because the pay of a Government clerk in England did not increase in the same ratio as the income-tax. As a matter of fact, he did not wear a canary-coloured livery, and his prison was as near an approach, people said, to an earthly Paradise as could well be conceived. With its encircling chains of mountains, folded one around the other, it was like a mighty rose, tossed from the Creator's hand into the desolate Southern Ocean. Here to his right towered purple Mount Wellington, with rugged cliffs gleaming forth from a purple background. To his left the wide Derwent shone and sparkled in blue robe and silver spangles, like the Bay of Naples, he had been told. Well, he had never seen the Bay of Naples, but there were times when he would have given all the beauty here, and as much more to spare, for a strip of London pavement in front of his old club. Mr. Paton's world, indeed, was out of joint. Perhaps twelve years of unthinking acquiescence in the flogging and hanging of convicts had distorted his mental focus. As for the joys of home-life, he told himself that those which had fallen to his share brought him but cold comfort. His sister was a Puritan, and she was making his children hypocrites, with the exception, perhaps, of Truca. Another disagreeable subject of reflection was the one that his groom Richard was about to leave him. In a month's time, Richard, like his royal namesake, would be himself again. For the past five years he had been only No. 213, expiating in that capacity a righteous blow aimed at a cowardly ruffian who had sworn to marry his sister – by fair means or by foul. The blow had been only too well aimed. Richard was convicted of manslaughter, and sentenced to seven years' transportation beyond the seas. His sister, who had sought to screen him, was tried and condemned for perjury. Of the latter, nothing was known. Of the former, Mr. Paton only knew that he would be extremely loth to part with so good a servant. Silent as the Slave of the Lamp, exact as any machine, performing the least of his duties with the same intelligent scrupulousness, his very presence in the household was a safeguard and a reassurance. It was like his luck, Mr. Paton reflected in his present pessimistic mood, to have chanced upon such a fellow, just as by his d — d good conduct he had managed to obtain a curtailment of his sentence. If Richard had been justly dealt with, he would have had two good years left to devote to the service of his employer. As to keeping him after he was a free man, that was not to be hoped for. Besides which, Mr. Paton was not sure that he should feel at all at his ease in dealing with a free man. The slave-making instinct, which is always inherent in the human race whatever civilisation may have done to repress it, had become his sole rule of conduct in his relations with those who served him.

There was one means perhaps of keeping the young man in bondage, but it was a means that even Mr. Paton himself hesitated to employ. By an almost superhuman adherence to impossible rules, Richard had escaped hitherto the humiliation of the lash; but if a flogging could be laid to his charge, his time of probation would be of necessity prolonged, and he might continue to groom the mare and tend the garden for an indefinite space of time, with the ever intelligent thoroughness that distinguished him. A slip of paper in a sealed envelope, which the victim would carry himself to the nearest justice of the peace, would effect the desired object. The etiquette of the proceeding did not require that any explanation should be given.

Richard would be fastened to the triangles, and any subsequent revolt on his part could only involve him more deeply than before. Mr. Paton had no wish to hurt him; but he was after all an invaluable servant, and perhaps he would be intelligent enough to understand that the disagreeable formality to which he was subjected was in reality only a striking mark of his master's esteem for him.

Truca's father had arrived thus far in his meditations when the gig pulled up before the Factory gate. It was a large bare building, with white unshaded walls, but the landscape which framed it gave it a magnificent setting. The little girl was allowed to accompany her father indoors, while a man in a grey prison suit, under the immediate surveillance of an armed warder, stood at the mare's head.

Mr. Paton's mission was a delicate one. To gently scan his brother man, and still gentler sister woman, did not apply to his treatment of convicts. He brought his sternest official expression to bear upon the aspirants who defiled past him at the matron's bidding, in their disfiguring prison livery. One or two, who thought they detected a likely looking man behind the Government official, threw him equivocal glances as they went by. Of these he took no notice. His choice seemed to lie in the end between a sullen-looking elderly woman, whom the superintendent qualified as a 'sour jade', and a half-imbecile girl, when his attention was suddenly attracted to a new arrival, who stood out in such marked contrast with the rest, that she looked like a dove in the midst of a flock of vultures.

'Who is that?' he asked the matron in a peremptory aside.

'That, sir,' – the woman's lips assumed a tight expression as she spoke, – 'she's No. 27 – Amelia Clare – she came out with the last batch.'

'Call her up, will you?' was the short rejoinder, and the matron reluctantly obeyed.

In his early days Truca's father had been a great lover of Italian opera. There was hardly an air of Bellini's or Donizetti's that he did not know by heart. As No. 27 came slowly towards him, something in her manner of walking, coupled with the half-abstracted, half-fixed expression in her beautiful grey eyes, reminded him of Amina in the *Sonnambula.* So strong, indeed, was the impression, that he would hardly have been surprised to see No. 27 take off her unbecoming prison cap and jacket, and disclose two round white arms to match her face, or to hear her sing *'Ah! non giunge'* in soft dreamy tones. He could have hummed or whistled a tuneful second himself at a moment's notice, for the matter of that. However, save in the market scene in *Martha*, there is no precedent for warbling a duet with the young person you are about to engage as a domestic servant. Mr. Paton remembered this in time, and confined himself to what the French call *le stricte nécessaire.* He inquired of Amelia whether she could do fine sewing, and whether she could clear-starch. His sister had impressed these questions upon him, and he was pleased with himself for remembering them.

Amelia, or Amina (she was really very like Amina), did not reply at once. She had to bring her mind back from the far-away sphere to which it had wandered, or, in other words, to pull herself together first. When the reply did come, it was uttered in just the low, melodious tones one might have expected. She expressed her willingness to attempt whatever was required of her, but seemed very diffident as regarded her power of execution. 'I have forgotten so many things,' she concluded, with a profound sigh.

'*Sir*, you impertinent minx,' corrected the matron.

Amelia did not seem to hear, and her new employer hastened to interpose.

'We will give you a trial,' he said, in a curiously modified tone, 'and I hope you won't give me any occasion to regret it.'

The necessary formalities were hurried through. Mr. Paton disregarded the deferential disclaimers of the matron, but experienced, nevertheless, something of a shock when he saw Amelia divested of her prison garb. She had a thorough-bred air that discomfited him. Worse still, she was undeniably pretty. The scissors that had clipped her fair locks had left a number of short rings that clung like tendrils round her shapely little head. She wore a black stuff jacket of extreme simplicity and faultless cut, and a little black bonnet that might have been worn by a Nursing Sister or a *grande dame* with equal appropriateness. Thus attired, her appearance was so effective, that Mr. Paton asked himself whether he was not doing an unpardonably rash thing in driving No. 27 down Macquarie Street in his gig, and introducing her into his household afterwards.

It was not Truca, for she had 'driven and lived' that morning, whose *mauvais quart-d'heure* was now to come. It was her father's turn to fall under its infuence, as he sat, stern and rigid, on the driver's seat, with his little girl nestling up to him as close as she was able, and that strange, fair, mysterious presence on the other side, towards which he had the annoyance of seeing all the heads of the passers-by turn as he drove on towards home.

Arrived at Cowa Cottage, the young gardener ran forward to open the gate; and here an unexpected incident occurred. As Richard's eyes rested upon the new arrival, he uttered an exclamation that caused her to look round. Their eyes met, a flash of instant recognition was visible in both. Then, like the night that follows a sudden discharge of electricity, the gloom that was habitual to both faces settled down upon them once more. Richard shut the gate with his accustomed machine-like precision. Amelia looked at the intangible something in the clouds that had power to fix her gaze upon itself. Yet the emotion she had betrayed was not lost upon her employer. Who could say? As No. 213 and No. 27, these two might have crossed each other's paths before. That the convicts had wonderful and incomprehensible means of communicating with each other, was well known to Mr. Paton. That young men and young women have an equal facility for understanding each other, was also a fact he did not ignore. But which of these two explanations might account for the signs of mutual recognition and sympathy he had just witnessed? Curiously enough, he felt, as he pondered over the mystery later in the day, that he should prefer the former solution. An offensive and defensive alliance was well known to exist among the convicts, and he told himself that he could meet and deal with the difficulties arising from such a cause as he had met and dealt with them before. That was a matter which came within his province, but the taking into account of any sentimental kind of rubbish did *not* come within his province. For some unaccountable reason, the thought of having Richard flogged presented itself anew at this juncture to his mind. He put it away, as he had done before, angered with himself for having harboured it. But it returned at intervals during the succeeding week, and was never stronger than one afternoon, when his little girl ran out to him as he sat smoking in the verandah, with an illustrated volume of *Grimm's Tales* in her hands.

'Oh, papa, look! I've found some one just like Amelia in my book of Grimm. It's the picture of Snow-White. Only look, papa! Isn't it the very living image of Amelia?'

'Nonsense!' said her father; but he looked at the page nevertheless. Truca was right. The snowmaiden in the woodcut had the very eyes and mouth of Amelia Clare – frozen through some mysterious influence into beautiful, unyielding rigidity. Mr. Paton wished sometimes he had never brought the girl into his house. Not that there was any kind of fault to be found with her. Even his sister, who might have passed for 'She-who-must-be-obeyed,' if Rider Haggard's books had existed at that time, could not complain of want of docile obedience to orders on the part of the new maid. Nevertheless, her presence was oppressive to the master of the house. Two lines of Byron's haunted him constantly in connection with her –

So coldly sweet, so deadly fair,
We start – for life is wanting there.

If Richard worked like an automaton, then she worked like a spirit; and when she moved noiselessly about the room where he happened to be sitting, he could not help following her uneasily with his eyes.

The days wore on, succeeding each other and resembling each other, as the French proverb has it, with desperate monotony. Christmas, replete with roses and strawberries, had come and gone. Mr. Paton was alternately swayed by two demons, one of which whispered in his ear, 'Richard Cole is in love with No. 27. The time for him to regain his freedom is at hand. The first use he will make of it will be to leave you and the next to marry Amelia Clare. You will thus be deprived of everything at one blow. You will lose the best man-servant you have ever known, and your sister, the best maid. And more than this, you will lose an interest in life that gives it a stimulating flavour it has not had for many a long year. Whatever may be the impulse that prompts you to wonder what that ice-bound face and form hide, it is an impulse that makes your heart beat and your blood course warmly through your veins. When this fair, uncanny presence is removed from your home, your life will become stagnant as it was before.' To this demon Mr. Paton would reply energetically, 'I won't give the fellow the chance of marrying No. 27. As soon as he has his freedom, I will give him the sack, and forbid him the premises. As for Amelia, she is my prisoner, and I would send her back to gaol to-morrow if I thought there were any nonsense up between her and him.'

At this point demon No. 2 would intervene: 'There is a better way of arranging matters. You have it in your power to degrade the fellow in his own eyes and in those of the girl he is after. There is more covert insolence in that impenetrable exterior of his than you have yet found out. Only give him proper provocation, and you will have ample justification for bringing him down. A good flogging would put everything upon its proper footing, - you would keep your servant, and you would put a stop to the nonsense that is very probably going on. But don't lose too much time; for if you wait until the last moment, you will betray your hand. The fellow is useful to him, they will say of Richard, but it is rather rough upon him to be made aware of it in such a way as that.'

One evening in January, Mr. Paton was supposed to be at his club. In reality he was seated upon a bench in a bushy part of the garden, known as the shrubbery - in parley with the demons. The night had come down upon him almost without his being aware of it - a night heavy with heat and blackness, and noisy with the cracking and whirring of the locusts entombed in the dry soil. All at once he heard a slight rustling in the branches behind him. There was a light pressure of hands on his shoulders, and a face that felt like velvet to the touch was laid against his cheeks. Two firm, warm feminine lips pressed themselves upon his, and a voice that he recognized as Amelia's said in caressing tones,' Dearest Dick, have I kept you waiting?'

Had it been proposed to our hero some time ago that he should change places with No. 213, he would have declared that he would rather die first. But at this instant the convict's identity seemed so preferable to his own, that he hardly ventured to breathe lest he should betray the fact that he was only his own forlorn self. His silence disconcerted the intruder.

'Why don't you answer, Dick?' she asked impatiently.

'Answer? What am I to say?' responded her master. 'I am not in the secret.'

Amelia did not give him time to say more. With a cry of terror she turned and fled, disappearing as swiftly and mysteriously as she had come. The words 'Dearest Dick' continued to ring in Mr. Paton's ears long after she had gone; and the more persistently the refrain was repeated, the more he felt tempted to give Richard a taste of his quality. He had tried to provoke him to some act of overt insolence in vain. He had worried and harried and insulted him all he could. The convict's constancy had never once deserted him. That his employer should have no pretext whereby he might have him degraded and imprisoned, he had acted upon the scriptural precept of turning his left cheek when he was smitten on the right. There were times when his master felt something of a persecutor's impotent rage against him. But now at least he felt he had entire justification for making an example of him. He would teach the fellow to play Romeo and Juliet with a fellow-convict behind his back. So thoroughly did the demon indoctrinate Mr. Paton with these ideas, that he felt next morning as though he were doing the most righteous action in the world, when he called Richard to him after breakfast, and said in a tone which he tried to render as careless as of custom, 'Here, you! just take this note over to Mr. Merton with my compliments, and *wait for the answer.*'

There was nothing in this command to cause the person who received it to grow suddenly livid. Richard had received such an order at least a score of times before, and had carried messages to and fro between his master and the justice of the peace with no more emotion than the occasion was worth. But on this particular morning, as he took the fatal note into his hands, he turned deadly pale. Instead of retreating with it in his customary automatic fashion, he fixed his eyes upon his employer's face, and something in their expression actually constrained Mr. Paton to lower his own.

'May I speak a word with you, sir?' he said, in low, uncertain tones.

It was the first time such a thing had happened, and it seemed to Richard's master that the best way of meeting it would be to 'damn' the man and send him about his business.

But Richard did not go. He stood for an instant with his head thrown back, and the desperate look of an animal at bay in his eyes. At this critical moment a woman's form suddenly interposed itself between Mr. Paton and his victim. Amelia was there, looking like Amina after she had awoken from her trance. She came close to her master, – she had never addressed him before, – and raised her liquid eyes to his.

'You will not be hard on – my brother, sir, for the mistake I made last night?'

'Who said I was going to be hard on him?' retorted Mr. Paton, too much taken back to find any more dignified form of rejoinder. 'And if he is your brother, why do you wait until it is dark to indulge in your family effusions?'

The question was accompanied by a through and through look, before which Amelia did not quail.

'Have I your permission to speak to him in the day-time, sir?' she said submissively.

'I will institute an inquiry,' interrupted her master. 'Here, go about your business,' he added, turning to Richard; 'fetch out the mare, and hand me back that note. I'll ride over with it myself.'

Three weeks later Richard Cole was a free man, and within four months from the date upon which Mr. Paton had driven Amelia Clare down Macquarie Street in his gig, she came to take respectful leave of him, dressed in the identical close-fitting jacket and demure little bonnet he remembered. Thenceforth she was nobody's bondswoman. He had a small heap of coin in readiness to hand over to her, with the payment of which, and a few gratuitous words of counsel on his part, the leave-taking would have been definitely and decorously accomplished. To tell her that he was more loth than ever to part with her, did not enter into the official programme. She was her own mistress now, as much or more so than the Queen of England herself, and it was hardly to be wondered at if the first use she made of her freedom was to shake the dust of Cowa Cottage off her feet. Still, if she had only known – if she had only known. It seemed too hard to let her go with the certainty that she never did or could know. Was it not for her sake that he had been swayed by all the conflicting impulses that had made him a changed man of late? For her that he had so narrowly escaped being a criminal awhile ago, and for her that he was appearing in the novel *rôle* of a reformer of the convict system now? He never doubted that she would have understood him if she *had* known. But to explain was out of the question. He must avow either all or nothing, and the all meant more than he dared to admit even to himself.

This was the reason why Amelia Clare departed sphinx-like as she had come. A fortnight after she had gone, as Mr. Paton was gloomily smoking by his library fire in the early dark of a wintry August evening, a letter bearing the N.S.Wales postmark was handed to him. The handwriting, very small and fine, had something familiar in its aspect. He broke open the seal, – letters were still habitually sealed in those days – and read as follows: –

'SIR, – I am prompted to make you a confession – why, I cannot say, for I shall probably never cross your path again. I was married last week to Richard Cole, who was not my brother, as I led you to suppose, but my affianced husband, in whose behalf I would willingly suffer again to be unjustly condemned and transported. I have the warrant of Scripture for having assumed, like Sarah, the *rôle* of sister in preference to that of wife; besides which, it is hard to divest myself of an instinctive belief that the deceit was useful to Richard on one occasion. I trust you will pardon me. – Yours respectfully,

'AMELIA COLE.'

The kindly phase Mr. Paton had passed through with regard to his convict victims came to an abrupt termination. The reaction was terrible. His name is inscribed among those 'who foremost shall be damn'd to Fame' in Tasmania.

III

RENEGOTIATING SEXUAL ROLES

ELLEN CLACY
Leaves from a Young Lady's Diary

Saturday, September 25. – Having been a week in Australia, it is time I re-commenced my diary with some account of this strange country. Not only are we at the antipodes in point of situation from England, but everything here is the very reverse of all that we have been accustomed to at home. Eagles here are white and swans are black; cockatoos and parrots are as common as our hedge-sparrows; it is winter in July, and summer in January; night here when our friends at home have broad daylight, and, of course, *vise versâ*. The leaves of Australian trees do not fall, but, instead, the trees shed their bark; the flowers are mostly without perfume, and the birds without song; owls hoot only by day; the north winds are warm, and the east winds healthy; and last, not least of these marvels, there is a fruit called the wild cherry which actually grows with the stone outside.

These are some of the natural wonders of Australia; but, after having been only a few days in Melbourne, the social ones that I have met with are even more striking. Ladies are at a premium, and have no lack of suitors; using your hands is not considered debasing; those that were the poorer classes are richer than the fine gentlemen who land here, and servants are accustomed to have the upper hand of their masters and mistresses.

In spite of all these strange things, I like my present life amazingly. Mrs. Dormer is a very kind old lady, and more cheerful than I expected to have found her, considering it is only a year since her husband's death. How frequently it happens in this world that what occasions the deepest sorrow to one is the source of great happiness to others; had she not been left a widow in a strange land, she would, perhaps, never have remembered the orphan child of her old friend and schoolfellow, who was leading a miserable existence as the under-paid, over-worked English teacher at the Misses R.'s fashionable seminary for young ladies.

Brought up by a harsh step-father, without brothers or sisters to love – then half-teacher, half-pupil at the Misses R.'s, where I was only taught how to instruct the junior classes – and at last promoted to be under teacher, with my very thoughts chained down to the monotonous routine of school-life – I never in those days knew what it was to enjoy existence.

Now, seated outside our wooden cottage, the soft Australian air blowing gently upon me, with a friend who loved my mother and already feels affection for myself – with no conventional rules dinned momentarily into my ears to shackle my free enjoyment of all around – from the depths of my heart I thank God for the most blessed of all his gifts – life.

We reside at Collingwood, in quite a rustic sort of habitation; it is built principally of boards, and has only three rooms – all on the ground – a kitchen, bedroom, and sitting-room. We keep no servant: it would be useless; for in such a tiny place there would be nothing for her to do, and I am becoming, under Mrs. Dormer's instructions, quite an extraordinary cook. The distance from here to Melbourne gives me a pleasant walk now and then, and I am beginning to know my way about the town. I was most struck with the drays, each drawn by eight oxen, which perambulate the streets, and are as plentiful as omnibuses in London.

The quantity of newly arrived emigrants is surprising; where they all find room to settle in, is an unexplained mystery to me. Melbourne, they say, is too full now, yet thousands keep pouring in, and manage to exist somewhere.

Thursday, September 30. – To-day, a horticultural show at the Botanical Gardens, which are situated close to Melbourne, on the Yarra-Yarra. It was a very gay sight, and some of the shrubs and flowers were most beautiful. The showy dresses amused me greatly; and on one person who was there, arm in arm with a roughly arrayed digger, I counted all the colours of the rainbow. Light blue kid shoes with pink rosettes; purple silk dress, shot with red; lace mantle, lined with orange and trimmed with the same colour; pink silk bonnet, trimmed with a wreath of green leaves, and a gaudy ribbon, in which every imaginable tint had been assembled; yellow kid gloves, and a sky-blue parasol lined with rose colour. She strutted about, evidently thinking herself the centre of attraction, which she certainly was, though not altogether of a complimentary description.

Friday, October 1. – I took a longer stroll than usual this morning, so as to give myself a good view of the surrounding scenery. Almost all the trees have drooping foliage, which is of a dingy tint – nothing fresh-looking as in England, although this time of year is the spring – the grass too, has a burnt appearance. I collected a number of wild flowers, blue and pink, some of them very elegant.

Thursday, 7th. – Two days ago, I saw an advertisement in the *Argus* from a gentleman who wished to place his daughter in some quiet family, whilst he was engaged in mercantile pursuits to and from the diggings; and, as I have really more time on my hands than I know what to do with, I have persuaded Mrs. Dormer to let me undertake the care of her. Accordingly I wrote, and this afternoon received a reply, in which she says that he will call to-morrow morning to see if we can arrange it.

Friday, 8th. – Mr. Handley called, and is evidently willing to leave his little girl in our charge. He is a widower. His terms are very liberal, so I shall feel myself not so great a burden upon my friend, whose income is little suited for this expensive place. He is to bring the little Janette to us tomorrow.

Saturday, 9th. – Mr. Handley came, but no Janette. She is not well, and he thought the walk might be too fatiguing for her. He was here talking for more than two hours: I thought he never intended to depart; but, as it amused Mrs. Dormer, I ought not to grudge the waste of my time listening to him.

Sunday, 10th. – I went to St. Peter's Church this morning, which was filled almost to suffocation. People in England have an idea, I believe, that in this money-making country religion is at a discount; but I never saw church or chapel so full of attentive, earnest congregations as they are here.

Tuesday, 12th. – Never was I so astonished in my whole life. A proposal! and from Mr. Handley! I looked so surprised, I could scarcely answer him. But I must begin at the beginning.

Mrs. Dormer had gone to lie down, the day being very warm, so I was forced to receive him alone. After apologising for not having brought Janette (I now verily believe her illness is all a pretence), he was quite silent, till, on a sudden, he said – 'he had been thinking the matter over, and would I be a mother to his little girl instead of her governess?'

I was so unprepared for this, that, for a few moments, I believe I only stared at him; and then, telling him that I declined his offer (of what words I made use I have not the slightest idea), I rushed into Mrs. Dormer's room, and, like a goose, began to cry. Mr. Handley took his departure, and I could see him from the window slowly walking towards Melbourne.

Wednesday, 13th. – At Mrs. Dormer's suggestion, I have written to-day to Mr. Handley, to say that, after our interview yesterday, I could not take charge of his little girl. This was the only course to pursue. I wonder what sort of a reply I shall receive. As for promising to marry a person I have only seen thrice, it would be too absurd, thought quite *à la colonies* – not but that I fancy I could have loved him, if he had not been so precipitate.

Saturday, November 27. – Week after week glides by in a very comfortable manner. The weather is now becoming dreadfully warm, and affects Mrs. Dormer greatly: fortunately, it appears to agree with me. I now give lessons in drawing at one of the ladies' schools in Melbourne: among the pupils there I met Janette Handley – I presume, the same young lady for whom I was bespoken as step-mother. She seems an affectionate, clever child. Mr. Handley, in partnership with another, has set up one of the largest stores at Forest Creek, and is said to be very rich. I am thankful I so promptly refused him; for to have your husband imagine that he was accepted only for his wealth, must be a miserable state of matrimonial life.

Tuesday, 30th. – How can I describe what has just happened! Mr Handley has been brought into Melbourne almost murdered. He was coming to town with a party of others, when they were attacked in the Black Forest; and, although the robbers were worsted and took to flight, they had severely wounded two of the party. The other victim died on the road home; but Mr. Handley is still alive, though in great danger, the joltings of the dray having considerably increased his sufferings.

As soon as he arrived at the boarding-house where he usually stays when in town, he implored his attendants to send for me. I entirely forgot to reflect whether it was right or wrong to go, until I found myself by his bed-side talking about Janette. I have promised to do all I can to console her.

Monday, December 6. – Janette is stopping with us, and Mr. Handley himself is coming here as soon as he is able to be moved. Doctor M. first suggested it. He said, 'Get him out of this hot, noisy town, with its oppressive atmosphere, or he'll be carried off in a high fever before long.' Mrs. Dormer offered to receive him. How we shall be able to accommodate an invalid, I cannot tell.

Wednesday, 22nd. – Mr. Handley is now here. He had a slight relapse, brought on by moving; but I think he has not only recovered from that, but is gaining strength quickly. Janette is so good and so useful, that we get on far better than I anticipated. He must have always been a kind father to her, or she would not show such intense grief at his illness.

Tuesday, January 4. – Mr. Handley is up again, and almost convalescent. He carries one arm in a sling, which has a most interesting apearance. He has never made any reference to his former proposal, nor expressed a wish for Janette to remain with us; but there is a painful look in his eyes, when they chance to meet mine, which grieves me. He leaves us in a few days, to return to Forest Creek: for Janette's sake, he ought to take more care of himself. I should like to persuade him to stop longer, and thoroughly recruit his strength; but, whenever I attempt to urge it, I feel myself colouring up and looking quite foolish.

Saturday, 15th. – Both Janette and her father have left us. I miss my little friend exceedingly, but I hope we shall meet often: she is to spend her Sundays with us.

Thursday, March 8. – Again I am alone in the world – my old friend gone! Dear, unselfish Mrs. Dormer! even in her last hours, she thought more of me than of herself, and regretted that her income, being derived from an annuity, would cease at her death. She was more uneasy on my account than I am myself. In this country, I have no fear of being unable to earn a livelihood. Janette, dear child, has been here consoling me. I was ungrateful to call myself alone.

Friday, 9th. – Mr. Handley has come down from Forest Creek for the express purpose of asking me to be his wife. Janette must have written to inform him of Mrs. Dormer's death. I refused again – not because I could not love him (those days he resided here taught me differently), but because I am too proud to accept, when I am penniless, what I refused when I was not so friendless as I now am. He shall never be able to fancy that I marry, where I do not love, for the sake of a comfortable home.

This evening Janette came and sat beside me; she looked very sad, and took my hand between her tiny ones; then kissed me.

'You do not love me,' said she.

'Oh, Janette!'

'You do not love me; you will not be my mother.'

Her tone of voice was so melancholy – her looks so sorrowful – that I could only say, 'Hush, darling, hush,' and endeavour to stifle my tears.

'Poor papa!' continued she, in a low sad tone, as if talking to herself; 'yet you called him "dear" in your sleep last night. I told him that this morning, and he looked, ah! so pleased; but he was unhappy again directly. Poor papa!'

I laid my face in my hands and sobbed unrestrainedly: pride was fairly conquered.

'Do be my mamma,' pleaded the gentle voice; and the little arms were twined fondly round my neck. 'Ah! you mean yes! I'll tell papa so;' but he was already beside us.

I cannot exactly recollect all that passed, but I have promised that, six months hence, if God spares our lives, Janette shall have a mother.

ADA CAMBRIDGE
A Sweet Day

Lord Thomas de Bohun had been married twice – and more. In fact, he was sick and tired of womenkind. And that is why he came out to Australia. He thought a year or two of travel in a savage country, free of all the trammels of civilization, would give him a rest. Besides, the second Lady Thomas had been rather nice to him, and she had died pathetically, and he missed her. Wherefore he loathed the British matchmaker for the present, and was glad to get as far away from her as possible.

He was not a *roué* and a reprobate, such as this introduction might imply. Nothing of the sort. A better-natured or more charming young man – he was on the right side of forty still – was not to be found in London. But he was the son of a duke, poor fellow, with a great deal of money, and no work to do – misfortunes for which the fair-minded reader will make a large allowance.

In the beginning, Australia did not quite answer his expectations. Whereas he had imagined a dress-suit to be a thing unknown, he found himself obliged to wear one nightly, and he was just as ducal in our city clubs and drawing-rooms as he would have been at home – indeed, a great deal more so. But as soon as he escaped into the country he was all right. Clad in moleskins and a Crimean shirt, with a soft felt hat on his head, and big spurs on his heels, he galloped about at kangaroo hunts and cattle musters, a simple bushman of the bush (while his servant played the gentleman in Melbourne), enjoying health and happiness and the unrivalled charm of novelty to a degree unknown before. Anybody could get him who had no right to him. The great country houses, flattering themselves that they alone could entertain him suitably, found it a most difficult matter to drop salt on his elusive tail.

He was at a bush hotel one evening, spending a convivial hour with perfect strangers, who did not know he was Lord Thomas. Having heard his name was De Bohun, they called him Mr Bone, and were quite satisfied with that. So was he. The talk turned upon agricultural machinery as used by English and Australian

151

farmers respectively; and a member of the latter class, as Lord Thomas supposed, was most anxious to show him a five-furrow plough and various modern implements – American 'notions' of the labour-saving kind.

'You come home with me,' said the jolly old man, 'and you shall see 'em working. Now do, Mr Bone. Pot-luck, you know, but a hearty welcome.'

Lord Thomas jumped at the chance, for amongst other delightfully novel pursuits, he had set himself to the improvement of his mind in these matters, as a responsible landlord and potential duke.

'But your family?' he objected. 'Would it not inconvenience them to receive a stranger without warning, and at so late an hour?'

'Not a bit of it, Mr Bone. There's always a bed ready for anybody that may turn up. Mrs. Kemp will be charmed to see you.'

'In that case,' said Lord Thomas, 'I accept with pleasure.'

A pair of rough horses, in a ramshackle American wagon, were brought round, and they set forth on a ten-mile voyage through the bush, with neither lamps nor moon to steer by. At a long, swinging trot, never hastening and never loitering, the shabby animals did it in an hour without making a false step, and were as fresh at the end as at the beginning. The mysterious, illimitable gloom and the romantic solitude were very refreshing to the London man, and so was his host, who was full of merry tales and valuable information. Lord Thomas, in short, enjoyed his adventure thoroughly.

But he was taken aback by the sight of Mr. Kemp's house. Instead of the shanty of his anticipations, he beheld a tall and imposing structure, cutting a great block out of the starry midnight sky. A sweet place by daylight – ivied, virginia-creepered, grape-vined all over its mellow brick walls and decaying verandahs, with a great garden and magnificent trees around it.

'Built by my father in the early days,' said Mr. Kemp. 'The first big house in this district, and the only one for nigh twenty years. We've been rich folks in our time, Mr. Bone, but the ups and downs, you know – things ain't what they used to be, especially since the Boom. However, we've still got a roof over us, thank God, and a crust to share with a friend.'

The family had retired, and the guest, having been warmed with whisky, was escorted to his bedroom by the host. It was a kind of bedroom to make him feel slightly nervous about meeting the hostess next morning. The bed creaked with age, and so did the carpetless floor beneath it; but the linen was fine and the pillow soft, the handsome old rosewood furniture shone like glass, and there was an impalpable air about everything that bespoke the house of a lady.

'I don't know whether you like the windows shut?' said Mr. Kemp, hospitably bustling about. 'We always keep them open, and the blinds up. Nobody to overlook us here you know.' He tried to pull down a sash which stuck in the frame, but at Lord Thomas's request desisted.

'Leave it as it is,' said the guest. 'I like them open. It's so Australian!'

And he presently lay down on his lavender-perfumed couch, feeling – after his experience of bush inns – that it was the nicest bed he had ever occupied. And that scent of the earth and of the night, coming in through open windows, how exquisite it was! He blew out his candle – a home-made candle in an old chased silver candlestick – and slept like a baby.

Not for long, however. Voices called him through those open windows, and before six o'clock he was leaning out of one of them, awake and alive as he had rarely been at such an hour.

What an Arcadian world was this, in which he felt like a man new born! Air as clear as crystal, and dew shining on shrubs and trees; giant acacias and native white cedars, and pink and white oleanders that could have swallowed an ordinary bush house; the morning moon still gleaming like a jewel over the saffron sunrise and the intensely dark-blue hills. He had heard curlews in the night and frogs at the break of dawn; now the magpies were fluting all over the place, cheerful fowls were crowing, laughing jackasses shouting 'Ha-ha-ha!' and 'Hoo-hoo-hoo!' to one another. Delicious sounds! But none so acutely audible as the immense silence at the back of them.

'This,' said he to himself, 'is the real bush, that we have heard so much about, at last.'

He looked down from his window, and saw the sparrows at the ripe grapes now loading the eaves of the verandah; saw a hare limping along the gravelled paths, where no hare should be. He looked over the garden hedges to the peaceful fields outside, where cows were feeding quietly, throwing shadows on the wet grass; flocks of cockatoos were screaming amongst them, and sprinkling themselves like white flowers over the fresh-ploughed land; and an army of dusky jays held the vineyard on the hill, whence their joyous gabble rose continuously. It was not his property they were destroying, and he saw and heard them with delight – those denizens of the wild bush – that was healing him, body and soul, of the ills of excessive civilization.

The pink dawn spread and glowed, quenching the horned moon and dimming sapphire hues of the distant ranges. Then some white bee boxes gleamed conspicuously to the right of the flower garden – an orderly encampment, like tents on a field of battle – and he could see the busy swarms going forth to their day's labour. He could even hear them humming, they were in such myriads. And another thing he heard – a faint, muffled clatter – which he traced to a little building near the gate of the bees' enclosure; a shed made of reeds, with two windows and a door in it – doubtless the honey-house, in which someone was early at work. As he listened to the noise within, he watched the door, which faced his view, and presently he saw a girl come out of it. She wore a pink cotton sun-bonnet, veiled with a bushman's fly net, and an all-embracing tight apron, which made her look like the toy figures of a Noah's ark. In each hand she carried a long tin box, one heavier than the other, by rough loops of fencing wire; and she marched with them down an alley between the beehives. Mr. Kemp had casually mentioned his daughter, who, at the time, Lord Thomas had not regarded as affecting him in any way. Evidently this was she, and the circumstances of the house disposed him to take another view of her.

He saw her put the boxes on the grass and set the lids open, then lift the roof from one of the wooden hives. A cloud of angry insects rose to her stooping face and buzzed about her; it made him tingle to see them, but she heeded them no more than if they had been motes in the sun-rays that now lighted up her figure so effectively. She puffed something that smoked into the open hive from a sort of little bellows arrangement, and then lifted out the frames of comb, held them dangling in the air while she brushed black masses of bees off them, and placed them edgewise in one of the boxes on the grass until she had quite filled it. Out of the other she took similar frames, which she dropped into the emptied chamber, and shut down there. Then he saw her labouring towards the honey house with the weighted box, and was exasperated to note how it dragged her down. She passed it from hand to hand to ease the strain, but could not carry it without a twist of her supple body, a staggering gait, and pantings that he seemed to hear, though of course he could not.

'What a shame!' he inwardly ejaculated. And he withdrew into his room, emptied a can of water into a battered old bath, and dressed in haste. The clatter in the honey-house, which had ceased while she was amongst the bees, showing that she worked single-handed, began again.

'I wonder,' quoth Lord Thomas, 'what she's doing in there?'

He thought he would go down to see, and went, stepping softly, so as not to disturb the rest of the family, who did not seem to rise so early as she. As usual in the bush, no locks or bolts impeded him; he turned the handle of the hall door, and noiselessly slipped out.

What a morning indeed! Freshly autumnal – for it was the end of March – though the day would be all summer until the sun was low again; cool almost to coldness, with an air that washed the lungs and invigorated the heart in a manner to make mere living an ecstasy, even to a lord – the air of the spacious, untainted bush, and of nowhere else in the wide world. He stood a moment on the steps of the verandah to drink it in – to sniff the wholesome odour of gum trees and the richer scent of the perennial orange flower starring the thick green walls of the orchard paths. Then he strolled down one of those perfumed lanes – the one that divided the back garden from the front – and presented himself at the gate of the bee enclosure just as Miss Kemp, with one of her tin boxes, dashed out of the honey-house and slammed the door behind her, disappointing the expectations of a cloud of besieging bees.

She saw him and stopped short, evidently taken aback, and conscious of her coarse apron and limp sun-bonnet, not worn for company. He hesitated for a moment in sympathetic confusion, but, being immediately aware that the form thus plainly outlined was a charming one, as also the pink face in the frame of pink calico, stood his ground and modestly accosted her. He lifted his cap gracefully, and a bee got under it.

'Good morning – you brute!' was what he said.

'Don't come,' she cried in answer, waving him back. Then she pulled off a sticky glove and held a bare hand over the gate, regardless of bees, expressing a polite astonishment at his being up so soon.

'I heard of your arrival, Mr. Bone,' said she. 'I hope you slept well. I hope you like Australia, as far as you have seen it.'

They chatted conventionally for some minutes. He apologized for his presence, and she reassured him, on behalf of the family, with an easy frankness that seemed to say he was but one of dozens of Mr. Bones flowing in a continuous stream through the house, like tramps through a casual ward. And then he begged to be allowed to help her in her work. 'I am sure,' said he, 'you must want somebody to carry that heavy box – oh, conf —— ! They know I am a stranger, evidently.'

'Go away.' she laughed. 'You have no business here. I don't want help – I am quite used to doing it all – and you'd better go and sit on the verandah, where you can be at peace. Or wouldn't you like a stroll round? With a pipe, perhaps?'

'Will you show me round?'

'I'm sorry I can't; I must be busy here. The honey is coming in so fast this weather – which may break at any moment – that I can't gather it quickly enough. I get on an average nearly a quarter-of-a-ton per day.'

She looked at him with an air of professional pride, forgetting her costume; and he looked at her. The closer view showed freckles and a *retroussé* nose, without at all detracting from her charm. He could gaze full into her face without being rude, because her eyes were continually following the movements of the bees that buzzed about him. Every now and then her fingers skirmished round his head like a flight of butterflies.

Five minutes more, and she was tying a large apron round his waist, over a very old coat that did not fit him, and he was planting on his aristocratic head an aged straw hat, flounced with mosquito netting. In this costume, finished off with a pair of good gloves of his own, cheerfully sacrificed, he was allowed to pass through the gate and take up the box by its handles of fencing-wire. The sun was well above the ranges now, and every dewy leaf and blade of grass glittering.

'What a heavenly morning!' he sighed ecstatically.

'Isn't it?' she assented, and then fell to work again with an energy interesting to contemplate in a person of her sex and years. She walked between the rows of hives till she came to the one to be operated on; he walked after her, inwardly nervous, but with an air of utmost valour.

'Now be careful,' said she, as she seized her little bellows. 'Tuck that net into your waistcoat in front, and then lift the lid off for me.'

He did as she bade him, and gasped at the spectacle presented. How all those bees managed to breathe and move, let alone work, in the space they occupied, was more than he could understand. She had no time to explain just now. While he stood rigid, and imagined bees under the hems of his trousers – for they were thick in the grass he stood on – she rapidly smoked the hive and drew out the frames of comb, heavy with honey, brushed thousands of stinging things off them, and placed them in the empty tin. From the full one she took the frames filled only with hollow cells, which she had brought from the honey-house; and these she dropped into the hive amid the masses of bees, leaving less than an inch between one wall of comb and another.

'And you make the same wax do again?' he inquired, thirsting for knowledge.

'Many times,' she replied, pleased to inform his ignorance. 'That comb will be refilled in about ten days. Put the lid on again, please. Gently – don't crush more than you can help. Now . . .'

She straightened her back and looked at him.

'Now what?' he inquired eagerly.

'Well, if you would, you might be filling the other box while I extracted.'

But this was rather more than his courage was equal to. He said he was afraid he did not know enough about it yet.

'Very well; we will go and extract the lot we have.'

They went to the honey-house together, and she quickly shut the door as soon as both were in. He smiled to himself as he saw her do it. The situation to him was – well, noticeable; to her it was absolutely without sentimental suggestions. The honey-house was the place for work, not for play.

It was a stuffy and sticky place, for its windows, as well as the door, had to be closed to keep the bees out. Ventilation depended on the loosely-woven canvas lining the reed-thatched walls. Half of the floor was raised above the other half, so that the honey from the extractor, pouring from the spout upon a fine sieve, could flow downwards to the great tank, and from that into the tins which conveyed it to market. Five tons' weight of these tins were stacked on the lower floor, all filled and soldered up; and many more, Miss Kemp stated, were stored in the house.

'I used to get sixpence a pound for it,' she informed him, with an anxious business look in her pretty grey eyes; 'but now the stores won't give more than threepence. It really doesn't seem worth while, at that price, taking railway charges and all; do you think it does?'

Lord Thomas did not, emphatically.

'So I am going to try exporting. I have the regulation boxes and tins – fifty-six pounds in a tin, and two tins in a case – and, as soon as I can get my hands free here, I shall prepare a consignment for the London market. I *do* hope that will pay! You are an Englishman, Mr. Bone – what is your opinion of the chances of a trade in Australian honey?'

With the confidence of utter ignorance, Lord Thomas assured her that there was a splendid opening. He knew people – heaps of people – who would snap it up gladly; and proposed to himself to be her purveyor to those people, comprising all the De Bohuns and his numerous lady friends.

'Oh, I am so *thankful* to hear you say that!' Miss Kemp ejaculated, with a heave of the chest. 'You see wool is down, and cattle selling for nothing and the value of places like this dropped to less than what they are mortgaged for; therefore something *must* be done. I've begun with honey, so I want to go on with it. I can increase to any extent. If I can only get a regular and paying market.'

He was oddly touched, and more interested and amused than he had ever been in his life, to see a pretty girl regarding her destiny from such a point of view. It was something quite out of his experience. She really wanted to work, and not to flirt - to do something for men, instead of being done for by them. And yet there was nothing of the new woman about her. She was sweetly old-fashioned.

For instance, it gave her a visible shock to learn, in the course of miscellaneous conversation, that he had a baby ten-months-old and had left it behind in England.

'What!' she exclaimed tragically, 'without either father or mother to look after it?'

'Oh,' said he, 'there are plenty of people to look after it.'

'Who will - who *could* - like its own parents?'

'Well, you wouldn't have a fellow travel about the world with a nursery in his train - now would you?'

'I don't know how you can travel, under such circumstances.'

He thought this very funny. And yet he liked it. Lady Thomas the first had detested children; Lady Thomas the second, a mother for a day, had shown no feeling for them. This girl's evident concern for his virtual orphan - who, as she said, might die of croup or convulsions without his knowing it, while he idly gadded about like an irresponsible bachelor - struck him as very interesting. She asked questions about it in an earnest way, and made him feel quite fatherly and serious. He wondered if the poor little brat was really being cared for properly, and determined to make strict inquiries by the next mail.

Conversation was not allowed to hinder business. While she talked in this friendly, human fashion, Miss Kemp worked as he had never seen a lady work before, as he had never worked himself since he was born. With a frame of comb in one hand, and in the other a big knife, kept hot in a tin of water standing on an oil-fed flame, she sheared off the capsules from the cells that had been filled and closed, leaving those that had bees in them, with the rapidity and dexterity of a performing conjuror. Then she dropped the frames into the wheel arrangement inside the extractor, and turned the handle violently - no, he turned it for her while she prepared more frames, full ones for the machines and empty ones for the tin box, and cleared up the shreds of wax, and so on. She had no regard for attitudes, nor for the state of her complexion, and it was clearly evident that she valued Lord Thomas for his services and not for himself. He had never been in such a position since he was a fag at school; in relation to a woman, never. It chagrined him a little, but pleased him much. He determined to remain Mr. Bone for the present.

Called to breakfast, he made the acquaintance of just such a hostess as he had expected - a faded woman, with a refined face and voice, English-born, and homesick for her own country. He exercised upon her that art of pleasing, of which he was a master, and she was so charmed with him that she begged him to stay a little, not to run away immediately, unless bored by the dullness of the place. Her husband abetted her, with the unquestioning hospitality of the bush, which asks no more of a guest than that he shall know how to behave himself.

'And I'll show you all my improvements,' said Mr. Kemp. 'A good deal more than you could run through in a hour or two, or even in a day.'

'Thanks, thanks,' Lord Thomas murmured. 'Just at present I am more interested in the honey industry than in anything else. I intend to keep bees myself when I get back, and it is a great chance for me to see all the working of the thing as it is done here. Er – er – how clear and beautiful that is!' He looked at a dish containing a square block of honey in the comb, neatly removed from the wooden frame it was made in. Letty hastened to pass it to him.

'Isn't it?' she crooned, surveying it with a maternal air. 'And this is what I get only threepence for in the local market! I can't but think there must be ways of exporting it in sections, with careful packing. Don't *you* think if it could be brought on English breakfast tables in the comb like this there would be a great demand for it? I am sure they haven't honey to surpass our honey.'

Lord Thomas was equally sure of it – convinced, indeed, that benighted England never tasted anything like it in its life. Mrs. Kemp smiled a superior British smile. Mr. Kemp pooh-poohed the fuss his daughter made over comparative trifles. What was honey, as a topic of interest for an Englishman anxious to improve his mind, compared with ensilage, and irrigation, and six-furrow ploughs?

For two precious hours Lord Thomas found himself obliged to attend to these latter subjects with what interest he could muster, and he only got away from them so soon by force of misleading insinuations to the effect that bees were his natural hobby and beekeeping his proposed profession. At eleven o'clock he resumed his sticky apron and gloves, his old coat and his veiled old hat, with more delight than he had ever taken in clothes before – ridiculous as it seemed, even to himself – and rushed to the heated and messy honey-house as he had never rushed to a royal garden party.

Letty's hot face lighted up at sight of him. Beads of perspiration lay like dew under her clear eyes and over her pretty lips, but she cared not, neither did he. This sort of thing did not spoil the effect, as usual.

'Oh, how good of you!' she exclaimed. And at once she set him to work. He buckled to with might and main, as if his life and hers depended on the amount of honey they could extract in a given time. They had two hours together, talking while they worked, growing better friends every minute.

'Labour-saving machines,' said she, still harping on the one string, 'are splendid, I know; but they run away with money when there isn't any money. My plan is just the opposite of father's. It mightn't be such good economy in other circumstances, but as things are it is my idea of economy. I don't know what you think.'

He told her what he thought, and she told him it was beside the point. So it was. So he wanted it to be. Hard as he worked at the handle of the extractor, he worked still harder at trying to change the subject. But, though she might be led aside a step or two, she could not be wholly drawn from it.

It was worse after lunch. She said to him with the firm air of a general directing military manœuvres, 'Now you know all that is to be done in the house, so you can attend to that while I am changing the frames in the hives. Oh, never mind the box; I can carry it quite easily. And we shall get on twice as fast.'

He found he had to do it – the uncapping with the hot knife, and all the rest of it – while she went back and forth outside. It was a long afternoon, and the little shed was stifling. The perspiration poured from his brow and trickled down his neck as he strained every nerve to be ready for her each time she brought the full box in. And his wages were next to nothing.

But at last the sun went down, and his long struggle to get the better of his rivals seemed over. They came straggling home in the golden twilight to their well-earned rest, and Letty Kemp prepared to follow their example when it was too dark to work any more.

'There,' said she, with a sigh of utter weariness and satisfaction, 'we have done well, haven't we? I can't tell you how much obliged to you I am, Mr. Bone.'

Suddenly he felt tired of being Mr. Bone and a casual labourer, so he said awkwardly, 'Er – er – I think you haven't got my name quite correctly. It is De Bohun – Thomas de Bohun.'

'Oh, I beg pardon,' she returned, in an airy manner; and he perceived that she was not enlightened. 'You know, Mr. de Bohun, there is a little talk and movement about eucalyptus honey just now. Some chemist people at home have been praising its medicinal properties. And it is everything in these cases to strike while the iron is hot.'

'Ye – es,' drawled Lord Thomas absent-mindedly. Actually she had been so absorbed in those blessed bees as not to have heard of him in his proper character.

They took off their sticky overalls and returned to the house to prepare for the evening meal. And when Miss Kemp came downstairs, washed and brushed, in a pale-blue frock, a white muslin fichu, and a rose, Lord Thomas thought her beautiful. Yes, in spite of freckles and a turned-up nose. Never had he seen in woman's shape such pure health and such an absence of self-consciousness. Of all the charming novelties surrounding him, these were the most charming.

'I suppose she's too busy to notice what a sweet creature she is,' he thought, as he sat down to the juicy slice of mutton for which he had earned so keen an appetite. And he anticipated with joy the leisure hours he now expected to spend with her, undisturbed by bees, in the somewhat threadbare drawing-room.

All went thither together at the conclusion of the meal – the comfortable tea-dinner of the bush. Mr. Kemp, desiring to talk ploughs and ensilage, proposed a smoke. His guest, yearning for tobacco, aching in every limb, declined. Mrs. Kemp sent her daughter to the piano, and Letty played – admirably Lord Thomas thought – the intermezzo from *Cavalleria*, and a few things of that sort; and while he tried to listen, and to feed his sense of the girl's many-sided excellence, his hostess babbled about London as she remembered it, and wanted a thousand and one details of the dear city as it was now. During a laborious description of the Thames Embankment, Letty rose from the music-stool, and softly moved about the room. Her admirer flattered himself that she was listening to him, but was shortly undeceived. She vanished at a moment when his face was turned from the door, and never came back.

'Does she actually *leave* me!' he dumbly groaned. 'Is she so lost to all the feelings of her sex as to imagine that I won't miss her while I have this old woman to talk to?' It was enough to drive any titled gentleman to extremities.

Soon he was hunting the dim verandahs round and round, in search of the fugitive. He explored the passages of the house; he walked about the garden, smelling so strongly of orange blossom, in the pure night air; and he used bad language under his breath. At last he was drawn to a light shining like a thread of incandescent wire through a certain outhouse door. He lifted the latch and looked in.

There she was. Kneeling on a piece of sacking in the middle of the floor, with her blue skirt pinned up round her waist under a large apron, and with all the mess of a station workshop and lumber-shed around her, she was busily engaged in painting her brand on honey tins. A kerosene lamp shed effective rays on her dainty figure, her fair, clear skin, her shining chestnut hair. In short, Lord Thomas stood and looked at her, fascinated. Of the thousands of pretty women that he had admired in his time, not one had ever appeared to such advantage in the matter of background and grouping. Yet he protested at the sight.

'Oh, I *say*! Haven't you done enough work for one day, Miss Kemp? Are you trying to kill yourself?'

She looked up at him with a laugh; and her eyes, focusing the light, were like stars in the grubby gloom.

'Oh, I beg your pardon, Mr. de Bohun! I thought, as you were talking to mother, you would not notice if I slipped away for half-an-hour.'

'*Did* you?' said Lord Thomas, entering and shutting the door behind him.

'I want so badly to get my consignment away next week. And I thought if I painted the tins tonight, they would be dry for packing in the morning.'

She continued to dab her black brush upon a slip of perforated zinc, but her quick hand became slightly unsteady, and she blushed visibly, even in that bad light. The fact was that Lord Thomas – not as Lord Thomas, but as a man – was a delightful fellow, and it was not in nature that a healthy, heart-whole girl could spend a long and intimate day with him without being more or less affected in the usual way. As yet her bees were of more consequence than lovers – he was resentfully aware of it – but that did not prevent her feeling hourly more conscious that the toil was sweetened by his participation therein. She was pleased that he had found her. She was more pleased when he took the black brush from her, asked leave to remove his coat, turned up his cuffs, and began to paint honey tins himself.

'I am not a very practised hand at this sort of thing,' he confessed. 'You must tell me if I don't do it right.'

'You are quite as practised at that as I am looking on while others do my work,' she said.

'So I suppose,' he rejoined thoughtfully.

They had a happy hour, unmolested by the parents, who never supposed that their practical Letty could lend herself to foolishness. Lord Thomas painted all the tins successfully. He could not well go wrong while she held the lettered label straight. Their two heads were within an inch of touching as they bent over their job; a handkerchief might have covered their four hands while the branding was in process. They looked at each other's fingers continually.

'Mine,' said Letty, 'are quite rough compared with yours. I don't think I ever saw such beautiful nails. It's my belief you never did a stroke of work in your life until you came here.'

'Well,' said Lord Thomas, colouring a little, 'I am afraid I haven't done much. You make me awfully ashamed of myself, Miss Kemp.'

They fell into serious talk at this stage – the first serious talk Lord Thomas had ever had with a young lady, all his experiences notwithstanding.

'I wish,' he abruptly remarked, 'you'd teach me to be as useful as you are.' There was much feeling in his voice.

She seemed to think the matter over. Then she asked him when he intended to return home. He said he was not sure.

'Soon, I suppose?'

'Oh, I suppose so.'

'You *must* go soon,' she urged. 'You must, for the sake of that poor baby, left to the tender mercies of hired people.'

'Well,' he said, 'I will.'

'Then you will have an opportunity to be very, *very* useful. You can look after my honey for me in London – oh!'

He flung the paint-brush into the pot.

'I suppose it is useless,' he exclaimed, through grinding teeth, 'to expect you to care a straw for anything except honey and bees!'

There were but two courses open to a self-respecting man, titled or otherwise – to make her do it, or die in the attempt.

She is Her Grace the Duchess now. And an excellent duchess into the bargain. The smart folks laugh at her for not 'knowing her way about', but the duke does not. He thoroughly realizes that she knows it better than they do. When, as a surprise present to her, he established a magnificent apiary in the castle grounds, and then found she did not care for it, he was a little disappointed; but soon woke to the fact that bees had been merely the makeshift of circumstance until worthier objects for the exercise of her splendid abilities were provided. With great households to administer and young dukes to rear – not to speak of a thousand matters of more public moment – she advisedly transferred her interest in honey to the wives of her husband's tenants.

'But they will never make honey like mine,' she says, shaking her coroneted head. 'It wants the taste of the eucalyptus in it.'

ALBERT DORRINGTON
A Bush Tanqueray

The coach creaked round a path hewn out of the grey sandstone, leading to the road that ran white and bare over the summit of a hill. The driver pulled up. Away down in the smoke-laden hollow a number of men gathered and sent up a faint cheer. Then a shirt of many colours, supported by yellow moleskin trousers, rose solemnly from the box-seat and made some parabolic gestures in return. The driver touched his leader tenderly on the flank, and the coach wound through lichen-covered boulders into a dingy mulga background. Simultaneously the crowd below adjourned to the public-house. A mottle-faced old whaler peeped in at the door to remark, for the fifth time, that 'water was bad, and the road too stinkin' for anything.' No one noticed him until, pressed by a great thirst, he hazarded another cast of the die:

'Anybody want to 'ear a song – a real blanky song without funny business? Ever 'eared "When Molly marries the Ringer"? I'd sing "Billy the Bound'ry", only I'm gone in the 'igh notes through sleepin' in the wet without a bluey.'

A derisive, withering reply sent him hobbling to the kerb to examine further the grey ridges that bounded an everlasting plain, and the question of his life – the road. Conversation in the bar turned upon Benjamin Stokes, the man who had just left by coach for Sydney. Everybody admitted that Ben was too reserved and sullen. In the first place, his life had been spent beyond the enlightening influence of his fellow-townsmen, in long night-watches with stamping herds and vicious colts. 'And the result,' said Tackler, the school-master, 'is a product as rough as Nature, his god. Gentlemen,' continued Tackler, seizing a gin-and-peppermint, 'the man Stokes is a heathen idolater.'

And Mottle-face went lamely over the hill, his tattered clothes flapping weirdly through a vista of white dust.

Ben's trip was to last a month, and each week of his absence was duly notched off on the post outside the pub. When the notches grew to ten, and he did not return, the circumstance was referred to in the *Deep Creek Dabbler*.

Ben had never seen a train before; his ideas of city life had been drawn from the rough word-pictures of bushmen. The cause of his prolonged absence was explained in the first page of his new pocket-book –

Stoping two Teath, one ginny. Millysent Lee – cab – Mattrymonal agenc, 3£. 2s. 6d.

One afternoon the coach dropped them at the door of a hut near the creek. The driver shook hands with Ben, winked at Ben's wife, and flogged his horses over the wooden bridge to the township. They stood watching the coach till attention was claimed by a tabby cat which brought out several blind kittens for inspection. Her sinful pride led to painful consequences, for a few minutes later the anxious mother mewed piteously near the tank, while Benjamin did strange things with her blind offspring in a bucket of water.

Millicent threw herself wearily on a biscuit-box and slowly took out her hat-pins. The room was stuffy and dark; the tiny window and the little tin mirror filled her with profound astonishment. In a corner was a narrow bed that met the requirements of a long single man, and its presence plainly indicated that the whole wedlock business was unpremeditated. A sporting print on the wall depicted 'Jimmy the Biff' going sweet and fresh after ten hard rounds with 'Mick the Nipper' from Bendigo.

Through a large hole in the wall near the fire-place Ben apologised for the speckled condition of the nuptial chamber – due, he explained, to the goats and fowls. By-and-by he might nail up the hole with a bag; it was getting too big. Some night an enterprising cow would squeeze through and breathe over a married couple – he'd nail it up now. He rushed away, and there were sounds of a man chopping wood.

The next day was Sunday. Ben took out a concertina from the hollow log where it had lain for weeks; and tucking it under his arm, stole down to the creek bend, where the belt of coolabahs would hide his musical proceedings from Mill. He began to wonder if she were really fond of music. Anyhow, he would practise a bit before submitting anything to her judgment. She had lived all her life in swell boarding-houses where the aristocracy sat down to the piano and gave it what for. He reckoned that Mill would be very hard to please; still, a concertina was as good as a piano, and if he could only get hold of a few rattling tunes he'd spring 'em on her suddenly – he'd go marching up the track swinging his instrument over his head and filling the bush with an imitation of cathedral bells. His mother used to say he had a grand forehead for music. He looked back over his shoulder to see if Mill were watching him from the door. A screw of smoke trailed from the tiny chimney, winding like a scarf across the roof of the bush.

How different the country seemed since he had returned! The blazed eucalypt that had always reminded him of a crucified man looked quite cheerful; the cattle were in better condition; the very atmosphere held some hidden witchery that set him aglow as if he had drunk wine from the billy instead of tea.

He sat on a boulder hugging his concertina. The coming of this grey-eyed town-girl would change his life. There were times when he used to sit alone clasping his knees and smoking until he felt sick and giddy. People said he was sulkier than a calf. Yet there were hundreds of lads who lived as he had lived, with the unresponsive bush for a mistress and slavering red-eyed cattle for comrades.

The first few notes from his concertina seemed to wake the morning stillness; a couple of inquisitive magpies chortled back melodiously as if defying the big sun-tanned stripling to out-clamour them.

He rose suddenly and pitched a stone in their direction. 'Go way, yer blooming cadgers! yous sneak about when yous ain't wanted. Gerrout!'

'*Ha, ha, ha! ho, ho ho!*'

A kingfisher sailed over the hut roof and settled on the lower branch of a gum.

'*Ho, ho, ho!*'

The savage, insulting laughter cracked discordantly along the hollow.

For a moment the hot blood swam in Ben's cheeks; the same bird had shed laughter a thousand times over his hut, but never till now had he felt how closely the cackle resembled the fierce mockery from a human throat.

When he returned Mill was clearing out the garnered litter of his bachelor days – leaky, rust-eaten billies, old boots and bridle straps, fearsome pictures of groggy pugilists and bush racehorses. He whistled softly, with his body half in the door-way, wondering whether he had better take off his hat before entering.

After breakfast Millicent hinted weakly about going to church. 'Right, Mill!' said Ben, dropping the saw he was greasing, 'we'll go now, though I've never been before. Put on your grey dress and the hat with the big black feather.'

He followed her inside.

When they started Ben walked ahead swinging his arms so that the shortness of his sleeves might not attract Mill's attention. For the first time in his life he took an interest in the long shadow that stretched about six fathoms ahead. In the middle of it was a hideous kink where the saddle had pressed his coat-tail outwards. The ridiculous shape of it hurt Ben beyond words.

Mill panted after him – he was sublimely unconscious that his terrific pace distressed her. She caught his hand: he slackened instantly and blushed a peony red.

The track swung over a boulder-strewn hillock where the scattered cairns of pick-torn stone recalled a one-time mining camp. They rested awhile: Ben propped himself against a blue-gum.

'Yer git a good breeze here on hot nights, Mill. Grand place fer a breeze.'

She did not answer; her fingers were shut over his, her parted lips drank the mountain air.

The rocks filtered great drops of mouth-cooling water into their outstretched hands: the sun stalked valiantly across the naked East over treeless gullies and rolling downs. Through the still scrub they caught the moving gleams of tawny light radiated from leaf to leaf into the deeps of ebon shadows. He touched her hand unconsciously, and the wanton blood leaped to her throat and temples. She looked at him, and he seemed to her a part of the big, secret bush. The light of morning was in his eyes, a fierce young light that she had seen in the eyes of men who lurked under gasaliers and crouched over desks. He was staring absently at the red cattle wallowing in the reed-choked lagoon. He turned suddenly; his long arm went out towards the tin-roofed box in the hollow.

'It ain't a flash place I've brought yer to, Mill. Yer might have done better.'

Mill tugged at her cheap gloves and laughed softly. 'Yer right, Ben, it ain't flash; but, Lord! we'll pull through.'

'Course we will.' He glanced at her stealthily, and noted the handful of half-dead violets tucked cunningly under the brim of her straw hat. There wasn't a woman in the township who could fix violets over her little ear in the same way. He moistened his lips.

'We oughter be happy here, Mill,' he said, 'seein' it's me an' you.'

'Yes, Ben,' she acquiesced.

'They're alright people in Pyers when you know 'em,' went on Ben; 'an' they're bound to take to you – being friendly with me, yer see.'

She rose and took his arm. 'O' course, Ben.'

He stretched himself on his disengaged side and breathed

lustily. The world seemed so young and glorious – it made his eyes water. His voice trembled a little as he said, 'Yer wouldn't believe what a place this is fer a breeze.'

They moved onwards.

He chose a seat directly under the pulpit. 'Keep yer 'ead agin the mahogany, Mill; they'll be dyin' to see yer face when they come in; don't let 'em!'

The church at this time was empty; but it filled – filled to overflowing. 'Don't forgit the mahogany, Mill,' whispered Ben behind his hand.

Their pew remained as sacred as a Hindu cow. The coach-driver pointed them out from a crowded porch, and his audience appeared spasmodically grateful for the information concerning Mrs. Ben. The driver admitted regretfully that his friend, Sam Hopkins, knew her pretty well, thanks – 'wished I knew her as well.' Still, it wasn't for him to take away the character of a respectable married woman. Heard that she could cook as good a feed as anybody in Pyers, and if —— The organ took it up, and sent out a moaning 'Adeste Fideles.'

The minister thundered at his stoic congregation, and charged the air with strange, charitable precepts. At the end he waved a calm benediction over his respectable flock: 'Go in peace, and sin no more!'

The men leered at Ben and Mill as they passed out; young girls gathered up skirts and scattered; obese wives and mothers cannoned in circling, agitated groups.

'Thank God the roof didn't fall on us this blessed day! The idea!'

Ben lifted his head and eyed the hostile gathering; some of them had known him for years – since the time when he used to drive about Pyers in a billy-goat tandem. A shout of mocking laughter followed them to the gate. Ben clinched his mouth; an unknown shame spread to his neck and face: something gripped his arm, and a word hummed in his ear that an ordinary woman never uses at any period of her life.

So they tramped along, voiceless and sullen, through paddocks where flowers nodded to a caressing wind, while the sun warmed perfumes from the moist Spring earth. Mill's right hand bruised her breast savagely; the other held his sleeve.

She glanced furtively at him across the room – his head down, his chin resting in the heel of his palm.

'Did I ever say I was a good girl, Ben? I ain't, Gawd 'elp me!'

She thrust herself beside him, shaking and trembling. Then

Benjamin Stokes listened, almost for the first time in his life, to the commonest story in the world – a betrayal, a little shame, a gradual hardening, a world-defiance.

'The old woman at the boardin'-house said she'd clear me out unless I was obligin' and civil to the gentlemen. So there was presents for Mill, and gloves planted in my bed . . . It all helped to take my head away from the damned 'ard scrubbin'. I ain't old – nineteen ain't very old, is it? Gimme a chance, Ben – gimme a chance!'

Something simmered in the fireplace; plates clattered; a shadowy girl moved about him all the afternoon in a dull, half-frightened way. He stumbled outside to the wood-heap, and the soft-eyed collie hung at his heels for a word.

The sun dropped to the edge of the plains, drenching the far off hills with yellow mist. A rush of cool air brought the clang of bells; he raised a rough and haggard face and spoke a word to the night – a word he used when punching cattle through an overflow. The dog fawned joyously . . . 'Away, you beast!' – and a savage kick sent it howling down the track.

A candle flickered in the little bedroom, throwing a shape across the chintz curtain. 'That bell again!' He walked a short distance from the house. How everyone knew! How everyone guessed the truth! What had happened at the church to-day would happen again with sickening regularity. He might force the men to respect him with his fists; but that cackling brood in the porch! He struck a match and groped into the room to fling a word of hate at this Magdalen– and fell into a chair, silenced. The face was so pretty, so weak – prey for every libertine. The minister had said something about a woman who wiped the feet of Christ with her long meshes of hair; nobody believed it, of course; if they did, why was Mill treated as she had been? He sat through the long night, heavy-browed and brooding, until a grey light from the east whitened the window-pane.

'Mill!' She smiled sleepily at the word.

'Mill!' The sound of his voice made her crouch on the rough pallet; she stared at the white haggard face in the half-light.

'Don't be frightened, Mill! – don't be frightened; I shan't hit yer. I've been thinkin'; and we ain't goin' to church again to let 'em worry us. I'll build another place over at Red Point on the hundred-acre patch; if they come there to carry on I'll be about to receive 'em.'

Her face was hidden from him, but her hand crept into his big palm.

A few hours later Ben led a bay horse to the front and hopped into the saddle. She came to the door, her white arms splashed with milk and flour.

'It's a long way to the Point, ain't it, Ben?'

'Yeh!'

She stole nearer – obviously to examine the horse. He threw himself forward and kissed her on the lips.

GEORGE ESSEX EVANS
The Women of the West

They left the vine-wreathed cottage and the mansion on the hill,
The houses in the busy streets where life is never still,
The pleasures of the city, and the friends they cherished best:
For love they faced the wilderness – the Women of the West.

The roar, and rush, and fever of the city died away,
And the old-time joys and faces – they were gone for many a day;
In their place the lurching coach-wheel, or the creaking bullock
    chains,
O'er the everlasting sameness of the never-ending plains.

In the slab-built, zinc-roofed homestead of some lately-taken run,
In the tent beside the bankment of a railway just begun,
In the huts on new selections, in the camps of man's unrest,
On the frontiers of the Nation, live the Women of the West.

The red sun robs their beauty, and, in weariness and pain,
The slow years steal the nameless grace that never comes again;
And there are hours men cannot soothe, and words men cannot
    say –
The nearest woman's face may be a hundred miles away.

The wide Bush holds the secrets of their longings and desires,
When the white stars in reverence light their holy altar-fires,
And silence, like the touch of God, sinks deep into the breast –
Perchance He hears and understands the Women of the West.

For them no trumpet sounds the call, no poet plies his arts –
They only hear the beating of their gallant, loving hearts.
But they have sung with silent lives the song all songs above –
The holiness of sacrifice, the dignity of love.

Well have we held our fathers' creed. No call has passed us by.
We faced and fought the wilderness, we sent our sons to die.
And we have hearts to do and dare, and yet, o'er all the rest,
The hearts that made the Nation were the Women of the West.

LOUISA LAWSON
Lines Written During a Night Spent in a Bush Inn

I wish now this heart with its pleading refrain
Would freeze and be still, then this tumult of pain
That mortals call living would end, and the cast
Of life be as nought but a pestilence past.

This robe I am wearing, as white as a cloud,
With neatly sewn border, would do for a shroud,
And thus I'd be ready, pain-shriven and meet,
With only to straighten my hands and my feet.

No sign would I make when Death's hand on me lay,
No sob would I utter when passing away;
For those in the house need the rest, all too short,
To heal the fatigue that a hard day has brought.

Out on the verandah, asleep on the floor,
With weary feet blistered, and aching and sore,
The tramp dreams of home with his head on his swag,
Nor recks he of drought, or the dry water-bag.

And soundly asleep, with a sun-blistered face,
The drover now dreads not the 'breaks' he must chase.
But he must be up at the first peep of light
To 'fetch up' the yards for his cattle at night.

And while all the sheep in the hurdles are snug
The black boy must rest on his old 'possum rug.
In dust and in heat he has shouted all day,
And sunrise must see him again on his way.

I looked in the face of Death once, when alone,
And met the grim King without shudder or moan,
So I will not shiver nor shriek with affright
If I have to go with him into the night.

And then they would take me to where I love best,
To where I know well that my spirit would rest,
Where gaudy birds chatter and wild cherries wave,
And sunset would throw a red haze o'er my grave –

Away on the gap, 'neath the big kurrajong
That stretches its branches the granites among,
And forms with its shelter a natural tomb
With rest in its stillness, and peace in its gloom.

And some one among them, with grief in his breast,
Might register roughly the place of my rest
By carving in letters cut deep on its bole
These plain words: 'A Woman. May God rest her soul.'

In ground that is hallowed let happy folk lie,
But give me a grave in the bush when I die.
For have I not lived, loved, and suffered alone?
Thus making it meet that my grave be unknown.

The sound of the stockwhip away on the hill.
Ah, God! It is day, and I'm suffering still!

CHARLES HARPUR
from *Note* to *'A Wanton'*

Though constitutionally disposed well nigh to worship Women
and to stickle for her rights also with an ultra liberality; I know
at the same time, that Man is her natural superior – her born head.
Of this fact, their comparative persons & dispositions with every
sexual, social and domestic relation subsisting between them, is
unmistakably demonstrative. His bodily structure is firm and
angular, hers yielding and round. He is adventurous in spirit and
out-seeking in habit; she is unspeculative and retired. He is
endowed with the higher fortitude of soul for their mutual
defence; and with the greater physical energy and endurance for
their joint manual support; while the mere results of this conjugal
intercourse are often such as to render her utterly helpless and
dependent upon him. Nay, finally, in the very perpetuation of
the species, he is the *cause* and she only the procreative
medium. – The poetry above was written in my youth; this note
to it in my manhood.

BARBARA BAYNTON
Squeaker's Mate

The woman carried the bag with the axe and maul and wedges; the man had the billy and clean tucker-bags; the cross-cut saw linked them. She was taller than the man, and the equability of her body, contrasting with his indolent slouch, accentuated the difference. 'Squeaker's mate' the men called her, and these agreed that she was the best long-haired mate that ever stepped in petticoats. The Selectors' wives pretended to challenge her right to womanly garments, but if she knew what they said, it neither turned nor troubled Squeaker's mate.

Nine prospective posts and maybe sixteen rails – she calculated this yellow gum would yield. 'Come on,' she encouraged the man; 'let's tackle it.'

From the bag she took the axe, and ring barked a preparatory circle, while he looked for a shady spot for the billy and tucker bags.

'Come on.' She was waiting with the greased saw. He came. The saw rasped through a few inches, then he stopped and looked at the sun.

'It's nigh tucker time,' he said, and when she dissented, he exclaimed, with sudden energy, 'There's another bee! Wait, you go on with the axe, an' I'll track 'im.'

As they came, they had already followed one and located the nest. She could not see the bee he spoke of, though her grey eyes were as keen as a Black's. However, she knew the man, and her tolerance was of the mysteries.

She drew out the saw, spat on her hands, and with the axe began weakening the inclining side of the tree.

Long and steadily and in secret the worm had been busy in the heart. Suddenly the axe blade sank softly, the tree's wounded edges closed on it like a vice. There was a 'settling' quiver on its top branches, which the woman heard and understood. The man, encouraged by the sounds of the axe, had returned with an armful of sticks for the billy. He shouted gleefully, 'It's fallin', look out.'

But she waited to free the axe.

With a shivering groan the tree fell, and as she sprang aside, a thick worm-eaten branch snapped at a joint and silently she went down under it.

'I tole yer t' look out,' he reminded her, as with a crow-bar, and grunting earnestly, he forced it up. 'Now get out quick.'

She tried moving her arms and the upper part of her body. Do this; do that, he directed, but she made no movement after the first.

He was impatient, because for once he had actually to use his strength. His share of a heavy lift usually consisted of a make-believe grunt, delivered at a critical moment. Yet he hardly cared to let it again fall on her, though he told her he would, if she 'didn't shift.'

Near him lay a piece broken short; with his foot he drew it nearer, then gradually worked it into a position, till it acted as a stay to the lever.

He laid her on her back when he drew her out, and waited expecting some acknowledgment of his exertions, but she was silent, and as she did not notice that the axe, she had tried to save, lay with the fallen trunk across it, he told her. She cared almost tenderly for all their posessions and treated them as friends. But the half-buried broken axe did not affect her. He wondered a little, for only last week she had patiently chipped out the old broken head, and put in a new handle.

'Feel bad?' he inquired at length.

'Pipe,' she replied with slack lips.

Both pipes lay in the fork of a near tree. He took his, shook out the ashes, filled it, picked up a coal and puffed till it was alight – then he filled hers. Taking a small firestick he handed her the pipe. The hand she raised shook and closed in an uncertain hold, but she managed by a great effort to get it to her mouth. He lost patience with the swaying hand that tried to take the light.

'Quick,' he said, 'quick, that damn dog's at the tucker.'

He thrust it into her hand that dropped helplessly across her chest. The lighted stick falling between her bare arm and the dress, slowly roasted the flesh and smouldered the clothes.

He rescued their dinner, pelted his dog out of sight – hers was lying near her head – put on the billy, then came back to her.

The pipe had fallen from her lips; there was blood on the stem.

'Did yer jam yer tongue?' he asked.

She always ignored trifles, he knew, therefore he passed her silence.

He told her that her dress was on fire. She took no heed. He put it out, and looked at the burnt arm, then with intentness at her.

Her eyes were turned unblinkingly to the heavens, her lips were grimly apart, and a strange greyness was upon her face, and the sweat-beads were mixing.

'Like a drink er tea? Asleep?'

He broke a green branch from the fallen tree and swished from his face the multitudes of flies that had descended with it.

In a heavy way he wondered why did she sweat, when she was not working? Why did she not keep the flies out of her mouth and eyes? She'd have bungy eyes, if she didn't. If she was asleep, why did she not close them?

But asleep or awake, as the billy began to boil, he left her, made the tea, and ate his dinner. His dog had disappeared, and as it did not come to his whistle, he threw the pieces to hers, that would not leave her head to reach them.

He whistled tunelessly his one air, beating his own time with a stick on the toe of his blucher, then looked overhead at the sun and calculated that she must have been lying like that for 'close up an hour.' He noticed that the axe handle was broken in two places, and speculated a little as to whether she would again pick out the back-broken handle or burn it out in his method, which was less trouble, if it did spoil the temper of the blade. He examined the worm-dust in the stump and limbs of the newly-fallen tree; mounted it and looked round the plain. The sheep were straggling in a manner that meant walking work to round them, and he supposed he would have to yard them to-night, if she didn't liven up. He looked down at unenlivened her. This changed his 'chune' to a call for his hiding dog.

'Come on, ole feller,' he commanded her dog. 'Fetch 'em back.' He whistled further instructions, slapping his thigh and pointing to the sheep.

But a brace of wrinkles either side the brute's closed mouth demonstrated determined disobedience. The dog would go if she told him, and by and bye she would.

He lighted his pipe and killed half an hour smoking. With the frugality that hard graft begets, his mate limited both his and her own tobacco, so he must not smoke all afternoon. There was no work to shirk, so time began to drag. Then a goanner crawling up a tree attracted him. He gathered various missiles and tried vainly to hit the seemingly grinning reptile. He came back and sneaked a fill of her tobacco, and while he was smoking, the white tilt of a cart caught his eye. He jumped up. 'There's Red Bob goin' t'our place fur th' 'oney,' he said. 'I'll go an' weigh it an' get the gonz' (money).

He ran for the cart, and kept looking back as if fearing she would follow and thwart him.

Red Bob the dealer was, in a business way, greatly concerned, when he found that Squeaker's mate was "avin' a sleep out there 'cos a tree fell on her.' She was the best honey-strainer and boiler that he dealt with. She was straight and square too. There was no water in her honey whether boiled or merely strained, and in every kerosene tin the weight of honey was to an ounce as she said. Besides he was suspicious and diffident of paying the indecently eager Squeaker before he saw the woman. So reluctantly Squeaker led to where she lay. With many fierce oaths Red Bob sent her lawful protector for help, and compassionately poured a little from his flask down her throat, then swished away the flies from her till help came.

Together these men stripped a sheet of bark, and laying her with pathetic tenderness upon it, carried her to her hut. Squeaker followed in the rear with the billy and tucker.

Red Bob took his horse from the cart, and went to town for the doctor. Late that night at the back of the old hut (there were two) he and others who had heard that she was hurt, squatted with unlighted pipes in their mouths, waiting to hear the doctor's verdict. After he had given it and gone, they discussed in whispers, and with a look seen only on bush faces, the hard luck of that woman who alone had hard-grafted with the best of them for every acre and hoof on that selection. Squeaker would go through it in no time. Why she had allowed it to be taken up in his name, when the money had been her own, was also for them among the mysteries.

Him they called 'a nole woman,' not because he was hanging round the honey tins, but after man's fashion to eliminate all virtue. They beckoned him, and explaining his mate's injury, cautioned him to keep from her the knowledge that she would be for ever a cripple.

'Jus' th' same, now then fur 'im,' pointing to Red Bob, 't' pay me, I'll 'ev t' go t' town.'

They told him in whispers what they thought of him, and with a cowardly look towards where she lay, but without a word of parting, like shadows these men made for their homes.

Next day the women came. Squeaker's mate was not a favourite with them – a woman with no leisure for yarning was not likely to be. After the first day they left her severely alone, their plea to their husbands, her uncompromising independence. It is in the ordering of things that by degrees most husbands accept their wives' views of other women.

The flour bespattering Squeaker's now neglected clothes spoke eloquently of his clumsy efforts at damper making. The women gave him many a feed, agreeing that it must be miserable for him.

If it were miserable and lonely for his mate, she did not complain; for her the long, long days would give place to longer nights – those nights with the pregnant bush silence suddenly

cleft by a bush voice. However, she was not fanciful, and being
a bush scholar knew 'twas a dingo, when a long whine came from
the scrub on the skirts of which lay the axe under the worm-eaten
tree. That quivering wail from the billabong lying murkily mystic
towards the East was only the cry of the fearing curlew.

Always her dog – wakeful and watchful as she – patiently
waiting for her to be up and about again. That would be soon,
she told her complaining mate.

'Yer won't. Yer back's broke,' said Squeaker laconically. 'That's
wot's wrong er yer; injoory t' th' spine. Doctor says that means
back's broke, and yer won't never walk no more. No good not
t' tell yer, cos I can't be doin' everythin'.'

A wild look grew on her face, and she tried to sit up.

'Erh,' said he, 'see! yer carnt, yer jes' ther same as a snake w'en
ees back's broke, on'y yer don't bite yerself like a snake does w'en
'e carnt crawl. Yer did bite yer tongue w'en yer fell.'

She gasped, and he could hear her heart beating when she let
her head fall back a few moments; though she wiped her wet
forehead with the back of her hand, and still said that was the
doctor's mistake. But day after day she tested her strength, and
whatever the result, was silent, though white witnesses, halo-
wise, gradually circled her brow and temples.

"'Tisn't as if yer was agoin' t' get better t'morrer, the doctor says
yer won't never work no more, an' I can't be cookin' an' workin'
an' doin' everythin'!'

He muttered something about 'sellin' out,' but she firmly
refused to think of such a monstrous proposal.

He went into town one Saturday afternoon soon after, and did
not return till Monday.

Her supplies, a billy of tea and scraps of salt beef and damper
(her dog got the beef), gave out the first day, though that was
as nothing to her compared with the bleat of the penned sheep,
for it was summer and droughty, and her dog could not unpen
them.

Of them and her dog only she spoke when he returned. He
d—d him, and d—d her, and told her to 'double up yer ole broke
back an' bite yerself.' He threw things about, made a long-range
feint of kicking her threatening dog, then sat outside in the shade
of the old hut, nursing his head till he slept.

She, for many reasons, had when necessary made these trips
into town, walking both ways, leading a pack horse for supplies.
She never failed to indulge him in a half pint – a pipe was her
luxury.

The sheep waited till next day, so did she.

For a few days he worked a little in her sight; not much – he never did. It was she who always lifted the heavy end of the log, and carried the tools; he – the billy and tucker.

She wearily watched him idling his time; reminded him that the wire lying near the fence would rust, one could run the wire through easily, and when she got up in a day or so, she would help strain and fasten it. At first he pretended he had done it, later said he wasn't goin' t' go wirin' or nothin' else by 'imself if every other man on the place did.

She spoke of many other things that could be done by one, reserving the great till she was well. Sometimes he whistled while she spoke, often swore, generally went out, and when this was inconvenient, dull as he was, he found the 'Go and bite yerself like a snake,' would instantly silence her.

At last the work worry ceased to exercise her, and for night to bring him home was a rare thing.

Her dog rounded and yarded the sheep when the sun went down and there was no sign of him, and together they kept watch on their movements till dawn. She was mindful not to speak of this care to him, knowing he would have left it for them to do constantly, and she noticed that what little interest he seemed to share went to the sheep. Why, was soon demonstrated.

Through the cracks her ever watchful eyes one day saw the dust rise out of the plain. Nearer it came till she saw him and a man on horseback rounding and driving the sheep into the yard, and later both left in charge of a little mob. Their 'Baa-baas' to her were cries for help; many had been pets. So he was selling her sheep to the town butchers.

In the middle of the next week he came from town with a fresh horse, new saddle and bridle. He wore a flash red shirt, and round his neck a silk handkerchief. On the next occasion she smelt scent, and though he did not try to display the dandy meerschaum, she saw it, and heard the squeak of the new boots, not bluchers. However he was kinder to her this time, offering a fill of his cut tobacco; he had long ceased to keep her supplied. Several of the men who sometimes in passing took a look in, would have made up her loss had they known, but no word of compaint passed her lips.

She looked at Squeaker as he filled his pipe from his pouch, but he would not meet her eyes, and, seemingly dreading something, slipped out.

She heard him hammering in the old hut at the back, which served for tools and other things which sunlight and rain did not hurt. Quite briskly he went in and out. She could see him through the cracks carrying a narrow strip of bark, and understood, he was making a bunk. When it was finished he had a smoke, then came to her and fidgetted about; he said this hut was too cold, and that she would never get well in it. She did not feel cold, but, submitting to his mood, allowed him to make a fire that would roast a sheep. He took off his hat, and, fanning himself, said he was roastin', wasn't she? She was.

He offered to carry her into the other; he would put a new roof on it in a day or two, and it would be better than this one, and she would be up in no time. He stood to say this where she could not see him.

His eagerness had tripped him.

There were months to run before all the Government conditions of residence, etc., in connection with the selection, would be fulfilled, still she thought perhaps he was trying to sell out, and she would not go.

He was away four days that time, and when he returned slept in the new bunk.

She compromised. Would he put a bunk there for himself, keep out of town, and not sell the place? He promised instantly with additions.

'Try could yer crawl yerself?' he coaxed, looking at her bulk.

Her nostrils quivered with her suppressed breathing, and her lips tightened, but she did not attempt to move.

It was evident some great purpose actuated him. After attempts to carry and drag her, he rolled her on the sheet of bark that had brought her home, and laboriously drew her round.

She asked for a drink, he placed her billy and tin pint besides the bunk, and left her, gasping and dazed to her sympathetic dog.

She saw him run up and yard his horse, and though she called him, he would not answer nor come.

When he rode swiftly towards the town, her dog leaped on the bunk, and joined a refrain to her lamentation, but the cat took to the bush.

He came back at dusk next day in a spring cart – not alone – he had another mate. She saw her though he came a roundabout way, trying to keep in front of the new hut.

There were noises of moving many things from the cart to the hut. Finally he came to a crack near where she lay, and whispered the promise of many good things to her if she kept quiet, and that he would set her hut afire if she didn't. She was quiet, he need not have feared, for that time she was past it, she was stunned.

The released horse came stumbling round to the old hut, and thrust its head in the door in a domesticated fashion. Her dog promptly resented this straggler mistaking their hut for a stable. And the dog's angry dissent, together with the shod clatter of the rapidly disappearing intruder, seemed to have a disturbing effect on the pair in the new hut. The settling sounds suddenly ceased, and the cripple heard the stranger close the door, despite Squeaker's assurances that the woman in the old hut could not move from her bunk to save her life, and that her dog would not leave her.

Food, more and better, was placed near her – but, dumb and motionless, she lay with her face turned to the wall, and her dog growled menacingly at the stranger. The new woman was uneasy, and told Squeaker what people might say and do if she died.

He, scared at the 'do', went into the bush and waited.

She went to the door, not the crack, the face was turned that way, and said she had come to cook and take care of her.

The disabled woman, turning her head slowly, looked steadily at her. She was not much to look at. Her red hair hung in an un-curled bang over her forehead, the lower part of her face had robbed the upper, and her figure evinced imminent motherhood, though it is doubtful if the barren woman, noting this, knew by calculation the paternity was not Squeaker's. She was not learned in these matters, though she understood all about an ewe and lamb.

One circumstance was apparent – ah! bitterest of all bitterness to women – she was younger.

The thick hair that fell from the brow of the woman on the bunk was white now.

Bread and butter the woman brought. The cripple looked at it, at her dog, at the woman. Bread and butter for a dog! but the stranger did not understand till she saw it offered to the dog. The bread and butter was not for the dog. She brought meat.

All next day the man kept hidden. The cripple saw his dog, and knew he was about.

But there was an end of this pretence when at dusk he came back with a show of haste, and a finger of his right hand bound and ostentatiously prominent. His entrance caused great excite-ment to his new mate. The old mate, who knew this snake-bite trick from its inception, maybe, realised how useless were the terrified stranger's efforts to rouse the snoring man after an empty pint bottle had been flung on the outside heap.

However, what the sick woman thought was not definite, for she kept silent always. Neither was it clear how much she ate, and how much she gave to her dog, though the new mate said to Squeaker one day that she believed that the dog would not take a bite more than its share.

The cripple's silence told on the stranger, especially when alone. She would rather have abuse. Eagerly she counted the days past and to pass. Then back to the town. She told no word of that hope to Squeaker, he had no place in her plans for the future. So if he spoke of what they would do by and bye when his time would be up, and he able to sell out, she listened in uninterested silence.

She did tell him she was afraid of 'her,' and after the first day would not go within reach, but every morning made a billy of tea, which with bread and beef Squeaker carried to her.

The rubbish heap was adorned, for the first time, with jam and fish tins from the table in the new hut. It seemed to be understood that neither woman nor dog in the old hut required them.

Squeaker's dog sniffed and barked joyfully around them till his licking efforts to bottom a salmon tin sent him careering in a muzzled frenzy, that caused the younger woman's thick lips to part grinningly till he came too close.

The remaining sheep were regularly yarded. His old mate heard him whistle as he did it. Squeaker began to work about a little burning off. So that now, added to the other bush voices, was the call from some untimely falling giant. There is no sound so human as that from the riven souls of these tree people, or the trembling sighs of their upright neighbours whose hands in time will meet over the victim's fallen body.

There was no bunk on the side of the hut to which her eyes turned, but her dog filled that space, and the flash that passed between this back-broken woman and her dog might have been the spirit of these slain tree folk, it was so wondrous ghostly. Still, at times, the practical in her would be dominant, for in a mind so free of fancies, backed by bodily strength, hope died slowly, and forgetful of self she would almost call to Squeaker her fears that certain bees' nests were in danger.

He went into town one day and returned, as he had promised, long before sundown, and next day a clothes line bridged the space between two trees near the back of the old hut; and – an equally rare occurrence – Squeaker placed across his shoulders the yoke that his old mate had fashioned for herself, with two kerosene tins attached, and brought them filled with water from the distant creek; but both only partly filled the tub, a new purchase. With utter disregard of the heat and Squeaker's sweating brow, his new mate said, even after another trip, two more now for the blue water. Under her commands he brought them, though sullenly, perhaps contrasting the old mate's methods with the new.

His old mate had periodically carried their washing to the creek, and his mole-skins had been as white as snow without aid of blue.

Towards noon, on the clothes line many strange garments fluttered, suggestive of a taunt to the barren woman. When the sun went down she could have seen the assiduous Squeaker lower the new prop-sticks and considerately stoop to gather the pegs his inconsiderate new mate had dropped. However, after one load of water next morning, on hearing her estimate that three more would put her own things through, Squeaker struck. Nothing he could urge would induce the stranger to trudge to the creek, where thirst-slaked snakes lay waiting for someone to bite. She sulked and pretended to pack up, till a bright idea struck Squeaker. He fastened a cask on a sledge and harnessing the new horse, hitched him to it, and, under the approving eyes of his new mate, led off to the creek, though, when she went inside, he bestrode the spiritless brute.

He had various mishaps, any one of which would have served as an excuse to his old mate, but even babes soon know on whom to impose. With an energy new to him he persevered and filled the cask, but the old horse repudiated such a burden even under Squeaker's unmerciful welts. Almost half was sorrowfully baled out, and under a rain of whacks the horse shifted it a few paces, but the cask tilted and the thirsty earth got its contents. All Squeaker's adjectives over his wasted labour were as unavailing as the cure for spilt milk.

It took skill and patience to rig the cask again. He partly filled it, and just as success seemed probable, the rusty wire fastening the cask to the sledge snapped with the strain, and, springing free, coiled affectionately round the terrified horse's hocks. Despite the sledge (the cask had been soon disposed of) that old town horse's pace then was his record. Hours after, on the plain that met the horizon, loomed two specks: the distance between them might be gauged, for the larger was Squeaker.

Anticipating a plentiful supply and lacking in bush caution, the new mate used the half-bucket of water to boil the salt mutton. Towards noon she laid this joint and bread on the rough table, then watched anxiously in the wrong direction for Squeaker.

She had drained the new tea-pot earlier, but she placed the spout to her thirsty mouth again.

She continued looking for him for hours.

Had he sneaked off to town, thinking she had not used that water, or not caring whether or no? She did not trust him; another had left her. Besides she judged Squeaker by his treatment of the woman who was lying in there with wide-open eyes. Anyhow no use to cry with only that silent woman to hear her.

Had she drunk all hers?

She tried to see at long range through the cracks, but the hanging bed clothes hid the billy. She went to the door, and, avoiding the bunk looked at the billy.

It was half full.

Instinctively she knew that the eyes of the woman were upon her. She turned away, and hoped and waited for thirsty minutes that seemed hours.

Desperation drove her back to the door, dared she? No, she couldn't.

Getting a long forked propstick, she tried to reach it from the door, but the dog sprang at the stick. She dropped it and ran.

A scraggy growth fringed the edge of the plain. There was the creek. How far? she wondered. Oh, very far, she knew, and besides there were only a few holes where water was, and the snakes; for Squeaker, with a desire to shine in her eyes, was continually telling her of snakes – vicious and many – that daily he did battle with.

She recalled the evening he came from hiding in the scrub with a string round one finger, and said a snake had bitten him. He had drunk the pint of brandy she had brought for her sickness, and then slept till morning. True, although next day he had to dig for the string round the blue swollen finger, he was not worse than the many she had seen at the "Shearer's Rest" suffering a recovery. There was no brandy to cure her if she were bitten.

She cried a little in self-pity, then withdrew her eyes, that were getting red, from the outlying creek, and went again to the door. She of the bunk lay with closed eyes.

Was she asleep? The stranger's heart leapt, yet she was hardly in earnest as she tip-toed billy-wards. The dog, crouching with head between two paws, eyed her steadily, but showed no opposition. She made a dumb show. 'I want to be friends with you, and won't hurt her.' Abruptly she looked at her, then at the dog. He was motionless and emotionless. Besides if that dog – certainly watching her – wanted to bite her (her dry mouth opened), it could get her any time.

She rated this dog's intelligence almost human, from many of its actions in omission and commission in connection with this woman.

She regretted the pole, no dog would stand that.

Two more steps.

Now just one more; then, by bending and stretching her arm, she would reach it. Could she now? She tried to encourage herself by remembering how close on the first day she had been to the woman, and how delicious a few mouthfuls would be – swallowing dry mouthfuls.

She measured the space between where she had first stood and the billy. Could she get anything to draw it to her? No, the dog would not stand that, and besides the handle would rattle, and she might hear and open her eyes.

The thought of those sunken eyes suddenly opening made her heart bound. Oh! she must breathe – deep, loud breaths. Her throat clicked noisily. Looking back fearfully, she went swiftly out.

She did not look for Squeaker this time, she had given him up.

While she waited for her breath to steady, to her relief and surprise the dog came out. She made a rush to the new hut, but he passed seemingly oblivious of her, and, bounding across the plain began rounding the sheep. Then he must know Squeaker had gone to town.

Stay! Her heart beat violently; was it because she on the bunk slept and did not want him?

She waited till her heart quieted, and again crept to the door.

The head of the woman on the bunk had fallen towards the wall as in deep sleep; it was turned from the billy, to which she must creep so softly.

Slower, from caution and deadly earnestness, she entered.

She was not so advanced as before, and felt fairly secure, for the woman's eyes were still turned to the wall, and so tightly closed she could not possibly see where she was.

She would bend right down, and try and reach it from where she was.

She bent.

It was so swift and sudden, that she had not time to scream when those bony fingers had gripped the hand that she prematurely reached for the billy. She was frozen with horror for a moment, then her screams were piercing. Panting with victory, the prostrate one held her with a hold that the other did not attempt to free herself from.

Down, down she drew her.

Her lips had drawn back from her teeth, and her breath almost scorched the face that she held so close for the staring eyes to gloat over. Her exultation was so great that she could only gloat and gasp, and hold with a tension that had stopped the victim's circulation.

As a wounded, robbed tigress might hold and look, she held and looked.

Neither heard the swift steps of the man, and if the tigress saw him enter, she was not daunted. 'Take me from her,' shrieked the terrified one. 'Quick, take me from her,' she repeated it again, nothing else. 'Take me from her.'

He hastily fastened the door and said something that the

shrieks drowned, then picked up the pole. It fell with a thud across the arms which the tightening sinews had turned into steel. Once, twice, thrice. Then the one that got the fullest force bent; that side of the victim was free.

The pole had snapped. Another blow with a broken end freed the other side.

Still shrieking 'Take me from her, take me from her,' she beat on the closed door till Squeaker opened it.

Then he had to face and reckon with his old mate's maddened dog, that the closed door had baffled.

The dog suffered the shrieking woman to pass, but though Squeaker, in bitten agony, broke the stick across the dog, he was forced to give the savage brute best.

'Call 'im orf, Mary, 'e's eatin' me,' he implored. 'Oh corl 'im orf.'

But with stony face the woman lay motionless.

'Sool 'im on t' 'er.' He indicated his new mate who, as though all the plain led to the desired town, still ran in unreasoning terror.

'It's orl er doin',' he pleaded, springing on the bunk beside his old mate. But when, to rouse her sympathy, he would have laid his hand on her, the dog's teeth fastened in it and pulled him back.

ANONYMOUS (MARCUS CLARKE?)
The Rights of Woman (By a Brute)

Of course, they have their rights. Though I am not what is called 'a lady's man,' I freely concede this. I love my friend and my friend's wife as a good Christian should, but in general, I like the sex, and children, and brass bands, and amateur flute players – at a distance. It may be concluded, therefore, that I am not a marrying man. The estimable female with whom I have boarded and lodged since I became 'an orphan boy' is a 'lone lorn creetur,' who has attained the venerable age of seventy, and possesses the additional recommendation of being deaf and dumb. I began by confessing the righteousness of woman's rights. They have a right to become mothers. We must have mothers, you know. The necessity of fathers is not so apparent. 'It's a wise child, &c.' Then they have a right to nurse their own children, and become proficients in that mysterious infantile dialect which furnishes such terms as 'tootsicums,' 'petsey-wetsey,' and 'poppity-woppity.' They have a right to be young and plump, and rosy; with sweet, low voices, and soft, glancing eyes. They may also array themselves in bewitching bonnetlings and distracting boots. I allow further that they are only pursuing their natural vocation when swindling unhappy males at fancy bazaars, or running up soul-maddening bills for gloves and fal-lals at Moubray and Lush's. A married friend of mine once blew his brains out. A note on his dressing-table said he freely forgave his Emma, but the last bill for 'gloves and things' had driven him to the rash act. Man-hunting is another of woman's rights, and they may, like young lions, rend the prey that has fallen in the marriage warpath. A woman may also henpeck her husband – when he allows it. Some men like to be henpecked. A man I was once acquainted with liked to be kicked: he was frequently kicked.

But I deny women the right to cultivate whiskers, or enter the army, or ride *en chevalier*. I *don't* think they ought to be policemen or doctors. Mrs. MacStinger is cast in the antique Roman mould, it is true, and I could imagine her as X 55 putting a whole mob of small boys to flight. But her daughter Emma would disgrace any 'force.' She would faint at the sight of a burglar, and go into hysterics if sent out on 'night duty.' I think, too, we should combine to keep them out of Oxford and Cambridge. Fancy one courting Minerva Jones, M.A., or being the unfortunate better-half of a Mrs. Brown, L.L.D.! Do you think, my idiotic advocate of woman's right, that it is pleasant for a woman to set you right in a Latin quotation, or lay down the law in a disputed passage in Aeschylus? How would you like, my dear young Noodle, to get a three-cornered note written in Greek hexameters, and miss spending a pleasant evening with your lady love because you couldn't translate the invitation? Or, how would you feel if, at the moment you thought you were making such powerful running with that tall girl of Brown's in the conservatory, she asked you a poser concerning the bars of the solar spectrum, or the correct theory of light? No - no! The woman of time past, with her 'youth of folly and her age of cards,' was bad enough, but she was more attractive than Minerva Jones, M.A., or Mrs. Brown, L.L.D. But fancy yielding woman her great right - the franchise! Fancy further that, by sheer power of voting - for female voters would, of course, be the most numerous - female M.P.'s were created! I have often, in my school days, pitied poor Jupiter with two such vixens as Minerva and Juno to interfere in the councils of the gods. But imagine poor Mr. Speaker with two hundred Junos on either side of him! Scenes such as the following could be easily supposed:

MRS. FRUMP, a leading member of the opposition, *loquitur*. The hon. member is a nasty thing, and the meanness of her politics is almost as stingy as her hospitality. Her cook told my maid -

THE SPEAKER: I hope the hon. member will keep to the question before the House.

MRS. FRUMP: Such impudence! Question indeed! Well, I really couldn't support any measure proposed by a hon. member who wears such dowdy bonnets; and besides, she didn't invite us to her last party. (Derisive cheers from the hon. member attacked.) Not that I would have gone (with a hysterical giggle), for the greengrocer who was hired to wait -

THE SPEAKER: I must really call the hon. member to order. The subject before the House is 'Metropolitan Sewage,' and not parties and greengrocers.

MRS. FRUMP: I consider your remarks most insulting, sir. You shall hear from Mr. Frump in the morning, sir. I shall talk as I please, and about what I please; and her bonnets *are* dowdy, and she *is* a mean old creature, and *none* of her hair is her own - (order, order). Her maid told mine (opposition cheers), and my maid told me that her maid told her - I mean that the hon. member told her maid – only I'm flurried, I could put it plainer – that I was an ugly old thing, and that – that – my – teeth – were – not – my – (the hon. member here broke down, and was led out by a gentlemanly usher, weeping hysterically, amid a perfect forest of opposition smelling-bottles and handkerchiefs).

'DORA FALCONER'
(LOUISA LAWSON)
The Strike Question

10 000 WIVES TO BE CALLED OUT!!
MASS MEETING OF THE AMALGAMATED WIVES' ASSOCIATION
DEMANDS OF THE WOMEN!!
DOMESTIC LIFE PARALYSED!!

What would you say if you saw these headlines in your morning
paper? Yet why should you not see them? Wives suffer from long
hours of work, low wages, lack of rest, and oppression, and wom-
en are citizens entitled to just such rights and privileges [as] are
claimed by men, among these privileges being the right to cease
work, and to make terms for the betterment of their condition.

Working-men strike for higher wages, shorter hours, 'smoke
ohs,' or in defence of one of their number unjustly or despotically
treated, but though sensitive as to their own rights does it ever
occur to them to think of the women? Is there any one member
of all the affiliated Trades who has reflected that there is another
class more in need of union and of defensive leagues than he and
his fellows. Never! The social constitution may be turned upside
down and stood on its head so to speak, when men's demands
require hearing, but no one thinks of the women. Thousands of
pounds are spent on organisation, circulating newspapers, bands,
processions and free meals, and on the other side thousands on
special services of constables and military, while the grievances
of the men are being put to the test, but not a soul asks 'Have
the women any claims?'

In point of fact even working men themselves stand in the
position of employers, because just as under the wealthy there
is the less powerful class of labour, so, subject to the social
predominance of men, there are the women, weak, unorganised,
and isolated.

Does a man concede to his employee-wife, defined hours of rest,
fair pay, just and considerate treatment? The wife's hours of work
have no limit. All day the house and at night the children. There
is no Woman's Eight Hour Demonstration, though we can make

191

a public holiday because the men have won this right. A wife has no time to think of her own life and development, she has no money to spend, it is 'her husband's money,' the complete right to her own children is not yet legally hers, and she is not even in independent possession of her own body.

Surely it must be admitted that she needs the protection of a Union as much as a working man.

What is a wife's pay? It is certainly what no Union would allow any member to accept from an employer. She did not marry for pay, you may urge. True, but her work is worth as much as the man's. He married her to share equally in his disasters as in his successes, and if she has to suffer with him in troubled times, surely she has a right to share equally when finances are sound. 'She gets food, lodging, and clothes?' Yes, but who else could be hired day and night for a lifetime on those terms.

What of the treatment? Some are happy. Yes, and others bear a petty despotism, rough handling, rough language, selfish indifference, overwork. There are many of these. They endure far more than any man would tolerate from any master. Yet at first it seemed strange to talk of a Woman's Union and a strike of wives.

If men demanding rights and liberties would grant the same to their wives, and demand as much for all women, we might begin to flatter ourselves on our civilization, but this men do not do, and as for women they have no unions, no organisers, no speakers, no meeting halls, and no newspapers to represent their claims publicly and justly. Serious writers in newspapers do not touch woman's questions; such topics are left to the comic man, yet the wrongs of women are real and crying out for remedy.

Do not lay the flattering unction to your soul that a woman's excited imagination has invented woman's wrongs. Do not fancy that such wrongs are slight and tolerable because they are not known to bachelor clerks, nor quoted in newspapers, nor talked of in commercial circles; these things are to be learned by following men when work is over, to the secrecy of 'homes,' where sheltered in the privacy of an Englishman's castle, selfishness can be indulged, bitterness spoken, meanness practised. Men's wrongs are vented by public speakers in the Domain, women's wrongs are endured in the abominable seclusion of separate 'homes.' This may sound extreme but if you have ever seen a beaten woman, if you have seen a woman exhausted by house-work, if you have seen one broken down by perpetual suppression, or if you have ever talked with a doctor about his women patients, you may understand in what manner the great Strike Question presents itself to a woman.

'DORA FALCONER'
(LOUISA LAWSON)
The Divorce Extension Bill or,
The Drunkard's Wife

The fate of the Victorian divorce extension bill is a source of keen anxiety to many a miserable wife who has the misfortune to be linked for life to a drunkard.

In the helpless innocence of girlhood, she, in good faith, believing her lover all that he led her to think him, trustingly said 'I will,' and for better or worse, by this she must abide. No matter that he lied and deceived her knowingly. There is no law to punish a man for deceiving his wife. He may do violence to the best feelings of her nature; outrage the holiest emotions of her heart, and there is none to condemn. If he defrauds his fellow man of a shilling the law will deal with him. If he robs his wife by brutal deceit of all faith in mankind, health, peace, happiness, and of her life by the slow torture of a breaking heart – what of it? All he has to do is to bury her and seek another victim in another woman who believes him. All the consolation the wife of such a ghoul could reasonably expect from the world is 'Why did you marry him?' About as reasonable a question as asking a condemned criminal awaiting his execution why he committed the act that brought him there. What availeth her to say 'I was young, ignorant, inexperienced in the ways of the world; I believed and I loved him; he vowed that I should not want; he loved me and would love me for ever: all these promises he has broken. I have kept mine. He will not support me: he drinks and is cruel to me.' And the world's answer is: 'As you have made your bed so you must lie on it.' A wife's heart must be the tomb of her husband's faults. Verily, a girl must be as wise as a serpent and as harmless as a dove: she must have trusting innocence, implicit faith, loving devotion, and every soft and womanly attribute, and at the same time be an expert in physiognomy, phrenology and mind-reading, and a veritable woman of the world into the bargain, to ensure herself against matrimonial disaster. With all due reverence for the sanctity of marriage, can there be anything sacred in the bond which binds a good woman to a sot, felon, or brute?

Of the three the first is the worst, the felon disgraces her, the brute bruises her flesh, and perhaps breaks her bones, but the sot makes her perpetuate his ignoble race. What sober, strong, cleanly man would submit to share his bed with another in the worst stage of drunkenness? But the confirmed sot, if he possesses enough command of his tottering limbs to bring him to his lawful wife's chamber, may then collapse in abandoned beastliness upon the floor or conjugal couch if he reaches it, and proceed to make night hideous for her. A nerve of iron truly, must be possessed by frail women, who are expected to endure nightly this horrid ordeal, and put a cheerful face upon it in the morning, well knowing that this is her fate so long as her power of endurance holds out. How often does the patient wife quietly steal from the chamber of horrors to seek shelter by the bed of her sleeping children, content if but allowed to sit in peace until day brings temporary respite. What patience! what forgiveness must these martyrs possess. To what extent can our good Queen realise the position of these long-suffering women?

BARBARA BAYNTON
Day-birth

Pain-girt she stood and cried aloud –
  I heard the sea.
In agony her strong head bowed –
  Dew sprinkled me.
Night's red lips turned to east from west,
Her right hand drew them to her breast,
Her fair full breast – again the dew:
  (I thought of you).
She sighed content – I heard the breeze,
  Its rustling banners all unfurled.
  Below a wanderer's smoke upcurled
And amorous sought the quivering trees.
She smiled, Morn-Mother, victory won,
And oped her eyes – I saw the Sun.

To-morrow

    To-morrow?
Nay, I shall not fear – this is to-night –
  Nor sorrow.
Beside thee kneels thy son – first mine, then thine.
Amid the gloom thy face gleams white,
    Nor need we light
If thou but ope thine eyes – so shall mine shine.
Thy lips shew not where, moaning, mine have pressed.
The arms that folded lie upon thy breast
Stretch forth, Beloved! for thou are not dead . . .
Yet still, so still! Thy restless head
Furrowed the pillow ere but one hour sped.
Beloved! ever didst thou love the night . . .
Sleep on! I will not sorrow –
This is to-night – nor fear to-morrow.

'WAIF WANDER' (MARY FORTUNE)
The Spider and the Fly

'WANTED, HOUSEKEEPER: Position of trust.'

That's the advertisement that set so many female hearts in a flutter in and around Melbourne; and as I was very much personally interested in a mythical 'place of trust', I myself was among the number of 'ladies' who donned their best bibs and tuckers, and repaired to the place appointed, at or before the time appointed.

It is astonishing what different ideas of full dress are possessed by different women; and if you want an illustration of the fact, I could not recommend you to a better observatory than one of the said places of appointment. And while upon the subject, I should like to draw your attention to the number of advertisements you will meet with in *the* daily, making some hotel or other the place of rendezvous.

I have lately had some little experience in, and opportunity of, taking notes upon the way these affairs are generally conducted, and my conclusion is, that no hotel whatever, be it as respectable as it may, shall ever be honoured by the light of my countenance in search of a place of trust. I may be mistaken, as you know we are all liable to be, but I am more than suspicious that a good many of these advertisements are simply hoaxes.

It is easy for any person at all conversant with one of the many varieties of fast human nature masculine, to imagine the delightful 'fun' it must be to see forty or fifty gullible women flocking to their call, with faces more or less anxious, and with every pin in their several attires arranged to make a favourable impression upon the enviable 'gentleman'. I could have guessed all that without having seen the advertiser I am going to tell you of, so thoroughly enjoying himself and his levee.

I said forty or fifty, did I not? Well, that was about the number that, as the hour of two p.m. approached, managed to locate themselves in and around the side door of one of the first hotels in Melbourne. I have no doubt that many of the females felt as awkward as I myself did at applying in such a place, and would not have showed face near it had it not been well-known as a first-class hotel, and a noted rendezvous for country gentlemen.

Well, as I arranged my bonnet-ties, and put upon myself generally as attractive an air as I could muster, I entered the side passage, to find myself in the company of seven or eight females, every separate one of whom seemed as thoroughly uncomfortable as any woman could be. Some of them were making inquiries through a window into the hall of a barmaid, who in vain attempted to keep her countenance, and whose very face was quite a sufficient declaration that she at least considered the whole thing a most absurd farce.

Well, having received a reply from the said barmaid, the several applicants looked around for some place in which to dispose themselves until their turn came to be ushered into the presence of the great autocrat of their fates. There was little choice. On one side was a private sitting-room, already crammed with 'ladies' possessed of sufficient impertinence to intrude there. On the other, a door opening into the bar itself, on the seats of which were disposed some half score or so of persons very available for places or positions of trust.

Some vacillated between the bar and the sitting-room, afraid to encounter the number of excited persons who occupied the latter, each jealous and envious of the other, and disinclined to make so little of themselves as to seat themselves in the public bar. Indeed, there were 'ladies' who seemed to take it as a personal insult that the bar door had been left open for their accommodation, and turned up their nose visibly at those who availed themselves of it. I observed that every one of these ladies had furiously red faces, and about half a stone or so of mock jewellery on their persons.

I did not feel inclined to face the ladies in the parlour, and I could not hang about the doorway in the public streets. Certainly I might have followed the example of some confused and forward applicants, who pushed open a glass door leading into the more private portion of the hotel, and there stood congratulating themselves, no doubt, upon the more comfortable position they had obtained.

But I didn't – I had a fancy for seeing all that was to be seen, you see, and I walked straight into the bar. Once there, I seated myself between a gentle-looking woman in deep but rusty mourning with a little pale-faced girl on her knee, and a brazen-faced lady with a 'diadem' bonnet, three quarters high, upon her head. And then I began to enjoy myself thoroughly in my own especial way. Opposite to me was the bar, and inside the counter the barmaid; the latter was affecting to arrange her glasses, etc., but her risible faculties were not under the strongest control, and sometimes overcame her altogether.

And no wonder. If you had been there you would have laughed too; that is to say, if you had not been one of the 'unco guid' folk of poor Burns. I was fortunate in having the advantage of the poor girl, seeing that I could observe every movement of the ladies in the mirror behind her, without being observed; while she was obliged to face the crowd, and answer the hundred and one questions put to her by fresh arrivals.

Behind the bar went one applicant after another, and returned, some looking particularly sheepish, and some bold enough to terrify a troop of dragoons. It was evident that the sanctum of the wonderful and interesting gentleman who required the person of respectability for a position of 'trust' was somewhere inside in a corner; and do you know that for the life of me I could not help thinking of that favourably known composition, 'Will you walk into my parlour? said the Spider to the Fly.'

And such a great choice of flies had that hidden spider, that I began to have a decided curiosity to see him. I wondered if he was a huge, bloated spider, with small eyes and a grin, or a slender-limbed, black, sharp chap, that seemed on all sides at once, and with long crawling limbs, that were ready to grab any fly foolish enough to put herself within his clutches. And there was such a choice of flies, too, that I can fancy the spider, of whatever stamp he might be, aggravated to death that he could not grab them all at one haul.

There was a buzzing, restless mosquito, and the ubiquitous house-fly, of changeful hue and indomitable perseverance in attack. There was the ugly and disgusting big brown blow-fly, and the active and detestable, yet seemingly pretty bluebottle. There was the miserable little midge, and the silly moth, all gathering at the invitation of Mr Spider.

And he was not long invisible to me, seated in the bar parlour in a charming state of excitement, and licking his lips in a delightful state of anticipation, I could well imagine. Charming old Spider! Little he thought how open to inspection was every one of his movements, through the unpoliteness of an angry fly (of the bluebottle species), to whom his highness would not extend the top of his sceptre.

This fly was of ample proportions, and had a face of the hue of port wine stains. A number of tremulous red flowers, a profusion of metallic green silk, and blond, and beads, was raised above a quantity of shining black bepuffed hair, in the form of a bonnet wondrous to behold. A tight jacket of dark blue velvet stuck to her stout figure; and her skirt was a changeable silk, of chameleon hues. A chain - a watch - a brooch - a locket - rings upon an ungloved, puddingy hand, and *voilà!* the most dashing looking bluebottle fly you can imagine!

'You a gentleman!' she cried, bursting from the sanctum, and dashing the intervening door open against the wall. 'A good lambing is what the likes of you wants. Gentleman indeed! Advertises for respectable ladies, and then insults 'em.'

'My good woman,' remonstrated the invisible Spider, in a deprecatory tone of voice, which had no chance amid the thunder of indignation launched at him by the parting lady.

'A position of trust, indeed. Do I look like a person to do your dirty cooking and washing, and whatnot? Faugh!' And, amid an indignant rustling of silks and shaking of agitated red roses, evanished that disappointed fly, leaving the door wide open behind her.

Now I could well understand why the occupant of the bar parlour left the door open. To close it, he should have been obliged to expose himself to the eager gaze of many dozens of eyes – eyes now in a state of snapping curiosity as to the occasion of the departed female's anger.

So the door remained open, and the Spider behind it, in his corner, exposed to my delighted watch, reflected in the mirror opposite the door of his den.

There he sat, I say, and in a state of unpleasant excitement, as recipient of the lady's abuse. He *was* one of the bloated, cunning-looking spiders, with small green eyes; and he had grey bristly hair, that now stood up from his low forehead, most likely where he had desperately run his fingers through it at the moment of his late attack.

He grinned, and he shuffled in his chair, and he listened; and then he tapped at the bar partition, a signal that seemed understood by the barmaid, who had not yet recovered her gravity, which had been completely upset by the bluebottle's exit.

'You can go in now,' she at length managed to articulate, indicating at the same time one of the females in the bar.

'That she won't!' exclaimed a prim, conceited-looking woman, attired in a stuff gown, a black shawl, and an old straw bonnet. 'I've been here full an hour before her, and it's my turn, whether you like it or no,' and, suiting the action to the word, the dame pushed her way into the autocrat's den.

But she was a very unattractive fly, that elderly person with the old bonnet and the wrinkled face. The Spider required but a single glance to convince him that his web would be wasted in catching a 'lady' so unsuited for a 'position of trust'.

'I have engaged a person, ma'am,' he said, with a stiff nod at the woman, as she put her screwed-up nose around the door.

'Oh!' she said, with an indescribable toss of the head, as she emerged with a vinegar visage, 'He's engaged, ye needn't wait any longer.' And she too went out of the door, shaking, I have no moral doubt, the imaginary dust from her shuffling feet at its threshold.

At this instant a loud rapping from inside assured the barmaid that our gentleman required her instant attendance. From my post I could see that his highness was exceedingly irate, and soundly rated the barmaid for something or other. When she emerged, too, she shut the door, and I think I never saw so great a want of tact as that girl displayed in a position that she doubtless felt exceedingly awkward.

'Has the gentleman engaged?' – 'I never heard the like! Before he saw half the applications!' – 'He had no right to do it!' – etc., etc., – were some of the questions and observations with which she was assailed.

The girl looked hither and thither, and feigned to perform some extraordinary feat under the counter, casting all the time furtive looks from one to the other of the excited applicants. It amused me excessively to observe the way in which the poor girl was obliged to twist and turn her mouth to prevent an open exhibition of her merriment; while her face was perfectly scarlet from suppressed laughter.

At this awkward juncture arose a young woman, attired cheaply in an extravagantly fashionable style. I need not describe her – you may see her type every day on the street, and the impudent stare and conceited air are not attractive. She was one of that class of foolish young ladies who are happy in piling pads and bows of ribbon on their heads, and in trailing a yard of cheap material after them in the dirt, and in walking upon boots two sizes too small for them, and upon heels less comfortable than stilts. No need to describe her, is there? You know, by sight only, I hope, a round hundred of them.

Influenced by her movement, doubtless, stepped also forward an old frowsy woman of about fifty years, determined, as it would appear, not to lose any chance that might present itself of admission to *the* presence.

'I suppose I can go in?' she did not question, as she attempted to push aside the barmaid, and enter; while the fashionable 'young lady' stared at her insolent rival as if she would wither her with a look.

Again came that rap at the partition, and the poor go-between's face grew redder than ever.

'The gentleman is engaged, ma'am,' she half whispered to the frowsy woman, 'and it's no use for you to see him. He's engaged a person already.'

And she winked – yes, winked visibly with her left eye at the 'young lady'.

Another 'Oh!' from Mrs Frowsy, and out also went she, muttering as she went.

'Isn't it true that he is suited, then?' asked the smiling fashionable of the also smiling attendant of the bar and the Spider.

'Oh, he only says that to some he doesn't like the appearance of,' replied the maid. 'You can go in.'

And in swept the delighted young lady.

Now came the chief fun of the whole business. In the front door of the bar crept the most ludicrous figure you can well imagine in search of a 'position of trust'. I do not generally find much difficulty in describing to you such characters as make a forcible impression upon myself, but in this instance I confess to a fear of failure, so immeasurably beyond 'all my fancy painted her' was this old lady's absurdity of appearance, and conceit of manner.

She was tall and thin, and attired in the sparsest manner. From her appearance, it was to be judged that her dress consisted totally of the scrap of dirty black skirt and voluminous long cloak, that she drew tightly about her shoulders, always excepting the filthy muslin cap and old greasy, black*ish* bonnet, that but partially covered it.

Every line in her face had a downward tendency. From the sharp nose on her ash-coloured face, to the wrinkles at the corners of her thin mouth – even her flabby cheeks, or rather what remained of them, dropped visibly, as in a vain search to discover their proper level. But, in spite of all this, there was an impudence and a temper that asserted itself in the elevation of her sharp chin, and the twist of the most flexible nose I ever beheld in my life.

As I have said, she drew the voluminous but thin cloak tightly around her shoulders, and she drew it with both hands under her chin. That is to say, that with both hands concealed under the cloak, she clasped it across her flat chest, so that nothing remained exposed to view of her skinny person, save the ash-coloured face, and the narrow angular outline revealed by the tight black covering.

She moved toward the bar in such a noiseless manner, and with such suspicious looks at the 'ladies' in the place, that one might have come to the conclusion she had come on some errand in which she feared the intervention of the police; and as she curled up her nose, firstly at one, and secondly at another, and finally at myself, in proper person, it was but too evident that she looked down upon us separately and collectively with the most perfect contempt.

After disposing of us to her satisfaction she leaned her old, wretched visage across the counter, and accosted the retreating barmaid in a stage whisper.

'What sort of woman does he want, my dear?'

'I don't know, indeed; he's inside with one now,' was the reply, as the speaker seized her apron and hid her face from the old hag.

It was impossible to stand it any longer – the old creature was the last straw on the risible faculties of the women, who nearly choked in an attempt at coughing to hide a laugh, in which every one of the applicants joined as silently as they could.

'Housekeeper, eh?' in another stage whisper.

The speechless girl nodded again.

'Oh – um!' and the old face was turned *at* us over her shoulder, as she once more examined us with a grin of ineffable disgust. 'Oh, I know what he wants! An' if I'd a known afore I cum here, you wouldn't a seen *me* wid the likes!'

And the old creature drew her drapery still more tightly around her, to avoid contact with the 'ladies', who could not help laughing aloud as she made her stately exit.

And in a few minutes forth came the 'fashionable young lady', all smiles and pride, and announced to the envying applicants who waited 'at the gate' that she had been engaged by the 'gentleman'. There is no knowing what might have been the symptoms of some of the irate and disappointed women in the bar; for sundry tossing heads and mutterings, such as, 'A person of trust indeed!' 'Pretty person for a position of trust!' were beginning to be seen and heard, when to the rescue pops in at the door the old head of the skinny old woman.

'I told ye so!' she nodded and grinned at the barmaid. 'Ha, ha! I knew what he wanted – he, he! ho, ho!' and she was gone.

Retired we all discomfited. Retired the poor widow and her pale-faced child. What impudence *she* had to suppose that one without youth, and with sense, would be eligible for a position of trust under a bloated old Spider! Retired the barmaid, to laugh heartily behind the scenes, and to repeat the whole story to the hero of the hour, who called for a glass of brandy, and chucklingly began to consider if the silly fly, who had engaged with him would require a very intricate web to entrap her.

> Will you walk into my parlour? said the Spider to the Fly,
> 'Tis the prettiest little parlour that ever you did spy;
> The way into my parlour is up a winding stair,
> And I've many pretty things to show you there.

But I shall ever hereafter, in connection with a 'position of trust', remember the miserable old skinny face that chuckled through the doorway, and said,

'I told you so! Ha, ha! he, he!'

ADA CAMBRIDGE
Influence

As in the mists of embryonic night,
  Out of the deep and dark obscurities
  Of Nature's womb, the little life-germs rise,
Pushing by instinct upward to the light;
As, when the first ray dawns on waking sight,
  They leap to liberty, and recognize
  The golden sunshine and the morning skies
Their own inheritance by inborn right; –

So do our brooding thoughts and deep desires
  Grow in our souls, we know not how or why;
   Grope for we know not what, all blind and dumb.
So, when the time is ripe, and one aspires
  To free his thought in speech, ours hear the cry,
   And to full birth and instant knowledge come.

Vows

What worth are promises? We can pretend
  To constant passion and a life-long trust,
  As to all decorous virtues, if we must;
But you and I will speak the truth, my friend.
And can we say what fickle fate will send
  To lift us up or grind us into dust? –
  What bloom of growth or waste of moth and rust
Shall be our portion ere the final end?

No laws, no oaths can free-born souls confine.
  When vows have force, the treasured thing whereon
They stamped their pledge is neither yours nor mine;
  Wishing to go, it is already gone.
When faith and love needs bolts upon the door,
Then faith is faith and love is love no more.

Unstrung

My skies were blue, and my sun was bright,
And, with fingers tender and strong and light,
He woke up the music that slept before –
Echoing, echoing evermore!

By-and-by, my skies grew grey; –
No master-touch on the harp-strings lay, –
Dead silence cradled the notes divine:
His soul had wander'd away from mine.

Idly, o'er strange harps swept his hand,
Seeking for music more wild and grand.
He wearied at last of his fruitless quest,
And he came again to my harp for rest.

But the dust lay thick on the golden wires,
And they could not thrill to the old desires.
The chords, so broken and jarred with pain,
Could never be tender and sweet again.

ETHEL MILLS
A Box of Dead Roses

The old lady was a most amusing creature, and she had a past which was a record amongst pasts. Only that she was rich enough to buy the whole district, its 'society' would have 'cut' her long ago; as it was, people only talk about her with meaning looks and whispered condemnation. At least, the generation to which she belonged did that; the younger one only looked and wondered. Bent with rheumatism, bushy-browed, fierce-eyed and hard-featured – there remained no trace of the beauty and charm which (so report said) had sent more than one good man to the devil.

On sunny days she would have her chair moved on to the wide, vine-sheltered verandah. She liked to see what was going on; and she said that in Australia most things happened on verandahs. This particular one had been planned and built in early pioneering days, and had, no doubt, seen many ups and downs of varied incident.

One could listen to her by the hour when she was in the vein for remembering pages from her own life or from other lawless lives of early days, when all country west of the station was unknown Australia. Like most old people, she was given to repetition, but she told me a story once which neither I nor anyone else could ever induce her to tell again.

It was about a young wife – the most innocent of brides, who thought the world of her husband, and had no wish or look for other men. Yet the house was full of other men in those days, and they all gave thoughts or looks, more or less, to the prettiest woman in the district. Every evening she used to stand at her bedroom door, looking along the verandah, until she saw her husband returning from his work; and every evening he brought her a rose from the big bush by the steps. That was during the first months of her marriage. Next year, the rose-bush bore as abundantly as ever, but the man often forgot to pick a flower for her; and, after a time, he forgot altogether.

The young wife was painfully ideal and long-suffering, and never gave him a word of reproach; she was still so much in love with him that she was shy, and blushed like a girl when he came near her unexpectedly. 'Fancy: after two years of married life!' And the old lady smiled wickedly, and continued:

'She was tired one night, and went to bed early, leaving her husband smoking and reading in the dining-room; but it was so hot that she presently got up, threw on a gown, and strolled along the verandah in the shadow for a breath of cool air. The sultriness of the air brought out the strongest scent of the moonflowers. Just there, at the corner near the rose-bush, she saw her husband with his arms round a woman, kissing her lips over and over again – they were full, very red lips, such as men like to kiss.

'The woman was one of the housemaids – the soft-voiced, self-contained, velvet-footed one who usually brought in the tray for supper, and whose eyes never left the floor as she did so – a girl who seemed to have no thought beyond her duties.

'The wife heard enough to show her that the woman had thoughts for many things besides – enough to tell her that those kisses were not the first by any means; that the man's life had been a long lie, except, perhaps, during the very early days of marriage. She liked to think that he was all hers then. A delusion also, possibly; but a harmless one.

'As it was, she stole off to bed without saying a word. I call that a "verandah tragedy," my dear; because her whole nature changed in a few moments. Not that there was much to notice one way or the other at first – except that she said she could not bear the scent of the moonflowers, and had the creeper taken up at the roots. She did not even send away the housemaid. Why should she? But things were a great deal more pleasant for the "other men" afterwards – a great deal, my dear! She used to sing and play to them, and dance and flirt with them, and fill the house with visitors, and so on – in fact, she was a beauty, and had only just awakened to a knowledge of her power. You see, the station and money belonged to her; so she was freer than most wives.

'There was the baby, of course – a lovely, soft-faced little thing that used to take its midday sleep in a string hammock, swung up there by the trellis. She was fond of the child; yet, when it died and was buried by the lagoon in the garden, she used to sit dry-eyed, looking at the hammock that swung loosely in every breeze without its accustomed burden. She even said she was not sorry; because the boy might have grown up to break some woman's heart, and the world was well rid of the breed. Perhaps it was best so; though – looking at the other side of the question – he might have lived to blush for his mother.

'One day her husband was brought in, dead – kicked by the horse he was trying to catch in the yard. They carried him straight up the verandah to the big spare-room, and the blood was dripping, dripping all the way.

'She was a tidy, methodical woman always, and she sent for the housemaid – the velvet-footed one – and bade her wash the boards. The girl had a wonderful power of self-command usually, yet, at sight of that blood, she shivered and trembled like one with the palsy. Sentimental people said the wife was perfectly inhuman to think of the state of her verandah at such a time – and, of course, a kind friend told her. She laughed as she said, 'No! I am not heart-broken. I went through that experience two years ago.'

'Well, my dear' (and the old lady's voice sounded a little tired), 'she lived a long, long life, and rather a varied and interesting one, from an outsider's point of view, at any rate. I often sit and think of her and of many things that happened on this old verandah, but of late years I forget a great deal. I like best to remember the days when the young wife used to stand listening, listening for the husband's step – the sweetest music in the world to her.

'No doubt she was an arrant little fool and bored him to death. I think, now, that he was no worse than the majority of men: a clever, interesting woman could have managed him. She became all that afterwards – for other men; but, as I said before, she was a totally different woman. Live every inch of your life, my dear,' finished the old lady, impressively. 'One life, one love! – the idea is perfectly absurd.'

Two years later I saw the old lady again – feebler, worn in body and mind. She still sat in sunny weather on the verandah, but now she always had a little cardboard box on her lap, caressing it with her withered fingers.

'Look, my dear!' she said; 'this box is full of dead rose-leaves – they all came off that bush by the corner, years ago. Young people are *so* careless and forgetful. I may die at any moment, and unless I had it with me they would never remember to bury it in my grave. They are the dearest things I possess; the reason why they are so dear I shall carry a secret to my grave also.'

The old lady had forgotten that she had ever told me a story with roses in it.

ADA CAMBRIDGE
Reaction

Let us, dear friend, in mutual strength arise
   Against our tyrant Custom, and demand
   Free souls and bodies at our own command.
Let us defy the vulgar world's surprise,
Scorn brute convention and soft compromise,
   And, bold in proud revolt, and hand in hand,
   Cast in our lot and take our fearless stand
With the unsafe, improper, and unwise.

Let us abjure the comfortable creeds
   Approved by prudent minds, and revel free
In foolish thoughts and inexpedient deeds; –
   For thus alone can life for you and me
Out of this suffocating sloth revive,
And our small spark of good be kept alive.

An Answer

Thy love I am. Thy wife I cannot be,
   To wear the yoke of servitude – to take
   Strange, unknown fetters that I cannot break
On soul and flesh that should be mine, and free.
Better the woman's old disgrace for me
   Than this old sin – this deep and dire mistake;
   Better for truth and honour and thy sake –
For the pure faith I give and take from thee.

I know thy love, and love thee all I can –
   I fain would love thee only till I die;
But I may some day love a better man,
   And thou may'st find a fitter mate than I;
Some want, some chill, may steal 'twixt heart and heart.
And then we must be free to kiss and part.

ROSA PRAED
from *The Bond of Wedlock, ch. vi, 'A Foul Stroke'*

The rattling of the cab drowned Harvey Lomax's complaints as they drove back to Elizabeth Street. Ariana leaned forward as far away from her husband as possible. She thought of Sir Leopold going homeward in his luxurious brougham. She thought of his impassioned words, of all the pleasant and refined things which were a part of his life, of the possessions which he would so gladly share with her, of the hideous, horrible contrast between what was and what might have been.

The house was in darkness save for a lamp glimmering in the dining-room, as, after an angry colloquy with the cabman, Mr. Lomax let himself and his wife in. He went straight to the stuffy dining-room, where some refreshments were laid, and where a letter was placed on the table, so that it might be seen at once. He poured himself out a glass of brandy and water, and drank it off before he glanced at the superscription of the letter, and then, after he had read it, he fortified himself against its evil contents by some more brandy.

'By God!' he ejaculated, 'it's from Slade. He won't do anything about that bill; it falls due to-morrow. There will be the most infernal row with the partners, and a regular smash up if it's presented.'

Ariana stood still and helpless, with her candle in her hand.

Harvey paced the room muttering curses, and growing every moment more excited.

'How could I have been such a fool?' he cried, 'as to let things muddle themselves into this condition? I can't face the partners. It's ruin for me. Do you hear, Ariana? Have you nothing to say? Do you think you can help matters by standing stock-staring there?'

'I am very sorry,' she said feebly.

'You may well be sorry. You'll be sorrier still before we've done. You had better bestir yourself, and think of a way out of the mess. I owe it all partly to your extravagance – yours and your swindling father's. It's you that have brought me to this.'

'Oh! that is unjust,' exclaimed Ariana.

'I tell you the truth. You have never done a hand's turn to help me. It was the worst day in my life, the day I married you. Not only for the money part of it. Your airs and your temper, and your infernal coldness – it all wakes the devil in me. Did you ever in your life give me a kiss of your own accord, or show me that you looked upon me as anything but a bit of dirt? Your ingratitude sickens me. You make me hate coming inside my doors, for I know you'd rather that I was outside them.'

'Have you ever tried to win my affection?' she exclaimed, stung by his reproaches. 'Have you ever given me anything but coarse treatment and harsh words? Is it not your own doing that I am glad when you leave the house and sorry when you enter it?'

'You own it, then? You can tell me so to my face?'

'Why not? I am tired of deceit and sham. We had better have an understanding, and each go our own way. But you are not in a state to come to a clear understanding to-night,' she added, with unconcealed contempt. 'You had better go to bed, and leave business till tomorrow.'

The speech was an injudicious one.

'What do you mean? Do you mean that I am drunk? If you think I'm going to be made a fool of, you are very much mistaken. You don't think me good enough to talk to, do you?'

'I prefer talking to people who are more courteous to me,' said Ariana. 'Goodnight.'

'No, you are not going yet; you needn't put on airs, they won't do with me. They won't save us from being ruined. You think that you have got D'Acosta at your feet, and that you can defy me. You know very well that I can put a stop to that sentimental game if I choose, and by the Lord I will, too, unless your fine friends make it worth my while to let them hang on here. I'll forbid D'Acosta the house if he won't make himself pleasant and useful to me. What shall you say to that? Hot-house flowers and partridges won't pay my debts, and if it's an amusement to you to philander with him, it's none to me.'

'Oh, I know you well enough,' he went on after a pause, during which Ariana had remained silent, and he had made several strides up and down the room; 'there's no need to do outraged virtue. Is it any outrage on virtue to ask a trifling loan of a friend? If it is, then, by Jove, your father has outraged his virtue pretty often. No one has such good reasons as I have for knowing that you are the coldest and most selfish-hearted woman that ever existed. It isn't in you to go over the border; I'm not afraid of that. I'm not afraid that you'll bring disgrace on your child in that way.'

'No,' said Ariana, in a strange, hard tone, and with a face set like marble, 'you need not be afraid of that.'

'I'll have no man coming to my house and pretending honest and disinterested friendship who doesn't choose to act the friend to me and help to pull me out of a fix. If D'Acosta is your friend and my friend, we need have no scruple in asking him for the loan of a thousand or so, to get us out of our difficulties.'

Ariana stood perfectly rigid and silent.

'Well, have you nothing to say?'

'I have already said that I would rather starve than take money from Sir Leopold, as a loan or as a gift. It is the same thing.'

'You meant that, did you?'

He advanced threateningly to her.

'I meant it so thoroughly that, this very afternoon, when he offered me a loan I refused it - in those very words.'

'You did, did you? By God! I'll punish you for this!'

He came close to her. For a moment she seemed to see only the flash of fury from his reddened eyes. His heavy arm was raised and fell in a cruel blow - once, twice, thrice, upon her shoulder and half-bared neck. He was blind with drink and with passion, and scarcely realised what he was doing. Her unflinching courage maddened him. She uttered no sound; her large, clear eyes met his steadily; she did not attempt to evade the blow. Her face was as though it had been cut out of stone; every drop of blood seemed to have gone out of it. She staggered beneath the weight of his clenched hand, but reared herself again and stood erect. The pain made her dizzy; for a few moments everything was dark.

There was a silence between them - a strange tragic silence. The shock of what he had done, and the look in her eyes, sobered Harvey.

'Damn you!' he said. 'Go away from me; I can't answer for myself. If I've hurt you, it's your own fault.'

She made no answer, but went out of the room and dragged herself upstairs. When she reached her own room she bolted the door and in a dazed way sat down on a couch at the foot of the bed. She sat for several hours in complete darkness. She heard her husband go into his room, and knew that he would soon fall into a heavy slumber. But she, herself, sat on till dawn broke. She was as one stunned. When the grey light crept in through the curtains, she roused herself, and then she realised that she was bruised and aching, and that her left arm and shoulder were so swollen as to make it impossible for her to remove her dress without cutting the sleeve. She did this with a little difficulty. She scarcely dared look at the red angry flesh. A passion of wrath and humiliation and disgust came over her, but she shed no tears; she felt completely hardened. She crept into bed presently, and, by-and bye, fell into a stupefied slumber.

She was awakened late in the morning by Tottie's voice and loud rapping. The child was sent away, and she rose and dressed. Her arm was very painful, so painful that she could scarcely lift it, and the nurse, who came to do her hair, exclaimed in horror at the great bruise which could not be concealed: 'What had Madame done? – There must have been an accident, doubtless coming from the theatre? And Monsieur had roused no one! It was incredible! Should not a doctor be sent for?'

Ariana allowed her maid's ejaculations to flow unchecked, and neither confirmed nor contradicted her suppositions. What did it matter? She learned that Harvey had gone out, and had left a message that he would not be home till late. She put on a loose morning robe, and went slowly down to the drawing-room. She remembered that Sir Leopold had said that he was going to call. Well, let him come. She had a reckless disregard of what might be revealed to him. A gentleman was waiting for her, but it was her father, not Sir Leopold. Mr Vance saw, as she moved forward, that something was very much amiss.

'Nan, what is the matter?' he exclaimed.

'I am not very well,' she answered, in a mechanical manner. 'I have been hurt.'

'Hurt!' he repeated. 'How? Where? What has become of Harvey? If you are ill, why doesn't he get a doctor? He said nothing about it to me this morning.'

'You have seen him?'

'He roused me up at half-past nine, on his way to the City. He didn't get to the City; he acted on a suggestion of mine, instead. I think his mind is easier now; he was in a queer, excited state; he said he was in the deuce of a mess. Is this at the bottom of it all?'

She said nothing, but seated herself on the sofa, with her hands clasped in her lap and her dark eyes fixed straight before her. Her appearance, something tragic in her look, her strange apathy, frightened him.

'Nan, tell me what's the matter. You are not ill? It's something that has gone wrong with you. If it's about money, my dear, don't be unhappy; Sir Leopold has made it all right.'

'Sir Leopold!' she cried, with a despairing groan. 'Ah, it only wanted that! He could be so base! And you – you, father, what have you done?'

'The most natural thing in the world, Nan. Harvey came to me this morning and told me of the mess he was in. He asked me if I could help him – not much likelihood of that. He asked me if I could suggest any friend who would pull him out of the hole, and lend him two thou. on his note of hand. No good going to the Jews, you know; we've tried that game. I could only suggest one friend who I knew would cheerfully supply the stuff, and I named him. We went straight to Brook Street; it was the simplest transaction in the world.'

'He – you took the money!' Ariana covered her face with her hands and burst into a storm of sobs. They were the first tears she had shed. He tried to soothe her.

'Nan, don't, it goes to my heart. Nan, it's nothing, it's only what one friend might do for another any day; and to Sir Leopold D'Acosta, who is rolling in money, a thousand pounds is no more than a farthing to people like us. My dear girl, don't take it so seriously.' He laid his hand on her shoulder with an attempt at a caress; she winced and turned very white. He saw that she was in pain. 'Nan, what is the matter? How are you hurt? Good God! It can't be that he has dared to lift a hand against you? No, I must see. I'm your father, girl, and you are more to me than anything in the world. Nan . . .'

He broke short in a horrified cry, for he had unfastened the robe and raised the loose sleeve, and the great purple bruises on the delicate neck and shoulder were laid bare. It was a pitiable sight. The father, who, to do him justice, loved his daughter after his selfish fashion, felt it too deeply to storm or rave.

'He struck you last night? Tell me the truth, girl. Don't try to screen him – the villain! the brute!'

'He struck me; yes.'

'Was he drunk?'

'I believe he had been drinking. It was late at night, after the theatre.'

'That shouldn't have done the mischief. I know that Labarte's champagne never turned a gentleman into a beast. If Harvey would drink like a gentleman – but he *will* go in for brandy. What led to the row? I suppose it began about money?'

'He wanted me to get some money from Sir Leopold D'Acosta, and I angered him by saying that I had already refused to take it.'

'Ah!' Mr Vance uttered a low, prolonged ejaculation. He tenderly covered the bruised arm again, and sat silent for a minute, while he meditatively put his fingers together and performed his customary gesture, when in thought, of sawing the air. A new view of the situation had opened before him. 'I see, you had your own reasons, and very proper ones, for not wishing to be under any pecuniary obligation to Sir Leopold. I appreciate the delicacy of your conduct, Ariana, I had not clearly grasped the situation. Perhaps, for Harvey's sake, it was as well that I did not fully grasp it before our little transaction took place this morning.'

'Father,' exclaimed Ariana. 'If you had had any sympathy with my feelings, or any true regard for me, you would not have done what you did this morning. Why talk now of what you do not understand?'

'But I assure you that I do understand, Ariana, and I sympathise more deeply than I can express. My heart bleeds for you, my poor girl. You are placed in the most peculiar, the most trying, position. It is my duty, as your father, to alleviate it as far as lies in my power.'

'You have shamed and humiliated me,' she answered passionately – 'you and my husband. There is nothing more to be done or to be said. I made my lot, and I must endure it as best I can.'

'Something can be done,' said Mr Vance weakly. 'Something must be done. I will speak to Harvey. I cannot permit you to be so grossly ill-treated.'

'Do you think that if it were not for the child's sake I would remain another day under his roof?' said Ariana, the dark fire flashing from her moody eyes. 'You don't know the sort of feeling that a blow rouses in a woman. For Tottie's sake I must submit to be insulted – to be beaten. For Tottie's sake I must give up what I valued most, the friendship of a man who honoured me. I despised and disliked my husband before. I hate him now.'

'No, no, Nan, as a woman of the world you make a mistake. Never burn your ships, my love. I don't wonder at your indignation, but, my poor child, you will see when you think calmly over things, that giving up Sir Leopold will not make matters any better. I enter into your scruples. I am quite alive to your fear that this pecuniary obligation might colour your relations with Sir Leopold – might – in short, might give rise to misconstruction. It is your natural impulse, as a high-minded woman, to see no more of a man who you know has a strong affection for you. Your feelings in regard to Harvey's conduct, alas, is most natural and right. But we must take the world as we find it, Ariana. I speak as a man of the world to a woman who is no longer a child, and who is safe in the consciousness of her own rectitude. I speak as a father, Ariana.'

ADA CAMBRIDGE
The Future Verdict

How will our unborn children scoff at us
    In the good years to come –
    The happier years to come –
For that, like driven sheep, we yielded thus,
    Before the shearers dumb!

I know the words their wiser lips will say; –
    'These men had gained the light,
    These women knew the right;
They had their chance and let it slip away.
    They *did not* when they *might*.

'They were the first to hear the gospel preached,
    And to believe therein –
    Yet they remained in sin;
They saw the Promised Land they might have reached,
    And dared not enter in.

'They might have won their freedom, had they tried;
    No savage laws forbade –
    For them the way was made.
'They might have had the joys for which they cried;
    And yet they shrank, afraid.

'Afraid to face an honourable shame,
    The most they had to pay –
    Of what the world would say –
Not of the martyr's portion, rack and flame.
    Great God! what fools were they!'

And oh! could *we* look backward from those years
    When we have ceased to be,
    This wasted chance to see,
Should we not also cry, with bitter tears,
    'Alas! what fools were we!'

IV

THE QUEST FOR FULFILMENT

'AUSTRALIE' (EMILY MANNING)
The Emigrant's Plaint*

Song to the air of 'The Night Is Closing Around'

I'm far away from ye all, mother
   And the world is strange and new;
Not a well-known place, not one dear home-face!
   O'er the sea I weary for you.

The sky is sunny and bright, mother,
   For this Southern land is fair;
There is room for all, and no hunger is known,
   But little I reck or care.

The cold and want of the past, mother,
   Were easier far to bear
Than this aching want in my lonely heart,
   And this plenty with none to share!

Why did I leave my home, mother?
   I was wilful, and thoughtless, and wild –
I long'd to be free, a woman I'd be!
   Yet I weep as a motherless child.

I'm no one's daughter or pet, mother,
   But 'one of the emigrants' here.
I must do my duty, and work, without
   One friend to counsel or cheer.

O, how I long for a kiss, mother,
   Or a kind touch on my brow!
I wish you were here to scold me e'en, –
   It would seem like a blessing now!

----

* Suggested by the words of an emigrant as she lay sick in the Sydney
Infirmary.

The letters will soon be here, mother;
    How welcome each word will be!
Will you pluck a primrose sometimes, and send
    A bit of Old England to me?

Good-bye - so sorry I am, mother!
    As long as I e'er should live,
I would grieve ye no more, could I enter that door.
    - Ask father if he'll forgive!

ELLEN CLACY
from *A Lady's Visit to the Gold Diggings of Australia, in 1852–53*

Saturday, 18. – Fine day; we now approached Bendigo. The timber here is very large. Here we first beheld the majestic iron bark, *Eucalypti*, the trunks of which are fluted with the exquisite regularity of a Doric column; they are in truth the noblest ornaments of these mighty forests. A few miles further, and the diggings themselves burst upon our view. Never shall I forget that scene, it well repaid a journey even of sixteen thousand miles. The trees had been all cut down; it looked like a sandy plain, or one vast unbroken succession of countless gravel pits – the earth was everywhere turned up – men's heads in every direction were popping up and down from their holes. Well might an Australian writer, in speaking of Bendigo, term it 'The Carthage of the Tyre of Forest Creek.' The rattle of the cradle, as it swayed to and fro, the sounds of the pick and shovel, the busy hum of so many thousands, the innumerable tents, the stores with large flags hoisted above them, flags of every shape, colour, and nation, from the lion and unicorn of England to the Russian eagle, the strange yet picturesque costume of the diggers themselves, all contributed to render the scene novel in the extreme.

We hurried through this exciting locality as quickly as possible; and, after five miles travelling, reached the Eagle Hawk Gully, where we pitched our tents, supped, and retired to rest – though, for myself at least, not to sleep. The excitement of the day was sufficient cure for drowsiness. Before proceeding with an account of our doings at the Eagle Hawk, I will give a slight sketch of the character and peculiarities of the diggings themselves, which are of course not confined to one spot, but are the characteristics that usually exist in any auriferous regions, where the diggers are at work. I will leave myself, therefore, safely ensconced beneath a tent at the Eagle Hawk, and take a slight and rapid survey of the principal diggings in the neighbourhood from Saw-pit Gully to Sydney Flat.

*   *   *

Let us take a stroll around Forest Creek – what a novel scene! – thousands of human beings engaged in digging, wheeling, carrying, and washing, intermingled with no little grumbling, scolding and swearing. We approach first the old Post-office Square; next our eye glances down Adelaide Gully, and over the Montgomery and White Hills, all pretty well dug up; now we pass the Private Escort Station, and Little Bendigo. At the junction of Forest, Barker, and Campbell Creeks we find the Commissioners' quarters – this is nearly five miles from our starting point. We must now return to Adelaide Gully, and keep alongside Adelaide Creek, till we come to a high range of rocks, which we cross, and then find ourselves near the head-waters of Fryer's Creek. Following that stream towards the Loddon, we pass the interesting neighbourhood of Golden Gully, Moonlight Flat, Windless and Red Hill; this latter which covers about two acres of ground is so called from the colour of the soil, it was the first found, and is still considered as the richest auriferous spot near Mount Alexander. In the wet season, it was reckoned that on Moonlight Flat one man was daily buried alive from the earth falling into his hole. Proceeding north-east in the direction of Campbell's Creek, we again reach the Commissioners' tent.

The principal gullies about Bendigo are Sailor's, Napoleon, Pennyweight, Peg Leg, Growler's, White Horse, Eagle Hawk, Californian, American, Derwent, Long, Piccaninny, Iron Bark, Black Man's, Poor Man's, Dusty, Jim Crow, Spring, and Golden – also Sydney Flat, and Specimen Hill – Haverton Gully, and the Sheep-wash. Most of these places are well-ransacked and tunnelled, but thorough good wages may always be procured by tin dish washing in deserted holes, or surface washing.

It is not only the diggers, however, who make money at the Gold Fields. Carters, carpenters, storemen, wheelwrights, butchers, shoemakers, &c., usually in the long run make a fortune quicker than the diggers themselves, and certainly with less hard work or risk of life. They can always get from £1 to £2 a day without rations, whereas they may dig for weeks and get nothing. Living is not more expensive than in Melbourne: meat is generally from 4*d*. to 6*d*. a pound, flour about 1*s*. 6*d*. a pound, (this is the most expensive article in housekeeping there,) butter must be dispensed with, as that is seldom less than 4*s*. a pound, and only successful diggers can indulge in such articles as cheese, pickles, ham, sardines, pickled salmon, or spirits, as all these things, though easily procured if you have gold to throw away, are expensive, the last-named article (diluted with water or something less innoxious) is only to be obtained for 30*s*. a bottle.

The stores, which are distinguished by a flag, are numerous and well stocked. A new style of lodging and boarding house is in great vogue. It is a tent fitted up with stringy bark couches, ranged down each side the tent, leaving a narrow passage up the middle. The lodgers are supplied with mutton, damper, and tea, three times a day, for the charge of 5s. a meal, and 5s. for the bed; this is by the week, a casual guest must pay double, and as 18 inches is on an average considered ample width to sleep in, a tent 24 feet long will bring in a good return to the owner.

The stores at the diggings are large tents generally square or oblong, and everything required by a digger can be obtained for money, from sugar-candy to potted anchovies; from East India pickles to Bass's pale ale; from ankle jack boots to a pair of stays; from a baby's cap to a cradle; and every apparatus for mining, from a pick to a needle. But the confusion – the din – the medley – what a scene for a shop walker! Here lies a pair of herrings dripping into a bag of sugar, or a box of raisins; there a gay-looking bundle of ribbons beneath two tumblers, and a half-finished bottle of ale. Cheese and butter, bread and yellow soap, pork and currants, saddles and frocks, wide-awakes and blue serge shirts, green veils and shovels, baby linen and tallow candles, are all heaped indiscriminately together; added to which, there are children bawling, men swearing, store-keeper sulky, and last, not *least*, women's tongues going nineteen to the dozen.

Most of the storekeepers are purchasers of gold either for cash or in exchange for goods, and many are the tricks from which unsuspecting diggers suffer. One great and outrageous trick is to weigh the parcels separately, or divide the whole, on the excuse that the weight would be too much for the scales; and then, on adding up the grains and pennyweights, the sellers often lose at least half an ounce. On one occasion, out of seven pounds weight, a party once lost an ounce and three quarters in this manner. There is also the old method of false beams – one in favour of the purchaser – and here, unless the seller weighs in both pans, he loses considerably. Another mode of cheating is to have glass pans resting on a piece of green baize; under this baize, and beneath the pan which holds the weights, is a wetted sponge, which causes that pan to adhere to the baize, and consequently it requires more gold to make it level; this, coupled with the false reckoning is ruinous to the digger. In town, the Jews have a system of robbing a great deal from sellers before they purchase the gold-dust (for in these instances it must be *dust*): it is thrown into a zinc pan with slightly raised sides, which are well rubbed over with grease; and under the plea of a careful examination, the purchaser shakes and rubs the dust, and a considerable quantity adheres to the sides. A commoner practice still is for examiners of gold-dust to cultivate long finger-nails, and, in drawing the fingers about it, gather some up.

Sly grog selling is the bane of the diggings. Many – perhaps nine-tenths – of the diggers are honest industrious men, desirous of getting a little there as a stepping-stone to independence elsewhere; but the other tenth is composed of outcasts and transports – the refuse of Van Diemen's Land – men of the most depraved and abandoned characters, who have sought and gained the lowest abyss of crime, and who would a short time ago have expiated their crimes on a scaffold. They generally work or rob for a space, and when well stocked with gold, retire to Melbourne for a month or so, living in drunkenness and debauchery. If, however, their holiday is spent at the diggings, the sly grog-shop is the last scene of their boisterous career. Spirit selling is strictly prohibited; and although Government will license a respectable public-house on the *road*, it is resolutely refused *on* the diggings. The result has been the opposite of that which it was intended to produce. There is more drinking and rioting at the diggings than elsewhere, the privacy and risk gives the obtaining it an excitement which the diggers enjoy as much as the spirit itself; and wherever grog is sold on the sly, it will sooner or later be the scene of a riot, or perhaps murder. Intemperance is succeeded by quarrelling and fighting, the neighbouring tents report to the police, and the offenders are lodged in the lock-up; whilst the grog-tent, spirits, wine, &c., are seized and taken to the Commissioners. Some of the stores, however, managed to evade the law rather cleverly – as spirits are not *sold*, 'my friend' pays a shilling more for his fig of tobacco, and his wife an extra sixpence for her suet; and they smile at the store-man, who in return smiles knowingly at them, and then glasses are brought out, and a bottle produced, which sends forth *not* a fragrant perfume on the sultry air.

It is no joke to get ill at the diggings; doctors make you pay for it. Their fees are – for a consultation, at their own tent, ten shillings; for a visit out, from one to ten pounds, according to time and distance. Many are regular quacks, and these seem to flourish best. The principal illnesses are weakness of sight, from the hot winds and sandy soil, and dysentery, which is often caused by the badly-cooked food, bad water, and want of vegetables.

The interior of the canvas habitation of the digger is desolate enough; a box on a block of wood forms a table, and this is the only furniture; many dispense with that. The bedding, which is laid on the ground, serves to sit upon. Diogenes in his tub would not have looked more comfortless than any one else. Tin plates and pannicans, the same as are used for camping up, compose the breakfast, dinner, and tea service, which meals usually consist of the same dishes – mutton, damper, and tea.

In some tents the soft influence of our sex is pleasingly apparent: the tins are as bright as silver, there are sheets as well as blankets on the beds, and perhaps a clean counterpane, with the addition of a dry sack or piece of carpet on the ground; whilst a pet cockatoo, chained to a perch, makes noise enough to keep the 'missus' from feeling lonely when the good man is at work. Sometimes a wife is at first rather a nuisance; women get scared and frightened, then cross, and commence a 'blow up' with their husbands; but all their railing generally ends up in their quietly settling down to this rough and primitive style of living, if not without a murmur, at least to all appearance with the determination to laugh and bear it. And although rough in their manners, and not over select in their address, the digger seldom wilfully injures a woman; in fact, a regular Vandemonian will, in his way, play the gallant with as great a zest as a fashionable about town – at any rate, with more sincerity of heart.

Sunday is kept at the diggings in a very orderly manner; and among the actual diggers themselves, the day of rest is taken in a *verbatim* sense. It is not unusual to have an established clergyman holding forth near the Commissioners' tent, and almost within hearing will be a tub orator expounding the origin of evil, whilst a 'mill' (a fight with fisticuffs) or a dog fight fills up the background.

But night at the diggings is the characteristic time: murder here – murder there – revolvers cracking – blunderbusses bombing – rifles going off – balls whistling – one man groaning with a broken leg – another shouting because he couldn't find the way to his hole, and a third equally vociferous because he has tumbled into one – this man swearing – another praying – a party of bacchanals chanting various ditties to different time and tune, or rather minus both. Here is one man grumbling because he has brought his wife with him, another ditto because he has left his behind, or sold her for an ounce of gold or a bottle of rum. Donnybrook Fair is not to be compared to an evening at Bendigo.

CATHERINE HELEN SPENCE
from *Clara Morison, Impressions of the diggings and their effects*

From Henry Martin to Grace Elliot

Forest Creek

MY DEAREST GRACE, –
. . . Though we have all written often, I suppose I must take it
for granted that you have received none of our letters, and begin
at the beginning. We stayed only one night at Melbourne, in a
miserable lodging-house, where we three slept in the same room
with three other queer customers. There was a lame man, a very
deaf man, and one subject to fits, all bound for the diggings. It
cost us thirty shillings for the day and night, food and accommodation for three, which is not so bad as California used to be.

Next morning we set out on our eighty miles walk, and putting
our traps on a dray, we walked by the side of them, and camped
every night. We might have got up in three days easily if we had
not been obliged to stay with our goods; but the roads for vehicles
are horrible. The streets of Melbourne are highly praised, and are
really better than those of Adelaide; but once out of the town,
there is not a mile of made road in any direction. So we took six
days to reach Forest Creek, where we pitched our tent. It is
entirely occupied by Adelaide men, as the South Australians are
all called here, whether they come from Mount Remarkable or
Encounter Bay. They are wonderfully friendly among themselves,
and we were glad to hear familiar voices amongst them when we
came up.

It is a perfect lottery here; we have sunk nine holes already,
and have got nothing, while from holes close by us fellows have
taken pounds upon pounds of gold. I saw one party take eighteen
pounds' weight of gold from a hole that touched ours, in a day
and a half. We can only say, 'Better luck next time'; but I must
confess, my dear Grace, that I am ashamed of our first remittance,
for it *is* the first, – we have sent nothing before, either *via*
Melbourne, or by private hand. Here have we paid two months'
licence – that is nine pounds for three – we have worked like
slaves, and send you five ounces and a half of gold, worth here

only two pounds fifteen per ounce.

However, we have cleared our expenses hitherto, for we bought a lot of stuff from a party who were so busy nuggeting, that they would not take the trouble to wash for the smaller particles, and we hired a horse and cart, and took it four miles to wash it in the creek. Such dust we had to drive through! Adelaide is a joke to it, and even the Burra road is, comparatively speaking, a pure atmosphere. Oh, Grace! If you could have seen me there, with such a dirty face and hands, and looking as cross as the policemen do when they catch a chap working without a licence, I fear you would neither have known me when you saw me, nor liked me when you knew me. But it always did me good to remember your dear, gentle face, and I can tell you that one thought of you used to make me relax the muscles of my begrimed countenance, and give an afflicted sort of smile.

Five ounces and a half! This does not look like our getting married soon; but don't think I despair. If people will only persevere long enough, they will be successful in the end, and if we cannot raise the money for our licences next month, we shall go into some employment, and not be too proud to work for wages, till we can raise the thirty shillings a piece, and start afresh. If we could just clear two hundred each, and come back to find Adelaide so far recovered as to give us employment again, I think we need delay matters no longer. It is two years and a half now since we were engaged, and though I have been very patient hitherto, the thought that a lucky stroke may enable us to marry at once, makes my heart beat very restlessly, and sends my pickaxe down with double force. Now, write to me, dear Grace, to tell me how little you would be satisfied with, and also how things are going on, for we hear such confused accounts. It is of no use sending newspapers through the post-office, but if William Bell comes, make up a packet for him to bring us.

I have turned out a capital cook – decidedly the best of the party – so you will know who to apply to on an emergency. No doubt I made mistakes sometimes; the first plum-pudding we made was a singular production. I made George stone the plums, and Gilbert chop the suet, while I put on the pot to boil the pudding in, and made a damper. There was a pannikin full of plums, and another of suet; with this I mixed up five pannikins of flour, and kneaded it up as stiff as the damper. It was in vain that George told me puddings were made in a basin, and stirred with a spoon. I told him that these were delusive puddings, and not the substantial fare which working men required; so I tied it in a cloth, and boiled it for five hours. And was it not a stiff piece of work? We took three days to get through it; and the jokes that were perpetrated, as I chewed away at the cold pudding, were very aggravating. However, I am now quite proficient in the art, and some of our hungry neighbours like to drop in on a Sunday to take a share of Martin's pudding; for there are many here worse off than ourselves, who live in a sort of scrambling way upon chance hospitality; and they do clear everything before them. Many a time we have thought ourselves provisioned for two days, and half-a-dozen fellows would drop in, sometimes altogether, but generally by two and two, and polish of everything we had in the house, so that we were obliged to bake fresh damper for tea, and eat it without mutton; for it is only in the morning that the butchers will serve you, and then you must buy a whole quarter, or you will get none.

And, oh! Grace, the washing has been a dreadful business; we should have taken lessons from you before we went away, but we had a conceited idea that all women's work was easy, and could be done by instinct. And I had passed myself off to your brothers as completely up to the thing, and was entrusted with the management of the first washing. I took the clothes, and cut up half a bar of soap, and put them into the pot with a lot of stones and pebbles, thinking that the friction would be beneficial, and boiled all together for two or three hours. Then I took them out, saying that if they were not clean, they ought to be by this time; but the stewed shirts and trousers looked horrible; even the diggers were ashamed to wear them, for the dirt was completely boiled into them, – fast colours, and no mistake; and I felt so completely discomfited, that I let George and Gilbert wash by themselves next time; but their exploits were very little better than mine, which consoled me in some measure. However, one day I saw an old woman drawing water from a deserted hole, (these holes are all the wells we have here,) which was very hard work for her; she was the first woman I had seen on the diggings, and I was glad to have it in my power to help her. She was profuse in her thanks, and I insinuated that I should be more than repaid by a few plain directions about washing; these she gave me at considerable length, and my success has been brilliant ever since, though we find it very hard work. We are all very much shocked at the idea of your having to wash, now that we know how disagreeable it is, and hope that if we are successful, you will not need to do it in future. ·

We have a lot of Burra miners here, who have a bad trick of undermining other people's holes, and taking the gold out of them, so that when you fancy you are striking into the real good stuff, down comes your crowbar upon disappointing emptiness. They have not been uniformly successful, and I have seen a good many who regret their comfortable billets under the South Australian Mining Association.

We send you the escort receipt for the gold; it is in a chamois-leather bag, marked with your name. Next time you will have to pay two per cent, for its safe conveyance to Adelaide, but this Tolmer says is a labour of love; so you will have it all; and a miserable lot it is. It is part of what we washed out of Jones' party's rejected stuff; I believe it is likely to be published in the Adelaide newspapers, so there will be plenty of chaff flying about touching Elliot's party's large remittance.

I know it was you that put up the portfolio for us to write upon, and we are very glad of it; for it is unpleasant to write on one's knee, or even on the top of one's hat; I must now resign it to George, who looks volumes at me, and will, no doubt, write a voluminous letter to Annie.

And now, dear Grace, I must bid you farewell; you cannot think how reluctant I am to cease, when I think that you will really get my letter. God bless you, my dear girl, comfort you in all your troubles, and make me worthy of you, is the constant prayer of

Yours more than ever,
Henry Martin.

From William Bell to Margaret Elliot

Bendigo, 1852

My Dear Miss Margaret,

. . . I can give you no account of the diggings so good as you have had from your brothers; but as I stayed three days in Melbourne, while they came in at dusk and left next morning, I have the advantage of them there. Do not elevate your eyebrows, and say impatiently, 'What kept the idle fellow so long in that wretched town?' till you read my reasons. I had a small bill to settle with Mr. Campbell on my brother James's account, and like an honest man went to his place of business in Melbourne to pay it. He received me graciously, was glad I had remembered my debt, which he had forgotten completely, and begged me to sit down while he gave me the receipt. Then he told me in a good many words that he wanted a trust-worthy young man as clerk, for his last had gone to the diggings; and concluded by offering me a salary of two hundred and fifty, if I would promise to stay out the year. This was twice as much as I ever had before, and I promised to think over it, and give him an answer in two days.

So these two days I poked about from street to lane, and from lane to street. I inquired the price of lodgings, and what sort of accommodation I could get for thirty-five shillings a-week, the sum named by Mr. C., but in no case could I have a room to myself, and in every instance the parlour was full of those symptomatic sofas Mrs. Bantam liked so ill. Where I actually was I had the fourth part of a room; the inmates were all noisy and quarrelsome, and I had a good reason to believe, from the broad arrow on the night-cap of my nearest neighbour, that he was an old convict. Now, that is not at all my idea of comfortable lodgings, and though Miss Withering used to complain of the state of matters at Mrs. Brown's, you cannot think how superior Mrs. B.'s is to anything you could find in this Babel of a town. The houses are finer and the shops more splendid; there is a sort of centralization in Melbourne, which your scattered irregular town cannot boast of; but it seems to me that rich and busy as it is, there is very little enjoyment or happiness in it. It is uncomfortable, and indeed dangerous, to be out at night, and that to a man shut up in an office all day is a great deprivation. One had better remain in Adelaide with one hundred, where one had a room to oneself, and where it was perfectly safe, at least in a physical point of view, to walk over to your cottage of an evening, and chat with you and your sisters, than dwell in troubled Melbourne with two hundred and fifty.

It is true that the best society in Melbourne has always been considered by Scotch people superior to its counterpart in Adelaide; but how was a stranger and a clerk, with such very slender social talents as you know I have, to get into it? Where should I find a place in the universal overturn of society which is taking place in Victoria? The aristocratic members of the community are retreating when they can to England, to keep out of the crowd and discomfort; the mercantile are turning over money with unexampled rapidity, large profits and quick returns being the order of the day; and there is the same keen money-making look about them, which you used to observe in the frequenters of your Exchange, but with more feverish anxiety about the Melbourne men.

The town is densely crowded; places built in narrow lanes for stables are filled by human occupants, who live in dirt and discomfort, injuring the general health of the town. Owing to the stringent Building Act there have been many good streets built, because every man in buying his piece of land got the plan of the house to be erected towards the front; but as there was nothing to prevent the back being divided into lanes, the profit of the speculation has induced many to do it. It is shameful that with an unlimited extent of country, and in such a new town, people should be living in rows of houses only ten feet apart. You know a few such places in Adelaide; you know them to be nests for fever and sickness; and when I tell you that there are no fewer than two hundred and ninety of these private alleys in Melbourne not subject to the street regulations, you will not believe it can be a healthy city. Nor will you think so the more when you consider that a great proportion of the people are the sweepings of British jails, who have just made their way to a place where almost every description of crime may be committed with impunity. A feeble government, which is now led by a clique of squatters, a wretched police, and incompetent courts of law, is a great obstruction to the course of justice. I heard a gentleman say it was no bad thing for the colony that Melbourne was not a desirable place of residence; for that in a new state comfortable and luxurious cities impede the spread of the people and the subjugation of the soil. And there is some truth in that, but the only subjugation people think of now, is getting the gold out of the land; and every other description of industry is for the time paralyzed. I did not see much gambling in my peregrinations, at least not nearly so much as I expected, from our knowledge of its extent in California; but I suppose that the great medley of nations who find a common language and common sympathies over the gambling table, have not yet come to an understanding. But of drinking and swearing I saw more than enough. I thought Adelaide was not particularly moral, but it is infinitely better than this. Even gentlemen make a boast of swearing in Victoria, while few, except bullock-drivers, do so in South Australia.

I happened to look into a shop when an Irish orphan, who had come to the colony with scarcely a shoe to her foot, was buying white satin for a bridal dress at twelve shillings a yard, and scornfully rejecting any shawl under ten guineas. Marriages are very frequent, and on a few days' acquaintance. The disproportion of the sexes was always great, for Melbourne was peopled chiefly by independent emigrants and people from the other colonies; and not so much from free emigration, paid for out of the colony's land fund, in which case pains are taken to equalize them. The high upset price of crown lands has on the whole been a great benefit to South Australia; for when half the price was devoted to bringing out labour to improve the land it benefited both the mother country and the young colony.

Scarcely any wages will tempt a girl to remain in service, when she sees the foolish finery in which the foolish brides go off; and the ladies of Victoria are forced to do the meanest drudgery, even occasional assistance not being to be had. To them it is a special hardship, for they never were so independent of servants as the Adelaide ladies. I met Mr. Bantam in Great Collins-street one day, and he took me home to see his wife. Their cottage is nicely situated but very small. He is doing a good business as a commission-agent; but his wife seems to pine after Adelaide yet, and was pleased to hear that things were looking up a little when I left. They were both glad that Miss Morison had not found a situation, for they still hoped she would have no objection to join them at some future time.

So after my two days' researches, I determined to refuse Mr. Campbell's offer of a situation, and to set off immediately to join your brothers, and deliver your letters and messages. Mr. Campbell shook his head, called me a rash young man, and gave me back my money with some hesitation, seeming to fear that I could not be trusted with it. And thus I quitted Melbourne, with the conviction, that if the discovery of gold in South Australia would bring such characters there as I had seen poured into this devoted city, we ought to pray daily that God would not send such a curse upon us, as a punishment for our colonial sin of worldly-mindedness.

I lost no time on the road; and did not Elliot's party give me a shout of welcome! I consider myself remarkably fortunate in joining a party which has been unlucky hitherto; for I shall share all the good fortune they may justly expect in return. Our change of quarters also gives a prestige of success. I do not need to buy a cradle or a tent, and I am benefited by the experience of my comrades. Your brothers and Martin are all looking well, and seem to have excellent health. I hope that you will answer this long epistle, and remain,

Yours very faithfully,
William Bell

[Meanwhile the recipients of these letters are having their share of novel experiences too – ed.]

. . . 'Do you see the woman who is standing at the door of the 'pizé' cottage before us. She was our washerwoman long ago, and initiated me into the mystery. Let us go and ask for a drink of water. How do you do, Mrs. Tubbins? My cousin and I would be obliged to you for a drink of water.'

'You are welcome hearty, Miss Marget,' answered the person addressed, who had on a smart cap, but a dirty gown, with rather a slipshod appearance about the feet; 'come in and chat with me a bit, for I am lonesome now my master is off to them diggings again.'

Never had such an incongruous-looking abode greeted the eyes of the cousins. Into one room, which had a clay floor, and was indeed the only room in the house, there was crammed so much furniture, that there was scarcely standing room. A piano, by Collard and Collard, stood in one corner; a cheffonier, with a great array of decanters and glasses, graced another; there were two chests of drawers, wedged between a common stretcher and a heap of bedding, which seemed intended for a nightly shake-down. There was, in truth, an abundance of everything but chairs, and that deficiency was made up by a number of three-legged stools, which the children liked to lift on to the drawers, and, climbing by the handles, to perch themselves where they could reach the rafters of the unceiled house. A very small piece of matting lay under the table, but the legs of the piano and of all the valuable furniture rested on the earthen floor.

'Rather a change of days for us,' said Mrs. Tubbins, glancing complacently from her furniture to her visitors. 'Aint we snug now, Miss Marget? This is a prettier piany than yours, and cost more money too, I expect, for my master gin sixty guineas for it the week before he left me, that I might have something cheerful in the house; but the children are for ever strumming on it, and broke three of the prettiest of the brass wires no further gone than last night. They tear at the wires with their fingers, and scrape across them with an iron hoop they picked up, which aint doing justice to the piany. Just play us a tune, Miss Marget, to let them see how it should be done.'

Margaret found that the piano had suffered very much from the course of treatment which the young Tubbinses had pursued; she played very softly, in order to spare her own ears.

'Just try now, Fanny, if you can play like that,' said Mrs. Tubbins.

Fanny struck the notes at random, more gently than her wont, and her mother smiled approvingly, and said she knew she would come on if she had any one to tell her how to play. Then Clara was asked to give a tune, and as she was but a tyro, she could not moderate her style to the piano, but played as hard as she did on her cousin's.

'Your cousin beats you, Miss Marget; but if she would just put her foot on the stick below, it would make a wonderful improvement. It sounds quite grand, and booms in your ears; but I think there ought to be two sticks, one for each foot, that folk may have all their limbs helping the music; but yours had only one. Do you know anybody who would come in for a few hours every day to teach me and Fanny, for it would be grand to able to play to Mr. Tubbins when he comes back?'

'Have you any music?' asked Clara, wondering at the extraordinary tones of the handsome and apparently new piano.

'Oh! I beg your pardon, Miss. I should have given you the books. I never play without them myself.' And Mrs. Tubbins handed her a leaf of Jeannette and Jeannot, and another which had formed part of the overture to Tancredi, saying that she really ought to buy another book or two. 'I went to Platts' last week, and they wanted to sell me an instruction book, as they called it, and asked a guinea for it, but I saw they thought me green, for the book was more words than music; so I told the young man as served me that I knew chalk from cheese, and that was not the book for my money, and did not spend a brass farthing in the shop after all. You'll stop and have a glass of wine with me, Miss Marget? Fanny, run across to the public-house for a pint of sherry, the best they have got.'

'I wish Annie had been with us,' said Margaret, unable to repress a smile. 'She has not been well or in good spirits lately, and it would have done her good to have seen you in the midst of all your splendour.'

'I expect her young man is at the diggings, and she is pining about him; but it's far worse to have to pine after one's old man;' and Mrs. Tubbins heaved a sigh, but controlled her feelings at the sight of her piano.

'All our young men are at the diggings – George, Gilbert, and Henry Martin,' observed Margaret.

'That's the young man Miss Grace has married,' said Mrs. Tubbins.

'Only going to marry.'

'Dear, dear! how long you two misses have been in settling for yourselves! But here's Fanny with the wine and biscuits.'

'Give me my fourpenny, mother, for going your message.'

'I only said I'd give you twopence, and I can see you have been nibbling, and don't deserve a brass farthing, you little good-for-nothing! Oh, how I wish I had not lost my keys!'

'Bob has planted them somewhere, mother, to get at the plums and sugar. I've got my fourpenny, so I don't mind how soon you find them.' And Fanny ran away to the nearest lolly shop, and all her brothers and sisters followed her.

'Don't you send the childen to school? asked Margaret. 'It is very bad for them to be running about idle.'

'I did send them a bit, but Fanny got scolded, and Bob got thrashed; and the little ones were kept in, and got no dinner at all one day; so they just hate the school, and won't go to it no more.'

'You should make them go, whether they will or not,' said Margaret. 'You will ruin your children if you allow them to do as they please, and all the gold and all the fine furniture in the world will never make up to you for the misery disobedient children will give you. I speak seriously to you, Mrs. Tubbins; for I see great evils coming on this colony from money being thrown into the hands of people who, instead of teaching their children the uses and duties of wealth, indulge them in everything they ask for. Send your children to school regularly, and insist upon their obeying you at home, that their father may be proud of them when he returns, and may find, after all his toil and hardships, a happy fireside and an orderly family.'

'What you say is all very true, Miss Marget, but you are over hard on the likes of us, who never got no learning, and don't quite see the use of it'.

'If you don't see the use of their learning, make them work as they used to do.'

'They ain't got no call to work, for I have lots of clothes for them, and a silk gown for myself to go to town with; and where is the use of them slaving just as if we had not a penny.'

'I have not seen you at church for a long time,' said Margaret. 'Do you go to chapel now?'

'Indeed, I ain't got a sitting anywheres just at present, and I don't like getting my religion for nothing now, when I can afford to pay for it. Your church is not ours, and I am just wondering which one to join; but, after all, I never get time to go to church, for there is the dinner to make ready in the morning, and the children to put to bed at night, so it is ill convenient for me to get away.'

'But don't the children go to church or Sunday school? I remember your telling me how fond Fanny was of learning hymns and catechism.'

'So she was then, and I was glad to get an old frock of yours to make down for her, to look decent to go to school in; but we are much smarter now.'

And Mrs. Tubbins took from a very miscellaneous lot of things Fanny's pink satin bonnet and dress of green and lavender silk, saying that she thought them very genteel, and that they took her fancy in the shop at first sight. Then her own gorgeous attire for Sundays was brought out for Margaret's inspection and admiration; and she was busy telling how much every article had cost, when her two nieces, Sarah and Lucinda Hagget, came in.

'Oh, aunt, how vain you are of your finery!' said Miss Lucinda. 'You never let anybody miss the sight of it if you can help. I fancy you are prouder of that fine silk dress than you are of your piany, though it's the piany I envy,' – but the speaker looked very hard at the gown too.

'Have you left your places, girls, that you are both here at this time of day? – and such good places you had too,' said Mrs. Tubbins.

'I hadn't enough of wages,' said Sarah. 'How do people expect one to dress on seven shillings a-week? I sha'n't take a place again under eight, if I have washing to do. Lucinda had no washing, so she might have stopped.'

'Stopped at such a place! Why, it was so dull that you could hear the grass growing, for want of anything else to hear. If I could get a good cheerful place, I shouldn't mind taking six shillings a-week till we hear from father.'

'I know a lady who wants a girl; she would give you an easy place, and she is a good mistress – Mrs. Trueman,' said Margaret.

'A grass widow! – I won't go there,' cried Lucinda. 'It is enough to pull down any creature's spirits, to live with such whining people. You, aunt, are the cheerfullest of the lot, and me and Sarah have come to stop with you till we get suited.'

'Where are you all to sleep?' asked Margaret.

'Oh! I make up a bed on the piany every night,' replied Mrs. Tubbins; 'and it holds a good many of the little ones, and Sarah may go beside them. It is quite handy for a bed. I can manage, I warrant.'

Miss Lucinda meanwhile was busily engaged trying to make out a nigger melody, but could not manage it. She was just going to ask Margaret to tell her what notes should be struck, when the cousins rose to depart. Clara could not get over the idea of the handiness of the large square piano, and its being strummed on and raked with hoops all day, and slept on all night: she hurried out of hearing of the people inside, and indulged in a long and hearty fit of laughter.

'It is all very well for you to laugh,' said Margaret; 'but I must say it is no laughing matter. I remember Mrs. Tubbins a hard-working honest woman, who brought up her family better than the average of her class; and now this suddenly-acquired wealth is ruining them all. When his gold is spent, I suppose Tubbins will set off for more; and until the diggings are worked out, South Australia is none the better for that family.'

'Are you longing to see the end of the gold, Margaret?'

'Heartily!' was the answer . . .

HENRY KENDALL
from *The Men of Letters in New South Wales*

More than eighty-four years have elapsed since Arthur Phillip first landed, and initiated civilization on these shores. The marvellous progress that the colony has made since then is known, I presume, to almost every member of the community – that is to say, to almost every one of us who can read, write, and think. Where vast belts of forest used to stand, cities have started up almost as rapidly as Troy did to the music of Apollo; where there was once nothing for the eye to rest upon but brown, sun-baked waste, the iron horse now rushes between noble townships, and great breadths of cultivated country; and where the silence in the old days was only broken by the occasional footfall of the savage, or the monotonous cry of the curlew, the ridges and gullies at the present date resound with the songs of the miner, the blows of the pick, and the harsh, grating noises of the crushing-machine. There is little need, however, to go into all this. I only refer to the changes that have taken place just to remind the reader of the wonderful strides New South Wales has made in one direction, before proceeding to speak of her unique backwardness in another.

For while all this social and commercial progress has been going on – while every possible effort has been made by the colony for the attainment of physical prosperity and wealth – almost next to nothing has been done with regard to its intellectual advance; or, in other words, towards the creation and fostering of a native literature. Not that we have never had amongst us men with that aboriginal and plenary power which constitutes the authentic insignia – so to speak – of genius; on the contrary, I think I could point to several who, if they had been placed in happier worldly circumstances, and under a different face of heaven, would have secured a permanent and honorable footing in the world of letters.

... What then is the history of these people – these men acknowledged to be 'clever', and assuredly in straitened circumstances? Simply this. Many – indeed the most of them, enter the field [of letters] while mere youths, full of enthusiasm, elated with consciousness that in the unique life and scenery around them they can find ample material for the exercise of their respective gifts; but the end invariably is disappointment and sorrow. They

very soon come to realise that Australia is a new country; that
society here is still in an unsettled, chaotic state; that the large
bulk of the population have yet to get their money before they
can enjoy leisure; that the wealthy classes – the geebung aristocracy, as they are called – are formed for the most part of illiterate
people, who have risen from the ranks; and, in short, that there
is not the ghost of a chance for a writer attempting to get his living
by offering to the public work not lying within the domains of
journalism. So it comes to pass that those who happen to be lucky
enough, and who possess the necessary aptitude, join the Press,
and in due time forget their early aspirations and become
plodding, satisfied newspaper hacks. The men who are not so
fortunate – God help them!

MARCUS CLARKE
Grumbler's Gully

The mining township of Quartzborough, or as it is called in the
vernacular, Grumbler's Gully, is situated about twelve miles from
Bullocktown.

There are various ways of approaching Grumbler's Gully. If you
happen to be a commercial traveller, for instance, in the employment of Messrs. Gin and Bitters, and temporary owner of a
glittering buggy and trotting mare, you would most likely take
a tour by way of Killarney, Jerusalem, Kenilworth, Blair Athole,
St. Petersburg, Maimaitoora, Lucky Woman's, and Rowdy Flat,
thus swooping upon Grumbler's Gully by way of Breakyleg,
Shicersville, Bangatoora, and Bullocktown. If you were a squatter
residing at Glengelder, The Reeks, or Vaucluse, you would ride
across the Lonely Plains, down by Melancholy Swamp and
Murderer's Flat, until you reach Jack-a-dandy, where, as every
one knows, the track forks to Milford Haven and St. Omer. If you
were a Ballarat sharebroker, and wanted to have a look at the reefs
on the road, you could turn off at Hell's Hole, and making for
Old Moke's, borrow a horse and ride on to the Hanging Rock,
midway between Kororoot and Jefferson's Lead; this course
taking you into the heart of the reefing country, you could jog
easily from Salted Claim to Ballyrafferty, Dufferstown, and
Moonlight Reefs, calling at the Great Eastern, and entering
Grumbler's Gully from the north by way of the Good-morning-
Bob Ranges and Schwilflehaustein.

The first impression of Grumbler's Gully is, I confess, not a
cheering one. I think it was Mr. Caxton who replied, when asked
what he thought of his new-born infant, 'It is very red, ma'am.'
The same remark would apply to Grumbler's Gully. It is *very* red.
Long before you get to it you are covered with dust that looks
and feels like finely-powdered bricks. The haggard gum trees by
the road-side – if you can call it rightly a road-side – are covered
with this red powder. The white near leader seems stained with
bloody sweat, and the slices of bank that, as you approach the
town, fringe the track, look as though they were lumps of red
putty drying and crumbling in the sun. On turning the corner,
Grumbler's Gully is below us – a long, straggling street, under a
red hill that overlooks a red expanse of mud, flecked with pools

of red water, and bristling with mounds, shaft-sheds, and wooden engine-houses. The sun is sinking behind yonder mighty range, under whose brow stretches that belt of scrub and marsh and crag that meets the mallee wilderness, and minor mountains rise up all around us. Grumbler's Gully is shaped like a shoe with a lump in the middle of it, or rather, perhaps, like one of those cockboats that children make with folded paper. It is a ridge of quartz, rising in the midst of a long valley surrounded by mountains.

The place is undermined with 'sinkings,' and the inhabitants burrow like moles beneath the surface of the earth. It is no disgrace – quite the reverse – in Grumbler's Gully to wear moleskin trousers stained with the everlasting red clay. There is, indeed, a story afloat there to the effect that a leading townsman presided at a public dinner in those garments, and was not a whit less respectable than usual. In getting into the bar of the Golden Tribute Hotel, you become conscious that the well-dressed and intelligent gentleman, who in the whitest of shirt sleeves handed you 'Otard' (the brand then in fashion on the gully) and bid you help yourself, was a share-holder in a rich claim, and could, topically speaking, buy and sell you over again if he liked, without inconvenience. In drinking the said 'Otard' you become conscious of a thumping vibration going on somewhere, as if a giant with accelerated action of the heart was imprisoned under the flooring, and getting out into the back yard, where Mr. Merryjingle's pair-horse buggy is waiting for Mr. Merryjingle to finish his twentieth last glass, you see a big red mound surmounting the stable, and know that the engine is pumping night and day in the Golden Tribute Reef.

But all the hotelkeepers of Grumbler's Gully are not as elegant as Mr. Bilberry. There is Polwheal, for example, the gigantic Cornishman, who lives in the big red building opposite the courthouse. Polwheal considers his hotel a better one than the Golden Tribute, and swears largely when visitors of note stop at Bilberry's. For Polwheal's hotel is of brick, and being built in the 'good old times,' cost something like a shilling a brick to erect, whereas Bilberry's is but a wooden structure, and not very substantial at that. The inmate of Bilberry's can hear his right-hand neighbour clean his teeth, and can trace the various stages of his left-hand neighbour going to bed – commencing with the scratching of a safety match, and ending with the clatter of hastily deposited boots. When the County Court sits at Grumbler's Gully, and the Judge, Crown Prosecutor, and others put up there, it is notorious that Bilberry is driven politely frantic by his efforts to put Mr. Mountain, who snores like the action of a circular-saw, in some room where his slumber will not be the cause of wakefulness in others. It is even reported that a distinguished barrister, after plugging his ears in vain, was compelled one sultry night to take his blankets and 'coil' on the wood heap, in order to escape from the roaring of Mr. Mountain's fitful diapason. I, myself, tossing in agony three rooms off, have been enabled to accurately follow the breathing of that worthy man, and to trace how the grunt swells into a rumble, the rumble reaches a harsh grating sound, which broadens into the circular-saw movement, until glasses ring, roofs shake, and the terrified listener, convinced that in another instant Mountain must either suffocate or burst, hears with relief the terrific blast soften to a strangled whistle, and finally die away in a soothing murmur, full of deceitful promises of silence.

Now at Polwheal's you have none of this annoyance, but then Polwheal's liquor is not so good, and his table is not so well kept. How often, with the thermometer at 100, have I shuddered at a smoking red lump of boiled beef, with Polwheal in a violent perspiration looming above it in a cloud of greasy steam! But Polwheal has his patrons, and many a jorum of whiskey-hot has been consumed in that big parlour, where the *Quartzborough Chronicle* of the week before last lies perpetually on the table. Then there is Cock-eyed Harry's, where the 'boys' dance, and where a young lady known to fame as the 'Chestnut Filly' was wont to dispense the wine cup. Also Mr. Corkison's, called Boss Corkison, who dressed elaborately in what he imagined to be the height of Melbourne fashion, owned half the Antelope Reef, and couldn't write his own name. Boss was an ingenious fellow, however, and wishing to draw a cheque, would say to any respectable stranger, 'Morning, sir! A warm day! Have a drink, sir? Me name's Corkison! Philip, a little hard stuff! Me hand shakes, sir. Up last night with a few roaring dogs drinking hot whiskey. Hot whiskey is the Devil, sir!' Upon the stranger drinking, and strangers were not often backward in accepting hospitality, Boss would pull from his fashionable coat pocket a fat cheque-book, and would insinuatingly say, 'Sir, I will be obliged if you will draw a chick for me (he always spoke of chicks) for £10, sir. Jeremiah Corkison: I will touch the pen. Sir, I am obliged to you.' If the stranger was deceived by this subterfuge, Boss would waylay him for days with the 'chicks,' getting bigger and bigger and his hand shakier and more shaky. I may mention Tom Tuff's store, where one drank Hennessy in tin tots, and played loo in the back parlour; and the great Irish house, where you got nothing but Irish whiskey and patriotism. I have no time to do more than allude to the Morning Star, the Reefer's Joy, the Rough and Ready, or the twenty other places of resort.

Leaving hotels for a while, let us walk down Main-street. Society in Grumbler's Gully is very mixed. I suppose that the rich squatters who live round about consider themselves at the top of the tree, while the resident police magistrate, the resident barrister, the Church of England clergyman, the Roman Catholic priest, and the managers of the banks sit on the big limbs, leaving the solicitors, rich storekeepers, and owners of claims to roost on the lower branches, and the working miners, &c., to creep into the holes in the bare ground. Of course, the place is eaten up with scandal, and saturated with petty jealousy. The Church of England clergyman will not speak to the Presbyterian Minister, and both have sworn eternal enmity to the Roman Catholic priest. The wife of the resident magistrate is at feud with the wife of the resident barrister, and the wives of the bank managers don't recognise the wives of the solicitors. If you call on Mrs. M'Kirkincroft, she will tell you – after you have heard how difficult it is to get servants, and that there had been no water in the tank for two days – that shocking story, though, remember, only a rumour, of Mrs. Partridge and Mr. Quail from Melbourne, and how Mrs. Partridge threw a glass of brandy and water over Mr. Quail, and how Mr. Quail went into Mr. Pounce's office and cried like a child, with his head on a bundle of mining leases. If you call on Mrs. Pontifex she will inform you – after you have heard that there has been no water in the tank for two days, and how difficult it is to get servants – that Mrs. M'Kirkincroft's papa was a butcher at Rowdy Flat, and that M'Kirkincroft himself made his money by keeping a public-house on the road to Bendigo. Mrs. Partridge has a very pretty history of Mrs. Pontifex's aunt, who came out in the same ship with Mr. Partridge's cousin, and who was quite notorious for her flirtations during the voyage; and Mrs. Partridge, who is a vicious, thin-lipped, little dark woman, pronounces the word 'flirtation' as if it included the breaking of seven seventh [*sic*] commandments seventy times over. You hear how Tom Twotooth ran away with Bessy Brokenmouth, and how old Brokenmouth took his entire horse, Alexander the Great, out of the stable in the middle of the night and galloped to the Great Eastern, only to find the floods down below Proud's Ferry, and the roads impassable. You hear how Jack Bragford lost over £600 to Dr. Splint, and how Jack drew a bill which was duly dishonoured, thereby compelling poor Sugman Sotomayordesoto, the wine and spirit merchant (who is as generous as becomes a man in whose veins runs the blood of Old Castile,) to impoverish himself in order to pay the money. There are current in Grumbler's Gully marvellous scandals respecting the parson, the priest, and the police magistrate – scandals which, though they are visible lies, are nevertheless eagerly credited by dwellers round about. There are strong-flavoured stories – old jokes such as our grandfathers chuckled at – told concerning the publicans, the miners, and the borough councillors; and a resident of Grumbler's Gully would be quite indignant if you hinted to him that you had 'heard that story before.'

But to come back to Main-street. The architecture is decidedly irregular. A bank shoulders a public-house, a wooden shanty nestles under the lee of a brick-and-iron store. Everything is desperately new. The bricks even look but a few days baked, and the iron roof of the Grumbler's Gully Emporium and Quartz-borough Magazin des Modes has not as yet lost its virgin white-ness. The red dust is everywhere flying in blinding clouds. The white silk coat of Boss Corkison, looking for the stranger, is pow-dered with it; and the black hat, vest, trousers, and boots of Jabez Hick – Jabez *P.* Hick he insists on signing himself – are marked with red smudges. Mr. Hick is a very smart Yankee (there are one or two in Grumbler's Gully,) and is the proprietor of the Emporium. He has also a share in the General Washington United, and has been down to the dam this afternoon to look at the small amount of water which yet remains there. The dust lies thickly on the hood of Mr. Salthide's buggy standing at the door of Copperas the ironmonger, and ruins the latest Melbourne toilettes of Mrs. Partridge and Mrs. Pontifex, who continue to think Main-street Collins-street, and make believe to shop there daily from three to five. The peculiarity of Main-street is its incongruous newness. Around are solemn purple hills, with their hidden mysteries of swamp and wilderness; and here, on the back-bone of this quartz ridge, in the midst of a dirty, dusty, unsightly mudpatch, punched with holes and disfigured with staring yellow mounds, are fifty or sixty straggling wooden, iron, and brick buildings, in which live people of all ranks of society, of all nations, of all opinions, but every one surrounded by his or her particular aureole of civilisation and playing the latest music, drinking the most fashionable brand of brandy, reading the latest novels, and taking the most lively interest in the Election for President, the Duke of Edinburgh, the Spanish Question, the Prussian war, and the appalling fact that oysters in London are positively three shillings a dozen! A coach blundering and rattling at the heels of four smoking horses drops upon them twice a day out of the Bush, and the coachman delivers his mails, skims a local paper, has a liquor, retails the latest joke (made in Melbourne perhaps twenty-four hours before,) and then blunders and rattles away again through the lonely gum-tree forest, until he drops upon just such another place with just such another population, at the next quartz out-cropping, fifty miles away. Amidst all this there is no nationality; the Frenchman, German, and Englishman all talk confidently about "going home," and if by any chance some old man with married daughters thinks he will die in the colony, he never by any chance expresses a wish to leave his bones in the horribly utilitarian cemetery at Grumbler's Gully.

A word about this Grumbler's Gully cemetery. It is close to the hospital, a fine building containing fifty beds, and supported by voluntary contributions, and the patients can see the grave of the man who died yesterday quite readily. Grumbler's Gully can see no reason why they should not see it; sick people must die sometimes, of course. In the same spirit has the cemetery been built. It is a square patch of ground surrounded by a neat iron railing. Everything spick and span new; the railing not even rusted, the sordid red mounds not even overgrown with grass. No tenderness, no beauty, no association; an admirable place to hold the loathly corpses that were once human beings – a most useful graveyard, and nothing more. Nothing more, save that near these ugly red mounds, unpoetical, untaught, ill-dressed men and women will sometimes linger, sparing an hour from the common place toil of the practical place to foolishly weep, thinking on the friends that are gone. The hideously excellent cemetery of Grumbler's Gully always seemed to me to realise the life of the colony – the stern, practical, laborious, unleisured life of a young country, a life in which one has no time to think of others until they have left us and gone Home.

Close beside the hospital is the church, and over against the church the chapel, and glaring viciously at both of them, in an underbred way is the meeting-house. Religion, or rather difference of religion, is a noted feature in Grumbler's Gully. Formerly, the inhabitants might have been divided into two classes, Teetotalers and Whiskey-hot men. There was a club called the Whiskey-hot Club at Polwheal's, each member of which was pledged to drink ten whiskeys hot *per noctem*, the qualification for membership being three fits of *delirium tremens*, – but of late these broad distinctions have been broken down, and the town now boasts five sects, each of which devoutly believes in the ultimate condemnation of the other four. There is a Band of Hope at Grumbler's Gully, likewise a Tent of Rechab. The last has fallen into some disrepute since it was discovered by a wandering analytical chemist that Binks Brothers, who were affiliated Jonadabers in the third degree, and who supplied the camp with teetotal liquids, habitually put forty per cent. of proof spirit into the Hallelujah Cordial. There was quite a run upon Hallelujah

Cordial for a few days after this discovery. The moving religious element, however, in Grumbler's Gully is a Mr. Jark. Jark was a cabinetmaker when yet in darkness, and did not get 'called' until he had been twice insolvent. He went so near fraudulency the second time that it is supposed that his imminent danger converted him. Jark is a short, squab, yellow-faced, black-toothed, greasy-fingered fellow, with a tremendous power of adjective. When he prays he turns up his eyes until nothing but a thin rim of white is visible, over which the eyelids quiver with agonising fervour. When he prays he is very abusive to his fellow creatures, and seems to find intense consolation in thinking everybody around him deceitful, wicked, and hard-hearted. To hear him denounce this miserable world, you would think that, did he suddenly discover that some people were very hopeful and happy in it, he would suffer intense pain. He travels about the country 'preaching the word,' which means I am afraid, sponging on the squatters, and has written a diary, *Jark's Diary, published by subscription*, which sets forth his wanderings and adventures. Passages like this occur in that Christian work:

'Nov. 28th. My horse fell with me at Roaring Megs' (*a claim be it understood, not a lady,*) and I could not get him to rise. After poking him with sharp sticks for some time in vain, I bethought me of lighting a fire beneath the beast. This roused him, and I lifted up my heart in prayer. Isaiah xix. 22.'

'Nov. 29th. Came to Bachelor Plains, and put up at the home station. The overseer, an intelligent young man, put my horse into the stable and gave him some oats, the which he had not tasted for many months. In the evening, after an excellent repast, I ventured to commune in prayer, but the overseer pulled out a pipe, and began to play euker with a friend. I felt it my duty to tell them of the awful position in which they stood, and upon their still continuing to gamble, to curse them both solemnly in the name of the Lord:'

It will be seen by this that Jark is not averse to a little blasphemy. He is a self-seeking, cunning dog, who is fit for nothing but the vocation he follows, viz., that of 'entering widows' houses, and for a pretence making long prayers.' Yet he has a large following, and crowds the chapel when he preaches. The result is that all the rationalistic-going men in the township, and there are some half-dozen, disgusted with the hypocrisy and vulgarity of this untaught teacher, have come to consider all clergymen knaves or fools, and to despise all religion.

These enlightened persons hold meetings at the Morning Star Hotel, and settle the universe quite comfortably. They are especially great at such trifling subjects as 'The Cause of Poverty,'

'Our Social Relations,' 'The Origin of Species,' 'Is Polygamy or Polyandry Best Calculated to Insure the Happiness of the Human Race?' 'Whence do we Come?' 'Whither do we Go?' and so on. Indeed, Grumbler's Gully was at one time denounced by the opposition (Barker's Flat) journal as having dangerous tendencies to pure Buddhism. The local paper, however, retorted with some ingenuity that the Barker's Flats were already far gone in the pernicious doctrines of Fo, and that it was well-known that Hung Fat, the Chinese interpreter, held nightly *séances* in order to expound the teachings of Confucius.

A word about the local literature. The *Quartzborough Chronicle* and *Grumbler's Gully Gazette* is like all other country papers – whatever its editor chooses to make it. Local news is scarce. An inch of telegram, a borough council riot, or two police-court cases will not make a paper; and the leading article on the alluvial diggings, Mr. Tagrag's speech on the budget, Mr. Bobtail's proposition for levelling the Gipps Land Ranges to fill up the Sandridge lagoon, or what not, once written, 'cuttings' become things of necessity, and Daw, the editor, 'cuts' remarkably well. Daw is a capital amateur actor, and a smart journalist. His leaders can be good if he likes to put his heart into his work and every now and then a quaint original sketch or pathetic story gives Grumbler's Gully a fillip. Daw writes about four columns a day, and is paid £250 a year. His friends say he ought to be in Melbourne, but he is afraid to give up a certainty, so he stays, editing his paper and narrowing his mind, yearning for some intellectual intercourse with his fellow-creatures. To those who have not lived in a mining township, the utter dulness [sic] of Daw's life is incomprehensible. There is a complete lack of anything like cultivated mental companionship, and the three or four intellects who are above the dead-level to do their best to reduce their exurberant acuteness by excess of whiskey and water. The club, the reading-room, the parliament, the audience that testifies approval and appreciation are all found in one place – the Public-house Bar. To obtain a criticism or a suggestion, one is compelled to drink a nobbler of brandy. The life of an up-country editor is the life of Sisyphus – the higher up the hill he rolls his stone, with the more violence does it tumble back upon him. 'You want an editor?' said a hopeful new chum to the lucky job-printer who owned the *Blanket Flat Mercury*; 'I have the best testimonials, and have written largely for the English press.' The man of advertisements scanned the proffered paper. 'Clever! sober! industrious! My good sir, you won't do for *me*. I want a man as is blazing drunk half his time, and who can just knock off a smart thing when I tell him.' 'But who *edits* the paper, then?'

asked the applicant. 'Who?' returned the proprietor, flourishing his scissors over his head in indignant astonishment; 'why, *I* does! all you'll have to do is to correct the spellin' and put in the personalities!' It is remarkable that in this free colony, where everybody is so tremendously equal, the tyranny of cash is carried to a greater extent than in any other country on the face of the earth. Men come to Australia to get rich, and if they don't get rich they go to the wall. In Melbourne, one can in a measure escape the offensive patronage of the uneducated wealthy, but in a mining township, where life is nothing but a daring speculation, the brutal force of money is triumphant.

But it is time to 'have a drink' – the chief amusement of the place. If we cannot imitate these jolly dogs of reef-owners, who start from Polwheal's at ten a.m., and drink their way to Bilberry's by two p.m., working back again to unlimited loo and whiskey hot by sundown, it is perhaps better for us; but we must at all events conform to the manners and customs.

To sum up the jollity of Grumbler's Gully in two words – 'What's yours?'

A.G. STEPHENS
from *Introduction* to *The Bulletin Story Book*

The grotesque English prejudice against things Australian, founded on no better reason than that they are unlike English things, still remains to vitiate the local sense of local beauty; but every year is teaching us wisdom. We have learnt to laugh at the ridiculous and reiterated fiction that our flowers have no scent and our birds no song. Why, the whole Bush is scented; in no land is there a greater wealth of aromatic perfume from tree and shrub and blossom – making the daisied meadows of England, as honest Henry Kingsley suggests, tame and suburban by comparison. And when you go up beyond the tropic-line, and walk out of your tent at dawn, the air in many places is literally weighed down with the fragrance of a hundred brilliant flowers. What would they not give in England for ten acres of wattle-blossom on Wimbledon Common? and how many nightingales would they exchange for a flight of crimson lories at sunset? – a shower of flaming rubies. Did Marcus Clarke never hear the fluting of an Australian magpie? – so mellow, so round, so sweet. If the little brown English birds sing better than our vari-plumaged parrakeets, is not the strife at least equal? Does not fine colour yield as much pleasure to the artist eye as fine song to the artist ear? When will Englified city critics realise that Australia is a country which extends through forty degrees of latitude and thirty-five of longitude, and comprehends all climates, all scenery – snow-capped mountain and torrid desert, placid lake and winding river, torrent and brook, charm as well as grandeur, garden and homely field as well as barren solitude?

It is heredity and custom which again betray us. The rose is a beautiful flower, but the most beautiful only because thousands of years of care and cultivation have been lavished to bring it to perfection, because thousands of lovers have breathed its perfume, thousands of poets have apostrophised its exquisite form. Give the same care and cultivation to a hundred modest bush flowers, draw them from obscurity as the rose has been drawn from the parent wilderness, let them be worshipped and adored through centuries of sentiment – and we have here the rivals of the rose herself. Cluster the associations of the oak and yew around the yarran or the cedar (all the cedars of Lebanon were not more stately than those of the Herberton scrub), and the oak and yew will shrink, not indeed into insignificance, but into their proper proportion as regarded from Australia. In a word, let us look at our country and its fauna and flora, its trees and streams and mountains, through clear Australian eyes, not through bias-bleared English spectacles; and there is no more beautiful country in the world.

It will be the fault of the writers, not of the land, if Australian literature does not by-and-by become memorable. In the field of the short sketch or story, for example, – the field which includes this book, – what country can offer to writers better material than Australia? We are not yet snug in cities and hamlets, moulded by routine, regimented to a pattern. Every man who roams the Australian wilderness is a potential knight of Romance; every man who grapples with the Australian desert for a livelihood might sing a Homeric chant of victory, or listen, baffled and beaten, to an Aeschylean dirge of defeat. The marvels of the adventurous are our daily common-places. The drama of the conflict between Man and Destiny is played here in a scenic setting whose novelty is full of vital suggestion for the literary artist. In the twilit labour of the timber-getter in a Richmond scrub; in the spectacle of the Westralian prospector tramping across his mirage-haunted waste; in the tropic glimpse of the Thursday Island pearling fleet, manned by men of a dozen turbulent races, – the luggers floating so calmly above a search so furious; – here, and in a hundred places beside, there is wealth of novel inspiration for the writers who will live Australia's life and utter her message. And when those writers come, let us tell them that we will never rest contented until Australian authors reach the highest standards set in literature, in order that we may set the standards higher and preach discontent anew.

EDWARD DYSON
A Golden Shanty

About ten years ago, not a day's tramp from Ballarat, set well back
from a dusty track that started nowhere in particular and had no
destination worth mentioning, stood the Shamrock Hotel. It was
a low, rambling, disjointed structure, and bore strong evidence
of having been designed by an amateur artist in a moment
of vinous frenzy. It reached out in several well-defined angles,
and had a lean-to building stuck on here and there; numerous
outhouses were dropped down about it promiscuously; its walls
were propped up in places with logs, and its moss-covered
shingle roof, bowed down with the weight of years and a great
accumulation of stones, hoop-iron, jam-tins, broken glassware,
and dried possum skins, bulged threateningly, on the verge of
utter collapse. The Shamrock was built of sun-dried bricks, of an
unhealthy bilious tint. Its dirty, shattered windows were plugged
in places with old hats and discarded female apparel, and draped
with green blinds, many of which had broken their moorings, and
hung despondently by one corner. Groups of ungainly fowls
coursed the succulent grasshopper before the bar door; a moody,
distempered goat rubbed her ribs against a shattered trough
roughly hewn from the butt of a tree, and a matronly old sow
of spare proportions wallowed complacently in the dust of the
road, surrounded by her squealing brood.

A battered sign hung out over the door of the Shamrock,
informing people that Michael Doyle was licensed to sell fer-
mented and spirituous liquors, and that good accommodation
could be afforded to both man and beast at the lowest current
rates. But that sign was most unreliable; the man who applied
to be accommodated with anything beyond ardent bever-
ages – liquors so fiery that they 'bit all the way down' – evoked
the astonishment of the proprietor. Bed and board were quite out
of the province of the Shamrock. There was, in fact, only one
couch professedly at the disposal of the weary wayfarer, and this,
according to the statement of the few persons who had ever
ventured to try it, seemed stuffed with old boots and stubble; it
was located immediately beneath a hen-roost, which was the
resting-place of a maternal fowl, addicted on occasion to nursing
her chickens upon the tired sleeper's chest. The 'turnover' at the

Shamrock was not at all extensive, for, saving an occasional agricultural labourer who came from 'beyant' – which was the versatile host's way of designating any part within a radius of five miles – to revel in an occasional spree, the trade was confined to the passing cockatoo farmer, who invariably arrived on a bony, drooping prad, took a drink, and shuffled away amid clouds of dust.

The only other dwellings within sight of the Shamrock were a cluster of frail, ramshackle huts, compiled of slabs, scraps of matting, zinc, and gunny-bag. These were the habitations of a colony of squalid, gibbering Chinese fossickers, who herded together like hogs in a crowded pen, as if they had been restricted to that spot on pain of death, or its equivalent, a washing.

About a quarter of a mile behind the Shamrock ran, or rather crawled, the sluggish waters of the Yellow Creek. Once upon a time, when the Shamrock was first built, the creek was a beautiful limpid rivulet, running between verdant banks; but an enterprising prospector, wandering that way, and liking the indications, put down a shaft, and bottomed on 'the wash' at twenty feet, getting half an ounce to the dish. A rush set in, and within twelve months the banks of the creek, for a distance of two miles, were denuded of their timber, torn up, and covered with unsightly heaps. The creek had been diverted from its natural course half a dozen times, and hundreds of diggers, like busy ants, delved into the earth and covered its surface with red, white, and yellow tips. Then the miners left almost as suddenly as they had come; the Shamrock, which had resounded with wild revelry, became as silent as a morgue, and desolation brooded on the face of the country. When Mr. Michael Doyle, whose greatest ambition in life had been to become a lord of a pub, invested in that lucrative country property, saplings were growing between the deserted holes of the diggings, and agriculture had superseded the mining industry in those parts.

Landlord Doyle was of Irish extraction; his stock was so old that everybody had forgotten where and when it originated, but Mickey was not proud – he assumed no unnecessary style, and his personal appearance would not have led you to infer that there had been a king in his family, and that his paternal progenitor had killed a landlord 'wanst'. Mickey was a small, scraggy man, with a mop of grizzled hair and a little, red, humorous face, ever bristling with auburn stubble. His trousers were the most striking things about him; they were built on the premises, and almost contained enough stuff to make him a full suit and a winter overcoat. Mrs. Doyle manufactured those pants after plans and specifications of her own designing, and was mighty proud when Michael would yank them up to his armpits, and amble round, peering about discontentedly over the waistband. 'They was th' great savin' in weskits,' she said.

Of late years it had taken all Mr. Doyle's ingenuity to make ends meet. The tribe of dirty, unkempt urchins who swarmed about the place 'took a power of feedin' ', and Mrs. D. herself was 'th' big ater'. 'Ye do be atin' twenty-four hours a day,' her lord was wont to remark, 'and thin yez must get up av noights for more. Whin ye'r not atin' ye'r munchin' a schnack, bad cess t'ye.'

In order to provide the provender for his unreasonably hungry family, Mickey had been compelled to supplement his takings as a Boniface by acting alternately as fossicker, charcoal-burner, and 'wood-jamber'; but it came 'terrible hard' on the little man, who waxed thinner and thinner, and sank deeper into his trousers every year. Then, to augment his troubles, came that pestiferous heathen, the teetotal Chinee. One hot summer's day he arrived in numbers, like a plague, armed with picks, shovels, dishes, cradles, and tubs, and with a clatter of tools and a babble of grotesque gibberish, camped by the creek and refused to go away again. The awesome solitude of the abandoned diggings was ruthlessly broken. The deserted field, with its white mounds and decaying windlass-stands fallen aslant, which had lain like a long-forgotten cemetery buried in primeval forest, was now desecrated by the hand of the Mongol, and the sound of his weird, Oriental oaths. The Chows swarmed over the spot, tearing open old sores, shovelling old tips, sluicing old tailings, digging, cradling, puddling, ferreting into every nook and cranny.

Mr. Doyle observed the foreign invasion with mingled feelings of righteous anger and pained solicitude. He had found fossicking by the creek very handy to fall back upon when the wood-jambing trade was not brisk; but now that industry was ruined by Chinese competition, and Michael could only find relief in deep and earnest profanity.

With the pagan influx began the mysterious disappearance of small valuables from the premises of Michael Doyle, licensed victualler. Sedate, fluffy old hens, hitherto noted for their strict propriety and regular hours, would leave the place at dead of night, and return from their nocturnal rambles never more; stay-at-home sucking pigs, which had erstwhile absolutely refused to be driven from the door, corrupted by the new evil, absented themselves suddenly from the precincts of the Shamrock, taking with them cooking utensils and various other articles of small value, and ever afterwards their fate became a matter for speculation. At last a favourite young porker went, whereupon its lord and master, resolved to prosecute inquiries, bounced into the Mongolian camp, and, without any unnecessary preamble, opened the debate.

'Look here, now,' he observed, shaking his fist at the group, and bristling fiercely, 'which av ye dhirty haythen furriners cum up to me house lasht noight and shtole me pig Nancy? Which av ye is it, so't I kin bate him! ye thavin' hathins?'

The placid Orientals surveyed Mr. Doyle coolly, and, innocently smiling, said, 'No savee'; then bandied jests at his expense in their native tongue, and laughed the little man to scorn. Incensed by the evident ridicule of the 'haythen furriners', and goaded on by the smothered squeal of a hidden pig, Michael 'went for' the nearest Asiatic, and proceeded to 'put a head on him as big as a tank', amid a storm of kicks and digs from the other Chows. Presently the battle began to go against the Irish cause; but Mrs. Mickey, making a timely appearance, warded off the surplus Chinamen by chipping at their skulls with an axe-handle. The riot was soon quelled, and the two Doyles departed triumphantly, bearing away a corpulent young pig, and leaving several broken, discouraged Chinamen to be doctored at the common expense.

After this gladsome little episode the Chinamen held off for a few weeks. Then they suddenly changed their tactics, and proceeded to cultivate the friendship of Michael Doyle and his able-bodied wife. They liberally patronised the Shamrock, and beguiled the licensee with soft but cheerful conversation; they flattered Mrs. Doyle in seductive pigeon-English, and endeavoured to ensnare the children's young affections with preserved ginger. Michael regarded these advances with misgiving; he suspected the Mongolians' intentions were not honourable, but he was not a man to spoil trade – to drop the substance for the shadow.

This state of affairs had continued for some time before the landlord of the Shamrock noticed that his new customers made a point of carrying off a brick every time they visited his caravansary. When leaving, the bland heathen would cast his discriminating eye around the place, seize upon one of the sun-dried bricks with which the ground was littered, and steal away with a nonchalant air – as though it had just occurred to him that the brick would be a handy thing to keep by him.

The matter puzzled Mr. Doyle sorely; he ruminated over it, but he could only arrive at the conclusion that it was not advisable to lose custom for the sake of a few bricks; so the Chinese continued to walk off with his building material. When asked what they intended to do with the bricks, they assumed an expression of the most deplorably hopeless idiocy, and suddenly lost their acquaintance with the 'Inglishiman' tongue. If bricks were mentioned they became as devoid of sense as wombats, although they seemed extremely intelligent on most other points. Mickey noticed that there was no building in progress at their camp, also that there were no bricks to be seen about the domiciles of the pagans, and he tried to figure out the mystery on a slate, but, on account of his lamentable ignorance of mathematics, failed to reach the unknown quantity and elucidate the enigma. He watched the invaders march off with all the loose bricks that were scattered around, and never once complained; but when they began to abstract one end of his licensed premises, he felt himself called upon, as a husband and father, to arise and enter a protest, which he did, pointing out to the Yellow Agony, in graphic and forcible language, the gross wickedness of robbing a struggling man of his house and home, and promising faithfully to 'bate' the next lop-eared Child of the Sun whom he 'cot shiften' a'er a brick.'

'Ye dogs! Wud yez shtale me hotel, so't whin me family go insoide they'll be out in the rain?' he queried, looking hurt and indignant.

The Chinamen said, 'No savee.' Yet, after this warning, doubtless out of consideration for the feelings of Mr. Doyle, they went to great pains and displayed much ingenuity in abstracting bricks without his cognizance. But Mickey was active; he watched them closely, and whenever he caught a Chow in the act, a brief and one-sided conflict raged, and a dismantled Chinaman crawled home with much difficulty.

This violent conduct on the part of the landlord served in time to entirely alienate the Mongolian custom from the Shamrock, and once more Mickey and the Chows spake not when they met. Once more, too, promising young pullets, and other portable valuables, began to go astray, and still the hole in the wall grew till the after-part of the Shamrock looked as if it had suffered recent bombardment. The Chinamen came while Michael slept, and filched his hotel inch by inch. They lost their natural rest, and ran the gauntlet of Mr. Doyle's stick and curse – for the sake of a few bricks. At all hours of the night they crept through the gloom, and warily stole a bat or two, getting away unnoticed perhaps, or, mayhap, only disturbing the slumbers of Mrs. Doyle, who was a very light sleeper for a woman of her size. In the latter case the lady would awaken her lord by holding his nose – a very effective plan of her own – and, filled to overflowing with the rage which comes of a midnight awakening, Mickey would turn out of doors in his shirt to cope with the marauders, and course them over the paddocks. If he caught a heathen he laid himself out for five minutes' energetic entertainment, which fully repaid him for lost rest and missing hens, and left a Chinaman too heart-sick and sore to steal anything for at least a week. But the Chinamen's friends would come as usual, and the pillage went on.

Michael Doyle puzzled himself to prostration over this insatiable and unreasonable hunger for bricks; such an infatuation on the part of men for cold and unresponsive clay had never before come within the pale of his experience. Times out of mind he threatened to 'have the law on the yalla blaggards'; but the law was a long way off, and the Celestial housebreakers continued to elope with scraps of the Shamrock, taking the proprietor's assaults humbly and as a matter of course.

'Why do ye be shtealing me house?' fiercely queried Mr. Doyle of a submissive Chow, whom he had taken one night in the act of ambling off with a brick in either hand.

'Me no steal 'em no feah - odder feller, him steal 'em,' replied the quaking pagan.

Mickey was dumb-stricken for the moment by this awful prevarication; but that did not impair the velocity of his kick - this to his great subsequent regret, for the Chinaman had stowed a third brick away in his pants for convenience of transit, and the landlord struck that brick; then he sat down and repeated aloud all the profanity he knew.

The Chinaman escaped, and had the presence of mind enough to retain his burden of clay.

Month after month the work of devastation went on. Mr Doyle fixed ingenious mechanical contrivances about his house, and turned out at early dawn to see how many Chinamen he had 'nailed' - only to find his spring-traps stolen and his hotel yawning more desperately than ever. Then Michael could but lift up his voice and swear - nothing else afforded him any relief.

At last he hit upon a brilliant idea. He commissioned a 'cocky' who was journeying into Ballarat to buy him a dog - the largest, fiercest, ugliest, hungriest animal the town afforded; and next day a powerful, ill-tempered canine, almost as big as a pony, and quite as ugly as any nightmare, was duly installed as guardian and night-watch at the Shamrock. Right well the good dog performed his duty. On the following morning he had trophies to show in the shape of a boot, a scrap of blue dungaree trousers, half a pigtail, a yellow ear, and a large part of a partially-shaved scalp; and just then the nocturnal visits ceased. The Chows spent a week skirmishing around, endeavouring to call the dog off, but he was neither to be begged, borrowed, nor stolen; he was too old-fashioned to eat poisoned meat, and he prevented the smallest approach to familiarity on the part of a Chinaman by snapping off the most serviceable portions of his vestments, and always fetching a scrap of heathen along with them.

This, in time, sorely discouraged the patient Children of the Sun, who drew off to hold congress and give the matter weighty consideration. After deliberating for some days, the yellow settlement appointed a deputation to wait upon Mr. Doyle. Mickey saw them coming, and armed himself with a log and unchained his dog. Mrs. Doyle ranged up alongside, brandishing her axe-handle, but by humble gestures and a deferential bearing the Celestial deputation signified a truce. So Michael held his dog down, and rested on his arms to await developments. The Chinamen advanced, smiling blandly; they gave Mr. and Mrs. Doyle fraternal greeting, and squirmed with that wheedling obsequiousness peculiar to 'John' when he has something to gain by it. A pock-marked leper placed himself in the van as spokesman.

'Nicee day, Missa Doyle,' said the moon-faced gentleman, sweetly. Then, with a sudden expression of great interest, and nodding towards Mrs Doyle, "How you sissetah?"

'Foind out! Fwhat yer wantin'?' replied the host of the Shamrock, gruffly. 'T' shtale more bricks, ye crawlin' blaggards?'

'No, no. Me not steal 'em blick – odder feller; he hide 'em; build big house byem-bye.'

'Ye loi, ye screw-faced nayger! I seed ye do it, and if yez don't cut and run I'll lave the dog loose to feed on yer dhirty carcasses.'

The dog tried to reach for his favourite hold, Mickey brandished his log, and Mrs. Doyle took a fresh grip of her weapon. This demonstration gave the Chows a cold shiver, and brought them promptly down to business.

'We buy 'em hotel; what for you sell 'em – eh?'

'Fwhat! yez buy me hotel? D'ye mane it? Purchis th' primisis and yez can shtale ivery brick at yer laysure. But ye're joakin'. Whoop! Look ye here! I'll have th' lot av yez aten up in two minits if yez play yer Choinase thricks on Michael Doyle.'

The Chinamen eagerly protested that they were in earnest, and Mickey gave them a judicial hearing. For two years he had been in want of a customer for the Shamrock, and he now hailed the offer of his visitors with secret delight. After haggling for an hour, during which time the ignorant Hi Yup of the contorted countenance displayed his usual business tact, a bargain was struck. The yellow men agreed to give fifty pounds cash for the Shamrock and all buildings appertaining thereto, and the following Monday was the day fixed for Michael to journey into Ballarat with a couple of representative heathens to sign the transfer papers and receive the cash.

The deputation departed smiling, and when it gave the news of its triumph to the other denizens of the camp there was a perfect babel of congratulations in the quaint dialogue of the Mongol. The Chinamen proceeded to make a night of it in their own outlandish way, indulging freely in the seductive opium, and holding high carouse over an extemporized fantan table, proceedings which made it evident that they were getting to windward of Michael Doyle, licensed victualler.

Michael, too, was rejoicing with exceeding great joy, and felicitating himself on being the shrewdest little man who ever left the 'ould sod'. He had not hoped to get more than a twenty-pound note for the dilapidated old humpy, erected on Crown land, and unlikely to stand the wear and tear of another year. As for the business, it had fallen to zero, and would not have kept a Chinaman in soap. So Mr. Doyle plumed himself on his bargain, and expanded till he nearly filled his capacious garments. Still, he was harassed to know what could possibly have attached the Chinese so strongly to the Shamrock. They had taken samples from every part of the establishment, and fully satisfied themselves as to the quality of the bricks, and now they wanted to buy. It was most peculiar. Michael 'had never seen anything so quare before, savin' wanst whin his grandfather was a boy'.

After the agreement arrived at between the publican and the Chinese, one or two of the latter hung about the hotel nearly all their time, in sentinel fashion. The dog was kept on the chain, and lay in the sun in a state of moody melancholy, narrowly scrutinizing the Mongolians. He was a strongly anti-Chinese dog, and had been educated to regard the almond-eyed invader with mistrust and hate; it was repugnant to his principles to lie low when the heathen was around, and he evinced his resentment by growling ceaselessly.

Sunday dawned. It was a magnificent morning; but the rattle of the Chinamen's cradles and toms sounded from the creek as usual. Three or four suave and civil Asiatics, however, still lingered around the Shamrock, and kept an eye on it in the interest of all, for the purchase of the hotel was to be a joint-stock affair. These 'Johns' seemed to imagine they had already taken lawful possession; they sat in the bar most of the time, drinking little, but always affable and genial. Michael suffered them to stay, for he feared that any fractiousness on his part might upset the agreement, and that was a consummation to be avoided above all things. They had told him, with many tender smiles and much gesticulation, that they intended to live in the house when it became theirs; but Mr. Doyle was not interested – his fifty pounds was all he thought of.

Michael was in high spirits that morning; he beamed complacently on all and sundry, appointed the day as a time of family rejoicing, and in the excess of his emotion actually slew for dinner a prime young sucking pig, an extravagant luxury indulged in by the Doyles on state occasions. On this particular Sunday the younger members of the Doyle household gathered round the festive board and waited impatiently for the lifting of the lid of the camp-oven. There were nine children in all, ranging in years from fourteen downwards – 'foine, shtrappin' childer, with th' clear brain,' said the prejudiced Michael. The round, juicy sucker was at last placed upon the table. Mrs. Doyle stood prepared to administer her department – serving the vegetables to her hungry brood – and, armed with a formidable knife and fork, Michael, enveloped in savoury steam, hovered over the pig.

But there was one function yet to be performed – a function which came as regularly as Sunday's dinner itself. Never, for years, had the housefather failed to touch up a certain prodigious knife on one particular hard yellow brick in the wall by the door, preparatory to carving the Sunday's meat. Mickey examined the edge of his weapon critically, and found it unsatisfactory. The knife was nearly ground through to the backbone; another 'touch-up' and it must surely collapse, but, in view of his changed circumstances, Mr. Doyle felt that he might take the risk. The brick, too, was worn an inch deep. A few sharp strokes from Mickey's vigorous right arm were all that was required; but alas! the knife snapped, whereupon Mr. Doyle swore at the brick, as if holding it immediately responsible for the mishap, and stabbed at it fiercely with the broken carver.

'Howly Moses! Fwhat's that?'

The brick fell to pieces, and there, embedded in the wall, gleaming in the sunbeam, was a nugget of yellow gold. With feverish haste Mickey tore the brick from its bedding, and smashed the gold-bearing fragment in the hearth. The nugget was a little beauty, smooth, round, and four ounces to a grain.

The sucking pig froze and stiffened in its fat, the 'taters' and the cabbage stood neglected on the dishes. The truth had dawned upon Michael, and, whilst the sound of a spirited debate in musical Chinese echoed from the bar, his family were gathered around him, open-mouthed, and Mickey was industriously, but quietly, pounding the sun-dried brick in a digger's mortar. Two bricks, one from either end of the Shamrock, were pulverized, and Michael panned off the dirt in a tub of water which stood in the kitchen. Result: seven grains of waterworn gold. Until now Michael had worked dumbly, in a fit of nervous excitement; now he started up, bristling like a hedgehog.

'Let loose th' dog, Mary Melinda Doyle!' he howled, and uttering a mighty whoop, he bounded into the bar to dust those Chinamen off his premises.

'Gerrout!' he screamed – 'Gerrout av me primises, ye thavin' crawlers!' And he frolicked with the astounded Mongolians like a tornado in full blast, thumping at a shaven occiput whenever one showed out of the struggling crowd. The Chinamen left; they found the dog waiting for them outside, and he encouraged them to greater haste. Like startled fawns the heathens fled, and Mr Doyle followed them, howling:

'Buy the Shamrock, wud yez! Robbers! Thaves! Fitch back th' soide o' me house, or Oi'll have th' law onto yez all.'

The damaged escapees communicated the intelligence of their overthrow to their brethren on the creek, and the news carried consternation, and deep, dark woe to the pagans, who clustered together and ruefully discussed the situation.

Mr. Doyle was wildly jubilant. His joy was only tinctured with a spice of bitterness, the result of knowing that the 'haythens' had got away with a few hundreds of his precious bricks. He tried to figure out the amount of gold his hotel must contain, but again his ignorance of arithmetic tripped him up, and already in imagination Michael Doyle, licensed victualler, was a millionaire and a J.P.

The Shamrock was really a treasure-house. The dirt of which the bricks were composed had been taken from the banks of the Yellow Creek, years before the outbreak of the rush, by an eccentric German, who had settled on that sylvan spot. The German died and his grotesque structure passed into other hands. Time went on, and then came the rush. The banks of the creek were found to be charged with gold for miles, but never for a moment did it occur to anybody that the clumsy old building by the track, now converted into a hotel, was composed of the same rich dirt; never till years after, when by accident one of the Mongolian fossickers discovered grains of gold in a few bats he had taken to use as hobs. The intelligence was conveyed to his fellows; they got more bricks and more gold – hence the robbery of Mr. Doyle's building material and the anxiety of the Mongolians to buy the Shamrock.

Before nightfall Michael summoned half-a-dozen men from 'beyant', to help him in protecting his hotel from a possible Chinese invasion. Other bricks were crushed and yielded splendid prospects. The Shamrock's small stock of liquor was drunk, and everybody became hilarious. On the Sunday night, under cover of the darkness, the Chows made a sudden sally on the Shamrock, hoping to get away with plunder. They were violently received, however; they got no bricks, and returned to their camp broken and disconsolate.

Next day the work of demolition was begun. Drays were backed up against the Shamrock, and load by load the precious bricks were carted away to a neighbouring battery. The Chinamen slouched about, watching greedily, but their now half-hearted attempts at interference met with painful reprisal. Mr. Doyle sent his family and furniture to Ballarat, and in a week there was not a vestige left to mark the spot where once the Shamrock flourished. Every scrap of its walls went through the mill, and the sum of one thousand nine hundred and eighty-three pounds sterling was cleared out of the ruins of the hostelry. Mr. Doyle is now a man of some standing in Victoria, and as a highly respected J.P. has often been pleased to inform a Chinaman that it was 'foive pound or a month'.

A.B. ('BANJO') PATERSON
Clancy of The Overflow

I had written him a letter which I had, for want of better
  Knowledge, sent to where I met him down the Lachlan, years
    ago,
He was shearing when I knew him, so I sent the letter to him,
  Just 'on spec,' addressed as follows, 'Clancy, of The Overflow.'

And an answer came directed in a writing unexpected,
  (And I think the same was written with a thumb-nail dipped
    in tar)
'Twas his shearing mate who wrote it, and *verbatim* I will quote
    it:
  'Clancy's gone to Queensland droving, and we don't know
    where he are.'

In my wild erratic fancy visions come to me of Clancy
  Gone a-droving 'down the Cooper' where the Western
    drovers go;
As the stock are slowly stringing, Clancy rides behind them
    singing,
  For the drover's life has pleasures that the townsfolk never
    know.

And the bush hath friends to meet him, and their kindly voices
    greet him
  In the murmur of the breezes and the river on its bars,
And he sees the vision splendid of the sunlit plains extended,
  And at night the wond'rous glory of the everlasting stars.

I am sitting in my dingy little office, where a stingy
  Ray of sunlight struggles feebly down between the houses
    tall,
And the foetid air and gritty of the dusty, dirty city
  Through the open window floating, spreads its foulness
    over all.

And in place of lowing cattle, I can hear the fiendish rattle
   Of the tramways and the 'buses making hurry down the
     street,
And the language uninviting of the gutter children fighting,
   Comes fitfully and faintly through the ceaseless tramp of feet.

And the hurrying people daunt me, and their pallid faces
     haunt me
   As they shoulder one another in their rush and nervous
     haste,
With their eager eyes and greedy, and their stunted forms and
     weedy,
   For townsfolk have no time to grow, they have no time to
     waste.

And I somehow rather fancy that I'd like to change with
     Clancy,
   Like to take a turn at droving where the seasons come and
     go,
While he faced the round eternal of the cash-book and the
     journal –
   But I doubt he'd suit the office, Clancy, of 'The Overflow.'

HENRY LAWSON
Middleton's Rouseabout

Tall and freckled and sandy,
  Face of a country lout;
This was the picture of Andy,
  Middleton's Rouseabout.

Type of a coming nation,
  In the land of cattle and sheep,
Worked on Middleton's station,
  'Pound a week and his keep.'

On Middleton's wide dominions
  Plied the stockwhip and shears;
Hadn't any opinions,
  Hadn't any 'idears.'

Swiftly the years went over,
  Liquor and drought prevailed;
Middleton went as a drover,
  After his station had failed.

Type of a careless nation,
  Men who are soon played out,
Middleton was: – and his station
  Was bought by the Rouseabout.

Flourishing beard and sandy,
  Tall and robust and stout;
This is the picture of Andy,
  Middleton's Rouseabout.

Now on his own dominions
  Works with his overseers;
Hasn't any opinions,
  Hasn't any 'idears.'

HENRY LAWSON
The Union Buries Its Dead

While out boating one Sunday afternoon on a billabong across the river, we saw a young man on horseback driving some horses along the bank. He said it was a fine day, and asked if the water was deep there. The joker of our party said it was deep enough to drown him, and he laughed and rode farther up. We didn't take much notice of him.

Next day a funeral gathered at a corner pub and asked each other in to have a drink while waiting for the hearse. They passed away some of the time dancing jigs to a piano in the bar parlour. They passed away the rest of the time sky-larking and fighting.

The defunct was a young union labourer, about twenty-five, who had been drowned the previous day while trying to swim some horses across a billabong of the Darling.

He was almost a stranger in town, and the fact of his having been a union man accounted for the funeral. The police found some union papers in his swag, and called at the General Labourers' Union Office for information about him. That's how we knew. The secretary had very little information to give. The departed was a 'Roman', and the majority of the town were otherwise – but unionism is stronger than creed. Drink, however, is stronger than unionism; and, when the hearse presently arrived, more than two-thirds of the funeral were unable to follow. They were too drunk.

The procession numbered fifteen, fourteen souls following the broken shell of a soul. Perhaps not one of the fourteen possessed a soul any more than the corpse did – but that doesn't matter.

Four or five of the funeral, who were boarders at the pub borrowed a trap which the landlord used to carry passengers to and from the railway station. They were strangers to us who were on foot, and we to them. We were all strangers to the corpse.

A horseman, who looked like a drover just returned from a big trip, dropped into our dusty wake and followed us a few hundred yards, dragging his pack-horse behind him, but a friend made wild and demonstrative signals from a hotel verandah – hooking at the air in front with his right hand and jobbing his left thumb over his shoulder in the direction of the bar – so the drover hauled off and didn't catch up to us any more. He was a stranger to the entire show.

We walked in twos. There were three twos. It was very hot and dusty; the heat rushed in fierce dazzling rays across every iron roof and light-coloured wall that was turned to the sun. One or two pubs closed respectfully until we got past. They closed their bar doors and the patrons went in and out through some side or back entrance for a few minutes. Bushmen seldom grumble at an inconvenience of this sort, when it is caused by a funeral. They have too much respect for the dead.

On the way to the cemetery we passed three shearers sitting on the shady side of a fence. One was drunk – very drunk. The other two covered their right ears with their hats, out of respect for the departed – whoever he might have been – and one of them kicked the drunk and muttered something to him.

He straightened himself up, stared, and reached helplessly for his hat, which he shoved half off and then on again. Then he made a great effort to pull himself together – and succeeded. He stood up, braced his back against the fence, knocked off his hat, and remorsefully placed his foot on it – to keep it off his head till the funeral passed.

A tall, sentimental drover, who walked by my side, cynically quoted Byronic verses suitable to the occasion – to death – and asked with pathetic humour whether we thought the dead man's ticket would be recognized 'over yonder'. It was a G.L.U. ticket, and the general opinion was that it would be recognized.

Presently my friend said:

'You remember when we were in the boat yesterday, we saw a man driving some horses along the bank?'

'Yes.'

He nodded at the hearse and said:

'Well, that's him.'

I thought awhile.

'I didn't take any particular notice of him,' I said. 'He said something, didn't he?'

'Yes; said it was a fine day. You'd have taken more notice if you'd known that he was doomed to die in the hour, and that those were the last words he would say to any man in this world.'

'To be sure,' said a full voice from the rear. 'If ye'd known that, ye'd have prolonged the conversation.'

We plodded on across the railway line and along the hot, dusty road which ran to the cemetery, some of us talking about the accident, and lying about the narrow escapes we had had ourselves. Presently some one said:

'There's the Devil.'

I looked up and saw a priest standing in the shade of the tree by the cemetery gate.

The hearse was drawn up and the tail-boards were opened. The funeral extinguished its right ear with its hat as four men lifted the coffin out and laid it over the grave. The priest – a pale, quiet young fellow – stood under the shade of a sapling which grew at the head of the grave. He took off his hat, dropped it carelessly on the ground, and proceeded to business. I noticed that one or two heathens winced slightly when the holy water was sprinkled on the coffin. The drops quickly evaporated, and the little round black spots they left were soon dusted over; but the spots showed, by contrast, the cheapness and shabbiness of the cloth with which the coffin was covered. It seemed black before; now it looked a dusky grey.

Just here man's ignorance and vanity made a farce of the funeral. A big, bull-necked publican, with heavy, blotchy features, and a supremely ignorant expression, picked up the priest's straw hat and held it about two inches over the head of his reverence during the whole of the service. The father, be it remembered, was standing in the shade. A few shoved their hats on and off uneasily, struggling between their disgust for the living and their respect for the dead. The hat had a conical crown and a brim sloping down all round like a sunshade, and the publican held it with his great red claw spread over the crown. To do the priest justice, perhaps he didn't notice the incident. A stage priest or parson in the same position might have said, 'Put the hat down, my friend; is not the memory of our departed brother worth more than my complexion?' A wattlebark layman might have expressed himself in stronger language, none the less to the point. But my priest seemed unconscious of what was going on. Besides, the publican was a great and important pillar of the Church. He couldn't, as an ignorant and conceited ass, lose such a good opportunity of asserting his faithfulness and importance to his Church.

The grave looked very narrow under the coffin, and I drew a breath of relief when the box slid easily down. I saw a coffin get stuck once, at Rookwood, and it had to be yanked out with difficulty, and laid on the sods at the feet of the heartbroken relations, who howled dismally while the grave-diggers widened the hole. But they don't cut contracts so fine in the West. Our grave-digger was not altogether bowelless, and, out of respect for that human quality described as 'feelin's', he scraped up some light and dusty soil and threw it down to deaden the fall of the clay lumps on the coffin. He also tried to steer the first few shovelfuls gently down against the end of the grave with the back of the shovel turned outwards, but the hard, dry Darling River clods rebounded and knocked all the same. It didn't matter much – nothing does. The fall of lumps of clay on a stranger's coffin doesn't sound any different from the fall of the same things on an ordinary wooden box – at least I didn't notice anything awesome or unusual in the sound; but, perhaps, one of us – the most sensitive – might have been impressed by being reminded of a burial long ago, when the thump of every sod jolted his heart.

I have left out the wattle – because it wasn't there. I have also neglected to mention the heart-broken old mate, with his grizzled head bowed and great pearly drops streaming down his rugged cheeks. He was absent – he was probably 'Out Back'. For similar reasons I have omitted reference to the suspicious moisture in the eyes of a bearded bush ruffian named Bill. Bill failed to turn up, and the only moisture was that which was induced by the heat. I have left out the 'sad Australian sunset' because the sun was not going down at the time. The burial took place exactly at mid-day.

The dead bushman's name was Jim, apparently; but they found no portraits, nor locks of hair, nor any love letters, nor anything of that kind in his swag – not even a reference to his mother; only some papers relating to union matters. Most of us didn't know the name till we saw it on the coffin; we knew him as 'that poor chap that got drowned yesterday'.

'So his name's James Tyson,' said my drover acquaintance, looking at the plate.

'Why! Didn't you know that before?' I asked.

'No; but I knew he was a union man.'

It turned out, afterwards, that J.T. wasn't his real name – only 'the name he went by'.

Anyhow he was buried by it, and most of the 'Great Australian Dailies' have mentioned in their brevity columns that a young man named James John Tyson was drowned in a billabong of the Darling last Sunday.

We did hear, later on, what his real name was; but if we ever chance to read it in the 'Missing Friends Column', we shall not be able to give any information to heart-broken Mother or Sister or Wife, nor to any one who could let him hear something to his advantage – for we have already forgotten the name.

HENRY LAWSON
The Little World Left Behind

I lately revisited a western agricultural district in Australia after many years. The railway had reached it, but otherwise things were drearily, hopelessly, depressingly unchanged. There was the same old grant, comprising several thousands of acres of the richest land in the district, lying idle still, except for a few horses allowed to run there for a shilling a-head per week.

There were the same old selections – about as far off as ever from becoming freeholds – shoved back among the barren ridges; dusty little patches in the scrub, full of stones and stumps, and called farms, deserted every few years, and tackled again by some little dried-up family, or some old hatter, and then given best once more. There was the cluster of farms on the flat, and in the foot of the gully, owned by Australians of Irish or English descent, with the same number of stumps in the wheat-paddock, the same broken fences and tumble-down huts and yards, and the same weak, sleepy attempt made every season to scratch up the ground and raise a crop. And along the creek the German farmers – the only people there worthy of the name – toiling (men, women, and children) from daylight till dark, like slaves, just as they always had done; the elder sons stoop-shouldered old men at thirty.

The row about the boundary fence between the Sweeneys and the Joneses was unfinished still, and the old feud between the Dunderblitzens and the Blitzendunders was more deadly than ever – it started three generations ago over a stray bull. The O'Dunn was still fighting for his great object in life, which was not to be 'onneighborly,' as he put it. 'I *don't* want to be onneighborly,' he said, 'but I'll be aven wid some of 'em yit. It's almost impossible for a dacent man to live in sich a neighborhood and not be onneighborly, thry how he will. But I'll be aven wid some of 'em yit, marruk my wurrud.'

Jones's red steer – it couldn't have been the same red steer – was continually breaking into Rooney's 'whate an' bringin' ivery head av the other cattle afther him, and ruinin' him intirely.' The Rooneys and M'Kenzies were at daggers drawn, even to the youngest child, over the impounding of a horse belonging to Pat Rooney's brother-in-law, by a distant relation of the M'Kenzies, which had happened nine years ago.

The same sun-burned, masculine women went past to market twice a-week in the same old carts and driving much the same quality of carrion. The string of overloaded spring-carts, buggies, and sweating horses went whirling into town, to 'service,' through clouds of dust and broiling heat, on Sunday morning, and came driving cruelly out again at noon. The neighbours' sons rode over in the afternoon, as of old, and hung up their poor, ill-used little horses to bake in the sun, and sat on their heels about the verandah, and drawled drearily concerning crops, fruit, trees, and vines, and horses and cattle; the drought and 'smut' and 'rust' in wheat, and the 'ploorer' (pleuro-pneumonia) in cattle, and other cheerful things; that there colt or filly, or that there cattle-dog (pup or bitch) o' mine (or 'Jim's'). They always talked most of farming there, where no farming worthy of the name was possible – except by Germans and Chinamen. Towards evening the old local relic of the golden days dropped in and announced that he intended to 'put down a shaft' next week, in a spot where he'd been going to put it down twenty years ago – and every week since. It was nearly time that somebody sunk a hole and buried him there.

An old local body named Mrs. Witherly still went into town twice a-week with her 'bit av prodjuce,' as O'Dunn called it. She still drove a long, bony, blind horse in a long rickety dray, with a stout sapling for a whip, and about twenty yards of clothes-line reins. The floor of the dray covered part of an acre, and one wheel was always ahead of the other – or behind, according to which shaft was pulled. She wore, to all appearances, the same short frock, faded shawl, men's 'lastic sides, and white hood that she had on when the world was made. She still stopped just twenty minutes at old Mrs. Leatherly's on the way in for a yarn and a cup of tea – as she had always done, on the same days and at the same time within the memory of the hoariest local liar. However, she had a new clothes-line bent on to the old horse's front end – and we fancy that was the reason she didn't recognise us at first. She had never looked younger than a hard hundred within the memory of man. Her shrivelled face was the colour of leather, and crossed and recrossed with lines till there wasn't room for any more. But her eyes were bright yet, and twinkled with humour at times.

She had been in the Bush for fifty years, and had fought fires, droughts, hunger and thirst, floods, cattle and crop diseases, and all the things that God curses Australian settlers with. She had had two husbands, and it could be said of neither that he had ever done an honest day's work, or any good for himself or any one else. She had reared something under fifteen children, her own and others; and there was scarcely one of them that had not given her trouble. Her sons had brought disgrace on her old head over and over again, but she held up that same old head through it all, and looked her narrow, ignorant world in the face – and 'lived it down.' She had worked like a slave for fifty years; yet she had more energy and endurance than many modern city women in her shrivelled old body. She was a daughter of English aristocrats.

And we who live our weak lives of fifty years or so in the cities – we grow maudlin over our sorrows (and beer), and ask whether life is worth living or not.

I sought in the farming town relief from the general and particular sameness of things, but there was none. The railway station was about the only new building in town. The old signs even were as badly in need of retouching as of old. I picked up a copy of the local 'Advertiser,' which newspaper had been started in the early days by a brilliant drunkard, who drank himself to death just as the fathers of our nation were beginning to get educated up to his style. He might have made Australian journalism very different from what it is. There was nothing new in the 'Advertiser' – there had been nothing new since the last time the drunkard had been sober enough to hold a pen. There was the same old 'enjoyable trip' to Drybone (whereof the editor was the hero), and something about an on-the-whole very enjoyable evening in some place that was tastefully decorated, and where the visitors did justice to the good things provided, and the small hours, and dancing, and our host and hostess, and respected fellow-townsmen; also divers young ladies sang very nicely, and a young Mr. Somebody favoured the company with a comic song.

There was the same trespassing on the valuable space by the old subscriber, who said that 'he had said before and would say again,' and he proceeded to say the same things which he said in the same paper when we first heard our father reading it to our mother. Farther on the old subscriber proceeded to 'maintain,' and recalled attention to the fact that it was just exactly as he had said. After which he made a few abstract, incoherent remarks about the 'surrounding district,' and concluded by stating that he 'must now conclude,' and thanking the editor for trespassing on the aforesaid valuable space.

There was the usual leader on the Government; and an agitation was still carried on, by means of horribly-constructed correspondence to both papers, for a bridge over Dry-Hole Creek at Dustbin – a place where no sane man ever had occasion to go.

I took up the 'unreliable contemporary,' but found nothing

there except a letter from 'Parent,' another from 'Ratepayer,' a leader on the Government, and 'A Trip to Limeburn,' which latter I suppose was made in opposition to the trip to Drybone.

There was nothing new in the town. Even the almost inevitable gang of city spoilers hadn't arrived with the railway. They would have been a relief. There was the monotonous aldermanic row, and the worse than hopeless little herd of aldermen, the weird agricultural portion of whom came in on council days in white starched and ironed coats, as we had always remembered them. They were aggressively barren of ideas; but on this occasion they had risen above themselves, for one of them had remembered something his grandfather (old time English alderman) had told him, and they were stirring up all the old local quarrels and family spite of the district over a motion, or an amendment on a motion, that a letter – from another enlightened body and bearing on an equally important matter (which letter had been sent through the post sufficiently stamped, delivered to the secretary, handed to the chairman, read aloud in council, and passed round several times for private perusal) – over a motion that such letter be received.

There was a maintenance case coming on – to the usual well-ventilated disgust of the local religious crank, who was on the jury; but the case differed in no essential point from other cases which were always coming on and going off in my time. It was not at all romantic. The local youth was not even brilliant in adultery.

After I had been a week in that town the Governor decided to visit it, and preparations were made to welcome him and present him with an address. Then I thought that it was time to go, and slipped away unnoticed in the general lunacy.

MILES FRANKLIN
from *My Brilliant Career*
Impediments to female authorship

The morning came, breakfast, next Harold's departure. I shook my head and slipped the note into his hand as we parted. He rode slowly down the road. I sat on the step of the garden gate, buried my face in my hands, and reviewed the situation. I could see my life, stretching out ahead of me, barren and monotonous as the thirsty track along which Harold was disappearing. To-day it was washing, ironing to-morrow, next day baking, after that scrubbing – thus on and on. We would occasionally see a neighbour or a tea-agent, a tramp or an Assyrian hawker. By hard slogging against flood, fire, drought, pests, stock diseases, and the sweating occasioned by importation, we could manage to keep bread in our mouths. By training and education I was fitted for nought but what I was, or a general slavey, which was many degrees worse. I could take my choice. Life was too much for me. What was the end of it, what its meaning, aim, hope, or use?

In comparison to millions I knew that I had received more than a fair share of the goods of life; but knowing another has leprosy makes our cancer none the easier to bear.

My mother's voice, sharp and cross, roused me – 'Sybylla, you lazy unprincipled girl, to sit scheming there while your poor old mother is at the wash-tub. You sit idling there, and then by-and-bye you'll be groaning about this terrible life in which there's time for nothing but work.'

How she fussed and bothered over the clothes was a marvel to me. My frame of mind was such that it seemed it would not signify if all our clothes went to the dogs, and the clothes of our neighbours, and the clothes of the whole world, and the world itself for the matter of that.

'Sybylla, you are a dirty careless washer. You've put Stanley's trousers in the boil and the colour is coming out of them, and your father's best white handkerchief should have been with the first lot, and here it is now.'

Poor mother got crosser as she grew weary with the fierce heat and arduous toil, and as I in my abstraction continued to make mistakes, but the last straw was the breaking of an old cup which I accidently pushed off the table.

I got it hot. Had I committed an act of premeditated villainy I could not have received more lecturing. I deserved it, – I was careless, cups were scarce with us, and we could not afford more; but what I rail against is the grindingly uneventful narrowness of the life in which the unintentional breaking of a common cup is good for a long scolding.

Ah, my mother! In my life of nineteen years I can look back and see a time when she was all gentleness and refinement, but the polish has been worn off it by years and years of scrubbing and scratching, and washing and patching, and poverty and husbandly neglect, and the bearing of burdens too heavy for delicate shoulders. Would that we were more companionable, it would make many an oasis in the desert of our lives. Oh that I could take an all-absorbing interest in patterns and recipes, bargains and orthodoxy! Oh that you could understand my desire to feel the rolling billows of the ocean beneath, to hear the pealing of a great organ through dimly-lit arches, or the sob and wail of a violin in a brilliant crowded hall, to be swept on by the human stream.

Ah, thou cruel fiend – Ambition! Desire!

Soul of the leaping flame,
  Heart of the scarlet fire,
Spirit that hath for name
  Only the name – Desire!

To hot young hearts beating passionately in strong breasts, the sweetest thing is motion.

No, that part of me went beyond my mother's understanding. On the other hand, there was a part of my mother – her brave cheerfulness, her trust in God, her heroic struggle to keep the home together – which went soaring on beyond my understanding, leaving me a coward weakling, grovelling in the dust.

Would that hot dreary day never close? What advantage when it did? The next and the next and many weeks of others just the same were following hard after.

If the souls of lives were voiced in music, there are some that none but a great organ could express, others the clash of a full orchestra, a few to which nought but the refined and exquisite sadness of a violin could do justice. Many might be likened unto common pianos, jangling and out of tune, and some to the feeble piping of a penny whistle, and mine could be told with a couple of nails in a rusty tin-pot.

Why do I write? For what does any one write? Shall I get a hearing? If so – what then?

I have voiced the things around me, the small-minded thoughts, the sodden round of grinding tasks – a monotonous, purposeless, needless existence. But patience, O heart! surely I can make a purpose. For the present, of my family I am the most suited to wait about common public-houses to look after my father when he is inebriated. It breaks my mother's heart to do it; it is dangerous for my brothers; imagine Gertie in such a position! but me it does not injure, I have the faculty for doing that sort of thing without coming to harm, and if it makes me more bitter and godless, well, what matter?

'DORA FALCONER'
(LOUISA LAWSON)
from *About Ourselves*

'Woman is not uncompleted man, but diverse.' Says Tennyson, and being diverse why should she not have a journal in which her divergent hopes, aims, and opinions may have representation. Every eccentricity of belief, and every variety of bias in mankind allies itself with a printing-machine, and gets its singularities bruited about in type, but where is the printing-ink champion of mankind's better half? There has hitherto been no trumpet through which the concentrated voice of womankind could publish their grievances and their opinions. Men legislate on divorce, on hours of labor, and many other question intimately affecting women, but neither ask nor know the wishes of those whose lives and happiness are most concerned. Many a tale might be told by women, and many a useful hint given, even to the omniscient male, which would materially strengthen and guide the hands of law-makers and benefactors aspiring to be just and generous to weak and unrepresented womankind.

Here then is DAWN, the Australian Woman's Journal and mouthpiece – phonograph to wind out audibly the whispers, pleadings, and demands of the sisterhood.

Here we will give publicity to women's wrongs, will fight their battles, assist to repair what evils we can, and give advice to the best of our ability.

'WAIF WANDER'
(MARY FORTUNE)
Towzer and Co.

Being still, as you know I always was, the most unselfish being in existence, it is not to be wondered at that I hasten to introduce you, dear public, to three of the most interesting characters it has been my lot to come in contact with for some considerable time. Perhaps it is because my circle of observation has become unusually, but, I devoutly hope, temporarily limited of late, that I have devoted no small amount of time in amusing myself by contrasting and speculating upon the several characteristics of my new friends; but you know that I was always sadly addicted to that sort of thing, as well as to recording my conclusions for your behoof.

Well, then, under the roof which has the present honour – an honour which I fear it doesn't sufficiently appreciate – of sheltering me, reside the three individuals to whom I allude. That is to say, the said roof, surmounting some walls, is supposed to be their habitation; although two of them locate themselves during the night watches in a roofed box in the yard, and next door to the hen-house, while the third – dirty fellow! – displays an undoubted preference for a bed in the coal-house. Even under these debasing circumstances, however, I expect you to be interested in my three friends; and it is not to-day that you are told for the first time that even in worse places than fowl-houses and coal-holes you may find material for observation and reflection.

My three new friends are animals of the canine species. I might have said dogs at once; but I am fond of fine writing, you see, and never make use of a plain expressive English word when I can introduce a five or six syllabled one, expressive of nothing but my own want of common sense. But what would you have? We must swim with the stream, and nobody would accredit me with any refinement whatever if I used ordinary words on ordinary occasions. Bless you, this is an age of refinement; and, as one of our dailies remarked the other day, we have reached that pitch of it, that there isn't a woman left in the country – they are every single one of them *ladies* of the first water!

For my part, and *en parenthese* once more, I wish we had fewer ladies to deal with, and some more honest, downright, straight-forward women to encounter. In the sense in which the term is ordinarily used, I should take it as a decided insult to be dubbed a 'lady,' and some day I mean to give you my idea of the several divisions of the same lady species, but at present I am a chronicler of caninity, and so –

The oldest of my dog friends is named Keeper, and he is the remains of a not thoroughbred Newfoundland. I say the remains advisedly, for most assuredly is poor old Keeper the remains of his former self. You couldn't help feeling sorry for him, did you see him in his pitiable state of decay, and hear, as I do, many tales of his old prowess and faithful attachment.

Keeper is very old for one of his species: he has been for some fifteen or sixteen years in his present home. He is black and white; that is to say, ought to be black and white, for I am sorry to say, it is he who selects a resting place in a deep bed of coal-dust. Pray excuse him; if you were old and helpless, and had no woolly blankets and soft beds to curl your frail limbs up in, perhaps you, too, might become neglectful of appearances, and root for yourself a hole in the ash heap of the coal-hole, even though the contact might soil your white hair, if you had any left.

And poor Keeper is deaf – 'as deaf as a post;' and he looks piteously at you with his dull weak eyes, as he stands swaying in the sunshine on limbs that will hardly support him. Long ago, legend tells us that he accidentally, or otherwise, received a gun-charge in his hind-quarters, the effects of which are added to his age in paralysing, or partially paralysing, his poor limbs. When he walks he shuffles along, in a pitiable sort of way, with his head hanging, and his long dirty tail drooping inertly, and sadly reminds me of some old trembling man, who goes slowly on his friendless way, without one supporting arm or whispering word of cheer.

Little use it would indeed be to whisper words of cheer to old Keeper. You may shout if you like but he will not lift his heavy head from that sunny spot on the verandah. And you may scold him – if he is in your way, and you have the heart to do it – but he will gaze helplessly into your face with so touching an air of imbecility, that you wonder when the poor fellow readily obeys your pointing finger, and removes himself out of your path into his patch of sunshine.

I wonder if old Keeper thinks. I wonder if he feels that he is diseased, from the crown of his head to the sole of his foot; and is offensive to even his most pitying friends. I wonder if, when he lies with his huge head on his flaccid old paws, and watches the ducks and the hens blinkingly, he meditates sadly on the past or has any hope in the future. I wonder if, when he sleeps in the sun and lies stretched on his side, as nerveless looking as the — thing without strength which he is, and when he utters muffled barks, and moves his old feet spasmodically, I wonder, I say, is he dreaming of long ago days, when he was young, and bounded in the full enjoyment of animal vigour, after his beloved master's footsteps. Poor Keeper, is it a pity that one dare not believe in the doctrines of Pythagoras for your sake?

Be introduced to Towzer, one of the most perfect epitomes of dog cheekiness that you could discover in a month's search, even if you are a 'dog register' himself. Towzer is a well grown mongrel terrier, in colour a sort of iron-gray. He has got no hair, I venture to assert; the article which represents it being so nearly assimilated to bristles, that it stands up from his body in an aggressive manner entirely descriptive of his character. The remains of his ears, too, are erect, and *qui vive* looking; and so, most certainly is his stump of a tail, which sticks out at an angle of, say, forty-five degrees from his back, in all seasons and weathers. Indeed, the whole general appearance of Mr. Towzer is characteristic of stiffness; his little short legs are stiff, and the hair upon them is stiff; and he trots along in a jointless manner, that suggests the idea of a wooden dog, with the hinge in the small of his back, upon which he turns and twists as a vessel to the swing of her rudder. In short, Towzer is a matter-of-fact-looking dog, and sentiment could not possibly exist within a considerable radius of him.

And a politic dog is Mr. Towzer. There isn't a dog in Melbourne that knows better than he upon which side his bread is buttered. Oh! a regular time server he is, who will sneak into your good graces about dinner time, and muzzle the first poor little dog that has the misfortune to venture within ken of him. A splendid man of business would Towzer make. It would require no very special stretch of my imagination to picture him in an erect posture, with a pair of business-like inexpressibles covering his scrubby legs, and with a coat declaring the man upon his stiff back. I can fancy I see him at this moment, with a flower in his button-hole, and a bundle of papers – scrip, of course – sticking out of his pocket, and trotting down under the verandah, with a ready note-book in his hand. Why, his very air of *dogged* impudence would be a fortune to him; and silly speculators would study his firm, determined looking trot, and conclude that he, at least, knew where he was placing his feet. His air of indomitable self-satisfaction would, I say, be a fortune to Towzer & Co., for Towzer would be sure to have a 'Co.' for selfish reasons of his own, which, even as a dog, he at present indulges.

And now for Towzer's 'Co.' If you ever saw a miserable little cur, with the very stamp of helpless imbecility in the drop of its tail, you would recognise the character, or rather the want of it, in Towzer's 'Co.' A poor little trembling, yellowish-coloured mongrel, so nervous that a look is sufficient to set it shaking from 'stem to stern' is this nameless waif of caninity. It is nameless in that it crawled – off the street, I suppose – into its present quarters, and, having apparently found its vocation, will not leave them for any inducement. You may wonder what is the vocation of this poor little shaker; and when I tell you that it is to keep Mr. Towzer warm in the cold weather – to lie at the kennel door and keep off the rain in wet, to form a pillow of support for his highness when it suits him, and to toady him in a hundred ways, and to feel happy in the privilege of being permitted to do it, need I state to you the sex of selfish Towzer's 'Co.'

If you admire, between the sexes, an exhibition of the old simile of the oak and the ivy, doubtless it would delight you to see little Nameless muzzling around Mr. Towzer's bristly neck, and, after some vain attempts to relieve his lordship of some of his insect lodgers, lick his elevated nose as he, the consequential recipient of these proper attentions, blinks sleepily at the fire; and if you are one of Mr. Towzer's fraternity – in the sex way, of course, I mean – you will doubtless try and secure just such another 'Co.,' of your own, and blink indolently at the fire while *she* fusses around you, and studies your every shade of countenance and your smallest amount of taste, as a future guide for her own willing slavedom. I wonder if you will today find such a 'Co.,' my dear sir, or if the race has not nearly died out with the straightforward, sensible womanly fashions and ideas of our grand or great grandmothers?

But however one may try to admire the idea of a dependent and helpless femininity, one must rebel at times, for the honour of the sex, against too abject an exhibition of it, even in a dog. It is aggravating, to say the least of it, to see an animal cower to the ground in the extremity of trembling terror, when you extend your hand toward him with a bit of beef in it for acceptance; and yet you could not follow your first inclination of giving him (or her) a turn over with your foot, when you meet the poor little imploring eyes, and recognise in the prostration the utmost of humility as well as of cowardice; and so you simply call little Nameless a fool, and fling the beef at it (generally for Mr. Towzer to pick up and devour).

I wonder if any person could furnish me with a psychological reason why females all admire courage in the opposite sex, and inwardly look upon the coward as something wholly despicable.

In this one feeling, at least, I am a very woman (not 'lady' I beg you to observe), and recognise nothing so contemptible as cowardice, meet it in whatever shape or form it may exhibit itself. And yet, as we think a little over the position of poor little Nameless, we cannot help extending much of pity toward her to mingle with the occasional disgust her conduct inspires. It is, in reality, a homeless little stray, and only retains its present position by the most abject toadyism of Mr. Towzer. Should his lordship choose to take to burrowing in the coal-hole, like old Keeper, and so be able to dispense with the warmth of his present 'Co.' or should some other of the little canine waifs of this great city usurp the place poor Nameless at present holds within his dominions, woe to the future of the helpless little animal.

And, besides, who can tell how far the instinct of the intelligent race can go? Does Nameless know anything of that terrible dogman, and tremblingly anticipate the possibility that its services to the favoured Towzer may not be considered worth the yearly sum of five shillings? Does it (I hate to call it *she*!) while Towzer is dozing by the fire, or lolling his lazy weight upon the poor, frail little carcass, speculate hopelessly as to the sad end of homeless and houseless dogs who may be driven from the shelter of a roof for the paltry sum I have mentioned? Alas! little Nameless, for how many of *us* – the great human race – would a friendly hand be stretched out, with five shillings, to save from the same homeless condition that you may dread?

Take a leaf out of friend Towzer's book, ape his consequential strut, and cultivate his thorough and unmitigated selfishness. Fly at the beck of your master, and affect to fully believe him when he calls out 'Rat! rat!' in inconceivably odd moments, and most out-of-the-way places; and take out your revenge by bullying all the dogs smaller than yourself that may be unfortunate enough to fancy that it is a free country. Be irrepressibly impudent, and don't allow yourself to be put down by anybody whatever. That's the way to get on in the big world, my simple little friend. So fully do you now believe in Towzer, who condescends to extend his sceptre to you, and to permit you to bask in the light of his august countenance (weak little 'Co.'), that you do not hesitate to follow in his wake, assured that whatever he does is right; but you must act upon 'your own hook', little Nameless, if you wish to become independent of Towzer and the dogman.

The study of character is at all times an amusing and instructive one, and the idiosyncracies of those around us afford an unlimited source of gratification to one prone to such amusements, but they cannot be indulged in with pleasure at all times. A keen sense of the ridiculous is a troublesome aptitude to carry about with you, and it is grievously hard to wear the mask of a deaf and dumb person when, some absurdity being enacted or spoken, makes you want to fly out to the back premises for a genuine good laugh. Thus it is that I so enjoy the observation of my three new acquaintances; for I can make as many grotesque faces as I choose in watching the smug individuality of Mr. Towzer, or the helpless self-abandonment of poor little 'Co.'

Have you all heard of the minister's man, John, and the 'inference' he drew from the text furnished by his master? 'Ye've been a long time wi'me noo, John,' said the minister; 'I daresay ye could preach a pretty fair sermon yersel'.'

'Weel,' said John, in reference to the everlasting custom of Scotch ministers of winding up the firstly, secondly, and thirdly, etc., etc., with 'From this we may infer,' before the final 'application,' 'I think I could draw a gey guid inference.'

'Weel, noo, John, what inference would ye draw from the following text: "The ass snuffeth up the east wind"?'

'I'd infer, maister, that he'd no get very fat on it.'

Now, in humble imitation of the minister's man, John, I wonder if I could draw any 'inference' or make any 'application' of the lessons I at least *ought* to have learned from my comparisons of the several characteristics of my three friends. But morals are hateful things, as we all know; and should I be silly enough to moralise in the pages of the *Australian Journal*, Othello's occupation would soon be gone.

Still, it might be admissible for me to say that I should far rather be old and worn out, and my past spoken of in terms of grateful kindness as one of duty faithfully performed, than be irrepressible, and impudent, and selfish, and a thorough bully, like my acquaintance with the 'Co.'

But, irrespective of all that, there is nothing in Towzer's present life to envy, for his is no sinecure, I do assure you. It cannot be pleasant to be caught 'by the scruff of the neck' occasionally and held under the pump, or to be incarcerated and howl by the hour in the small tenement which does duty as a kennel. If he had a spark of honest independence, he would take his swag on his back and earn an honest living elsewhere, or, in default, drown himself in the big washing tub; but he hasn't, you see, and so he coolly trots into the drawing-room after his bath or his imprisonment, and impudently coils himself and his dirt up in the best arm-chair, and, of course, poor little silly follows him, as in duty bound, and keeps his back warm.

Well, such is life. I do not offer you this as an original quotation by any manner of means; but such really is life, all the world over. All over the world, and to the end of that strange thing we call

Time, there are, and will be, Towzers and old Keepers, and silly nonentities that are only suited to be 'Co.'s;' and, having no separate individuality of their own, must live, move, and have their being in that of some one else. That some one else will not always be a selfish, bouncible, bullying, and aggressive Towzer, to be sure; nor will, it is to be hoped, in the interest of future nameless, characterless waifs, those poor, soft unfortunates always be in terror of being evicted from even such a home as our little 'Co.'s' by any destiny, be it in the shape of the 'dog register' or any other shape whatever.

Towzer, having retired to his box (with the 'Co.' at his back, of course), and having resigned himself to hideous dreams of a huge rat, in form somewhat resembling a pump, who is pouring icy streams of water on his wretched scrubby back; and good, helpless old Keeper, having betaken himself to a fresh hole in the ashes, where he utters muffled barks at an aggravating dog he was acquainted with twenty years ago, I may cease to try and interest you on their behalf. Should you meet old Keeper some day trying to shuffle along Collins Street, in my wake, and observe him staring in a bewildered manner at some fine ladies who are 'doing the block,' I beg that you will excuse him. He is an old-fashioned fellow, you see, and in his day there were *women*, and they did not appear in public attired in a style which might suggest an asylum.

ADA CAMBRIDGE
The Physical Conscience

The moral conscience – court of last appeal –
   Our word of God – our Heaven-sent light and guide –
   From what high aims it lures our steps aside!
To what immoral deeds it sets its seal!
That beacon lamp has lost its sacred fire;
   That pilot-guide, compelling wind and wave,
   By slow, blind process, has become the slave
Of all-compelling custom and desire.

Not so the conscience of the body. This,
   Untamed and true, still speaks in voice and face,
In cold lips stiffened to the loveless kiss,
   In shamed limbs shrinking from unloved embrace,
In love-born passion, that no laws compel,
Nor gold can purchase, nor ambition sell.

Fallen

For want of bread to eat and clothes to wear –
   Because work failed and streets were deep in snow,
   And this meant food and fire – she fell so low,
Sinning for dear life's sake, in sheer despair.
Or, because life was else so bald and bare,
   The natural woman in her craved to know
   The warmth of passion – as pale buds to blow
  And feel the noonday sun and fertile air.

And who condemns? She who, for vulgar gain
   And in cold blood, and not for love or need,
    Has sold her body to more vile disgrace –
    The prosperous matron, with her comely face –
   Wife by the law, but prostitute in deed,
In whose gross wedlock womanhood is slain.

'TASMA' (JESSIE COUVREUR)
Barren Love

Chapter I

Only two veins standing out from a woman's neck – that was all!
The cynic told himself he was a fool, and telling himself so, walked
away to the farther end of the deck. Blue veins starting up from
a young throat! There was nothing, after all, in a phenomenon
of the sort – nothing, that is to say, that could not be explained
on physiological grounds. The cynic was accustomed to look at
manifestations of pain from a point of view purely scientific. Thus,
when you cut off the head of a dog-fish, the monster squirms with
the agony. Like the evil it typifies, there is a hold-fastness in its
grip of life. But you know, or you believe you know, of how much
account is all this resistant wrestling with death! What softer
sensation do you have than one of animosity towards the dog-
fish for dying so hard, and for giving you such a world of trouble
to get your blunt knife through a neck like animated indiarubber?

The cynic admitted a difference between the throat of a
placoidian and the throat of a young girl. But to watch the one
gasping its death-gurgle from a bleeding gash, and the other,
distorted, working against a sentimental grief, might not of itself
be a process provocative of intensely differing emotions. The
cynic, holding it as a theory that softening of the heart and
softening of the brain have meanings almost synonymous, pooh-
poohed his maudlin fancies, and walked resolutely back to his
old post by the bulwarks. Those obtrusive veins annoyed him!
In thirty or forty years' time they might ride up, if they chose.
Everything should be smooth in youth, even to the trunk of a
tree. Nature had given these veins a semi-opaque covering,
smoother and softer than the blossom of an arum. In their normal
condition they obliterated themselves behind it, or only started
into the faintest show of self-assertion when their home was
unsettled. And here they had risen like blue weals, raised by the
lash of an inward thong!

The cynic, feeling justified in his irritation, looked up from the
demonstrative neck to the face above it – and immediately
walked away. This time it was for good. He felt about as much
ashamed of himself as if he had torn open the girl's dress and

asked her where she was smarting.

Not that the cynic was unacquainted with the nature of tears – 'a limpid fluid secreted by the lachrymal gland,' &c. If you come to tears, nothing can shed them more profusely than a seal. The soft-eyed creature wails and cries on the score of her outraged maternity. She plants her unwieldy body in front of her little one and asks for mercy with streaming eyes. Tears, therefore, are nothing in themselves! Sterne shed them by the bucketsful, with much maudlin satisfaction to himself the while. The cynic loathed Sterne, and despised the sentimentalist for his perpetual flourish of handkerchiefs in the faces of his readers. But on the present occasion he came very near to despising himself. He wondered just when he would forget the strained eyes – every gleam of self-consciousness washed out of them – nothing but an intelligence of suffering left. He did not require to be told that from among the departing boats, fast turning into mere buoyant dots in the distance, one more than another must have magnetised the hopeless gaze.

Looking half-way across Plymouth harbour, by the light of a sudden burst of yellow sunshine, he could discern the outline of a man standing upright in the foremost boat of all.

The cynic was so quick in connecting the dejection of the man's attitude with the crushed aspect of the girl, that he would have despised himself with a fresh access of vigour if it had occurred to him to think about himself in the matter at all. Somehow, he forgot at the moment to make proper sport of his own show of human interest. The fluttering of a handkerchief in the boat called forth a curious corresponding signal on the part of the girl. Her hands, trembling all over, like the rest of her body, tugged at her collar-fastening and extracted a hidden white envelope. They carried it to her lips – she was past all heed of curious bystanders long ago! The passionate kissing of the unheeding paper – the stretching of it out towards the boat, as if so frantic a gesture might stay even the stolid Plymouth boatman – the effort that she made to restore it to its place and lay it as a sort of healing plaster against her gasping throat – all this might have been grotesque if it had been only one shade less humanly real. The cynic found a characteristic outlet for his unaccountable sensations by glaring with an expression of appalling severity at any unwary waif who might venture within three yards of the desolate girl. Long after the boat was out of sight she continued to stand in the same spot, stonily indifferent to the scene before her. For the last English sunset was sending the ship on her way in a rose-coloured light. People on the Plymouth pier saw her in a haze of burnished mist, moving airily away under gilded sails.

Chapter II

The cynic, who was not called Mr. Cynic, however, by those on board, but Mr. Ralph Grimwood, or Mr. Grimwood only, was very sea-sick. Between the intervals of his degradation he thought about dog-fishes and seals; he thought about the affections too – those perplexing equivalents in the sum total of the disturbing influences that control us. On principle, he execrated the affections – officious meddlers in the sound mechanical functions of the body. On principle, he was antagonistic to love, the mere display of which would have been nauseous if it had not been so ludicrous! But sea-sickness, it would seem, had rendered him illogical. As he lay in his bunk, careful not to look at the swinging port-hole, a mere glance at which seemed to heave him up into the watery clouds and drag him down into the watery depths, he fell to picturing what his life might have become if he could have changed personalities with the vague outline in the boat. Being weakened by so much diminution of bile, he was fain to indulge the fancy. He had never known what it was to be light-headed as yet. Instead, therefore, of controlling his impulse, according to his stern creed, he was constrained to let his impulse control him. And it controlled him utterly!

Now he could see the boat racing after the ship, while he himself was urging it on! Now he could see himself climbing up the ship's side, clothed always in the shadowy form he had distinguished. How soon he had kissed back into their white hiding-place the poor swollen veins! He had separated the helpless hands twisted into each other for their own support, and put them round his strong, surly shoulders. His lips had closed for one instant the heavily-weighted eyelids, that he might see the grey eyes open again with such a look as his touch would have restored to them. It need not be pointed out that the light-headed fancy was running riot through his brain.

Meanwhile a wind had set in that was driving away all traces of tears from the emigrant's cheeks, and blowing a fresher brininess against them instead. The ship, at the outset, swayed timorously along, like a child in leading-strings. The wind pushed her about, slapped her alternately on either side, tilted her forward, and hitched her back, till she jerked like a gibbing horse – finally took her by the hand and pulled her smoothly along across the Bay of Biscay. Then Mr. Grimwood came on deck.

The passengers up above were proudly displaying their newly-acquired sea-legs. They strutted along uncertainly, after the manner of ducks, – very much pressed for time to get nowhere at all. Mr. Grimwood watched them stumping past him, the same strained expression peculiar to landsfolk at the outset of a long voyage, stamping them all; the ruins of their eyes reddened by the wind.

The deck was a flush one, and amid-ships was a balustrade dividing the spaces allotted respectively to the first and second-class passengers. As it is always easier to lower one's social status than to raise it, on board ship as in the world, passengers from the first cabin were allowed the run of the space paid for by passengers from the second cabin. None of them, however, with the sole exception of Mr. Grimwood, seemed in any especial hurry to snatch at their privilege. Probably it was one of the cynic's eccentricities to like whiffs of a mixed character.

On the second-class deck the nostrils conveyed food to the mind in the shape of a hundred conjectures. For instance, on the weather side, it was impossible, after a few enforced sniffs, to abstain from speculations as to the state in which the fowls might be kept. On the lee side, the speculative mind might find a still wider range and lose itself in dwelling on the odoriferous origin of ship's grease. It is not certain whether these inducements allured Mr. Grimwood from the quarter-deck. If neither fowls nor ship's grease attracted him, it may be inferred that the people were worth a glance, albeit not from Mr. Grimwood's point of view – a cynic always sees a crumbling skeleton behind the most life-warm flesh.

They were of all varieties – the needy family man whose olive branches would have borne pruning, the runaway defaulter who looked even at the horizon with suspicion – the willing-to-better-herself spinster, who knew to a nicety how many of the ship's officers were married, and could have told off each mate to his watch on deck with less hesitation than the Captain himself. In none of these classes would you have included the one solitary passenger standing by herself on a coil of rope, with arms leaning on the bulwarks and eyes directed to the impalpable boundary-line of the sea. Neither would you have found her counterpart more readily among the first-class passengers. In the quiescence of her present attitude, as in the mute storminess of her grief, she seemed absolutely to ignore all human surroundings. Andromeda, chained to a rock, with foam leaping over her white limbs, could not have been more oblivious of the impression she was conveying than was this plaid-enveloped girl.

Mr. Grimwood had cultivated art even before he cultivated cynicism. To a stirring of the ancient art-impulse within him he sacrificed his reflections anent dog-fishes and seals. With such a model for an Andromeda, his cynicism might all have spent itself on the Dragon. Who can say? It is certain that some of his bile had spent itself already. Andromeda would not, perhaps, have worn a black felt hat or a green plaid shawl; but could even Andromeda's hair have been blown back into softer, silkier rings from whiter temples; could Andromeda's eyes – always granting that they were of the same transparent grey – have been hedged in by longer lashes; could Andromeda herself have shown a purer profile, or – now that the mutinous veins were laid to rest – have displayed a more rounded throat? Mr. Grimwood, gravely parading the second-deck, must have known all this by intuition. It was soon after his excursive walk along the hen-coops that he was seen in conversation with the Captain.

That same afternoon, the second-class steward, who was washing second-class plates in second-class slop, was half-deafened by a call from the Captain himself. The steward was to fetch him the young woman in plaid – Miss Leighton by name – and to look sharp about it.

The Captain was a sort of typical tar – one of a race not quite extinct; still to be met with on old colonial wool-ships, despite the new genus introduced by steam. He did not think about Andromeda when he saw Miss Leighton, but it partly occurred to him that it was a blank shame such an eternally fine girl should be spooking about the world by herself. It seemed that he had summoned her to give her a cheering piece of news. It appeared, according to the Captain's story, that a letter and a deposit had been put into his hands at starting, which, by some remarkable oversight, had never been opened until to-day. The letter bore no signature – over this part of his story the Captain blundered unaccountably. Somebody, about whose appearance the Captain was by no means clear, had entrusted the letter to his keeping. In fact, only as regarded the instructions, did the Captain express himself with anything like clearness, and on that head he was more than explicit. Miss Leighton was to travel as a saloon passenger, the deposit being sufficient not only to defray the cost of her passage-money, but to give her a cabin to herself. Here the Captain attempted an apology for his delay in imparting the news. Somehow, he blundered again, and stopped suddenly short.

Certainly Miss Leighton's mind must have been given to travelling on its own account. All the time the Captain was speaking, it seemed to be journeying back from some dreary distance, until it shone through her great abstracted eyes. Their lost, desolate look made way for the light that a warm sense of surrounding care brought into them. It was no longer Andromeda with the horror of the Dragon's presence in her white face, but Andromeda with uplifted eyes watching the glittering pathway of her deliverer through the air.

Poetical justice should have awarded Mr. Grimwood a seat next to Miss Leighton at the dinner-table, but poetical justice was not embodied in the head-steward – a ginger-hued little man, upon whom devolved the arrangement of the passengers' places. A constant suspicion that some outrage upon his dignity might be meditated had caused the little steward's eyes to protrude. His exalted position was a bar to his making any confidential friends. He was on speaking terms only with the cook, and spent his life with one eye upon the lazarete and the other on the look-out for a slight.

The cynic's post at the dinner-table was exactly in front of his cabin. When his eyes travelled along a row of ungainly noses on the same side of the table as his own, they invariably stopped at a small Greek profile, standing out like a cameo from among the irregular heads that flanked it. There was something embar-rassing in looking down a column of strongly-defined nose-tips. The cynic waited until the regulation plum-duff was put into its place; then he took a rapid glance to the rear. Out of all the assortment of heads, there was only one that could possibly correspond to the profile – a stately little head, very black and shining, perhaps a shade too upright, as if the knot of heavy hair on the nape had pulled it ever so slightly back.

And through all the swinging about in the Bay of Biscay, Mr. Grimwood continued to take his daily glance. It was not, perhaps, so fruitful of consequences as a nearer approach to the Andromeda might have proved itself. Sympathies have declared themselves on board ship between young men and women in proximity at meal-time, which otherwise must have been ever-lastingly ignored. What will not a constant adherence to black-currant tart in two young persons of different sexes engender? How steel yourself against a growing interest in the possessor of a plate that accompanies your own with such unswerving fidelity?

Only that the cynic was like nobody else on board ship or elsewhere, he would not have sat daily with an afflicted dowager and a failing octogenarian on either side of him. He would have found means to install himself in the place of one of the nondescript spinsters who enclosed Miss Leighton. But being unlike anybody else in any respect whatever, it was entirely consistent with his character to make a point of avoiding her. As to analysing his motives, that is another thing. It is not pretended that any man's intimate feelings are open to dissection.

There have been natures sufficiently high-flown to set a flesh-and-blood statue on an ideal pedestal, and to shrink from seeing the statue come down to its regular meals. There have been natures, high-flown too, to whom the quintessence of beauty lies in the bloom which covers it. Perhaps, in the cynic's eyes, the mystery surrounding the luxury of Miss Leighton's position was the bloom that covered its solid good. There are yet other natures, and these are not necessarily high-flown, who argue that only one passion can move a woman to so intense an agony of grief as that of which the cynic had been witness. Were such a passion immediately transferable, at what value must the new recipient place it in the sum of human emotions? Its sweetness might be just as transitory as its grief – all a piece of unconscious play-acting. Now the list of possible reasons is quite exhausted, it is hardly necessary to repeat that the cynic was unlike anybody else. As for the present of the cabin, there have been precedents in this direction. Amelia Sedley played on the piano Dobbin had restored to her, with something of the feeling that comforted Miss Leighton when she closed her eyes in the new cabin that the George Osborne of her dreams had chosen for her.

Chapter III

If Mr. Mantalini had ever been in the doldrums, he might have added to his experience of 'demmed moist unpleasant bodies.' A ship constrained to loiter there breaks out into a cold sweat. Everything she carries becomes clammy. In this respect there is not much difference between the animate and the inanimate bodies that she holds – unless it be that the first are pervaded with a warm stickiness, and the last with a cold stickiness. The most sanguineous of people assume the consistency of dough before it is kneaded. As for the spare folk, they look as if the scant supply of blood in their veins had turned to London milk. Then simple practical suggestions on the great question of 'demand and supply' occur to those unversed in the rudiments of political economy. The balance between the internal and the external moisture must be maintained; in maintaining it, panting passengers are reminded of 'Fair-shon's Son' –

'Who married Noah's daughter,
   And nearly spoilt ta Flood
By drinking up ta water.'

'Which he would have done,' adds his sceptical chronicler –

. . . . 'Had the mixture been
Only half Glenlivet.'

In emulation of the patriarch's convivial son-in-law, passengers only temper their drink with the tepid water served in regulation quantities to all on board. It is calculated that a little tepid water is very satisfying. Niggards, who depend upon it entirely, not using it as a tempering medium, but as a pure draught, are not taken into account on board a sailing-ship. They cannot even act upon Mr. Barlow's sage advice, and only 'drink when they are dry.' For they are always dry, and there is nothing to drink.

Under all ordinary and everyday circumstances the usual lot of the niggard at sea would have fallen to Miss Leighton's share. The Turkish bath atmosphere had wrapped her round, as it had enveloped her fellows. The cynic could see that his marble Andromeda was fast turning into an Andromeda of alabaster. Alabaster needs more tender handling than marble. The deposit placed in the Captain's hands seemed to have become self-fertilising like an oyster. How else could it be that a friendless young woman, who had come on board with nothing but a second-class ticket, a pair of strange grey eyes, and a Grecian profile, should find all her wants guessed at and gratified, before she had had time to acknowledge them as wants at all? The pompous little steward 'put himself in four' (as the French say) on her behalf. The easiest of easy-chairs was always in waiting for her, in the shadiest patch on deck so soon as the top of her straw-hat could be seen in the saloon beneath the skylight. While simmering dowagers wiped their faces, palm-leaf fans lay ready to hand, to beat away the too bold air resting in heavy heat on her pure cheeks. She could no longer look in the direction of the damp decanter with its freight of rusty warm water. So sure as she did so, the steward's eyes goggled at her meaningly. A moment later, in spite of all her laughing, wondering protestations, she was assailed with a whole battery of bottles. For peace's sake she was constrained to make choice from among the cool effervescent drinks drawn up before her. She was like Beauty in the enchanted palace, whose sensations were responded to as soon as they were born – but where was the BEAST?

The mystification gave rise to the sweetest of day-dreams. Whether the mysterious guardianship was exerted, like an electric wire of love, from the home she had left – whether it was held by some loyally-loving soul on board, she could not so much as conjecture. It was always there – like a soothing magnetic influence. Sometimes she fancied it must be very close to her – only there was nobody exactly like the Beast on board. The cynic, to be sure, in his aloofness from his kind, had something of the untamed beast about him; but then he never came to her to be stroked. He spoke rarely, and his rare speech was only exchanged with two persons – the Captain, who was 'boss' on deck, and the steward, who was 'boss' down below.

By the time the ship had passed through the Tropic Belt most of the resources in the way of amusement had been exhausted. The Trades, in rescuing the vessel from the doldrums, had been so much in earnest, that before long they would launch her into the 'roaring Forties' south of the Line. They had not quite abandoned her yet, but took her up and dropped her capriciously, treating her very much after the manner of a sovereign to a court favourite.

The cynic did not as yet admit to himself that he was well content they should drop her thus. He would never have allowed that, of his own accord, he indulged in the ridiculous visions that forced themselves upon him as he stood night after night intently watching the heaped-up glories in the west. Mad visions of finding the ship converted into a love-laden *Flying Dutchman* everlastingly sailing over such a glowing sea as this, to such an impalpable shore as the landscape in the clouds. With only one passenger, whom he would have chosen! The rest were for the most part sensible, prosaic folk, who would have looked properly disconcerted had it been suggested to them that, instead of sailing direct to Melbourne, they should make tracks for airy cities built up of glittering hues.

Chapter IV

The cynic did not drivel in the morning. It was his wont to wake himself early and think over a subject he had in his mind to write about. The subject was to bear upon the futility of giving the reins to the indulgence of the weakness called sentiment. He had his arguments all ready before coming on board. The perplexing part of it was, that although he was as much convinced of their soundness as ever, he did not see his way to putting them as clearly as he would have wished. He woke himself up on purpose to think of them at such an early hour, one morning in particular, that his ideas respecting sentiment were rather confused. They were mixed up with a sort of apathetic wonder at the noise of the swishing of water overhead. He supposed, lazily, that the middies must be washing the deck earlier than usual.

He felt no curiosity, however, about the change of time, being in the condition of sleepy receptiveness which makes everything indifferent to us. Neither did he trouble himself so far as to open his half-closed eyelids, even when a sort of red glare pervaded the darkness before them. Half-raising them at last, he saw – always with the same dream-like stolidity of gaze – that the sunrise seemed to illuminate his cabin in bursts of crimson light, and that the calm sea, lying tranquilly before his port-hole, was stained a deep carmine. He would have shut his eyes again on this phenomenon, if his sight had been the only sense appealed to. But a vigorous call was suddenly made upon his hearing and smelling perceptions as well.

Through the tarred planks over his head came the discordant sound of a woman's agonised scream – through the chinks and crannies of his cabin came a sickening scent of burning. Away went the thread of his argument against sentiment; away went the fag-end of his meaningless dream! As he bounded on to the cabin floor, a hundred trembling wretches, waking to so cruel a mockery of the morning sun, shrieked and raved to the Captain and the Omnipotent to save them from the flames.

Mr. Grimwood's cynicism ensured his keeping a cool head. One glance at the deck was enough to convince him that in a very few hours the ship would be nothing more than a flaming tar-barrel. The fire, he could see, must have been working in an underhand way in the hold, from the mouth of which it was coming up now as from the bottomless pit. There was something so sublime in its greed of prey, as it rolled up in scorching volumes of transparent blood-colour, that he stood watching it for a few seconds, unheeding the yells of the passengers.

There was a show being made of keeping the triumphant flames at bay, whereat they crouched like a panther preparing for a final spring. But Mr. Grimwood could see through this pretence from the first. The real work of the moment lay in the getting out of the boats for escape. But two of the boats were already useless, and the others could never have held the souls, all counted, on board. The cynic's theories about sentiment were strangely revolutionised as he went below and passed the open cabin-doors. Of all the distorted faces that he saw, how many would ever shape themselves into a laugh again?

The one cabin-door that he stopped at was ajar. In his hurry he hardly made a show of knocking before he pushed it open. Already there was a thin smoke spreading itself over the saloon. Inside the cabins the air was unnaturally warm. The cynic knew that all this was real. He knew that he had no more proprietorship over the girl he had come to save than he had over the ship itself. Yet it would have been just as easy to tell the upstart flames overhead to lie down and lick at empty space as to tell his own foolish heart to stop beating with unreasonable, exultant joy while he edged his way into the little cabin. He had hungered for it so often in his dreams – for just what had come to pass now!

Only, as a dying man, he might speak without attuning his voice to a pitch of artificial coldness – he might look without dreading lest the love-light in his eyes should betray him. He had forced his way through with the one thought only uppermost in his mind. The sinister glare from above – the crackling noise of the flames as they ran around the mainmast – the ugly chorus of screams overhead – screams of vitality that will not be tortured out of being, and protests against surrendering itself: all these were ministers to his absorbing passion. Now that he had passed into the cabin, pity and tenderness for its occupant swallowed up the egotistic triumph.

She was crouched on her berth like one waiting; partly smothered up in the worn plaid shawl, an old-fashioned covering of modern date, invested with all the grace of ancient drapery in the cynic's eyes – partly wrapped round by layers of brightly-dark hair, that lost itself somewhere in the blankets beneath her. Through all the terror in her drawn face, there was a something of expectation in the startled eyes – a vague trust that the guardianship she had taken refuge in would not forsake her in this pass. It could not be that the unknown power so quick to divine her wants, to forestall her fancies, to humour her passing whims, should leave her here, until her white skin shrivelled away with the heat and her voice was strangled by the smoke in the middle of its prayer for help. She had not so much as uttered one cry as yet. When Mr. Grimwood made his way in she broke into a sob of relief.

'I knew you would come,' she said. 'You are come to take care of me!'

Perhaps if the goggle-eyed little steward had come in she would have said the same thing. Any one appearing at this crisis must be the embodiment of the invisible love that had cherished her. Only it is doubtful whether, even at this supreme moment, the red light could have transformed the perky expression of the little steward as it had transformed Mr. Grimwood's. Women's rights' champions are without doubt altogether right. They have no end of solid grievances to redress. Let them bring about – if they can – social, intellectual, and muscular equality between the sexes. There is a certain sentimental instinct they can never do away with – the blind, unreasoning sense of comfort a trembling, frightened woman feels when a strong, earnest man takes her under his protection in a moment of danger.

There was such a volume of father-like, lover-like tenderness in Mr. Grimwood's tone as he came closer to reassure her – if the fire had curled itself round her doorway as the faint wreaths of smoke were beginning to curl she could not but have taken hope. He did not even hurry her unduly, though he knew that every second lost was a chance of life gone. He kneeled down by her berth – she had held out her hands to him as he came in – and holding her hands he spoke.

'She should go in the first boat,' he told her; 'the sea was so calm that the journey would be an easy one – they were within a hundred miles of Cape Town – he knew she was a brave girl and would do as he told her – he guaranteed to save her, but she must dress without loss of time – never mind what she put on – he would bring her a cloak and wraps from his cabin – in a minute he would be back again for her – only she must not lose any time.'

He was happier than he had ever been in his life as he scrambled together the coverings in his cabin that were to protect her from the chill sea-air. He dived into his trunk for a small treasure-box filled with his money and valuables, and carried it out with the wraps. When he returned to Miss Leighton's cabin the saloon was already dusky with smoke. She was waiting for him, dressed as when she came on board, and held close to his arm as he piloted her through the tumult below to the deck.

She could not help clinging to him afresh, with a gasp of horror, when she saw the scene above. It is all very well for people to die when they are let down to it by long illness or age! To be forced out of life so summarily – to be whipped into the green deep water, from which all your body shrinks, by the tingle of an unnatural smart against your flesh, is enough to make you shriek and protest. To see your own belongings in the same plight is enough to make you blaspheme. As for the sense that your kind is suffering along with you – there is not much comfort to be got out of it. Companionship in the search for glory is quite another thing. Warfare is as much a preparation for death as an illness without the bodily attenuation. A company of soldiers incite each other to mount a breach. On board a burning ship there is no glory to be gained – no predominant feeling for the most part, but a frenzied desire to save self. Nothing but a system of discipline can prevent the weak from being sacrificed to the strong.

There was just so much discipline on board, that the Captain's roaring order to call up the women and children was attended to. They were wailing as they were hustled into the boat. No mother set her foot in it until every child belonging to her had been tumbled in before her. Wives were in a sad pass. They clutched at their husbands and smuggled them into the boat at the risk of upsetting it.

Just as it was about to be pushed off, Mr. Grimwood's peremptory voice was raised high. 'Stop a moment!' he called loudly; 'another lady!'

At the instant of Miss Leighton's leaving him he put his small strong-box into her hands. She remembered afterwards that he had spoken quietly, but with wonderful quickness and clearness, as if these few last sentences were the outcome of a whole world of thought he had been fain to conceal. She seemed to read in his face that he looked for nothing but death after she had gone from him, and that as death only it would not be loathsome to him. She would have thought herself contemptible if at such a moment she had fettered her demonstrations by any apprehensions as to the after-construction that might be put upon them. She raised her face to his, put both her arms about his neck, and kissed him on the lips, as if in tearing her body away she were leaving her soul in his keeping. Then it was that he said what was on his mind.

'I can't help myself, darling! It's just as well that I should be going out of the world. We couldn't have made things square, I know! I only want you to remember that I would rather die like this than live as I did before I saw you.'

If he had more to explain, there was no time for it.

The sad boat pushed off, and already a wild fight for the means of salvation was raging all round him. The cynic watched the little boat so long as it remained within sight. It was cheering to see it pass out from the ghastly red influence of the ugly flames, into the sweet gold-scattering light of the morning sun. When it was lost in the brightness of those wholesome beams, the apotheosis of the cynic had begun. Who will say he was to be pitied? A barren life is not such a boon that any, save the timorous, need cling to it. But it is worth living even through a barren life to know an instant's unalloyed happiness at the last. What if the happiness involve the surrender of all your finely-constructed theories? – if it prove that you have been blundering from the beginning? What if the discovery come too late for you individually? You could not have made such a discovery without incorporating yourself so far with humanity as to die Christ-like – hoping for all! For to know the rapture of merging your spiritual being into that of another is dimly to conceive the possibility of an after-fulness of content for all that part of your nature which is not entangled with the bodily mechanism. That is why – since materialists logically maintain that the heart is nothing more than a muscular viscus, and the brain a whitish viscus, and tell us that the dissolution of these two means the annihilation of the keenly-conscious self – we, being unable to gainsay in truth a single reason advanced by materialists, may find an aimless life atoned for by an unreasoning flash of hope at the last. No matter how it is brought about, to die while you are in possession of it is to rejoice that you were born. Who would refuse the alternative?

Perhaps Miss Leighton, finding the cynic's money heavy and cold compared with the cynic's love, wished in after-years that she had flung it into the boat and stayed behind herself, to share in a hope-crowned death. Perhaps the shadowy outline in the Plymouth harbour developed into a prosaic husband, who liked modern cooking better than Greek art. Perhaps his wife thought sometimes of a tranquil southern sea, all aglow with a lurid stain – a sea ready to take into mysterious depths of changing colour two tightly-locked bodies that should never have been separated. Perhaps she dreamed all this after a futile fashion of her own. It is one thing to poetise about going to the bottom of the sea when in a cheerful sitting-room with a bright fire, and another thing to be brought face to face with it on a flame-shrouded ship a hundred miles from land.

As for deciding whether the cynic's fate or the girl's was the better one – it is for each one to judge according to his lights.

V

EXISTENTIAL ANXIETIES

'WAIF WANDER'
(MARY FORTUNE)
Brockman's Folly

No one who has not encountered it can understand the trouble
and difficulty a house and land agent has to encounter in his
business. I have been in Melbourne and in the business I have
named for fifteen years, and I am going to tell you a story about
it.

I did collecting for Mr. Julian Brockman for many years. He was
an active man himself, and I thought rather hard on his tenants.
He used to accuse me of being too easy, but he paid me all the
same, and, as I understood him, we never quarrelled.

I always rendered my accounts up faithfully every week. He
lived in one of his own houses, a place that somehow would not
let. Mr. Brockman had no family living with him, but had, as I
and everyone understood, a son who was a scapegrace, and had
run away to sea some fourteen years before he appointed me his
agent.

I have been accustomed to mark down dates, you know, and
so I can tell you the very day and year that Mr. Brockman told
me I must let the house he himself occupied at any and every
risk.

I was surprised, and I said so.

'The house is in bad repair, Mr. Brockman, and the rent is too
heavy,' I said.

'The rent shall be reduced and the house shall be put in repair,'
he answered, crabbedly.

'May I ask the reason of this sudden determination?' I questioned.

'You may ask, and I shall tell you,' was the most unexpected
reply; and then there was a long silence.

I began to fidget with my papers, for I wanted to go home, but
he took no notice, seeming immersed in thought. I knew how
useless it would be to try and push Mr. Brockman any way but
the way he wanted to go, and so I did not attempt to break the
silence.

'I can trust you, Barton,' Mr. Brockman said at length; 'I think
you are a man to be trusted.'

'I don't know what you mean, Mr. Brockman; but I think you have proved that I have not deceived you in one penny.'

'I know it, and that's the reason I trust you, Barton. Sit closer to the desk, and I will tell you the reason why I wish to let this house.'

'I will listen, sir; but may I suggest that you change the name?'

'The name of the house? Bah! What does the name matter?'

'I think it matters a great deal, Mr. Brockman. It is an uncanny name.'

'Do you think so?'

'I do, sir. Who would take a house with such a name?'

I turned over my books, and found the name 'Brockman's Folly'.

'Yes, it was a Folly, and I am sorry for having been such a fool as to erect a Folly. But now, Barton, let me tell you the reason why I wish to leave this house. You have heard of my son, I daresay?'

'I have heard the story, sir.'

'He ran away from me when he was fifteen years old, and I know that he was lost at sea. Well, I have seen that son of mine two nights now in succession.'

'You saw him?'

'I did, Barton, here in this room, last night and the night before.'

'Had you certain proof, Mr. Brockman?'

'Proof of my son's death, do you mean?'

'Yes.'

'I had the best proof that money could purchase.'

'Look here, Barton!' he added, suddenly. 'You have a right to stop and see this out! You are my paid servant.'

'I am your paid agent, Mr. Brockman, but no servant of yours.'

I was angry, and I showed it. I was making for the door, when I felt the grip of Mr. Brockman on my arm.

'You will stop?' he whispered. 'You will stop? I am afraid.'

I wondered to hear this usurer (for he was nothing else) actually requesting *me* to stay with him.

'I will stop,' I replied; 'if it will do you any good, but you must recollect, Mr. Brockman, that I have somebody waiting at home.'

'Yes, I remember,' he said, bitterly. 'Well, wait and see *my* family.'

'I will wait, Mr. Brockman,' I replied; 'but you will excuse me, I must take the date down in my book.'

'You can do as you like.'

I took the date down, and here it is:

Brockman's Folly.

I, John Barton, take this date down because I see something abnormal in the appearance of Mr. Julian Brockman. I have promised to stop with Mr. Julian Brockman, but if I see more signs of insanity I shall call in the aid of the police.

(Signed)   JOHN BARTON.

11 o'clock at night, 16th June, 18—.

I took this leaf of my note-book, and went to the door.

'Where are you going?' Mr. Brockman asked, quickly.

'I am going to your old housekeeper, sir. I have several things to do, among them to see that we shall be supplied with food. You forget, Mr. Brockman, that I have left a home, and that I cannot sit up with you without food.'

'Yes, I had forgotten; but don't be long.'

But I have not yet described to you 'Brockman's Folly'.

It was a large brick house of two storeys, with deep bay windows in front, and a heavy portico with stone copings. There was nothing peculiar in the style of the building; it was the situation in which it had been built that had given it the name of Brockman's Folly.

Mr. Julian Brockman had chosen as the site of his house – twenty years previous to the date of my tale – a swamp. There is no plainer term to call it, for it was a bit of low-lying, undrainable land. However, he built Brockman's Folly on it, and the walls of the house were now, after all those years, stained with damp, and most uninviting in appearance. The house was surrounded on three sides by high brick walls, and it had been another of Mr. Brockman's follies to plant the top of the walls with the common yellow stone-crop that doubtless reminded him of his boyhood's home in England.

So much for the appearance of the house; now I shall resume my story.

I went down the rambling stairs of this rambling old house with the double purpose in view of sending my wife some intelligence that might relieve her of natural fears on my behalf, and of communicating with the police if Brockman should really prove to be, as I suspected, insane. I could not see any signs of habitation until I came to the basement, and there I saw an old woman sitting by the low fire in a blackened kitchen chimney.

She heard my step the moment I entered, and looked up, but without showing any signs of fear or discomfiture; the old face turned toward me was pale and wrinkled, and a yellow-white cap, badly and hastily washed, covered her forehead with its broad borders.

'What is it you want?' she asked, in as quiet a tone as if she had known me all her life.

'Before I answer the question,' I replied, 'I think I will have a talk with you'; and I seated myself within the light of the wretched tallow candle that burned near her on the hob.

'What is your talk, sir?'

The question was not put insultingly, but in a quiet way, as if the answer could be of no personal interest to her.

'My talk is to be about Mr. Brockman,' I replied. 'Do you think there is anything wrong with him?'

'Mr. Brockman is mad, sir,' was the quiet reply.

'If you think so, why have you not called in some help?' I asked.

'Why should I, sir? I have eaten his bread for nearly thirty years; I was his wife's friend and his son's nurse.'

'I never knew there was a wife,' was my foolish response.

'There was a wife and a son; and now please tell me what you want in my kitchen.'

The sudden change in the woman's manner startled me. She had risen from her seat and turned toward me a face pale with anger. I could not understand her, and I said so.

'What do you want in my kitchen?' she repeated. 'But you needn't answer me, for I know; you want information, but will get none!'

'You are a very strange housekeeper,' I said, as I went toward the door. 'I came down here with Mr. Brockman's permission to get some food – if you cannot carry a tray *I* can.'

'You are going to sit up with him? Ha, ha! You want to see his ghosts! Well, a wilful man must have his way. *Now* leave my kitchen!'

I climbed up the old staircase again and wondered what I should do to send the note I had addressed to my wife, but I all at once remembered that Mrs. Barton knew where I was going to when we parted, and that she also knew what an unpleasant business it was at any time to settle with Mr. Julian Brockman.

'She will tell our neighbour, Constable Strong,' I thought, 'and *he* will hunt me up.'

When I entered the room Mr. Brockman was sitting where I had left him. He seemed to me to be half asleep, but he heard the door opening, and raised his head from the folded arms on the desk before him.

'What did she say to you?' he asked, putting down his head again.

'She turned me out of the kitchen.'

'Most likely,' he returned, with great bitterness.

'I must say that I do not see any use in stopping here to-night, Mr. Brockman. I think that to see a medical man would be the most judicious step you could take. These hallucinations – '

'Hallucinations!' He was sitting up now, and staring behind me with such fear in his face that I turned, just as a woman in a white dress glided past me, and, approaching Brockman, laid her thin white hand on his shoulder. I saw her leaning her pale face close to his bowed head, and saw him shrink under the touch of that thin hand. I saw her only for a moment, and then she had vanished as if the floor had swallowed the shadowy figure up.

In an instant he had risen and faced me.

'You were always a fool, Barton!' he said, sternly, 'but now you will believe, because you have seen her.'

'Yes, I have seen a woman,' I replied.

'A dead woman! Now you will believe in the ghost of Brockman's Folly?'

While I was feeling more bewildered than ever, and fancying myself the victim of some imposition, the old housekeeper made her appearance in the room. She went straight to Mr. Brockman and touched him on the shoulder.

'You have forgotten yourself, Julian Brockman,' she said; 'there is business awaiting you that your agent cannot attend to – come at once with me.'

At first he did not seem to understand the order (for that was what it appeared to me), but he eventually followed her quietly as an obedient child.

I was puzzled by the whole affair, and very suspicious of the housekeeper. I scarcely knew how to act, but I was determined now on seeing the matter out. I hoped that every moment would bring me help, remembering that I had an anxious and loving wife waiting for me at home.

And I had another idea – if Mr. Brockman was, as the old woman had told me, mad, it was my duty to help him if I could. I had better wait. He was the victim of some mania in which I could help him, so I sat still and waited.

I had not waited five minutes when I saw a young man, who was so like Mr. Brockman that I guessed at once it was his scapegrace son, Julian Brockman. I had been thinking wonderingly about the old woman taking Brockman away when he seemed to stand before me all at once, and addressed me.

'Mr. Barton, do you not know me?'

I looked at him – a fine, handsome young man, not exactly resembling his father, but yet with something in air and manner

306 Existential Anxieties

sufficient to establish his identity; and I replied:

'Yes, I can see a resemblance. You are Julian Brockman, junior, and it is you who have been personating the ghost in your father's house.'

'You are right, sir; it is I who have done so.'

'For what purpose, may I ask?'

'I must suppose that a Mighty Power has sent you here to help us. I am here to make Julian Brockman answer for a crime committed ten years ago.'

'A crime!'

'Yes, a crime. And now my father is coming back. I leave him to you, but, remember, you have not seen the ghost.'

The young man left the room by a door that seemed to lead into a bedchamber, which was one of those communicating with the front of the house, where the bay windows were. If I had not noticed his appearance so much I might have believed I had never seen him at all, but had been 'dreaming a dream'.

His appearance was this: he was dark-haired and tall, and was as stern in expression as his father. He was dressed in black clothes from head to foot, and had a broad band of crape round his left arm. He was honest-looking in spite of my suspicions, and had the eyes of a man who could meet the look of any other man without flinching.

'And this,' I thought to myself, 'this is the run-away son! If ever I saw the face of an honourable man I saw it now.'

I had now more than one question to ask myself. For what purpose had the old woman taken Brockman away, and why had young Julian confided in me so far?

These were the answers I gave myself to these questions:

'For what purpose had the old housekeeper taken Brockman away?'

'To give him warning of something.'

'Why had young Julian confided in me so far?'

'Because he had heard of me and could trust me.'

Then the result was that there was something hidden that it was hoped I would help young Julian to find out. I must wait and watch. I have hinted before how hard waiting is.

Mr. Brockman came back in a short time and sat down moodily beside me; it appeared to me that he had been taught a lesson and had done his best to learn it well.

'Barton,' he whispered to me; 'I thought I could depend on you?'

'So you can, as far as honesty is concerned, Mr. Brockman,' I returned.

'And you will let them arrest me?'

'Arrest you?' I repeated, at the same time more convinced than ever that the man was a lunatic.

'Yes. Old Nance called me out just now to tell me that you had sent word to the police to have me arrested.'

'Old Nance was mistaken,' I replied.

'Most likely so,' he answered; 'she is often mistaken. *She* often sees the spirits when *I* do not.'

'What spirits?'

'You have seen them, Barton!' he exclaimed, turning on me firecely; 'at least, you have seen one of them!'

'I have seen no spirits, Mr. Brockman.'

'Perhaps you have seen realities?'

He asked me as in a question, and I answered him thus:

'Most likely I have, sir. I do not believe in ghosts.'

'You are an unbeliever, Barton.'

'In many ways I am afraid that I am, Mr. Brockman,' I quietly replied; 'but what is it that you wish me to believe?'

He did not answer me, and again hid his head on his arms. I began to be afraid of the man.

There was just then the soft sound of gravel being quietly thrown against the window, and, gladly expecting some intelligence from the outer world, I walked toward it. A heavy curtain of some dark stuff was drawn across the recess. I had only to step inside it to be face to face with the darkness outside.

I, Mark Sinclair, continue this story of 'Brockman's Folly'. On the night of the sixteenth of June, 18—, one of our men reported to me that a man was missing from L— street, and that his wife was in the office. I went out to hear her explanation, which was in substance as follows:

The husband was a house and land agent residing in L— street, and had for years acted as collecting agent for Mr. Julian Brockman. He had left home early in the evening to render his accounts to Mr. Brockman, and had not returned. Constable Strong, who, it seems, was Mr. Barton's neighbour, had advised her application to our office, and accompanied the woman when I interrogated her.

When she had told her errand, I questioned Strong.

'Why did you bring Mrs. Barton here? Could you not have gone to the place yourself and inquired for Mr. Barton?'

'Why, you surely have not taken notice of the name of the place, Sinclair, or you would not have asked me such a question.'

'The name of the place?'

'Yes; it is Brockman's Folly, the place that has been so often reported.'

'Brockman's Folly? I remember nothing connected with any report about Brockman's Folly.'

'The place reported as being haunted and suspected of – '

'Oh, now I have you, Strong; and is it at Brockman's Folly that this woman's husband is?'

'It is there that he is supposed to be.'

'Have you told this woman anything about the suspicion?'

'I am afraid I did. She had heard something about the place being haunted.'

'You have done a very foolish thing, Strong, and now you can take this poor woman home again. When you have taken her home you can join me at Brockman's Folly.'

'You are going yourself then, Sinclair?'

'I am going myself.'

I pitied that poor woman who stood so patiently aside while I was talking to Strong, and I said to her, as gently as I could:

'Mrs. Barton, Strong will take you home; I am going to look for your husband myself.'

'Look for him?' she asked, wistfully; 'do you think that you will find him?'

'I am sure I shall find him. Will you tell me why you are so frightened about nothing?'

'I have heard such stories of Brockman's Folly.'

'Never mind stories, my good lady; go home with Strong, and be certain I shall find your husband for you.'

Before I started for Brockman's Folly I provided myself with a bull's-eye lantern and a revolver. It was after eleven when I left the office, and my way across the swamp was difficult, because I had not travelled it before; but I saw the dark walls looming up before me darker than the other shadows, and I made the most direct way I could toward them.

Turning under the north wall, I saw a faint light in a bow-window at the front of the house. Something hinted to me that I must climb up to that window. There was a portico at hand, and struggling to grasp, I got hold of a salient point and began to climb.

When I had reached a level with the window I seized some of the damp mortar I had dislodged and threw it softly against the panes. Someone heard it and lifted the curtain. As soon as I saw this someone I recognised from the description the lost husband.

'Let me in,' I whispered. 'I am a policeman, and your wife has sent me to find you. Lift up the side window, and leave the rest to me.'

In a moment the window was lifted, and I had crawled into the room. Barton did not say a word.

There was a heavy curtain behind him, and I caught the folds to peep through. It was a cold and damp-looking room into which I looked. There was an oak desk somewhere about the middle of it, and at the desk a man was seated, with his face resting on his folded arms.

I have never forgotten that man as he sat there, and he will always be as plain to my memory as he was when I first set eyes on him. He did not seem to see or hear me when I entered, and so I quietly took my seat on an old couch, where Barton told me he had sat all the time of his enforced visit.

'Mr. Brockman,' I said, quietly, 'tell me the story of your ghost.' He did not hear me at first, but I repeated it.

When the man lifted his face and looked at me I saw that he was ill – ill beyond all belief, and sick with suffering of both body and mind.

'You are sick,' I said, as I went to him and lifted him from the unsteady stool on which he was seated. 'Come with me, and lie down on this couch.'

'Who *are* you?' he asked, as he tried to do as I had told him.

'I am a friend.'

'People like me have no friends.'

'I want you to tell me the story of your ghost.'

'Why do you want to hear it?'

'To drive it away from you. There are *no* ghosts at Brockman's Folly.'

'No one believes.'

He said it wearily, and knowing that the poor man was really ill, I did not annoy him by speaking again at that time.

'If,' Mr. Barton questioned, '*if* you could give me some explanation I should be glad.'

'You shall have the explanation in good time, sir; in the meantime, please tell me your experiences since you entered this house to-night'.

He related them to me simply enough, while Brockman seemed to sleep, but with such an expression of suffering on his face as I have never seen equalled.

'And you have seen the son?' I asked.

'Certainly; I saw him here alive, and he spoke to me, as I have told you. He was in search of a crime committed ten years ago, so he said.'

'I think I have a clue to the mystery,' I observed, as I walked toward the door. 'Watch by Mr. Brockman; I will send for a doctor instantly.'

I went downstairs, and sitting in the same place where Barton said he had seen her was the ugliest old woman I had ever seen in my life.

It was not her ugliness of feature exactly; it was the fiendish expression with which she turned on me as she heard me fumbling down the old stairs.

'So, you've come?' she sneered.

'Yes; did you expect me?'

'I did, you are always a sly, crawling lot. *Now* what do you want in *my* kitchen?'

The same question she had asked Barton, but I replied to it differently.

'I want to find out the secret of the ghost,' I said, 'and I'll thank you to tell it to me at once.'

'Tell it to you? Ha, ha! tell it to a spy and informer! Who are *you*, anyhow?'

'I am not Barton, the agent,' I answered. 'At all events, I am not him.'

'I see you are not,' she said, shortly, as she resumed her seat. 'I fancied you were at first, but I see you are not now. Well, who has sent you this time?'

'No one has sent me. I have come myself to look after your ghosts.'

'I have no ghosts in my kitchen.'

'You have a good many, Nance Dwyer, and I hereby arrest you for the murder of Helena Brockman.'

When I clapped the handcuffs on the woman she stared at me like a terrified animal; then she cried out loudly as she struggled and tried to get the steel bracelets off. In the middle of the noise and my attempts to hold the old woman, to my astonishment Mr. Brockman appeared on the scene.

'Tell the truth, woman!' he exclaimed; 'tell the truth. I am dying; let me die in peace.'

'It is my duty to warn the prisoner that anything she may say will be taken down as evidence against her.'

'I will say nothing, and tell nothing!' she exclaimed; 'and now that I hold my tongue you had better confess and commit yourself, Julian Brockman.'

'I am going to do it,' the unhappy man said, as he turned to retrace his steps, 'and I shall escape, though *you* will not.'

There was here a knock at the kitchen door, and I admitted Constable Strong. Into his charge I gave my prisoner as I followed Mr. Brockman up the damp, miserable stairs to the first story.

I found him fainting in the arms of Barton, who explained to me:

'I thought he was asleep, and before I knew he had got out of the door. Oh, Mr. Sinclair, is he mad?'

'No, he is only dying. Carry him in, and I will look for his son.' I went to the door of that bedroom from which Mr. Barton had told me that young Brockman had appeared and disappeared, and I looked around me.

I was in a room so dark that I was glad to turn the small light of my 'bull's-eye' on it. Peering through the gloom I saw a large bedstead of old-fashioned make and of wood, with a heavy tester and a curtain of crimson. Someone was sitting on the bed in the dark, half hidden behind the curtains. When I flashed the light into his face I saw that it was that of the young man I had expected to see.

'Who are you?' he asked, quickly.

'I am a friend of your father's,' I replied; 'get up, Julian Brockman, and come with me.'

'Do you mean that I am under arrest?' he asked, as he rose and drew himself up.

'No, I do not mean that, but I mean that your father is dying, and I want you to comfort him if you can.'

'Dying!'

There was no need to say more. The young man followed me at once, and, after one swift glance, was bending by the couch where his father lay.

'Father!' he whispered. 'Father! it was not you I suspected.'

'I know that, Julian. I have been suspected too long.'

'Who do you suspect, dear father?'

'I do not suspect; I know.'

'Oh, father! if you know tell me, that I may avenge her and you.'

'It was Nance Dwyer – she did it.'

By this time we were supporting him, Brockman shaking like a leaf, and I raising him up to see his son.

'It is I, my father, it is I – your own Julian. Don't you know me? don't you know me?'

'I know you, my son, I know you well; but I thought you were drowned.'

'You fancied so, father; but I am here.'

'Was it a fancy?' questioned the dying man.

'It was a fancy, father, for I am here.'

That is how I, Mark Sinclair, recall the two faces – the old one and the young one – so close together, and yet so painfully alike: the one the living picture of the father as he had once been; the father dying, and yet with such a strange resemblance to the son.

'And I must leave you, my boy,' he said, softly; 'I must leave you. I'm going to a strange land, my son; shall we ever meet again?'

'As sure as the sun is the Lord's enlightener, and the grand belief true, dear father, we shall meet again.'

'Then, son, I believe you; we shall meet again.'

Doubtless they will meet again! When the Great Judge opens our eyes we shall see and rejoice in those we have loved on earth.

I never felt more pity than I did for that son. He would scarcely believe that his father was dead. When we lifted Brockman from his arms, he staggered and would have fallen only that we held him up.

'I wished to do well and I have done wrong,' he moaned.

'You have done well so far,' I said, encouragingly, 'and you must remember there is a mother to be found and avenged.'

The young man suddenly found all his strength and stood up facing me.

'I know what you mean,' he said, quietly. 'I will go with you to Nance Dwyer, but you will look after my father?'

'*I* will look after him,' Barton said, as he laid his hand on young Brockman's shoulder; 'trust him to me.'

He followed me down the damp staircase to the kitchen, in which I had left the old housekeeper in charge of Strong. She was sitting there just as I had left her, and with her handcuffs clasped upon her hands.

He sat down on a little stool close beside her, and she took no more notice of him than she did of the policeman on guard behind her.

'Do you know me?' he asked; and the reply startled me.

'I know no one, Julian Brockman.'

'You don't know me?'

'Yes, I know you; I nursed you on my bosom.'

'And murdered the mother that bore me. Oh, woman! if you have a conscience, and hope for mercy, speak out and tell the truth!'

It came from the man's agonised heart, and it struck even the heart of that hard old woman.

'I will tell the truth,' she said, 'and save my soul. Listen to my confession. It was I who murdered Mrs. Brockman.'

'Make a full confession now that you have begun.'

'I have confessed. I did the deed, but I will tell no more. You are detectives; find out the rest for yourself.'

'And that is what you call a confession?' Julian asked, bitterly. 'Oh, Nance, your sins lie lightly on your conscience.'

'You used to call me granny once,' the old creature said, as she turned a softening face toward the young man. 'Can you see me with these on me and feel no pity for me?'

She raised her manacled hands as she was speaking, and then let them fall again on her lap.

'God knows I pity you,' Julian replied; 'but I had a mother once, and I have a duty to perform.'

'Is it true that your father is dead?' she asked, in a low voice.

'It is true, Nance.'

'Then I can die too.'

Not another word could we extract from the woman. She went to the lock-up uncomplainingly. Only once I saw some sign of feeling: it was when we passed under the bow-window, which she doubtless knew was all that separated her from her dead master; she looked up suddenly, and gave a sort of gasping sigh, but the next moment she was her own hard self again.

I now think that it will be better for me to tell you exactly how the house known as Brockman's Folly came to be marked as suspicious in the detective office. You know already that Constable Strong was a neighbour of Mr. Barton's and that they were friendly. Well, it was Constable Strong who first gave us a hint that all was not right at the old house in the swamp.

'Barton is rather a soft sort of fellow,' Strong said to me one day, when we met accidentally; 'honest and quick in his business, and all that, but yet a little inclined to talk over a glass of an evening, and that old Brockman is on his brain, I think.'

'Brockman on his brain? What do you mean?'

'Barton is agent for Brockman, you know. Well, Barton is rather afraid of Brockman, who seems to be an ill-tempered old fellow.'

'What has this to do with this story of a suspected house?'

'I am going to tell you. I was on that beat for over two months – a most uncomfortable beat it was, too – and first one and then another began to complain that Brockman's place was haunted. Screams have been heard, and the shadow of a woman been passing behind the blind of that bow-window at night. At first I thought it would be a handy place for coiners to hide, and I watched it.'

'And what did you see?'

'I saw an old woman rambling about at night, and heard her muttering to herself queer words.'

'And you suspect something, Strong?'

'Yes. There is a mystery altogether about the house and Brockman's family. It seems there was a son who ran away to sea when he was fifteen. Then there was the mother – here one day, and away the next.'

'Here one day, and away the next?'

'Exactly. She was seen by some hawker of vegetables on the 10th June, 18—, and she was never seen again.'

'How did you find all this out, Strong?'

'By the gossip of neighbours, and my own eyes and ears. Now I leave the case in your hands, Sinclair.'

'You may. We are not busy just now, and I can devote myself to Brockman's Folly.'

And I devoted myself that morning to making notes of what Strong had told me.

'10th and 11th June, 18—,' I muttered, as I marked down the dates. 'Why, it's over nine years ago. Much chance there is of my being able to elucidate this so-called mystery of Brockman's Folly.'

Even as I was putting the note-book in my pocket a young man accosted me.

'You are Detective Sinclair?' he asked.

'I am,' I replied.

'I am Julian Brockman; have you heard the name at all?'

'Julian Brockman!'

I was more than surprised at the sound of the name – the very name I had been putting in my note-book a moment or two before.

'Yes, that is my name. I ran away to sea now more than fourteen years ago, and I am the son of Julian Brockman, of Brockman's Folly.'

'I know the place, but what do you want with me?'

'Because I dream,' he returned, with a wistful smile. 'I have had such dreams of my mother.'

'Dreams of your mother! God gracious, young man, do you think a detective office is a place to relate dreams in?'

'It might be the proper place sometimes; at all events I have come by sea and land to tell the police of Melbourne my dreams.'

'Tell them if it will relieve you.'

'I was in Corio Bay one day in June of last year, and being off duty lay down in the forecastle to sleep – it was on that occasion that I had my first dream.

'I thought that I saw my mother sitting by my bed, and that she laid a hand as cold as death on my forehead. I seemed to hear her say:

'Go home, my son, and look for your mother.'

'What date was that in June?' I asked him.

'It was on the 11th of June.'

'Well, go on; you dreamed again?'

'Yes, I did not trouble much about that dream, for I used to think a good deal about my mother; but the day before yesterday I dreamed the same dream again.'

'The day before yesterday was the 11th of June again.'

'It was; so I was determined to find out this thing for myself, and I came. I went to Brockman's Folly, and know now that my mother died on the 11th June.'

'Who told you?'

'I heard it from an old friend.'

'Did you see your father?'

'No, I am afraid of my father.'

'Your ship is still in Corio Bay?'

'It is.'

'Well, now, take my advice – go back to your ship. Did you ever hear anything come of dreams or a dreamer? If your mother is dead you cannot bring her to life. My dear fellow, give me your address, and when I want you I will send for you.'

We parted on the best of terms, though I have no doubt that he thought me hard and unsympathetic.

I never believed one word about the dreams, but as Strong had mentioned the matter to me, I investigated it in my own way. One's own way is not always the best, but I came to the conclusion that the gossip about Brockman's Folly *was* gossip, and nothing more. You know already how my attention was recalled to the old house in the swamp, and how we had arrested Nance Dwyer for the murder of her mistress.

We searched the premises at Brockman's from garret to cellar, and found nothing. The old murderess remained obdurate, and was deaf to the pleadings of her foster-son, the young sailor. One day, however, an accident discovered her secret and rendered her amenable to the law, for you know we could not prove a person guilty of murder when there was no proof that a murder had been committed.

Young Brockman had taken up his residence at Brockman's Folly with the sole hope of yet discovering his mother's body. On the arrangement of his late father's affairs he was found to be very comfortably situated as far as the world's goods were concerned, and so he devoted himself to the discovery he had so much at heart.

One day, then, he was overseeing some repairs in the damp kitchen that old Nance had claimed as her own, when the hearthstone was lifted. I do not wish to dwell upon details that must always be unpleasant, but the remains of Mrs. Brockman were hidden under the very spot where the murderess had sat night after night.

And no one yet knows the mystery of that murder, nor can they ever know now until the secrets of all hearts are revealed.

316 Existential Anxieties

Strong has his theory – I have mine; and I do not doubt but that Julian, now far at sea in a ship of his own, has another idea about the manner of his mother's death. But I think that as Mr. Barton, the house and land agent, commenced this story he ought to finish it in his own words.

Mr. Strong has requested me to put down in writing my opinion of the manner of the late Mrs. Brockman's death, and I do so now with the firmest conviction. Constable Strong has discovered that for some time previous to Mrs. Brockman's disappearance the old woman Nance was in the habit of disposing of articles of jewellery. Mrs. Brockman was known by her son to have been possessed of many valuable trinkets, belonging to her by will from her family, and I think it most likely that the old woman's cupidity had proved her ruin, as well as that Mrs. Brockman's discovery of the theft had cost her her life.

As to the apparition, or seeming apparition, I am satisfied, in my own mind, that Julian had, at first, suspected his father, and dressed himself to represent the spirit of his mother in the hope of working on Brockman's fears, and getting him to confess. If such was the case, it is no wonder that the young man should be ashamed to confess the fact when he discovered his father's innocence.

But my wife is of a different opinion, and thinks that old Nance herself must have been the personator of the ghost. However it may have been, it was very real to me at the time, and I remember with a shudder yet the white form that glided past me in the so-called haunted house.

MARCUS CLARKE
Human Repetends

We had returned from a 'Seance', and were discussing that which every one discusses without being anything the wiser – the future of the soul.

'Come,' I cried at last, 'our thinly-clad intellects will take cold if we venture so far up the mountain. Let us hasten to take refuge at the fireside of the great DON'T KNOW.'

'Ay,' said Hylton, the surgeon, 'it is best. The secrets of the grave are in safe keeping. Who has held parley with one risen from the dead?'

'You are sure, then, that the spirits of the dead do not re-visit us?' asked the sad voice of Pontifex, from out the gloom.

'Ay, as sure as of anything in this unstable world. But *you* are no convert to the "spiritualistic" doctrine. You are no believer in the ghost of Benjamin Franklin's small clothes.'

'I speak of spirits clad in flesh – ghosts who live and move amongst us – ghosts who, tenants of bodies like our own, mingle in the practical life of a methodical age, fulfilling a destiny, in the accomplishment of which some of us, all unwittingly, may be involved.'

'What do you mean, man?' asked Hylton, frowning down an involuntary stare of alarm.

'Did you never meet one of these embodied ghosts?' said Pontifex. 'Have you never, when dining in a public room or walking in a crowd, been conscious of the presence of something evil? Have you not known men, whose voice, silence, attitude, gait, feature, gave token of crime undetected? These are the ghosts of our modern day. They are with us, but not of us. We turn to look after them, and yet avoid them, or meeting them, shrink from contact, shuddering we know not why.'

'Pontifex,' I cried, urged to utterance by the tones of the speaker, 'we have all known that you have a story. Tell it to us to-night.'

The young man fixed his hollow eyes upon the fire and laughed low.

'I have a story, and I will tell it to you, if you like, for the occasion is a fitting one. Listen.

'Most men, however roughly the world has used them, can recall a period in their lives when they were absolutely happy,

317

when each night closed with the recollection of new pleasures tasted, when the progress of each day was cheered by the experience of unlooked-for novelties, and when the awakening to another dawn was a pure physical delight, unmarred by those cankering anxieties for the fortune of the hour which are the burden of the poor, the ambitious and the intriguing. To most men, also, this golden time comes, when the cares of a mother, or the coquettish attention of sisters, aid to shield the young and eager soul from the blighting influences of worldly debaucheries. Thrice fortunate is he among us who can look back on a youth spent in the innocent enjoyments of the country, or who possesses a mind moulded in its adolescence by the cool fingers of well-mannered and pious women.

'My first initiation into the business of living took place under different auspices. The only son of a rich widower, who lived but for the gratification of a literary and political ambition, I was thrown, when still a boy, into the society of men thrice my age, and was tolerated as a clever impertinent in all those witty and wicked circles in which virtuous women are conspicuous by their absence. My father lived indifferently in Paris, or London, and, patronised by the dandies, artists, and scribblers who form, in both cities, the male world of fashionable idleness, I was suffered at sixteen to ape the vices of sixty. Indeed, so long as I was reported to be moving only in that set to which my father chose to ally himself, he never cared to inquire how I spent the extravagant allowance which his indifference rather than his generosity permitted me to waste. You can guess the result of such a training. The admirer of men whose successes in love and play were the theme of common talk for six months; the worshipper of artists whose genius was to revolutionise Europe – only they died of late hours and tobacco; the pet of women whose daring beauty made their names famous – for three years; I discovered, at twenty years of age, that the pleasurable path I had trodden so gaily led to a hospital or a debtor's prison, that love meant money, friendship, an endorsement on a bill, and that the rigid exercise of a profound and calculating selfishness alone rendered tolerable a life at once so deceitful and barren. In this view of the world I was supported by those middle-aged Mephistopheles (survivors of the storms which had wrecked so many argosies), those cynical, well-bred worshippers of self, who realise in the nineteenth century that notion of the devil which was invented by the early Christians. With these good gentlemen I lived; emulating their cynicism, rivalling their sarcasms, and neutralising the superiority which their existence gave them, by the exercise of that potentiality for present enjoyment which is the privilege of youth.

'In this society I was progressing rapidly to destruction, when an event occurred which rudely saved me. My father died suddenly in London, and, to the astonishment of the world, left – nothing. His expenditure had been large, but, as he left no debts, his income must have been proportioned to his expenses. The source of this income, however, was impossible to discover. An examination of his banker's book showed only that large sums (always in notes or gold) had been lodged and drawn upon, but no record of speculations or of investments could be found among his papers. My relatives stared, shook their heads, and insulted me with their pity. The sale of furniture, books, plate, and horses brought enough to pay the necessary expenses of the funeral, and leave me heir to some £800. My friends of the smoking-room and the supper-table philosophised on Monday, cashed my I.O.U.'s on Tuesday, were satirical on Wednesday, and "cut" me on Thursday. My relatives said that "something must be done," and invited me to stay at their houses until that vague substantiality should be realised. One suggested a clerkship in the War Office; another a stool in a banking-house; while a third generously offered to use his interest at head-quarters to procure for me a commission in a marching regiment. Their offers were generously made, but, *then*, stunned by the rude shock of sudden poverty, and with a mind debauched by a life of extravagance and selfishness, I was incapable of manly action. To all proposals I replied with sullen disdain; and, desirious only of avoiding those who had known me in my prosperity, I avowed my resolution of claiming my inheritance and vanishing to America.

'A young man, with money and a taste for *bric-à-brac*, soon gathers about him a strange collection of curiosities, and at the sale of my possessions I was astonished to find how largely I had been preyed upon by the Jews, print-sellers, picture-dealers, and vendors of spurious antiques. The "valuable paintings," the curious "relics," the inlaid and be-jewelled "arms," and the rare "impressions" of old prints were purchased by the "trade" for a third of the price which I had paid for them, doubtless to be re-sold to another man of taste as artless and extravagant as myself. Of the numberless articles which had littered my bachelor-house I retained but three or four of the most portable, which might serve as remembrances of a luxury I never hoped again to enjoy. Among these was a copper-plate engraving, said to be one of the first specimens of that art. The print bore the noted name of Tommasco Finiguerra, and was dated 1469. It was apparently a copy of a "half-length" portrait of a woman, dressed in the fashion of that age, and holding in her hand a spray of rue. The name of this *grande dame* was not given – indeed, as I need hardly say, the absence of aught but the engraver's signature constituted the chief value of the print.

'I felt constrained to preserve this purchase, for many reasons. Not only had I, one idle day, "discovered" it, as I imagined, on the back shelves of a print-shop, and regarded it as the prize of my artistic taste; not only had it occupied the place of honour over my mantelshelf, and been a silent witness of many scenes which yet lingered fondly in my memory; not only had I seemed to hold communion with it when, on some lonely evening, I was left to reflect upon the barrenness of my existence, but the face possessed a charm of expression which, acknowledged by all, had become for me a positive fascination. The original must have been a woman of strange thoughts, and (I fancied) of a strange history. The *pose* of the head was defiant, the compressed lips wore a shadowy smile of disdain, and the eyes – large, full, and shaded by heavy lashes – seemed to look through you, and away from you, with a glance that was at once proud and timid, as though they contemplated and dared some vague terror, of whose superior power they were conscious. We have all, I presume, seen portraits which, by accident or design, bear upon them a startling expression rarely seen upon the face of the original, but which is felt to be a more truthful interpreter of character than is the enforced composure which self-control has rendered habitual. So with the portrait of which I speak. The unknown woman – or girl, for she did not seem to be more than three-and-twenty – revealed, in the wonderful glance with which she had so long looked down upon me, a story of pride, of love, of shame, perhaps of sin. One could imagine that in another instant the horror would fade from those lovely eyes, the smile return to that disdainful lip, and the delicate bosom, which now swelled with that terror which catches the breath and quickens the pulse, would sink into its wonted peacefulness, to rise and fall with accustomed equanimity beneath its concealing laces. But that instant never came. The work of the artist was unchangeable; the soul which looked out of the windows of that lovely body still shuddered with a foreknowledge of the horror which it had expected four hundred years ago.

'I tried in vain to discover the name and history of this strange portrait. The artists or men of taste to whom I applied had neither seen another copy of the print, nor heard of the original painting. It seemed that the fascinating face had belonged to some nameless one, who had carried with her to the grave the knowledge of whatever mystery had burdened her life on earth. At last, hopeless of discovering the truth, I amused myself by speculating on what might perchance, have been the history of this unknown beauty. I compared her features with the descriptions left to us of women famous for their sorrows. I invented a thousand wild tales which might account for the look of doom upon her fair face, and at last my excited imagination half induced me to believe that the mysterious print was a forged antique, and represented, in truth, some living woman to whom I had often spoken, and with whom my fortunes were indissolubly connected.

'A wickeder lie was never uttered than that favourite statement of colonial politicians – more ignorant or more impudent than others of their class – that in Australia no man need starve who is willing to work. I have been willing to work, and I have absolutely starved for days together. The humiliation through which I passed must, I fancy, be familiar to many. During the first six months of my arrival I was an honorary member of the Melbourne Club, the guest of those officials to whom I brought letters of introduction, the welcomed of South Yarra tea-parties, and the butt of the local *Punch*, on account of the modish cut of my pantaloons. I met men who "knew my people," and was surprised to find that the mention of a titled friend secured for me considerable attention among the leaders of such second-hand fashion as is boasted by the colony. In this genial atmosphere I recovered my independence. Indeed, had my social derelictions been worse than those incurred by poverty, I was assured that society would find it in its colonial heart to forgive them all. I was Hugh Pontifex, who had supped with the Marquis of Carabas, and brought letters of introduction from Lord Crabs. Had Judas Iscariot arrived armed with such credentials South Yarra would have auburnised his red hair and had him to dinner. To my surprise, instead of being cast among new faces, and compelled to win for myself an independent reputation, I found that I was among old friends, whom I had long thought dead or in gaol. To walk down Collins-street was like pulling up the Styx. On either side I saw men who had vanished from the Upper World sooner than I. Tonkins was there to explain that queer story of the concealed ace. Jenkins talked to me for an hour concerning the Derby, which ruined him. Hopkins had another wife in addition to the one whom he left at Florence; while Wilkins assured me, on his honour, that he had married the lady with whom he had eloped, and introduced me to her during a dinner party at a trading magnate's. The game was made in the same old fashion, only the stakes were not so high. The porcelain was of the same pattern, only a little cracked.

'For six months life was vastly pleasant. Then my term of honorary membership finally expired, and I left the Club to live at Scott's. By-and-bye my money ran short. I drew a bill on England, and the letter which informed me of its payment contained a stern command to draw no more. I went on a visit to the "station" of an acquaintance, and, on returning to town, found that my hotel bill was presented weekly. I retired into cheaper lodgings, and became affiliated to a less aristocratic club. Forced to associate with men of another set, I felt that my first friends remembered to forget me. My lampooned trousers began to wear out, and I wondered how I could have been once so reckless in the purchase of boots. I applied to Wilkins for a loan, then to Tomkins and Hopkins. I found that I could not repay them, and so avoided those streets where they were to be met. I discarded gloves, and smoked a short pipe publicly at noonday. I removed to a public-house, and, talking with my creditor-landlord at night, not unfrequently drank much brandy. I discovered that it is possible to be drunk before dinner. I applied for a clerkship, a messengership, a "billet" in the Civil Service; I went on the stage as a "super," I went up the country as a schoolmaster, I scribbled for the newspapers, I wrote verses for the Full and Plenty eating-house. I starved in "genteel" poverty until fortune luckily put me in the way of prosperity by suggesting coach-driving and billiard-marking. Thanks to an education at a public school, a licensed youth, a taste for pleasure, and the society of the "best men about London," I found myself, at three-and-twenty, master of two professions, driving and billiard-playing. You will understand now that my digression concerning pictures was necessary to convince you that all this time I never sold the mysterious print.

'One Sunday evening, towards the end of August, when the windy winter had not yet begun to melt into sudden and dusty spring, I was walking up Bourke-street. All you folks who have made a study of Melbourne city know what a curious appearance the town presents on a Sunday evening. The deserted road, barren of all vehicles save a passing cab, serves as a promenade for hundreds of servant-maids, shod boys, and idlers, while the pavement is crowded with young men and women of the lower middle class, who, under pretence of "going to church," or of "smoking a cigar," contrive to indulge their mutual propensities for social enjoyment. Those sewing-girls who, at six o'clock in the evening, are to be nightly seen debouching from Flinders-lane or Collins-street, frequent these Sunday evening promenades, and, in all the pride of clean petticoats and kid gloves, form fitting companions for the holiday-making barbers or soft-goods clerks, who, daring rakes! seek a weekly intrigue in the *Peacock* on the unsavoury strength of a "Sunday" cigar. Examining these groups as I walked, I found myself abreast of Nissen's Café, impeding the egress of a lady. I turned with an apology, but the words melted on my lips when, beneath the black bonnet of the stranger, *I found the counterpart of my unknown print.*

'For an instant surprise rendered me incapable of action, and then, with a beating heart and bewildered brain, I followed the fleeting figure. She went down Bourke-street, and turned to the left into Swanston-street. When she reached the corner where the Town Hall now stands, a man suddenly crossed the moonlit street and joined her. This man was wrapped in one of those Inverness cloaks which the slowly travelling fashion of the day had then made imperative to the well-being of the Melbourne dandies. A slouch hat of the operatic brigand type shaded his face, but, in the brief glance that I caught of him, I fancied that I recognised those heavy brows, that blunt nose, and that thin and treacherous mouth. The two met, evidently by appointment, and went onward together. It was useless to follow. I turned and went home.

'I passed the next day in a condition of mind which it is impossible to describe. So strange a coincidence as this had surely never happened to man before. A woman has her portrait engraved in the year 1469; I purchase the engraving, try in vain to discover the original, and meet her face to face in the prosaic Melbourne of 1863. I longed for night to come, that I might wander through the streets in search of her. I felt a terrible yearning tug at my heartstrings. I burned to meet her wild, sad eyes again. I shuddered when I thought that, in my wildest dreams, I had never sunk that pictured face so deep beneath the social waters as this incarnation of it seemed to have been plunged. For two nights I roamed the streets in vain. On the morning of the third day a paragraph in the *Herald* explained why my search had been fruitless. The body of a woman had been "found in the Yarra." Society – especially unmarried society – has, as a matter of course, its average of female suicides, and, as a rule, respectable folks don't hear much about them. The case of this unfortunate girl, however, was different. She was presumed to have been murdered, and the police made investigations. The case is sufficiently celebrated in the annals of Melbourne crime to excuse a repetition of details. Suffice it to say that, against the many persons who were presumed to be inculpated in the destruction of the poor girl, no proof was forthcoming. The journals aired Edgar Poe and the "Mystery of Marie Roget" for a day or so, but no one was sent for trial, and an open verdict left the detectives at liberty to exercise their ingenuity without prejudice. There was some rumour of a foreigner being implicated in the deed, but as the friends of the poor outcast knew of no such person, and as my evidence as to seeing a man of such appearance join the deceased was, in reality, of little value (for I was compelled to admit that I had never seen the woman before in my life, and that my glimpse of her companion was but momentary), the supposition was treated with contempt, and the "case" dismissed from the memory of the public.

'It did not fade so easily from my mind. To speak the truth, indeed, I was haunted by the hideous thing which I had been sent to "view" upon the coarse table of that wretched deadhouse which then disgraced our city. The obscure and cruel fate of the unhappy woman, whose portrait had so long looked down upon me, filled me not only with horror but with apprehension. It seemed to me as if I myself was implicated in her fate, and bound to avenge her murder. The fact of my having speculated so long upon her fortunes, and then having found her but to lose her, without a word having passed between us, appeared to give me the right to seek to know more of her. The proud queen of many a fantastic dream-revel: the sad chatelaine of many an air-built castle: had this portrait leapt to life beneath my glances, as bounded to earth the nymph from beneath the chisel of Pygmalion? Had the lost one, who passed me like a ghost in the gloaming, come out of the grave in which they had placed her four hundred years ago? What meant this resurrection of buried beauty? What was the mysterious portent of this living presentment of a dead and forgotten sin? I saw the poor creature buried. I wept – no unmanly tears, I trust – over her nameless grave. And then I learned her history. 'Twas no romance, unless the old story of a broken home and the cold comfort of the stony-hearted streets may be called romantic. She was presumed to have been well born – she had been a wife – her husband had left her – she was beautiful and poor – for the rest, ask Mother Carey, who deals in chickens. She can tell you entertaining histories of fifty such.

'At the inquest I met Warrend – you remember old Tom, Hylton? – and he sought me out and took me home with him. We had been schoolfellows; but although my taste for prints and pictures had now and then brought me into his company, I had seen but little of him. He was – as we know him – kindly, tender, and generous. He offered me his help. He was in good practice, and could afford to give me shelter beneath his bachelor roof. He wrote for the *Argus*; knew the editor, would try and procure work for me. That meeting laid the foundation of such independence as I now claim. Shaken in health by my recent privations, and troubled in mind by the horrible and inexplicable mystery upon which I seemed to have stumbled, I was for some weeks seriously ill. Warrend saw that something preyed upon my spirits, and pressed me to unbosom myself. I told him the story and produced the print.

'I must beg your grace for what I am about to tell you. You may regard the story as unworthy of credit, or sneer at it as the result of a "coincidence." It is simply true, for all that.

'Warrend became grave.
' "I have a copy of that print," said he, in a tone altogether without the pride usual in a collector. "I think a unique copy. It is the portrait of a woman round whose life a mystery spun itself. See here."
'He opened the portfolio, and took out the engraving. It was an exact copy of mine, but was a proof after letters, and bore, in the quaint characters of the time, the name, *Jehanne La Gaillarde*.
'I fell back upon the sofa as if I had been struck in the face. The name of the poor girl whom I had buried was Jenny Gay.
' "Warrend," said I, "there is something unholy about this. I met, a week ago, the living original of that portrait, and now you, a man whose name re-echoes that of the Italian artist who engraved it, tell me that you know the mystery of her life. What is it, then? for, before you speak, I know *I* figure in the scene."
'Warrend, or Finiguerra, took from the book-shelf a little book, published by Vander Berghen, of Brussels, in 1775, and handed it to me. It was called *Le Coeur de Jehanne La Gaillarde*, and appeared to be a collection of letters. In the advertisement was a brief memoir of the woman whose face had so long puzzled me. I glanced at it, and turned sick with a nameless terror. Jehanne la Gaillarde was a woman whose romantic amours had electrified the Paris of Louis XI. She was murdered by being thrown into the Seine. "All attempts to discover the murderer were vain, but, at length, a young man named Hugues Grandprête, who, though he had never seen the celebrated beauty, had fallen in love with her picture, persuaded himself that the murderer was none other than the Sieur De la Forêt (the husband of the beautiful Jehanne), who, being a man of an ill-life, had been compelled to fly from Paris. Grandprête communicated his suspicions to none but his intimate friends, followed De la Forêt to Padua, and killed him."
As I read this romance of a man who bore a name which reflected my own, I shuddered, for a sudden thrill of recollection lighted up the darkness of the drama as a flash of lightning illumes the

darkness of a thundercloud. The face of the man in the cloak was recalled to me as that of a certain gambling lieutenant, who was cashiered by a court-martial, so notorious that the sun of India and the snows of the Crimea have scarce burned out or covered the memory of his regiment's nickname.

'As Jehanne La Gaillarde was the double of Jenny Gay: as Hugues Grandprête lived again in Hugh Pontifex: as the Italian artist was recalled to life in the person of the man at my side, so Bernhard De la Forêt worked once more his wicked will on earth in the person of the cashiered gambler, Bernard Forrester. If this was a "coincidence," it was terribly complete.'

'But 'twas a mere coincidence after all,' said Hylton, gently. 'You do not think men's souls return to earth and enact again the crimes which stained them?'

'I know not. But there are in decimal arithmetic repeated "coincidences" called *repetends*. Continue the generation of numbers through all time, and you have these repetends for ever recurring. Can you explain this mystery of numbers? No. Neither can I explain the mystery of my life. Good-night. I have wearied you.'

'Stay,' cried I, rashly; 'the parallel is not yet complete. You have not yet met Forrester?'

'No,' cried Pontifex, his large eyes blazing with no healthy fire; 'I have prayed that I might not meet him. I live here in Melbourne at the seat of his crime because it seems the least likely place again to behold him. If, by accident, in the streets I catch sight of one who resembles him, I hurry away. But I *shall* meet him one day, and then my doom will be upon me, and I shall kill him as I killed him in Padua 400 years ago!'

HENRY KENDALL
The Voyage of Telegonus

'Telegonus, a son of Ulysses and Circe, was born in the island of Aeaea,
where he was educated in the arts of hunting, war, &c. When he had
reached the years of manhood, he went to Ithaca to make himself known
to his father, but he was shipwrecked on the coast, and, being destitute
of provisions, he plundered some of the inhabitants of the island. Ulysses
and Telemachus came to defend the property of their subjects against
this unknown invader; a quarrel arose, and Telegonus killed his father
without knowing who he was.' – Lemprière.

Ill fares it with the man whose lips are set
To bitter themes and words that spite the gods:
For, seeing how the son of Saturn sways
With eyes and ears for all, this one shall halt
As on hard hurtful hills; his days shall know
The plaintive front of Sorrow; level looks
With cries ill-favoured shall be dealt to him;
And *this* shall be that he may think of peace
As one might think of alienated lips
Of sweetness touched for once in kind warm dreams.
Yea, fathers of the high and holy face,
This soul thus sinning shall have cause to sob
'Ah, ah,' for sleep, and space enough to learn
The wan wild Hyrie's aggregated song
That starts the dwellers in distorted heights,
With all the meaning of perpetual sighs
Heard in the mountained deserts of the world,
And where the green-haired waters glide between
The thin lank weeds and mallows of the marsh.

But thou to whom these things are like to shapes
That come of darkness – thou whose life slips past
Regarding rather these with mute fast mouth –
Hear none the less how fleet Telegonus,
The brass-clad hunter, first took oar and smote
Swift eastward-going seas, with face direct
For narrowing channels and the twofold coasts
Past Colchis and the fierce Symplegades
And utmost islands washed by streams unknown.

For in a time when Phasis whitened wide
And drove with violent waters blown of wind
Against the bare salt limits of the land,
It came to pass that, joined with Cytheraea,
The black-browed Ares, chafing for the wrong
Ulysses did him on the plains of Troy,
Set heart against the king; and when the storms
Sang high in thunder and the Thracian rain,
The god bethought him of a pale-mouthed priest
Of Thebes, kin to ancient Chariclo,
And of an omen which the prophet gave
That touched on Death and grief to Ithaca;
Then, knowing how a heavy-handed fate
Had laid itself on Circe's brass-clad son,
He pricked the hunter with a lust that turned
All thoughts to travel and the seas remote;
But chiefly now he stirred Telegonus
To longings for his father's exiled face,
And dreams of rest and honey-hearted love,
And quiet death with much of funeral flame
Far in the mountains of a favoured land
Beyond the wars and wailings of the waves.

So past the ridges where the coast abrupt
Dips greyly westward, Circe's strong-armed son
Swept down the foam of sharp-divided straits
And faced the stress of opening seas. Sheer out
The vessel drave; but three long moons the gale
Moaned round; and swift strong streams of fire revealed
The labouring rowers and the lightening surf,
Pale watchers deafened of sonorous storm,
And dripping decks and rents of ruined sails.
Yea, when the hollow ocean-driven ship
Wheeled sideways, like a chariot cloven through
In hard hot battle, and the night came up
Against strange headlands lying East and North,
Behold a black wild wind with death to all
Ran shoreward, charged with flame and thunder-smoke,
Which blew the waters into wastes of white
And broke the bark, as lightning breaks the pine;
Whereat the sea in fearful circles showed
Unpitied faces turned from Zeus and light,
Wan swimmers wasted with their agony,
And hopeless eyes and moaning mouths of men.

But one held by the fragments of the wreck,
And Ares knew him for Telegonus,
Whom heavy-handed Fate had chained to deeds
Of dreadful note with sin beyond a name.
So, seeing this, the black-browed lord of war,
Arrayed about by Jove's authentic light,
Shot down amongst the shattered clouds and called
With mighty strain, betwixt the gaps of storm,
'Oceanus, Oceanus!' whereat
The surf sprang white, as when a keel divides
The gleaming centre of a gathered wave;
And, ringed with flakes of splendid fire of foam,
The son of Terra rose halfway and blew
The triple trumpet of the water-gods,
At which great winds fell back and all the sea
Grew dumb, as on the land a war-feast breaks
When deep sleep falls upon the souls of men.
Then Ares of the night-like brow made known
The brass-clad hunter of the facile feet
Hard clinging to the slippery logs of pine,
And told the omen to the hoary god
That touched on Death and grief to Ithaca;
Wherefore Oceanus with help of hand
Bore by the chin the warrior of the North,
A moaning mass, across the shallowing surge,
And cast him on the rocks of alien shores
Against a wintry morning shot with storm.

Hear also thou how mighty gods sustain
The men set out to work the ends of Fate
Which fill the world with tales of many tears,
And vex the sad face of Humanity:
Six days and nights the brass-clad chief abode
Pent up in caverns by the straightening seas,
And fed on ferns and limpets; but the dawn
Before the strong sun of the seventh, brought
A fume of fire and smells of savoury meat,
And much rejoicing, as from neighbouring feasts;
At which the hunter, seized with sudden lust,
Sprang up the crags, and, like a dream of Fear,
Leapt, shouting, at a huddled host of hinds
Amongst the fragments of their steaming food;
And, as the hoarse wood-wind in Autumn sweeps
To every zone the hissing latter leaves,

So, fleet Telegonus, by dint of spear
And strain of thunderous voice, did scatter these
East, South, and North: 'twas then the chief had rest,
Hard by the outer coast of Ithaca,
Unknown to him who ate the spoil and slept.
Nor stayed he hand thereafter; but, when noon
Burned dead on misty hills of stunted fir,
This man shook slumber from his limbs, and sped
Against hoar beaches and the kindled cliffs
Of falling waters; there he waded through,
Beholding past the forest of the West
A break of light, and homes of many men,
And shining corn, and flowers, and fruits of flowers;
Yea, seeing these, the facile-footed chief
Grasped by the knot the huge Aeaen lance,
And fell upon the farmers; wherefore they
Left hoe and plough, and crouched in heights remote
Companioned with the grey-winged fogs; but he
Made waste their fields and throve upon their toil –
As throve the boar, the fierce four-footed curse
Which Artemis did raise in Calydon
To make stern mouths wax white with foreign fear,
All in the wild beginning of the World.

So one went down and told Laertes' son
Of what the brass-clad stranger from the straits
Had worked in Ithaca: whereat the King
Rose, like a god, and called his mighty heir,
Telemachus, the wisest of the wise;
And these two, having counsel, strode without,
And armed them with the arms of warlike days –
The helm, the javelin, and the sun-like shield,
And glancing greaves and quivering stars of steel!
Yea, stern Ulysses, rusted not with rest,
But dread as Ares, gleaming on his car
Gave out the reins; and straightway all the lands
Were struck by noise of steed and shouts of men,
And furious dust, and splendid wheels of flame,
Meanwhile the hunter (starting from a sleep
In which the pieces of a broken dream
Had shown him Circe with most tearful face),
Caught at his spear, and stood, like one at bay
When Summer brings about Arcadian horns
And headlong horses mixt with maddened hounds;

The huge Ulysses, like a fire of fight,
Sprang sideways on the flying car, and drave
Full at the brass-clad warrior of the North
His massive spear; but fleet Telegonus
Stooped from the death, but heard the speedy lance
Sing like a thin wind through the steaming air,
Yet he, dismayed not by the dreadful foe –
Unknown to him – dealt out his strength, and aimed
A strenuous stroke at great Laertes' son,
Which missed the shield, but bit through flesh and bone,
And drank the blood, and dragged the soul from thence!
So fell the King! and one cried, 'Ithaca!
Ah, Ithaca!' and turned his face and wept.

Then came another – wise Telemachus –
Who knelt beside the man of many days
And pored upon the face; but lo, the life
Was like bright water spilt in sands of thirst,
A wasted splendour swiftly drawn away.
Yet held he by the dead: he heeded not
The moaning warrior who had learnt his sin –
Who waited, now, like one in lairs of pain,
Apart with darkness hungry for his fate;
For, had not wise Telemachus the lore
Which makes the pale-mouthed seer content to sleep
Amidst the desolations of the world?
So therefore he who knew Telegonus,
The child of Circe by Laertes' son,
Was set to be a scourge of Zeus, smote not
But rather sat with moody eyes, and mused,
And watched the dead. For who may brave the gods?

Yet, O my fathers, when the people came,
And brought the holy oils and perfect fire,
And built the pile, and sang the tales of Troy –
Of desperate travels in the olden time,
By shadowy mountains and the roaring sea,
Near windy sands and past the Thracian snows –
The man who crossed them all to see his sire,
And had a loyal heart to give the King,
Instead of blows – this man did little more
Than moan outside the fume of funeral rites,
All in a rushing twilight full of rain,
And clap his palms for sharper pains than swords.

Yea, when the night broke out against the flame,
And lonely noises loitered in the fens,
This man nor stirred nor slept, but lay at wait,
With fastened mouth. For who may brave the gods?

MARCUS CLARKE
from *Civilization without Delusion*

Much has been said concerning the 'world-smart', the weariness of life, the melancholy of modern thinkers. The melancholy of the age arises from this growing conviction, that the Religion of old time is insufficient for present needs, that the tender time of trustfulness in the supernatural is well-nigh over, and that the faith of our fathers is passing away from us . . .

The predicted change has begun, and on all sides are warning notes – 'ancestral voices prophesying war' – of coming ruin. The seasons run their course; the gentle spring of Christianity, its fierce summer, its liberal autumn, are ended, and louder in the ears of the pious believer in the stability of the rock-founded creed of Christendom, sounds the prophetic dirge of doom. The struggle of the reason and the emotions will tear in pieces the 'well-built nest' of Faith:

> Its passions will rock thee,
> As the storms rock the ravens on high,
> Bright reason shall mock thee
> Like the sun in a wintry sky.
> From thy nest every rafter
> Shall rot, and thine eagle home
> Leave thee naked to laughter
> When leaves fall and cold winds come.

The leaves are fast falling, and the cold winds are blowing. Where shall the human heart next build its sanctuary?

ALBERT DORRINGTON
Quilp

I have sold tea on a large and small scale around Geelong and Mount Brown. I have originated a peculiar brand of dyspepsia from Murray Bridge to the Towers. My blends are unequalled. And I know my business. An ordinary man may sell tea, if he has a decent moustache, a pair of legs, and can talk lies over the fence. It happens, however, that in appearance I am but once removed from the ape.

Years ago a man discovered me on the Circular Quay. He gave me some advice and half-a-sovereign, because I was uglier than anything he had ever seen. 'Go into the country,' he said, 'and sell something. Tell fortunes, you ugly little beggar!' This man put bread in my way when he taught me the trick of fortune-telling.

I detest your cities – your Melbourne, Sydney, Adelaide, Brisbane – bah! What a race of weaklings you are – and what mongrel species! The cinematograph-man in quest of local colour couldn't do better than visit Coogee some Sunday afternoon; he'll find colour, and in plenteous shades; ebony and cinnamon – especially cinnamon; and your tawny, silk-coated Jap. stalking hither, stalking thither, jingling cash. Last Sunday I was at Coogee, the gilded horror rolled up precisely at three – a shapely girl of eighteen, lissom of body, alert, and cursed with a fair face and skin. At the first glance she appeared alone, but from the tail of her eye she was watching the crawlsome Thing in her wake – an undersized Chow, very undersized, almost lacking arm-power to carry his own nasty infant. Angelina evinced no shame at the obvious relationship; she had kept ahead because the blood of meat ran in her veins, and she could not help out-distancing this slant-eyed product of a cabbage – her husband.

Suddenly she swung round, arms akimbo and threatening: 'Don't dashed well fall down with that precious kid! Hurry, you thing – hurry!' Parts of him looked young, but the salient skull was older than Yorick's. He spurted obediently, and nearly fainted; he wasn't a healthy Chow.

Some climax came along the beach – half-a-dozen Ah Goons out for the Seventh. Angelina snickered over her ribboned shoulder, naming them fluently in a guggling half-Chow lingo;

how they squirmed and wriggled, these old flames of hers! (A soft curse from a ginger-whiskered man in the shade.) Up strolled some girl-friends of Angelina's. They were unfeignedly glad to see her, and greeted Ah Cow with cheerful blasphemy; and Cow, wrung to his parental depths, introduced baby – a beady-eyed little squeaker. 'He was christened this morning at the Army,' said Angelina, with simple pride; 'we are calling him Reggy.'

Cow blinked feebly in the sun – Cow, the father of Reginald. (God ha' mercy, gentlemen!) 'Pitty ickle sing!' Kisses one, two, three – twice round; kisses on his Mongol lips, kisses on his little flipper. Various narrow-girthed ladies hovered round, attracted, interested to the sympathy-point.

Mesdames, get ye to a Chinkery!

Bah to your cities – bah! and bah again! The human can overcome the brutal in the Bush – can, does, will; because there is in the Bush sweating work to drive forth the animal – not now, not all at once, but sooner or later; and there is Nature's salt to keep the maggots from the carcase. What matter if she be fierce and cruel! she is sweet. But I'll tell you what I saw in Melbourne once – what I saw and watched in a suburban slum street.

There was a woman seated in a doorway – a study in feline immobility; yet her half-closed eyes saw each living thing that moved in the street. And there was an urchin toiling in the rain-flushed gutter before her, the object of her ferocious interest. She knew that the piling of rotting garbage in the floodway meant the swamping of her house; and he was labouring with impish stealth to reach that end.

A denizen of the street stopped with a mortar-board over his shoulder. 'Them two are at it again,' he confided to me. 'She hates the little bloke like poison: dunno why; he uster play with her dead kid, and they've been fightin' ever since the funeral. See!'

The boy had found that his dam was producing some effect – the water swirled over the pavement and touched the woman's feet. She did not move. Then the boy doubled forward and laughed – laughed in jerks with his hands gripping his knees.

The slow venom in his laugh brought the woman to a sitting posture. Her mouth twitched as though something had cut it. She began to sing, and the boy ceased capering in the filth. The words of her song caricatured his ill-shaped head, his squinting eyes, his dubious parentage. She was Irish, and had doubtless discovered long before that it is easier to wound in rhyme than in prose. Her feet beat time in the slush. She clasped her hands fervently and jeered.

The boy stood white and palpitating in his childish fury. Then suddenly he moved away, affecting a grotesque limp that only permitted him to pass her with painful slowness. She stopped singing; something in his pretended limp struck her into a fit of blind coughing that left her grovelling in the doorway.

'By cripes, look at her!' said the man. 'The kid beats her. Y'see, her Jimmy wot pegged out uster limp like that; an' this kid's imitatin' it – makes her think a bit, y'see. By cripes, look at her!'

And the boy went limping up the street.

In the Bush I have seen many things to shudder at; but nothing with the hell-sought malice of those mockers. On the contrary . . . *

Once, on a dusty track of western New South Wales, a bark humpy appeared near the mirage-haunted horizon. I hurried forward. A woman was crouching on a sand heap in front. And her face! O, Tussaud! it was supreme in its ugliness – the teeth and mane of a lion, and with a skin so scrofulous that it suggested leprosy. I was Apollo by the side of her. She was whining a baby-song, and every time her dry lips opened I could hear the clash of teeth. At the sound of my footsteps she picked herself up and hopped across the track, her red eyes squinting east and west.

'Do you want a drink, sir?'

She collared my bridle and stood like the embodiment of Dirt beside my clean horse.

'No, Madam Nightmare, I do *not* want a drink. Go away. Cover your head.'

She followed me some distance, screaming invitations to return and look at her baby. Curiosity gripped me at last, and I followed her back to her kennel. The place was miraculously clean inside.

In the centre of the hovel was a wicker cradle; she lifted the snowy covering and exposed the sweetest baby I have ever seen – a clutching, crowing bit of white humanity. I stooped for a moment and permitted its rosy fingers to grip mine, while thoughts of wicked enchanters held me for six heart-beats. Out into the road again, hat in hand, and face turned from the woman.

'Good-bye, mother. God be with you!' Felt that I had to say it.

'He is, mister – He is.' She flung out a claw towards the cherub in the cradle.

I shall never forget how, at the end of one hot January day, I dragged myself along the sun-split road that follows the Darling

* These dots appear in the original. They do not signify an ellipsis (ed.).

into Wilcannia. A woman's voice crooned from a tidy little cottage; there was a smell of new bread and pastry. I hurried past. Suddenly her voice filled the air, and the household swarmed to the gate. 'Here's Quilp! quick, come and see Quilp!' I turned in the middle of the road and put on a Cheshire smile. God! how those kids howled when I limped off like Richard the Third!

There's a piece of country on the Darling that I bar at present. I'm living down something I said there a year ago.

It was getting late when I crawled into Puncher's Crossing, with the horse going on three legs. Several cockies passed me on the way, but they had always pulled up for a chat and a kindly word. Into their ears went my secret, the secret that fled to every homestead within ten miles before sundown. 'Monsieur Pompadour, the magician, is coming – the magician who pierces heart's depths by glancing at your little fat hand. Spread the happy tidings!'

Fin Maloney owned the pub, store, and newspaper at Puncher's; and after being sniffed at by a regiment of wall-eyed cattle-pups and mongrels, into Fin's pub. I hobbled.

Maloney's pub is misnamed 'The Swag and Pannikin'; it should have been called 'The Coffin and Grave.' Maloney looked in to my room and asked me if I would take a stiff nobbler of his lightning whisky. I was lying on the bed, and I snored gently. Maloney went away.

It was eight o'clock when I ventured from my room. There were noises in the parlour; heavy breathings and suppressed mirth, as if the whole female community of Puncher's Crossing had collected in the little oven of a room. I threw myself into a chair on the verandah, and waited for the ladies to stir. It was three minutes before I discovered that a mop of yellow hair was peering at me from the half-closed door. I maintained a commendable silence. Eve spoke.

'Say, mister, would yer like ter come inside?'

I glanced at her tenderly, and made a sweeping gesture of assent. I usually planted a few hundredweight of tea after each performance; and buiness is business. I followed the elderly baby with the hair.

There were fifteen girls inside, and one big man. He offered me some tobacco, which was taken as men take salt in the East. Then he spoke to Maloney's portrait by a Chinese artist, hanging just over my head:

'My gel here heard as you were pretty good at readin' fortunes. She's worried at me till I had to bring her over. These are my gel's friends, mister.'

I bowed. Lord! how pretty are some of my countrywomen: peeping brown faces, all too quickly sullied by the wicked shadows of men!

Fortune-telling out-back requires brains. Each one must have something different, and there are some awful combinations in fifteen. In the majority of cases, you may kill husband the first with perfect safety, providing that the void created is filled. They are touchy anent the old dying relative, and the old, old pile.

I married the first one right away to six-feet of gum. 'Would I describe him?' Certainly. He never wore a waistcoat, summer, or winter; he could sit any horse south of the line. Didn't go in for shearing now, but when he did he was a 'ringer.' On Saturday nights it was his custom to fight about three men. Tight pants – and big feet.

There was a great clapping of hands, a lot of pushing and laughter. Everyone recognised him immediately; the name, 'Jim Saunders,' was whispered through the room. The girl fled to the verandah to hide her flaring, happy face. All the others made similar journeys when the dark, tall gentleman turned up. (It is always a safe card to keep out short men: they don't live up there. Every man is longer than Adam.)

Now there remained one who had sat quiet throughout, although she was frequently whispered to. She was partially hidden by a screen of heavy cloth, but I knew hers was the sweetest face in the room.

In the midst of the babble I caught her hand gently – small, white, baby fingers that did not shrink from mine as others had. Her face became filled with an intense eagerness. I muttered, racking my brains for sweet dreams. Into her future I wove those bright phantasms that crowd the minds of children. I built her a tiny castle near the sea. Gulls drowsed over the palm-lined beach, and flew out to cry above the white ships that swam to all the islands of the world.

A strange silence crept over all. For one brief minute I knelt at her feet. It was not for Quilp to touch that wondrous hand with his hideous, twisted lips: enough if the gabbling tongue had put one iota of pleasure into her fancy.

And yet I had made a mistake: it was in every face. I stood up, still holding her hand. She was crying softly, her head down in the cushions. I limped to the door, a fraud, a failure.

What I said to that blind child let me not recall.

CATHERINE MARTIN
Wrecked!

Was it a dream? I cannot tell –
   I seem to see it all again;
It holds me as with magic spell,
   I try to shut it out in vain:
     Again, again I seem to hear
     That cry of horror and of fear.

I saw a man stand all alone
   Upon a rock within the sea, –
He uttered neither cry nor moan,
   He watched the seething breakers flee,
     With furious might and savage roar
     Around the rocks, gaunt, bare, and hoar.

The shrieking sea-fowls sought their rest,
   Circling above the barren heights,
While the great sun sank in the west
   Amid fierce crimson throbbing lights,
     Which faded from the sky away
     Until all heaven was cold and grey.

And all around those barren cliffs
   The waves rose up to meet the sky;
Upon a line of hungry reefs
   Some broken masts lay beach'd and dry;
     And ever with a thundering swell
     The heaving ocean rose and fell.

And still with gaze fast fixed afar
   Unmoved stood that silent form,
Until the solemn evening star
   Rose high above each earthly storm:
     Save for the wail of bird and wave
     The spot was silent as the grave.

Over the waste the moonbeams fair
   Fell like a peaceful dream,
The man alone in still despair
   Stood in their placid gleam.
     'Wrecked for all Time!' The awful cry
     Ascended to the star-lit sky.

What gleams in the mysterious light
   Of moon and stars upon the ocean?
What flutters nearer strangely white
   With an uncertain rapid motion?
     Thank God! at last, a sail, a sail
     Flying before the driving gale!

The silvery light was overcast
   With a stray fleecy cloud,
That round the moon as on its past,
   Wound closely like a spotless shroud;
     And nearer still that snowy sail
     Flew on before the driving gale.

'Help ho!' the man cried loud and long,
   No answer came to his wild call,
But far-off sounds as of a song
   Upon the boundless waters fall:
     Sounds as of strange unearthly pain
     That rose and fell, and rose again.

Once more the man cried loud and long,
   The startled sea-fowls made reply; –
The moon crept from its silvery shroud,
   The foam-wreathed breakers rose on high;
     And then the sail unto the rock
     Stole without grating sound or shock.

The sail was long and broad and white,
   And underneath its shadow there –
O God! it was an awful sight –
   A woman lay, surpassing fair,
     In anguish, like a spirit lost,
     With golden hair around her tost.

The man looked on that ashen face,
　His gaze met those strange sleepless eyes, -
A wail for Christ's high pardoning grace
　　Rose to the calm unpitying skies;
　　　The sobbing of the waves around,
　　　Prolonged the deep despairing sound.

The sail was long and broad and white,
　And underneath its shadow there -
O God! it was an awful sight -
　　A man lay writhing in despair.
　　　The words rose high above the sea,
　　　'Wrecked! wrecked! through all eternity!'

BARBARA BAYNTON
A Dreamer

A swirl of wet leaves from the night-hidden trees decorating the little station, beat against the closed doors of the carriages. The porter hurried along holding his blear-eyed lantern to the different windows, and calling the name of the township in language peculiar to porters. There was only one ticket to collect.

Passengers from far up-country towns have importance from their rarity. He turned his lantern full on this one, as he took her ticket. She looked at him too, and listened to the sound of his voice, as he spoke to the guard. Once she had known every hand at the station. The porter knew everyone in the district. This traveller was a stranger to him.

If her letter had been received, someone would have been waiting with a buggy. She passed through the station. She saw nothing but an ownerless dog, huddled, wet and shivering, in a corner. More for sound she turned to look up the straggling street of the township. Among the she-oaks, bordering the river she knew so well, the wind made ghostly music, unheeded by the sleeping town. There was no other sound, and she turned to the dog with a feeling of kinship. But perhaps the porter had a message! She went back to the platform. He was locking the office door, but paused as though expecting her to speak.

'Wet night!' he said at length, breaking the silence.

Her question resolved itself into a request for the time, though this she already knew. She hastily left him.

She drew her cloak tightly round her. The wind made her umbrella useless for shelter. Wind and rain and darkness lay before her on the walk of three bush miles to her mother's home. Still it was the home of her girlhood, and she knew every inch of the way.

As she passed along the sleeping street, she saw no sign of life till near the end. A light burned in a small shop, and the sound of swift tapping came to her. They work late to-night, she thought, and, remembering their gruesome task, hesitated, half-minded to ask these night workers, for whom they laboured. Was it someone she had known? The long dark walk – she could not – and hastened to lose the sound.

342

The zigzag course of the railway brought the train again near to her, and this wayfarer stood and watched it tunnelling in the teeth of the wind. Whoof! whoof! its steaming breath hissed at her. She saw the rain spitting viciously at its red mouth. Its speed, as it passed, made her realise the tedious difficulties of her journey, and she quickened her pace. There was the silent tenseness, that precedes a storm. From the branch of a tree overhead she heard a watchful mother-bird's warning call, and the twitter of the disturbed nestlings. The tender care of this bird-mother awoke memories of her childhood. What mattered the lonely darkness, when it led to mother. Her forebodings fled, and she faced the old track unheedingly, and ever and ever she smiled, as she foretasted their meeting.

'Daughter!'

'Mother!'

She could feel loving arms around her, and a mother's sacred kisses. She thrilled, and in her impatience ran, but the wind was angry and took her breath. Then the child near her heart stirred for the first time. The instincts of motherhood awakened in her. Her elated body quivered, she fell on her knees, lifted her hands, and turned her face to God. A vivid flash of lightning flamed above her head. It dulled her rapture. The lightning was very near.

She went on, then paused. Was she on the right track? Back, near the bird's nest, were two roads. One led to home, the other was the old bullock-dray road, that the railway had almost usurped. When she should have been careful in her choice, she had been absorbed. It was a long way back to the cross roads, and she dug in her mind for landmarks. Foremost she recalled the 'Bendy Tree,' then the 'Sisters,' whose entwined arms talked, when the wind was from the south. The apple trees on the creek – split flat, where the crows and calves were always to be found. The wrong track, being nearer the river, had clumps of she-oaks and groups of pines in places. An angled line of lightning illuminated everything, but the violence of the thunder distracted her.

She stood in uncertainty, near-sighted, with all the horror of the unknown that this infirmity could bring. Irresolute, she waited for another flash. It served to convince her she was wrong. Through the bush she turned.

The sky seemed to crack with the lightning; the thunder's suddenness shook her. Among some tall pines she stood awed, while the storm raged.

Then again that indefinite fear struck at her. Restlessly she pushed on till she stumbled, and, with hands out-stretched, met some object that moved beneath them as she fell. The lightning showed a group of terrified cattle. Tripping and falling, she ran, she knew not where, but keeping her eyes turned towards the cattle. Aimlessly she pushed on, and unconsciously retraced her steps.

She struck the track she was on when her first doubt came. If this were the right way, the wheel ruts would show. She groped, but the rain had levelled them. There was nothing to guide her. Suddenly she remembered that the little clump of pines, where the cattle were, lay between the two roads. She had gathered mistletoe berries there in the old days.

She believed, she hoped, she prayed, that she was right. If so, a little further on, she would come to the 'Bendy Tree.' There long ago a runaway horse had crushed its drunken rider against the bent, distorted trunk. She could recall how in her young years that tree had ever after had a weird fascination for her.

She saw its crooked body in the lightning's glare. She was on the right track, yet dreaded to go on. Her childhood's fear came back. In a transient flash she thought she saw a horseman galloping furiously towards her. She placed both her hands protectingly over her heart, and waited. In the dark interval, above the shriek of the wind, she thought she heard a cry, then crash came the thunder, drowning her call of warning. In the next flash she saw nothing but the tree. 'Oh, God, protect me!' she prayed, and diverging, with a shrinking heart passed on.

The road dipped to the creek. Louder and louder came the roar of its flooded waters. Even little Dog-trap Gully was proudly foaming itself hoarse. It emptied below where she must cross. But there were others, that swelled it above.

The noise of the rushing creek was borne to her by the wind, still fierce, though the rain had lessened. Perhaps there would be someone to meet her at the bank! Last time she had come, the night had been fine, and though she had been met at the station by a neighbour's son, mother had come to the creek with a lantern and waited for her. She looked eagerly, but there was no light.

The creek was a banker, but the track led to a plank, which, lashed to the willows on either bank, was usually above flood-level. A churning sound showed that the water was over the plank, and she must wade along it. She turned to the sullen sky. There was no gleam of light save in her resolute, white face.

Her mouth grew tender, as she thought of the husband she loved, and of their child. Must she dare! She thought of the grey-haired mother, who was waiting on the other side. This dwarfed every tie that had parted them. There was atonement in these difficulties and dangers.

Again her face turned heavenward! 'Bless, pardon, protect and guide, strengthen and comfort!' Her mother's prayer.

Steadying herself by the long willow branches, ankle-deep she began. With every step the water deepened.

Malignantly the wind fought her, driving her back, or snapping the brittle stems from her skinned hands. The water was knee-deep now, and every step more hazardous.

She held with her teeth to a thin limb, while she unfastened her hat and gave it to the greedy wind. From the cloak, a greater danger, she could not in her haste free herself; her numbed fingers had lost their cunning.

Soon the water would be deeper, and the support from the branches less secure. Even if they did reach across, she could not hope for much support from their wind-driven, fragile ends.

Still she would not go back. Though the roar of that rushing water was making her giddy, though the deafening wind fought her for every inch, she would not turn back.

Long ago she should have come to her old mother, and her heart gave a bound of savage rapture in thus giving the sweat of her body for the sin of her soul.

Midway the current strengthened. Perhaps if she, deprived of the willows, were swept down, her clothes would keep her afloat. She took firm hold and drew a deep breath to call her child-cry, 'Mother!'

The water was deeper and swifter, and from the sparsity of the branches she knew she was nearing the middle. The wind unopposed by the willows was more powerful. Strain as she would, she could reach only the tips of the opposite trees, not hold them.

Despair shook her. With one hand she gripped those that had served her so far, and cautiously drew as many as she could grasp with the other. The wind savagely snapped them, and they lashed her unprotected face. Round and round her bare neck they coiled their stripped fingers. Her mother had planted these willows, and she herself had watched them grow. How could they be so hostile to her!

The creek deepened with every moment she waited. But more dreadful than the giddying water was the distracting noise of the mighty wind, nurtured by the hollows.

The frail twigs of the opposite tree snapped again and again in her hands. She must release her hold of those behind her. If she could make two steps independently, the thicker branches would then be her stay.

'Will you?' yelled the wind. A sudden gust caught her, and, hurling her backwards, swept her down the stream with her cloak for a sail.

She battled instinctively, and her first thought was of the letter-kiss she had left for the husband she loved. Was it to be his last?

She clutched a floating branch, and was swept down with it. Vainly she fought for either bank. She opened her lips to call. The wind made a funnel of her mouth and throat, and a wave of muddy water choked her cry. She struggled desperately, but after a few mouthfuls she ceased. The weird cry from the 'Bendy Tree' pierced and conquered the deep-throated wind. Then a sweet dream voice whispered 'Little Woman!'

Soft, strong arms carried her on. Weakness aroused the melting idea that all had been a mistake, and she had been fighting with friends. The wind even crooned a lullaby. Above the angry waters her face rose untroubled.

A giant tree's fallen body said, 'Thus far!' and in vain the athletic furious water rushed and strove to throw her over the barrier. Driven back, it tried to take her with it. But a jagged arm of the tree snagged her cloak and held her.

Bruised and half conscious she was left to her deliverer, and the back-broken water crept tamed under its old foe. The hammer of hope awoke her heart. Along the friendly back of the tree she crawled, and among its bared roots rested. But it was only to get her breath, for this was mother's side.

She breasted the rise. Then every horror was of the past and forgotten, for there in the hollow was home.

And there was the light shining its welcome to her.

She quickened her pace, but did not run – motherhood is instinct in woman. The rain had come again, and the wind buffeted her. To breathe was a battle, yet she went on swiftly, for at the sight of the light her nameless fear had left her.

She would tell mother how she had heard her call in the night, and mother would smile her grave smile and stroke her wet hair, call her 'Little woman! My little woman!' and tell her she had been dreaming, just dreaming. Ah, but mother herself was a dreamer!

The gate was swollen with rain and difficult to open. It has been opened by mother last time. But plainly her letter had not reached home. Perhaps the bad weather had delayed the mail boy.

There was the light. She was not daunted when the bark of the old dog brought no one to the door. It might not be heard inside, for there was such a torrent of water falling somewhere close. Mechanically her mind located it. The tank near the house, fed by the spout, was running over, cutting channels through the flower beds, and flooding the paths. Why had not mother diverted the spout to the other tank!

Something indefinite held her. Her mind went back to the many times long ago when she had kept alive the light while mother fixed the spout to save the water that the dry summer months made precious. It was not like mother, for such carelessness meant carrying from the creek.

Suddenly she grew cold and her heart trembled. After she had seen mother, she would come out and fix it, but just now she could not wait.

She tapped gently, and called, 'Mother!'

While she waited she tried to make friends with the dog. Her heart smote her, in that there had been so long an interval since she saw her old home, that the dog had forgotten her voice.

Her teeth chattered as she again tapped softly. The sudden light dazzled her when a stranger opened the door for her. Steadying herself by the wall, with wild eyes she looked around. Another strange woman stood by the fire, and a child slept on the couch. The child's mother raised it, and the other led the now panting creature to the child's bed. Not a word was spoken, and the movements of these women were like those who fear to awaken a sleeper.

Something warm was held to her lips, for through it all she was conscious of everything, even that the numbing horror in her eyes met answering awe in theirs.

In the light the dog knew her and gave her welcome. But she had none for him now.

When she rose one of the women lighted a candle. She noticed how, if the blazing wood cracked, the women started nervously, how the disturbed child pointed to her bruised face, and whispered softly to its mother, how she who lighted the candle did not strike the match but held it to the fire, and how the light bearer led the way so noiselessly.

She reached her mother's room. Aloft the woman held the candle and turned away her head.

The daughter parted the curtains, and the light fell on the face of the sleeper who would dream no dreams that night.

BARBARA BAYNTON
The Chosen Vessel

She laid the stick and her baby on the grass while she untied the
rope that tethered the calf. The length of the rope separated them.
The cow was near the calf, and both were lying down. Feed along
the creek was plentiful, and every day she found a fresh place
to tether it, since tether it she must, for if she did not, it would
stray with the cow out on the plain. She had plenty of time to
go after it, but then there was baby; and if the cow turned on
her out on the plain, and she with baby, – she had been a town
girl and was afraid of the cow, but she did not want the cow to
know it. She used to run at first when it bellowed its protest
against the penning up of its calf. This satisfied the cow, also the
calf, but the woman's husband was angry, and called her – the
noun was cur. It was he who forced her to run and meet the advancing cow, brandishing a stick, and uttering threatening words
till the enemy turned and ran. 'That's the way!' the man said, laughing at her white face. In many things she was worse than the cow,
and she wondered if the same rule would apply to the man, but
she was not one to provoke skirmishes even with the cow.

It was early for the calf to go 'to bed' – nearly an hour earlier
than usual; but she had felt so restless all day. Partly because it
was Monday, and the end of the week that would bring her and
baby the companionship of its father, was so far off. He was a
shearer, and had gone to his shed before daylight that morning.
Fifteen miles as the crow flies separated them.

There was a track in front of the house, for it had once been
a wine shanty, and a few travellers passed along at intervals. She
was not afraid of horsemen; but swagmen, going to, or worse,
coming from the dismal, drunken little township, a day's journey
beyond, terrified her. One had called at the house to-day, and
asked for tucker.

Ah! that was why she had penned up the calf so early! She
feared more from the look of his eyes, and the gleam of his teeth,
as he watched her newly awakened baby beat its impatient fists
upon her covered breasts, than from the knife that was sheathed
in the belt at his waist.

She had given him bread and meat. Her husband she told him
was sick. She always said that when she was alone, and a

swagman came, and she had gone in from the kitchen to the bedroom, and asked questions and replied to them in the best man's voice she could assume. Then he had asked to go into the kitchen to boil his billy, but she gave him tea, and he drank it on the wood heap. He had walked round and round the house, and there were cracks in some places, and after the last time he had asked for tobacco. She had none to give him, and he had grinned, because there was a broken clay pipe near the wood heap where he stood, and if there were a man inside, there ought to have been tobacco. Then he asked for money, but women in the bush never have money.

At last he had gone, and she, watching through the cracks, saw him when about a quarter of a mile away, turn and look back at the house. He had stood so for some moments with a pretence of fixing his swag, and then, apparently satisfied, moved to the left towards the creek. The creek made a bow round the house, and when he came to it she lost sight of him. Hours after, watching intently for signs of smoke, she saw the man's dog chasing some sheep that had gone to the creek for water, and saw it slink back suddenly, as if the man had called it.

More than once she thought of taking her baby and going to her husband. But in the past, when she had dared to speak of the dangers to which her loneliness exposed her, he had taunted and sneered at her. She need not flatter herself, he had coarsely told her, that any body would want to run away with her.

Long before nightfall she had placed food on the kitchen table, and beside it laid the big brooch that had been her mother's. It was the only thing of value that she had. And she left the kitchen door wide open.

The doors inside she securely fastened. Beside the bolt in the back one she drove in the steel and scissors; against it she piled the table and the stools. Underneath the lock of the front door she forced the handle of the spade, and the blade between the cracks in the flooring boards. Then the prop-stick, cut into lengths, held the top, as the spade held the middle. The windows were little more than portholes; she had nothing to fear through them.

She ate a few mouthfuls of food and drank a cup of milk. But she lighted no fire, and when night came, no candle, but crept with her baby to bed.

What woke her? The wonder was that she had slept – she had not meant to. But she was young, very young. Perhaps the shrinking of the galvanized roof – yet hardly, since that was so usual. Something had set her heart beating wildly; but she lay quite still, only she put her arm over her baby. Then she had both round it, and she prayed, 'Little baby, little baby, don't wake!'

The moon's rays shone on the front of the house, and she saw one of the open cracks, quite close to where she lay, darken with a shadow. Then a protesting growl reached her; and she could fancy she heard the man turn hastily. She plainly heard the thud of something striking the dog's ribs, and the long flying strides of the animal as it howled and ran. Still watching, she saw the shadow darken every crack along the wall. She knew by the sounds that the man was trying every standpoint that might help him to see in; but how much he saw she could not tell. She thought of many things she might do to deceive him into the idea that she was not alone. But the sound of her voice would wake the baby, and she dreaded that as though it were the only danger that threatened her. So she prayed, 'Little baby, don't wake, don't cry!'

Stealthily the man crept about. She knew he had his boots off, because of the vibration that his feet caused as he walked along the veranda to gauge the width of the little window in her room, and the resistance of the front door.

Then he went to the other end, and the uncertainty of what he was doing became unendurable. She had felt safer, far safer, while he was close, and she could watch and listen. She felt she must watch, but the great fear of wakening baby again assailed her. She suddenly recalled that one of the slabs on that side of the house had shrunk in length as well as in width, and had once fallen out. It was held in position only by a wedge of wood underneath. What if he should discover that! The uncertainty increased her terror. She prayed as she gently raised herself with her little one in her arms, held tightly to her breast.

She thought of the knife, and shielded her child's body with her hands and arms. Even its little feet she covered with its white gown, and baby never murmured – it liked to be held so. Noiselessly she crossed to the other side, and stood where she could see and hear, but not be seen. He was trying every slab, and was very near to that with the wedge under it. Then she saw him find it; and heard the sound of the knife as bit by bit he began to cut away the wooden support.

She waited motionless, with her baby pressed tightly to her, though she knew that in another few minutes this man with the cruel eyes, lascivious mouth, and gleaming knife, would enter. One side of the slab tilted; he had only to cut away the remaining little end, when the slab unless he held it, would fall outside.

She heard his jerked breathing as it kept time with the cuts of the knife, and the brush of his clothes as he rubbed the wall in his movements, for she was so still and quiet, that she did not even tremble. She knew when he ceased, and wondered why. She stood well concealed; she knew he could not see her, and that he would not fear if he did, yet she heard him move cautiously away. Perhaps he expected the slab to fall. Still his motive puzzled her, and she moved even closer, and bent her body the better to listen. Ah! what sound was that? 'Listen! Listen!' she bade her heart – her heart that had kept so still, but now bounded with tumultuous throbs that dulled her ears. Nearer and nearer came the sounds, till the welcome thud of a horse's hoof rang out clearly.

'Oh, God! Oh, God! Oh, God!' she cried, for they were very close before she could make sure. She turned to the door, and with the baby in her arms tore frantically at its bolts and bars.

Out she darted at last, and running madly along, saw the horseman beyond her in the distance. She called to him in Christ's name, in her babe's name, still flying like the wind with the speed that deadly peril gives. But the distance grew greater and greater between them, and when she reached the creek her prayers turned to wild shrieks, for there crouched the man she feared, with outstretched arms that caught her as she fell. She knew he was offering terms if she ceased to struggle and cry for help, though louder and louder did she cry for it, but it was only when the man's hand gripped her throat, that the cry of 'Murder' came from her lips. And when she ceased, the startled curlews took up the awful sound, and flew shrieking over the horseman's head.

'By God!' said the boundary rider, 'it's been a dingo right enough! Eight killed up here, and there's more down in the creek – a ewe and a lamb, I'll bet; and the lamb's alive!' And he shut out the sky with his hand, and watched the crows that were circling round and round, nearing the earth one moment, and the next shooting skywards. By that he knew the lamb must be alive; even a dingo will spare a lamb sometimes.

Yes, the lamb was alive, and after the manner of lambs of its kind did not know its mother when the light came. It had sucked the still warm breasts, and laid its little head on her bosom, and slept till the morn. Then, when it looked at the swollen disfigured face, it wept and would have crept away, but for the hand that still clutched its little gown. Sleep was nodding its golden head and swaying its small body, and the crows were close, so close, to the mother's wide-open eyes, when the boundary rider galloped down.

'Jesus Christ!' he said, covering his eyes. He told afterwards how the little child held out its arms to him, and how he was forced to cut its gown that the dead hand held.

It was election time, and as usual the priest had selected a candidate. His choice was so obviously in the interests of the squatter, that Peter Hennessey's reason, for once in his life, had over-ridden superstition, and he had dared promise his vote to another. Yet he was uneasy, and every time he woke in the night (and it was often), he heard the murmur of his mother's voice. It came through the partition, or under the door. If through the partition, he knew she was praying in her bed; but when the sounds came under the door, she was on her knees before the little altar in the corner that enshrined the statue of the Blessed Virgin and Child.

'Mary, Mother of Christ! save my son! Save him!' prayed she in the dairy as she strained and set the evening's milk. 'Sweet Mary! for the love of Christ, save him!' The grief in her old face made the morning meal so bitter, that to avoid her he came late to his dinner. It made him so cowardly, that he could not say good-bye to her, and when night fell on the eve of the election day, he rode off secretly.

He had thirty miles to ride to the township to record his vote. He cantered briskly along the great stretch of plain that had nothing but stunted cotton bush to play shadow to the full moon, which glorified a sky of earliest spring. The bruised incense of the flowering clover rose up to him, and the glory of the night appealed vaguely to his imagination, but he was preoccupied with his present act of revolt.

Vividly he saw his mother's agony when she would find him gone. At that moment, he felt sure, she was praying.

'Mary! Mother of Christ!' He repeated the invocation, half unconsciously. And suddenly, out of the stillness, came Christ's name to him – called loudly in despairing accents.

'For Christ's sake! Christ's sake! Christ's sake!' called the voice. Good Catholic that he had been, he crossed himself before he dared to look back. Gliding across a ghostly patch of pipe-clay, he saw a white-robed figure with a babe clasped to her bosom.

All the superstitious awe of his race and religion swayed his brain. The moonlight on the gleaming clay was a 'heavenly light' to him, and he knew the white figure not for flesh and blood, but for the Virgin and Child of his mother's prayers. Then, good Catholic that once he was, he put spurs to his horse's sides and galloped madly away.

His mother's prayers were answered.

Hennessey was the first to record his vote – for the priest's candidate. Then he sought the priest at home, but found that he was out rallying the voters. Still, under the influence of his blessed vision, Hennessey would not go near the public houses, but wandered about the outskirts of the town for hours, keeping apart from the towns-people, and fasting as penance. He was subdued and mildly ecstatic, feeling as a repentant chastened child, who awaits only the kiss of peace.

And at last, as he stood in the graveyard crossing himself with reverent awe, he heard in the gathering twilight the roar of many voices crying the name of the victor at the election. It was well with the priest.

Again Hennessey sought him. He sat at home, the house-keeper said, and led him into the dimly-lighted study. His seat was immediately opposite a large picture, and as the house-keeper turned up the lamp, once more the face of the Madonna and Child looked down on him, but this time silently, peacefully. The half-parted lips of the Virgin were smiling with compassion-ate tenderness; her eyes seemed to beam with forgiveness of an earthly mother for her erring but beloved child.

He fell on his knees in adoration. Transfixed, the wondering priest stood, for mingled with the adoration, 'My Lord and my God!' was the exaltation, 'And hast Thou chosen me?'

'What is it, Peter?' said the priest.

'Father,' he answered reverently, and with loosened tongue he poured forth the story of his vision.

'Great God!' shouted the priest, 'and you did not stop to save her! Have you not heard?'

Many miles further down the creek a man kept throwing an old cap into a water-hole. The dog would bring it out and lay it on the opposite side to where the man stood, but would not allow the man to catch him, though it was only to wash the blood of the sheep from his mouth and throat, for the sight of blood made the man tremble.

CHRISTOPHER BRENNAN
Under a sky of uncreated mud

Under a sky of uncreated mud
or sunk beneath the accursed streets, my life
is added up of cupboard-musty weeks
and ring'd about with walls of ugliness:
some narrow world of ever-streaming air.

My days of azure have forgotten me.

Nought stirs, in garret-chambers of my brain,
except the squirming brood of miseries
older than memory, while, far out of sight
behind the dun blind of the rain, my dreams
of sun on leaves and waters drip thro' years
nor stir the slumbers of some sullen well,
beneath whose corpse-fed weeds I too shall sink.

The yellow gas is fired from street to street

The yellow gas is fired from street to street
past rows of heartless homes and hearths unlit,
dead churches, and the unending pavement beat
by crowds – say rather, haggard shades that flit

round nightly haunts of their delusive dream,
where'er our paradisal instinct starves: –
till on the utmost post, its sinuous gleam
crawls in the oily water of the wharves;

where Homer's sea loses his keen breath, hemm'd
what place rebellious piles were driven down –
the priestlike waters to this task condemn'd
to wash the roots of the inhuman town! –

where fat and strange-eyed fish that never saw
the outer deep, broad halls of sapphire light,
glut in the city's draught each nameless maw:
– and there, wide-eyed unto the soullness night,

methinks a drown'd maid's face might fitly show
what we have slain, a life that had been free,
clean, large, nor thus tormented – even so
as are the skies, the salt winds and the sea.

Ay, we have saved our days and kept them whole,
to whom no part in our old joy remains,
had felt those bright winds sweeping thro' our soul
and all the keen sea tumbling in our veins,

had thrill'd to harps of sunrise, when the height
whitens, and dawn dissolves in virgin tears,
or caught, across the hush'd ambrosial night,
the choral music of the swinging spheres,

or drunk the silence if nought else – But no!
and from each rotting soul distil in dreams
a poison, o'er the old earth creeping slow,
that kills the flowers and curdles the live streams,

that taints the fresh breath of re-risen day
and reeks across the pale bewilder'd moon:
– shall we be cleans'd and how? I only pray,
red flame or deluge, may that end be soon!

BIOGRAPHICAL NOTES

Astley, William ('Price Warung', 1855–1911)
Born in Liverpool, England, he spent his early life in Richmond, Melbourne. His pseudonym drew on his mother's maiden name and the Aboriginal designation for Sydney. He allegedly spent two decades investigating exhaustively the convict system (official and private documents, verbal histories, etc.) which he turned to good account in the 1890s, when he was the *Bulletin's* most prolific contributor. The reprinted story appeared as No. XX in the series 'Tales from "The System"'. Gradual physical decline, linked with drug addiction and a spinal complaint, hampered his career, and he died destitute in Sydney.

Baynton, Barbara (1857–1929)
Born in Scone, rural New South Wales. While governessing she met her first husband, a selector. Deserted and left with three young children, she entered into a second marriage ten years later in 1890 with Dr Thomas Baynton in Sydney. There she flourished and began to contribute to the *Bulletin*. Unable to find a local publishers for *Bush Studies* (1902) she went to England, where she eventually cemented her social standing by marrying her third husband, Lord Headley, in 1921. Her final years were spent between England and Australia.

Brennan, Christopher John (1870–1932)
Born in Sydney, and influenced by his Irish Catholic background and education, he began a promising academic career with a travelling scholarship to Berlin and significant work on the classics. His major poetry appeared in the collection *Poems* (1913), which bears the imprint of Mallarmé and the French Symbolists. Later he became a notorious university and café figure in Sydney. He was dismissed from the University of Sydney in 1925, and his final years were marked by a struggle with alcoholism and poverty.

Cambridge, Ada (1844–1926)

Born in Norfolk, England, she moved to country Victoria with her clergyman-husband in 1870. There they experienced a variety of rural postings, before settling eventually in Williamstown, Melbourne, in 1893. Throughout this period she developed rapidly as a writer, publishing numerous well-received novels, of which the best known today is *A Marked Man* (1890). She also continued to write verse, which is often more personal in expression and outspoken on social issues, culminating in the anonymous publication of *Unspoken Thoughts* (1887), less controversial parts of which were reissued in *The Hand in the Dark* (1913).

Clacy, Ellen (1830?–?)

Born in England, she visited Australia during the goldrushes, first treading 'the golden shores of Victoria' on 24 May 1852, and combined homeward voyage and honeymoon to return to England on 27 February of the following year. She published various works, some under the pseudonym 'Cycla', and her two Australian-based books, represented here, testify both to the immediacy of her experiences, and to current metropolitan interest in antipodean material, particularly when accompanied by lively descriptions and an acute perception of local characteristics.

Clarke, Marcus (1846–81)

Disappointed in his hopes of a significant inheritance, he moved from London to Melbourne in 1863, where he became a versatile journalist and prominent member of the Yorick Club. Writing under a variety of pen-names, he established an enviable reputation, commenting on town and country life, and producing poetry, prose and drama; though this was not sufficient to stave off bankruptcy. *Humbug*, which he edited, was one of his magazine failures, and it is possible that he wrote 'The Rights of Women (By a Brute)'. For a decade he was employed at the Public Library of Victoria, and died suddenly (like his father), leaving his wife and six children unprovided for.

Clifton, Louisa (1816?–?)

One of fourteen children, she emigrated with her parents to Western Australia, where they entertained hopes of economic betterment. Her father, a Fellow of the Royal Society, had been appointed chief commissioner of the Western Australia Company, and Louisa's diary charts the conflicting pulls exercised by absent friends and by the interest generated by a novel land. Our entries focus on the family's arrival in Australind, as the new colony was then known.

Couvreur, Jessie ('Tasma', 1848–97)

Born at Highgate, London, she came to Tasmania as a child. Her first marriage took her to rural Victoria, to Malmsbury south of Bendigo, where she launched her writing career, and which provides part of the setting for *Uncle Piper of Piper's Hill* (1889). Long trips were undertaken to Europe, where she established herself as a lecturer and author, and where she met her second husband, Auguste Couvreur, journalist and politician. Her second marriage anchored her in the expansive intellectual climate of Brussels, and saw the publication of her major fiction.

Dorrington, Albert (1874?–1953)

Born in London, he later travelled widely in Australia before making Sydney his home in 1895. There he began a fruitful association with the *Bulletin* and a number of local papers. The title of his story 'Quilp' is apparently based on a malicious dwarf of that name in Charles Dickens's *The Old Curiosity Shop*. Later, feeling that his talent had received insufficient local recognition, he returned to England in 1907, where he continued his writing career, contributing to the Fleet Street press and producing novels which were translated into five languages.

Dyson, Edward (1865–1931)

Born into the family of a mining engineer near Ballarat, he grew up in the country, and directly experienced the life of a miner and a factory worker, before becoming a freelance writer. This diverse experience, together with knowledge of the down-trodden, provided a rich quarry for his subsequent poetry and prose. One of the most professional of local writers, his fluency, humour and industry assured a successful career, which was fully launched when 'A Golden Shanty' was chosen as the title-story for the *Bulletin's* 1889 Christmas collection.

Evans, George Essex (1863–1909)

Born at Regent's Park in London, he came to Queensland in 1881, and later settled at Toowoomba. At various times he worked as farmer, teacher, journalist and public servant. He contributed to various newspapers, such as the *Queenslander*, produced descriptive works while literary director of the Intelligence and Tourist Bureau, and edited occasional literary annuals, including a joint venture with A. B. Paterson in 1897. His patriotic poems had brought him to national prominence by the time of his death.

Field, Barron (1786–1846)

He came from England to Sydney in 1817 to be a Supreme Court judge, and remained there until 1824. His versatile literary interests fall within the general competence of a cultured gentleman of the period, and often reveal a tension between the fascination exercised by the unfamiliar features of colonial experience and the Old World norms which shaped his categoric judgements. He later continued his judiciary career on Gibraltar, which also inspired a slim volume of poetry, *Spanish Sketches*, in 1841, the year of his pensioned retirement from colonial service.

Fortune, Mary ('W.W.' or 'Waif Wander', 1833–1910?)

Born in Belfast, she went with her father first as migrants to Canada, and then to the Victorian goldfields in 1855. Here she married a mounted constable, and later turned this experience to good use when she became a prolific contributor to the *Australian Journal*, and supported herself by the pen. She was best known for her crime stories featuring Mark Sinclair, the hero of the long-running series entitled 'The Detective's Album', and it was under this heading that 'Brockman's Folly' first appeared. She is believed to have died lonely and destitute in the decade after Federation.

Franklin, Miles (1879–1954)

Born in country New South Wales, she moved in 1889 to Bangalore near Goulburn, and to the more impoverished circumstances described in *My Brilliant Career* (1901). After this monotonous farm-life, she enjoyed an ever-increasing range of literary, nationalist and feminist acquaintance, centred first on Sydney, and later on the USA and England. Following over two decades abroad, she returned to Australia in 1827 and to her fiction writing, publishing the first of her six 'Brent of Bin Bin' novels in 1928, and worked tirelessly in literary and intellectual circles. She left her estate to establish the annual Miles Franklin Award for Australian writing.

Gordon, Adam Lindsay (1833–70)

Born in the Azores and educated in England, he came to South Australia in 1853, and subsequently earnt his living with the mounted police, farming, livery stables and horse-racing. With the failure of his hopes for a family inheritance in Scotland, he took his own life. Best known in his day as a bold horseman, posthumously such works as 'The Sick Stockrider' found increasing favour, and finally gained him a place in Poets' Corner of Westminster Abbey, London, as a representative of antipodean verse.

Harpur, Charles (1813–68)

Born of convict parents at Windsor, near Sydney, he struggled to make a living from the land and was for a time an assistant gold commissioner. One of the earliest 'currency lad' poets, he saw the celebration of his native country and the inculcation there of spiritual and republican principles as his special mission. Harpur died a disgruntled writer, but parts of his literary inheritance were passed on to future generations through the works of Henry Kendall.

Kendall, Henry (1839–82)

Born on the south coast of New South Wales, he worked as civil servant, freelance writer, timber merchant, and finally as inspector of forests. The major crisis of his life came in the late 1860s, when financial and personal problems forced him to flee Sydney for Melbourne. Their impact is evident in the works reprinted here, and in the ensuing collapse which led to him being admitted twice to the Gladesville Mental Asylum in the early 1870s at the nadir of his private fortunes.

Lawson, Henry (1867–1922)

Born at Grenfell, New South Wales. After a difficult childhood in the country, his move to Sydney with his mother in 1883 led to involvement in radical circles, and to close association with the *Bulletin*. Popularity, however, did not mean financial security. He travelled to Western Australia, New Zealand and, in 1900 to England, but nowhere could establish himself successfully. With his marriage and finances in tatters, he returned to Sydney in 1902. His best work was now behind him, and his final years were embittered by maintenance disputes, alcoholism and penury.

Lawson, Louisa ('Dora Falconer', 1848–1920)

Born in Mudgee, New South Wales. She left the goldfields there after years of a trying married life, and found greater scope for her energies and intellectual interests in Sydney after 1883. There, in the teeth of bitter male opposition, she founded the country's first feminist newspaper, *The Dawn*, in 1888, and agitated for womanhood suffrage; though even her ebullient nature was seriously darkened after the turn of the century by protracted and unsuccessful attempts to gain compensation from the Postal Department for a patented invention, and by a serious tram accident, from whose effects she never fully recovered.

Leakey, Caroline ('Oliné Keese', 1827–81)

Born in Exeter, England, into a pious, evangelical family, she spent five years in Tasmania with her married sister, much of it marred by ill-health, returning to England in 1853. The impressions gleaned here were turned to good account in *Lyra Australis, or Attempts to Sing in a Strange Land* (1854) and *The Broad Arrow* (1859), while in her convict heroine she offers insights into moral and gender dilemmas which are not always easy to reconcile with the work's ostensible espousal of orthodox standpoints.

MacNamara, Francis ('Frank the Poet', 1811–?)

Born in Belfast, he was transported to New South Wales in 1832 for stealing, and perhaps also for political involvement. Here and elsewhere he gained grim, first-hand experience which, when turned to literary account, earned him his sobriquet. Works attributed to him were often transmitted orally, and so exist in various forms. Our text of 'A Convict's Lament on the Death of Captain Logan' is apparently a later and polished version of earlier variants reprinted in John Meredith and Rex Whalan, *Frank the Poet* (Red Rooster, Melbourne, 1979).

Manning, Emily ('Australie', 1845–90)

Born into privileged circles in Sydney, she was well educated and partook of social activities centred on Government House. She later contributed to a number of local newspapers on belletristic issues as well as on subjects of topical interest, and was also a staff-member of the *Illustrated Sydney News*. Her pseudonym foregrounds a concern with local matter, which is supported by her detailed and frequently anthologised depictions of antipodean scenery.

Martin, Catherine (1847–1937)

Brought out from the Isle of Skye to South Australia in 1855 by her parents, she later turned her hand to teaching and journalism. Widely read and conversant in a number of languages, she was highly regarded as an original writer in her own day. Her subject matter was broad, ranging from her first book, *The Explorers and Other Poems* (1874), through works with local settings like *An Australian Girl* (1890), with its spirited engagement with contemporary issues, to her seminal attempt to recapture the life-experience of Aboriginal women in *The Incredible Journey* (1923).

Mills, Ethel
She contributed to the *Bulletin* at the turn of the century, from whence 'A Box of Dead Roses' was selected for inclusion in *The Bulletin Story Book* (1901).

Paterson, Andrew Barton ('The Banjo', 1864–1941)
Born near Orange, New South Wales, he later lived near Yass, and so near the high country immortalised in 'The Man from Snowy River'. His final schooling and legal training was in Sydney, before embarking on a roving, journalistic career. This involved travel in outback Australia, and he also covered the Boer War and Boxer Rebellion, as well as the beginning of the First World War. His diverse local experience provided material for poems and stories which made him a household name, while his pen-name, taken from a family race-horse, testifies to his strong identification with the land.

Praed, Rosa (1851–1935)
Born on a Queensland station, she later experienced Brisbane social life as the daughter of a state minister, and then primitive, pioneering conditions for two years on Curtis Island, near Gladstone, with her English husband. In 1875 they moved to England, where he entered the family brewing business, and she was immensely productive as a writer for nearly four decades, drawing successfully on her varied experience in the antipodes, and on burning, contemporary issues, as in *The Bond of Wedlock*.

Savery, Henry (1791–1842)
Born in Somerset, England, he was found guilty of forgery in 1825 after failure in business at Bristol. The death penalty was commuted at the eleventh hour to transportation for life. Hobart conditions inspired early sketches, and later the first Australian novel, *Quintus Servinton* (1830). His fortunes see-sawed, but he never worked his way beyond a conditional pardon, which was revoked after a repetition of his original offence. He ended his days at Port Arthur.

Sinnett, Frederick (1830–66)
He emigrated from Hamburg, Germany, to Adelaide in 1849, where he worked as a surveyor and later as an explorer in the region of Lake Torrens, South Australia. Then he shifted to Melbourne and to journalism, where he became a well-known and stimulating figure in literary circles, and helped to found the *Melbourne Punch*. 'The Fiction Fields of Australia' provided a landmark survey of fledgling colonial literature.

Spence, Catherine Helen (1825–1910)
She migrated from Scotland to South Australia with her family in 1839. There she worked first as a governess, but later came to prominence as a writer, public speaker and social reformer. Her ambitious work *Clara Morison* (1854) was singled out by Frederick Sinnett as the best local novel to date, and she produced further novels and utopian fiction. She also campaigned indefatigably for expanded suffrage and women's rights, both locally and abroad, while she interested herself in various related issues, ranging from child welfare through to education and political economy, and did much to expand the boundaries of permissible female engagement.

Stephens, Alfred George (1865–1933)
Born in Toowoomba, Queensland, he worked his way up in the newspaper world from an initial apprenticeship to a Sydney printer, through diverse journalistic and editorial posts with Queensland papers, until he achieved lasting fame with the *Bulletin*. There he was associated particularly with the Red Page or literary section, where he both welcomed local literary productions and introduced colonial readers to works from a wide range of English, European and American writers. He furthered the *Bulletin's* printing ventures, and oversaw the issuing of such local classics as *On Our Selection* (1899) and *Such Is Life* (1903).

Tucker, James (1808?–88?)
Born in Bristol, England, he was transported to Australia in 1827, and works attributed to him suggest that he spent time at penal settlements in New South Wales, Tasmania and Queensland, the horrors of which colour the pages of his major work, a manuscript novel originally entitled 'Ralph Rashleigh, or the Life of an Exile by Giacomo di Rosenberg'. The last certain record concerning Tucker refers to his receipt of a ticket-of-leave for Moreton Bay in 1853.

Vidal, Mary Theresa (1815–69)
Born in Devon, England, she was briefly in Australia from 1840 to 1845, and her writing career began as a natural extension of her sphere of influence as the wife of an Anglican clergyman. Her first work, *Tales for the Bush* (1844), consisted of stories with a strong moral and didactic purpose. It proved sufficiently popular to be reissued in an expanded form, when it concluded with the tale reprinted here; and she went on to draw more widely on her experience of colonial life in New South Wales in her major contribution to local fiction, the novel *Bengala: Or, Some Time Ago* (1860).

Woolls, William (1814–93)
Born in Hampshire, England, he came to Australia in his late teens, where he became a teacher and later an Anglican minister. One of his pupils was 'Rolf Boldrewood' (T. A. Browne), and his own works at times combine the fruits of a classical education with his life-long appreciation of local flora. He also produced diverse essays and scientific works, and achieved wide recognition as a botanist, corresponding with Ferdinand von Mueller and Caroline Atkinson on this common interest, and gaining a doctorate from the University of Tuebingen for his research.

TEXTUAL SOURCES

Apart from changes demanded by house style, or by occasional corrections of obvious typographical errors, texts are reprinted as in the sources listed below.

I THE CHALLENGE OF A NEW LANDSCAPE

Louisa Clifton, *Journal*, typescript copy (MS 2801, National Library of Australia); Barron Field, *Journal of an Excursion across the Blue Mountains of New South Wales*, from *Geographical Memoirs on New South Wales in Various Hands* (John Murray, London, 1829); Barron Field, 'The Kangaroo', from *First Fruits of Australian Poetry* (G. Howe, Sydney, 1819); William Woolls, 'The Beauties of Australia', from *Miscellanies in Prose and Verse* (G. Evans, Sydney, 1838); 'Australie' (Emily Manning), 'The Weatherboard Fall', from *The Balance of Pain and Other Poems* (George Bell & Son, London, 1877); Charles Harpur, 'The Kangaroo Hunt' (ML [Mitchell Library] MS A97); Charles Harpur, 'Dawn and Sunrise in the Snowy Mountains' (ML MS A87); Henry Kendall, 'Bell-Birds', from *Leaves from Australian Forests* (George Robertson, Melbourne, 1869); Charles Harpur, 'The Scenic Part of Poetry' (ML MS C380); Charles Harpur, 'The Creek of the Four Graves' (ML MS A87); Henry Kendall, 'A Death in the Bush', from *Leaves from Australian Forests* (George Robertson, Melbourne, 1869); Marcus Clarke, 'Preface' to Adam Lindsay Gordon, *Sea Spray and Smoke Drift* (Clarson, Massina & Co., Melbourne, 1876); Adam Lindsay Gordon, 'The Sick Stockrider', from *Bush Ballads and Galloping Rhymes* (Clarson, Massina & Co., Melbourne, 1870); Marcus Clarke, 'Pretty Dick', from *Holiday Peak and Other Tales* (George Robertson, Melbourne, 1873); Henry Lawson, 'Some Popular Australian Mistakes', from *Bulletin*, 18 November 1893; Henry Lawson, 'The Drover's Wife', from *The Country I Come From* (Blackwood & Sons, Edinburgh and London, 1901); Edward Dyson, 'The Conquering Bush', from *Below and on Top* (George Robertson, Melbourne, 1898); Henry Lawson, 'Rats', from *While the Billy Boils* (Angus & Robertson, Sydney, 1896).

II THE BURDEN OF THE PAST

Marcus Clarke, 'Port-Arthur', *Argus*, 26 July 1873; Anonymous, 'The Female Transport', from Susan Hampton and Kate Llewellyn (eds), *The Penguin Book of Australian Women Poets* (Penguin, Ringwood, Vic., 1986); 'Frank the Poet' (Francis MacNamara), 'A Convict's Lament on the Death of Captain Logan', from Russel Ward (ed.), *The Penguin Book of Australian Ballads* (Penguin, Ringwood, Vic., 1964); Henry Savery, *Quintus Servinton: A Tale Founded upon Incidents of Real Occurrence* (Henry Melville, Hobart Town, 1830); Mary Theresa Vidal, 'The Convict Laundress; A True Story', from *Tales for the Bush* (Francis & Rivington, London, 1852); Frederick Sinnett, 'The Fiction Fields of Australia', *Journal of Australasia*, vol. 1, July–December 1856; 'Oliné Keese' (Caroline Leakey), *The Broad Arrow: being Passages from the History of Maida Gwynnham, a Lifer* (Richard Bentley & Son, London, 1859) ch. xvi; James Tucker, *Ralph Rashleigh*, ed. by Colin Roderick (Angus & Robertson, Sydney, 1952) ch. xxiv; Marcus Clarke, *For the Term of His Natural Life* (George Robertson, Melbourne, 1885) bk. iii, ch. xxvii; A. G. Stephens, 'Marcus Clarke's Minor Writings', *Bulletin* 29 November 1890; 'Price Warung' (William Astley), 'Lieutenant Darrell's Predicament', *Bulletin*, 29 April 1899; 'Tasma' (Jessie Couvreur), 'An Old-Time Episode in Tasmania', from Harriet Patchett Martin (ed.), *Coo-ee: Tales of Australian Life by Australian Ladies* (Griffith Farran, London, 1891).

III RENEGOTIATING SEXUAL ROLES

Ellen Clacy, 'Leaves from a Young Lady's Diary', from *Lights and Shadows of Australian Life,* vol. II (Hurst & Blackett, London, 1854) vol. ii, chs iv, viii, ix; Ada Cambridge, 'A Sweet Day', from *At Midnight and Other Stories* (Ward, Lock & Co., London, 1897); Albert Dorrington, 'A Bush Tanqueray', from *Castro's Last Sacrament and Other Stories* (Bulletin Newspaper Co., Sydney, 1900); G. E. Evans, 'The Women of the West', from *The Secret Key and Other Verse* (Angus & Robertson, Sydney, 1906); Louisa Lawson, 'Lines Written During a Night Spent in a Bush Inn', from *The Lonely Crossing and Other Poems* (Dawn Office, Sydney, 1905); Charles Harpur, 'Note to "A Wanton" ' (ML MS C376); Barbara Baynton, 'Squeaker's Mate', from *Bush Studies* (Duckworth, London, 1902); Anonymous, 'The Rights of Woman (By a Brute)', *Humbug,* 13 October 1869; 'Dora Falconer' (Louisa Lawson), 'The Strike

Question', *Dawn*, 5 November 1890; 'Dora Falconer' (Louisa Lawson), 'The Divorce Extension Bill', *Dawn*, 5 March 1890; Barbara Baynton, 'Day-birth' and 'To-morrow', *Bulletin*, 9 December 1899; 'Waif Wander' (Mary Fortune), 'The Spider and the Fly', *Australian Journal*, November 1870; Ada Cambridge, 'Influence' and 'Vows', from *Unspoken Thoughts* (Kegan Paul, Trench & Co., 1887); Ada Cambridge, 'Unstrung', from *The Manor House and Other Poems* (Daldy, Isbister & Co., 1875); Ethel Mills, 'A Box of Dead Roses', *The Bulletin Story Book* (Bulletin Newspaper Co., Sydney, 1901); Ada Cambridge, 'Reaction' and 'An Answer', from *Unspoken Thoughts* (Kegan Paul, Trench & Co., London, 1887); Rosa Praed, *The Bond of Wedlock: A Tale of London* (F.V. White & Co., London, 1887); Ada Cambridge, 'The Future Verdict', from *Unspoken Thoughts* (Kegan Paul, Trench & Co., London, 1887).

IV   THE QUEST FOR FULFILMENT

'Australie' (Emily Manning), 'The Emigrant's Plaint', from *The Balance of Pain and Other Poems* (George Bell, London, 1877); Ellen Clacy, *A Lady's Visit to the Gold Diggings of Australia, in 1852–53* (Hurst & Blackett, London, 1853); Catherine Helen Spence, *Clara Morison: A Tale of South Australia during the Gold Fever* (J. W. Parker & Son, London, 1854) vol ii, chs iv, viii, ix; Henry Kendall, 'Men of Letters in New South Wales', *Punch Staff Papers*, 1872; Marcus Clarke, 'Grumbler's Gully', *Holiday Peak and Other Tales* (George Robertson, Melbourne, 1873); A. G. Stephens, 'Introduction' to *The Bulletin Story Book* (Bulletin Newspaper Co., Sydney, 1901); Edward Dyson, 'A Golden Shanty', from *Below and on Top* (George Robertson, Melbourne, 1898); A. B. ('Banjo') Paterson, 'Clancy of the Overflow', from *The Man from Snowy River and Other Verse* (Angus & Robertson, Sydney, 1895); Henry Lawson, 'Middleton's Rouseabout', from *In the Days When the World Was Wide* (Angus & Robertson, Sydney, 1896); 'The Union Buries its Dead', from *The Country I Come From* (Blackwood & Sons, Edinburgh and London, 1901); Henry Lawson, 'The Little World Left Behind', from *Joe Wilson and His Mates* (Blackwood & Sons, Edinburgh and London, 1901); Miles Franklin, *My Brilliant Career* (Blackwood & Sons, Edinburgh and London, 1901) ch. xxxvii; 'Dora Falconer' (Louisa Lawson), 'About Ourselves', *Dawn*, May 1888; 'Waif Wander' (Mary Fortune), 'Towzer and Co.', *Australian Journal*, August 1870; Ada Cambridge, 'The Physical Conscience' and 'Fallen', from *Unspoken Thoughts* (Kegan Paul, Trench & Co., London, 1887); 'Tasma' (Jessie Couvreur), 'Barren

Love', from *A Sydney Sovereign and Other Tales* (Truebner, London, 1890).

V EXISTENTIAL ANXIETIES

'Waif Wander' (Mary Fortune), 'Brockman's Folly', *Australian Journal*, November 1885; Marcus Clarke, 'Human Repetends', from *The Mystery of Major Molineux and Human Repetends* (Cameron, Laing, Melbourne, 1881); Marcus Clarke, *Civilization without Delusion* (F. F. Bailliere, Melbourne, 1880); Henry Kendall, 'The Voyage of Telegonus', from *Leaves from Australian Forests,* (George Robertson, Melbourne, 1869), the accompanying note prefixed it when first published in *Sydney Morning Herald,* 11 June 1866; Albert Dorrington, 'Quilp', from *Castro's Last Sacrament and Other Stories* (Bulletin Newspaper Co., Sydney, 1900); Catherine Martin, 'Wrecked!', from *The Explorers and Other Poems* (George Robertson, Melbourne, 1874); Barbara Baynton, 'A Dreamer' and 'The Chosen Vessel', from *Bush Studies* (Duckworth, London, 1902); Christopher Brennan, 'Under a sky of uncreated mud' and 'The yellow gas is fired from street to street', from *Poems* (G. B. Philip & Son, Sydney, 1913).

The Other Side of the Frontier   Henry Reynolds

Using documentary and oral evidence, much of it previously unpublished, Henry Reynolds sets out the Aboriginal reactions to the coming of the Europeans to Australia. Contrary to conventional beliefs the Aborigines were not passive; they resorted to guerilla warfare, sorcery, theft of white settlers' goods, crops and animals, retribution and revenge sallies, and the adaptation of certain of the newcomers' ways. In presenting this material, Reynolds challenges us to reconsider not only our interpretation of our history, but also the implications for future relations between the peoples of Australia.

Kenneth Slessor: The Enigma of a Poet   Geoffrey Dutton

Slessor, held by many to be Australia's finest poet, was a successful journalist and served as Australia's Official War Correspondent in the UK, Greece, the Middle East and New Guinea. He was also an engaging companion, a *bon viveur*, and a man prone to stormy relationships with the women in his life.

A major work on the life and times of Kenneth Slessor, written by Geoffrey Dutton, himself a respected writer and poet.

The Letters of Rachel Henning   Edited by David Adams

In 1854 at the age of twenty-eight Rachel Henning left the sheltered environment of her English home to settle in a new land – Australia. Pitchforked into the heat and the spartan conditions of the strange intense landscape, Rachel Henning, after an initial period of dislocation took to her new life with amazing gusto.

The evocative and detailed letters she wrote to her family build a picture of both the routine and the remarkable events of a world far from the drawing-rooms of England. Through them we glimpse the rigour and excitement of women's lives in nineteenth-century Australia.

Heroines: A Contemporary Anthology of Australian Women Writers
Edited by Dale Spender

Who are the heroines women look to? Twenty-two Australian writers of fiction, drama, poetry, journalism, TV scripts and non-fiction reflect on their heroines: from a rewriting of 'The Drover's Wife' to an unforgettable story of a mother in another land in the midst of a revolution.

There are ordinary women and extraordinary women; mothers, detectives, old women, teenagers, sisters, lesbians, rural women and urban; women who kill and women who resist violence; women who masquerade as men; women from the past and women from the present; there is comedy and music, satire and calls for action; a story that takes us back to the roots of human history and another that explores the impact of modern technology and the media on human consciousness.

PENGUIN – THE BEST AUSTRALIAN READING

The Law of the Land   Henry Reynolds

In this readable and dramatic book, Henry Reynolds reassesses the legal and political arguments used to justify the European settlement of Australia.

His conclusions form a compelling case for the belief that the British government conceded land rights to the Aborigines early in the nineteenth century.